Graz and Nölke have brought together a variety of perspectives on a whole sector of transnational arrangements that do not directly involve states and which are designed to regulate activities or to negotiate consensus on practices across national borders at both regional and international levels. They have derived from these different perspectives on particular cases some general propositions about the broader significance of these arrangements for world order. Their book raises important questions concerning the power relations that these arrangements reinforce. Do they bias outcomes in favour of the more powerful corporate entities? Do they privilege technocratic professionalism? Do they escape democratic accountability? Graz and Nölke are to be congratulated for bringing this complex phenomenon, which has sometimes been seen as a benign adjunct to globalizing neoliberalism, into a focus for critical evaluation.

Robert W. Cox, York University, Toronto, Canada

This is an important contribution to an expanding literature. The book makes an especially clear argument about the severe limits to the democratic accountability of private governance despite the frequent protestations about the openness of many stakeholder processes.

Craig N. Murphy, Wellesley College, USA

As the level and scope of cross-border integration increase, awkward questions arise concerning the appropriate nature and form of governance for this changing world of ours. Private actors have often filled the breach opened by the simultaneous erosion of state capacity to govern and a failure of public authorities to achieve adequate cross-border pooling of their 'sovereignty' to keep pace with cross-border activity of increasing complexity. Building on an already prodigious literature dating from the early 1990s on private actors in global governance, this fine study takes a fresh, insightful and, above all, *critical* look (in the best sense of the term) at the dilemmas which democratic policy-making processes face in such a context. Questions once raised by Susan Strange or Benjamin J. Cohen, such as 'who governs?' and 'in whose interest?' receive fresh and innovative analysis from Graz and Nölke and their contributors. Broadening the coverage of existing studies and deepening our understanding, this is a serious effort to understand better where and how private power and authority can and should fit in the governance of a transnational world which nonetheless aspires to a strong public domain under a democratic order. This study should inspire scholars and policy-makers alike to think more deeply and eschew the path of least resistance when it comes to resolving our problems of governance in a globalising world.

Geoffrey R.D. Underhill, Chair of International Governance,
University of Amsterdam, the Netherlands

Transnational Private Governance and its Limits

Transnational private governance is a core feature of the devolution of power that we observe in the global realm and that is bringing about new forms of authority. This book explores a variety of forms of transnational private governance where non-state actors co-operate across borders to establish rules and standards accepted as legitimate by agents not involved in their definition.

The book provides both theoretically and empirically informed insights into the interactions between states and non-state actors including domains beyond intergovernmental organizations, conventional non-governmental organizations, and multinational enterprises. It covers a wide range of arrangements, from highly formal devolutions of power to lax and informal platforms of interaction between private actors. In an attempt to overcome the divide between comparative and global political economy approaches, the book offers a systematic, yet flexible framework of analysis to understand how the interplay of structural constraints and actor-based processes drive the evolution of transnational private governance with significant normative implications. *Transnational Private Governance and its Limits* brings together experts whose background in political science is often completed by involvements in other fields, such as law, sociology, business studies, or economics. Contributing to the latest generation of globalization studies, the authors consider the relationship between states and markets as closely integrated and seek to broaden the scope of enquiry by including new patterns and agents of change on a transnational basis.

This book will be of great interest to researchers and students of political science, international relations, international political economy, economics, business studies, globalization, and law.

Jean-Christophe Graz is a Swiss National Science Foundation (SNF) Professor at the Institut d'études politiques et internationales of the University of Lausanne, Switzerland. **Andreas Nölke** is Professor of Political Science at the Institut für Politikwissenschaft of the Johann Wolfgang Goethe-Universität, Frankfurt am Main, Germany. He is also Programme Coordinator at the Amsterdam Research Center for Corporate Governance Regulation (ARCCGOR).

Routledge/ECPR studies in European political science

Edited by Thomas Poguntke

Ruhr University Bochum, Germany on behalf of the European Consortium for Political Research

The Routledge/ECPR studies in European political science series is published in association with the European Consortium for Political Research – the leading organisation concerned with the growth and development of political science in Europe. The series presents high-quality edited volumes on topics at the leading edge of current interest in political science and related fields, with contributions from European scholars and others who have presented work at ECPR workshops or research groups.

1 **Regionalist Parties in Western Europe**
Edited by Lieven de Winter and Huri Türsan

2 **Comparing Party System Change**
Edited by Jan-Erik Lane and Paul Pennings

3 **Political Theory and European Union**
Edited by Albert Weale and Michael Nentwich

4 **Politics of Sexuality**
Edited by Terrell Carver and Véronique Mottier

5 **Autonomous Policy Making by International Organizations**
Edited by Bob Reinalda and Bertjan Verbeek

6 **Social Capital and European Democracy**
Edited by Jan van Deth, Marco Maraffi, Ken Newton and Paul Whiteley

7 **Party Elites in Divided Societies**
Edited by Kurt Richard Luther and Kris Deschouwer

8 **Citizenship and Welfare State Reform in Europe**
Edited by Jet Bussemaker

9 **Democratic Governance and New Technology**
Technologically mediated innovations in political practice in Western Europe
Edited by Ivan Horrocks, Jens Hoff and Pieter Tops

10 **Democracy Without Borders**
Transnationalisation and conditionality in new democracies
Edited by Jean Grugel

11 **Cultural Theory as Political Science**
Edited by Michael Thompson, Gunnar Grendstad and Per Selle

12 **The Transformation of Governance in the European Union**
Edited by Beate Kohler-Koch and Rainer Eising

13 **Parliamentary Party Groups in European Democracies**
Political parties behind closed doors
Edited by Knut Heidar and Ruud Koole

14 **Survival of the European Welfare State**
Edited by Stein Kuhnle

15 **Private Organisations in Global Politics**
Edited by Karsten Ronit and Volker Schneider

16 **Federalism and Political Performance**
Edited by Ute Wachendorfer-Schmidt

17 **Democratic Innovation**
Deliberation, representation and association
Edited by Michael Saward

18 **Public Opinion and the International Use of Force**
Edited by Philip Everts and Pierangelo Isernia

19 **Religion and Mass Electoral Behaviour in Europe**
Edited by David Broughton and Hans-Martien ten Napel

20 **Estimating the Policy Position of Political Actors**
Edited by Michael Laver

21 **Democracy and Political Change in the 'Third World'**
Edited by Jeff Haynes

22 **Politicians, Bureaucrats and Administrative Reform**
Edited by B. Guy Peters and Jon Pierre

23 **Social Capital and Participation in Everyday Life**
Edited by Paul Dekker and Eric M. Uslaner

24 **Development and Democracy**
What have we learned and how?
Edited by Ole Elgström and Goran Hyden

25 **Do Political Campaigns Matter?**
Campaign effects in elections and referendums
Edited by David M. Farrell and Rüdiger Schmitt-Beck

26 **Political Journalism**
New challenges, new practices
Edited by Raymond Kuhn and Erik Neveu

27 **Economic Voting**
Edited by Han Dorussen and Michaell Taylor

28 **Organized Crime and the Challenge to Democracy**
Edited by Felia Allum and Renate Siebert

29 **Understanding the European Union's External Relations**
Edited by Michèle Knodt and Sebastiaan Princen

30 **Social Democratic Party Policies in Contemporary Europe**
Edited by Giuliano Bonoli and Martin Powell

31 **Decision Making Within International Organisations**
Edited by Bob Reinalda and Bertjan Verbeek

32 **Comparative Biomedical Policy**
Governing assisted reproductive technologies
Edited by Ivar Bleiklie, Malcolm L. Goggin and Christine Rothmayr

33 **Electronic Democracy**
Mobilisation, organisation and participation via new ICTs
Edited by Rachel K. Gibson, Andrea Römmele and Stephen J. Ward

34 **Liberal Democracy and Environmentalism**
The end of environmentalism?
Edited by Marcel Wissenburg and Yoram Levy

35 **Political Theory and the European Constitution**
Edited by Lynn Dobson and Andreas Follesdal

36 **Politics and the European Commission**
Actors, interdependence, legitimacy
Edited by Andy Smith

37 **Metropolitan Governance in the 21st Century**
Capacity, democracy and the dynamics of place
Edited by Hubert Heinelt and Daniel Kübler

38 **Democracy and the Role of Associations**
Political, organizational and social contexts
Edited by Sigrid Roßteutscher

39 **The Territorial Politics of Welfare**
Edited by Nicola McEwen and Luis Moreno

40 **Health Governance in Europe**
Issues, challenges and theories
Edited by Monika Steffen

41 **Republicanism in Theory and Practice**
Edited by Iseult Honohan and Jeremy Jennings

42 **Mass Media and Political Communication in New Democracies**
Edited by Katrin Voltmer

43 **Delegation in Contemporary Democracies**
Edited by Dietmar Braun and Fabrizio Gilardi

44 **Governance and Democracy**
Comparing national, European and international experiences
Edited by Yannis Papadopoulos and Arthur Benz

45 **The European Union's Roles in International Politics**
Concepts and analysis
Edited by Ole Elgström and Michael Smith

46 **Policy-making Processes and the European Constitution**
A comparative study of member states and accession countries
Edited by Thomas König and Simon Hug

47 **Democratic Politics and Party Competition**
Edited by Judith Bara and Albert Weale

48 **Participatory Democracy and Political Participation**
Can participatory engineering bring citizens back in?
Edited by Thomas Zittel and Dieter Fuchs

49 **Civil Societies and Social Movements**
Potentials and problems
Edited by Derrick Purdue

50 **Resources, Governance and Civil Conflict**
Edited by Magnus Öberg and Kaare Strøm

51 **Transnational Private Governance and its Limits**
Edited by Jean-Christophe Graz and Andreas Nölke

Also available from Routledge in association with the ECPR:
Sex Equality Policy in Western Europe, *Edited by Frances Gardiner*; **Democracy and Green Political Thought,** *Edited by Brian Doherty and Marius de Geus*; **The New Politics of Unemployment**, *Edited by Hugh Compston*; **Citizenship, Democracy and Justice in the New Europe**, *Edited by Percy B. Lehning and Albert Weale*; **Private Groups and Public Life,** *Edited by Jan W van Deth*; **The Political Context of Collective Action,** *Edited by Ricca Edmondson*; **Theories of Secession,** *Edited by Percy Lehning;* **Regionalism Across the North/South Divide**, *Edited by Jean Grugel and Wil Hout.*

Transnational Private Governance and its Limits

Edited by Jean-Christophe Graz and Andreas Nölke

Routledge
Taylor & Francis Group
LONDON AND NEW YORK

First published 2008
by Routledge
2 Park Square, Milton Park, Abingdon, Oxon OX14 4RN

Simultaneously published in the USA and Canada
by Routledge
270 Madison Ave, New York, NY 10016

Routledge is an imprint of the Taylor & Francis Group, an informa business

Typeset in Times by Wearset Ltd, Boldon, Tyne and Wear
Printed and bound in Great Britain by TJI Digital, Padstow, Cornwall

British Library Cataloguing in Publication Data
A catalogue record for this book is available from the British Library

Library of Congress Cataloging in Publication Data
A catalog record for this book has been requested

ISBN10: 0-415-41435-0 (hbk)
ISBN10: 0-203-93933-6 (ebk)

ISBN13: 978-0-415-41435-7 (hbk)
ISBN13: 978-0-203-93933-8 (ebk)

Contents

Illustrations

Figures

Tables

Contributors

Sven Bislev is Associate Professor at the Department of Intercultural Communication and Management, and Director of Undergraduate Studies at the Copenhagen Business School. His publications include *Deficient Institutionality – EU and NAFTA Integration* (Macmillan, 1999 – with K. Appendini, eds); 'Globalization, State Transformation and Public Security', *International Political Science Review*, 25, 3: 281–96, 2004.

Sebastian Botzem studied political science in Berlin and Granada, Spain. He is a Research Associate at the Social Science Research Center Berlin and a PhD Student at the doctoral program 'Research on Organizational Paths' at the Free University Berlin, Germany. His publications include 'Contested Rules and Shifting Boundaries: International Standard Setting in Accounting', in M.-L. Djelic and K. Sahlin-Andersson (eds), *Transnational Governance: Institutional Dynamics of Regulation* (Cambridge University Press, 2006 – with S. Quack).

George Christou is Assistant Professor in European Politics in the Department of Politics and International Studies at the University of Warwick. He was previously Research Associate on the ESRC-funded European Regulation of Internet Commerce project, at the Department of Information and Communications, Manchester Metropolitan University. He is author of *The EU and Enlargement: the Case of Cyprus* (Palgrave, 2004), and *The New Electronic Marketplace: European Governance Strategies in a Globalising Economy* (Edward Elgar, 2007 – with S. Simpson).

Thomas Conzelmann is Assistant Professor of International Relations at Darmstadt University of Technology and Coordinator of a Research Team on 'Soft Modes of Governance and the Private Sector: The EU and the Global Experience' (EU Network of Excellence CONNEX). Recent publications include 'Beyond the Carrot and the Stick: State Reporting Procedures in the WTO and the OECD', in J. Joachim *et al.* (eds) *International Organizations and Policy Implementation* (Routledge, 2007); and *Europäische Integration, europäisches Regieren* (VS Verlag, 2004 – with B. Kohler-Koch and M. Knodt).

Mikkel Flyverbom is Assistant Professor at the University of Southern Denmark. His research and teaching interests revolve around global communication, multi-stakeholder authority, global governance networks, and the sociopolitical consequences of new information and communication technologies. Recent publications include contributions in J. Hoff and H.K. Hansen (eds) *Digital Governance://Networked Societies* (Samfundslitteratur, 2006) and in H.K. Hansen and D. Salskov-Iversen (eds) *Critical Perspectives on Private Authority in Global Politics* (Palgrave-Macmillan, 2007).

Doris Fuchs is Professor of International Relations and European Integration at the University of Stuttgart. She is working on issues of private governance, sustainable development, and food policy and politics. Her publications include 'Commanding Heights? The Strength and Fragility of Business Power in Global Politics', *Millenium,* 33, 3: 771–80, 2005; and 'Sustainable Consumption Governance: A History of Promises and Failures', *Journal on Consumer Policy,* 28, 3: 261–88, 2005 (with S. Lorek).

Noemi Gal-Or is Professor at the Department of Political Science, and Director of the Institute for Transborder Studies, Kwantlen University College, British Columbia, Canada. Her most recent publications include 'A Reassessment of the International Wrong: Self-Help Remedies for International Wrongs & Countermeasures in Humanitarian Law, *35th Annual CCIL Conference Proceedings,* 2006; 'Outsourcing of Justice: A New International Orthodoxy?' in K. van der Pijl and K.-G. Giesen (eds) *Global Norms in the Twenty-First Century* (Cambridge Scholars Press, 2006).

Jean-Christophe Graz is a Swiss National Science Foundation (SNF) Professor at the Institut d'études politiques et internationales of the University of Lausanne, Switzerland. His publications include *La gouvernance de la mondialisation* (La Découverte, 2004); *Commerce international et développement soutenable* (Economica, 2001 – with M. Damian, eds); *Precursor of the WTO. The Stillborn Havana Charter, 1941–1950* (Droz, 1999). He is currently coordinating a research team on the global political economy of standards in services.

Otto Holman is Reader in International Relations at the Department of Political Science, University of Amsterdam. His publications include 'Asymmetrical Regulation and Multidimensional Governance in the European Union', *Review of International Political Economy,* 11, 4: 714–35, 2004; *Integrating Southern Europe: EC Expansion and the Transnationalization of Spain* (Routledge 1996); 'Introduction: Transnational Class Strategy and the New Europe', *International Journal of Political Economy,* 22: 1: 3–22, 1992.

Josep Ibáñez is Lecturer in International Relations at Pompeu Fabra University, Barcelona, Spain, and holds a PhD in Political Science. His publications include *El control de internet. Poder y autoridad en los mercados electrónicos* (Los Libros de la Catarata, 2005). His research interests focus on the political economy of information and communication technologies.

Jeroen Merk is PhD Student in International Relations at the University of Sussex and works for the Clean Clothes Campaign. His publications include 'Regulating the Global Athletic Footwear Industry: The Collective Worker in the Product Chain', in L. Assassi, D. Wigan and K. van der Pijl (eds), *Global Regulation: Managing Crises After the Imperial Turn* (Palgrave 2004).

Daniel Mügge is PhD student at the Amsterdam School of Social Science Research, University of Amsterdam. His publications include 'Reordering the Market Place: Competition Politics in European Finance', *Journal of Common Market Studies,* 44, 5: 989–1020, 2006; 'Private-Public Puzzles: Inter-firm competition and transnational private regulation', *New Political Economy,* 11, 2: 177–200, 2006; and 'Der Blinde Fleck der Zweiten Moderne. Globale Finanzmärkte und die Theorie reflexiver Modernisierung', *Soziale Welt,* 57, 1: 31–46, 2006.

Andreas Nölke is Professor of Political Science at the Institut für Politikwissenschaft of the Johann Wolfgang Goethe-Universität Frankfurt am Main, where he teaches international relations and international political economy. He is also Programme Coordinator at the Amsterdam Research Center for Corporate Governance Regulation (ARCCGOR). His recent publications include *The Transnational Politics of Corporate Governance Regulation* (Routledge, 2007 – with H. Overbeek and B. van Apeldoorn, eds) and a special issue of *Business and Politics* on the globalization of accounting standards (2005).

Karsten Ronit is Associate Professor at the Department of Political Science, University of Copenhagen. He has a long-time research interest in the problems of self-regulation and global politics and he has published a number of books, chapters and journal articles on this issue. His most recent contribution is the edited collection *Global Public Policy: Business and the Countervailing Powers of Civil Society* (Routledge, 2007).

Seamus Simpson is a Principal Lecturer at the Department of Information and Communications, Manchester Metropolitan University, UK. His research interests lie in European and global communications policy and regulation. He is author of two books: *Globalisation, Convergence and European Telecommunications Regulation* (E. Elgar, 2006 – with P. Humphreys); *The New Electronic Marketplace: European Governance Strategies in a Globalising Economy* (E. Elgar, 2007 – with G. Christou).

Stijn Smismans is Assistant Professor, Faculty of Sociology, University of Trento, Italy. His publications include *Law, Legitimacy and European Governance: Functional Participation in Social Regulation* (Oxford University Press, 2004); *Civil Society and Legitimate European Governance* (E. Elgar, 2006 – ed.).

Eleni Tsingou is Research Fellow at the Centre for the Study of Globalisation and Regionalisation, University of Warwick and Programme Manager of a

Network of Excellence on Global Governance, Regionalisation and Regulation: The Role of the EU. Her publications include 'Global governance and transnational financial crime: opportunities and tensions in the global anti-money laundering regime', ESRC CSGR Working Paper 161/05; and 'The governance of over-the-counter derivatives markets' in P. Mooslechner *et al.* (eds) *The Political Economy of Financial Market Regulation* (E. Elgar, 2006).

Frans van Waarden is Professor of public policy and organization at University College, Utrecht University, the Netherlands. His publications include 'Governance as a Bridge Between Disciplines: Cross-Disciplinary Inspiration Regarding Shifts in Governance and Problems of Governability, Accountability and Legitimacy', *European Journal of Political Research,* 43, 2: 141–73, 2004 (with K. van Kersbergen); 'Taste, Traditions, Transactions, and Trust: The Public and Private Regulation of Food', in C. Ansell and D. Vogel (eds), *What's the Beef? The Contested Governance of European Food Safety* (MIT Press, 2006).

Klaus Dieter Wolf is Professor of Political Science, Darmstadt University of Technology, Germany, and Research Group Director at the Peace Research Institute Frankfurt (PRIF). He was President of the German Political Science Association (DVPW) from 2003 to 2006. His publications include 'Contextualizing Normative Standards for Legitimate Governance Beyond the State', in J. Grote and B. Gbikpi (eds) *Participatory Governance* (Leske+Budrich, 2001); 'Private Actors and the Legitimacy of Governance Beyond the State: Conceptual Outlines and Empirical Explorations', in A. Benz and Y. Papadopoulos (eds) *Governance and Democracy* (Routledge, 2006).

Series editor's preface

Transnational private governance transcends two borders of traditional political analysis: the demarcation between the realm of the state and the sphere of civil society, and the borders between states. In the age of globalization, the blurring of these distinctions is interrelated and, to a considerable degree, mutually reinforcing. As the editors point out in their introduction, the central focus of this volume is on the 'ability of non-state actors to cooperate across borders in order to establish rules and standards accepted as legitimate by agents not involved in their definition'. In other words, it is about the privatization of rule making *and* the spatial extension of these patterns of rule making and rule enforcement beyond the nation state.

Arguably, the forces of globalization have necessitated patterns of private governance as a means of compensating for the inability of nation states to provide effective regulation. However, this is only one possible interpretation of transnational private governance, and others would argue that it should primarily be seen as underpinning the dominance of the neoliberal business model. Clearly, this is not the only controversy that is relevant in this context. Following a deliberately broad definition of 'private' and including all non-state actors, the editors discuss a range of problematic aspects related to transnational private governance.

First and foremost, the democratic legitimation of private regulatory bodies is precarious. While the delegation of powers formerly falling under the jurisdiction of the nation state to transnational private bodies may be justifiable on pragmatic grounds (because they may have superior expertise), important questions of democratic accountability remain as yet unanswered. Similarly, and relatedly, there is a transfer of sovereignty to private or semi-private bodies, and it is unclear to what degree such transfers are reversible.

General answers to such questions are difficult because there is clearly not one single model of transnational private governance. The scope and effectiveness of transitional private governance varies considerably according to the policy areas and the types of issues that need regulation. Such factors also explain the enormous variation of the institutional embeddedness of transnational private governance.

The book assembles detailed case studies covering four broad areas. Following the conceptual introduction by the editors, it begins with three analyses of the self-regulation of the financial sector, a policy area where transnational private governance is particularly developed. It then moves on to the role of business interests in transnational private governance in important issue areas such as labour, consumer interest, and environmental concerns and addresses issues of democratic control and a possible bias in favour of the status quo. The third section looks at the highly interesting issue of Internet regulation where states have had to regain ground and individual companies play a central role. Finally, the book moves on to examples on how structures for regional integration, namely the EU, increasingly use methods of transnational private governance as a method of regulation (or de-regulation).

The editors conclude that transnational private governance faces limits on three dimensions. First, there is a lack of conceptual clarity in that not 'all forms of transnational private governance have the same degree of "transnationality"'. Also, the term private is partially misleading because it does not mean that the state is 'completely out of the picture'. Rather, it signifies that private actors are also involved in rule making and rule enforcement, and the degree of their autonomy varies considerably across issue areas and sectors. In addition, the concept of 'governance' suggests a degree of non-hierarchical, consensual regulation that is empirically not always the case.

Second, transnational private governance does not work everywhere. The editors discuss the factors that are conducive to the emergence of patterns of transnational governance including; among others, a high need for specialized knowledge, oligopolistic market structures, and the dominance of neoliberalism. The study also shows that the EU is a key promoter of transnational private governance.

Finally, there are severe normative limitations that relate to problems of sovereignty and the precarious state of democratic legitimacy. While the 'output legitimacy' of transnational private governance may often be convincing in the sense that it can deliver regulation that is widely accepted, its 'input legitimacy' leaves a lot to be desired. In the age of the increasing role of intergovernmental cooperation and supranational political structures, transnational governance certainly represents a challenge to democratic theory.

Thomas Poguntke, Series Editor
Bochum

Preface

This book grew out of a workshop on 'Transnational Private Governance in the Global Political Economy' that we organised within the context of the ECPR Joint Sessions of Workshops in Granada, 14–19 April 2005. At that meeting, we benefited from papers and comments from several scholars who did not become further involved in the project, in particular Dirk Lehmkuhl, Michelle Micheletti, and James Perry. Besides the exceptional atmosphere of the workshop and the famous sense of hospitality provided by our host, we were struck from the outset by the depth and richness of the dialogue initiated at Grenada. We quickly realized that there were all the ingredients for constructing a tightly knit coherent collective book rather than a loose collection of chapters. The 'Spirit of Granada' has not only contributed to the timely completion of the book, but has also lead to a very intense process of collaboration during the drafting of the introductory and concluding chapters of the book. To do so, we certainly were painful on our contributors with the additional pressure this means in terms of responding to comments, revising chapters, engaging a common language, the back and forth of succeeding versions, not to speak of the considerable time pressure put in order to keep pace with a phenomena which provides new developments on an almost daily basis. We would like to express our gratitude to all the contributors for their willingness to comply with this pressure in going along with us in the same direction.

We would each like to thank Routledge and the European Consortium for Political Research for enabling us to publish the book in the Routledge/ECPR Studies in European political science. We are also deeply indebted to Thomas Poguntke and two anonymous referees for constructive comments on our book project, as well as to Heidi Bagtazo, Harriet Brinton and Amelia McLaurin at Routledge for their advise and support. Moreover, the volume could not have been pulled together without the big-hearted support in language editing of Liesl Graz, the contribution of Marc Raedler, Antoinette Lloyd, and Richard James Lloyd, as well as the editorial skill of Nafy Niang, Marcel Heires and Alexandre Sutlian in completing the final manuscript.

Jean-Christophe Graz would like to thank the generous support of the Swiss National Science Foundation (SNF), which has allowed him to study various issues of transnational private governance for many years, as well as the Institut d'études politiques et internationales and the Faculté des sciences sociales et politiques at the Universit of Lausanne, Switzerland, where he can now further explore this fascinating and fast-moving topic. Andreas Nölke has been conducting his research within the context of the Amsterdam Research Centre on Corporate Governance Regulation (ARCCGOR) in the Department of Political Science, Vrije Universiteit, Amsterdam. Financial support for this research from the Netherlandse Organisatie voor Wetenschappelijk Onderzoek (NWO) within the 'Shifts in Governance Programme' is gratefully acknowledged, as well support from the Netherlands Institute of Government (NIG) for the 'NIG Editing Grant' which helped in completing the book.

And most importantly, we would like to thank for their patience, their company, their insights, and their love, all our friends and our families, in particular Andrea, Anouk, and Antonia Nölke, as well as Gaspard, Zoé, Arthur, and Myriam Bickle Graz.

Abbreviations

ADR	Alternative Dispute Resolution
AIBD	Association of International Bond Dealers
AIDS	Acquired Immune Deficiency Syndrome
B2B	Business to Business
B2C	Business to Consumer
B2G	Business to Government
BCSC	British Columbia Supreme Court
BSE	Bovine Spongiform Encephalopathy
CAG	Competitiveness Advisory Group
CBOT	Chicago Board of Trade
CCC	Clean Clothes Campaign
ccTLD	Country Code Top-Level Domains
CEEP	European Centre of Enterprises with Public Participation
CERES	Coalition for Environmentally Responsible Economies
CESR	Committee of European Securities Regulators
CFTC	Commodities and Futures Trading Commission
CITES	Convention on International Trade in Endangered Species
CME	Chicago Mercantile Exchange
CPE	Comparative Political Economy
CSR	Corporate Social Responsibility
DGIS	Directorate General Information Society
DNS	Domain Name System
DR	Dispute Resolution
ECG	European Contact Group
EDI	Electronic Data Interchange
EEJ-Net	European Extra-Judicial Network
EES	European Employment Strategy
EFT	Electronic Fund Transfer
ERT	European Round Table of Industrialists
ETUC	European Trade Union Confederation
EU	European Union
EURID	European Registry of Internet Domains
FASB	Financial Accounting Standards Board

FDI	Foreign Direct Investment
FEE	Federation of European Accountants
Fin-Net	Network for Financial services
FLO	Fair Trade Labelling Organisations International
FSC	Forest Stewardship Council
FSF	Financial Stability Forum
FTAA	Free Trade Area of the Americas
FVA	Fair Value Accounting
G-30	Group of Thirty
GAAP	Generally Accepted Accounting Principles
GATS	Global Agreement on Trade in Services
GC	Global Compact
GCC	Global Climate Coalition
GMO	Genetically Modified Organism
GMP	Good Manufacturing Practices
GPE	Global Political Economy
GSC	Global Steering Committee
HACCP	Hazard Analysis and Critical Control Points
HIV	Human Immunodeficiency Virus
IAASB	International Auditing and Assurance Standards Board
IAS	International Accounting Standards
IASB	International Accounting Standards Board
IASC	International Accounting Standards Committee
ICANN	Internet Corporation for Assigned Names and Numbers
ICC	International Chamber of Commerce
ICCA	International Council of Chemical Associations
ICT	Information and Communication Technology
ICT4D	ICT for Development
IFAC	International Federation of Accountants
IFRS	International Financial Reporting Standards
IGF	International Governance Forum
IIF	Institute of International Finance
ILO	International Labour Organization
IMF	International Monetary Fund
IO	International Organization
IOSCO	International Organization of Securities Commissions
IPMA	International Primary Market Association
ISEAL	International Social and Environmental Accreditation and Labeling
ISO	International Organization for Standardization
ISOC	Internet Society
ITGLWF	International Textile, Garment, Leather Workers Federation
ITU	International Telecommunications Union
MNC	Multinational corporation
MoU	Memorandum of understanding
MSI	Multi-stakeholder initiatives

NAFTA	North American Free Trade Agreement
NGO	Non-Governmental Organization
NIC	Newly Industrialized Countries
OECD	Organisation for Economic Co-operation and Development
OMC	Open Method of Coordination
PCAOB	Public Company Accounting Oversight Board
PIOB	Public Interest Oversight Board
PPP	Private–Public Partnership
PPR	Public Policy Rules
RC	Responsible Care
RCGC	Responsible Care Global Charter
SARS	Severe Acute Respiratory Syndrome
SEC	Securities and Exchange Commission
SME	Small- and Medium-Sized Enterprise
SPS	Sanitary and Phytosanitary Measures
TAC	Transnational Auditors Committee
TBT	Technical Barriers to Trade
TCP/IP	Transmission Control Protocol/Internet Protocol
TEPG	Transnational Environmental Private Governance
TNC	Transnational Corporation
TPG	Transnational Private Governance
TLD	Top-Level Domain
TRIPS	Trade-Related Aspects of Intellectual Property Rights
UEAPME	European Association of Craft, Small- and Medium-Sized Enterprises
UN	United Nations
UNCED	United Nations Conference on Environment and Development
UNCITRAL	United Nations Commission on International Trade Law
UNEP	United Nations Environment Programme
UNICE	Union of Industrial and Employers' Confederations of Europe
W3C	World Wide Web Consortium
WBCSD	World Business Council on Sustainable Development
WGIG	Working Group on Internet Governance
WHO	World Health Organization
WIPO	World Intellectual Property Organisation
WSIS	World Summit on the Information Society
WTO	World Trade Organisation
WWF	World Wildlife Fund
WWW	World Wide Web

1 Introduction

Beyond the fragmented debate on transnational private governance

Jean-Christophe Graz and Andreas Nölke

Days before the collapse of the Berlin Wall in 1989, five US Army and Marine Corps officers introduced the concept of 'fourth-generation' warfare in an article published in the *Marine Corps Gazette*. Its basic outlines were as follows:

> In broad terms, fourth generation warfare seems likely to be widely dispersed and largely undefined; the distinction between war and peace will be blurred to the vanishing point. It will be nonlinear, possibly to the point of having no definable battlefields or fronts. The distinction between 'civilian' and 'military' may disappear. Actions will occur concurrently throughout all participants' depth, including their society as a cultural, not just a physical, entity.
>
> (Quoted in Jonathan Raban, 'The Truth about Terrorism', *New York Review of Books*, 52 (1), Jan. 13, 2005).

The above quotation may point out that the roots of the dramatic change in American strategic ambitions were planted long before the presidency of George W. Bush Jr. and the opportunity taken by his advisors to launch a 'war on terror' after 9/11 (Golub 2004). It also shows the extent to which a shift towards states' involvements with non-state actors cuts across diverse issues of political science. In the much-debated domain of globalisation studies, concerns about 'widely dispersed and largely undefined' phenomena, as well as claims about 'blurred distinctions', have contributed to the confusion. Attempts to clarify the economic and political transformations of contemporary capitalism have also led to a 'fourth generation' of scholarship – even though, on perspectivist grounds, the debate relates more on contending approaches than successive generations (Cameron and Palan 2003: 28). Whilst particular prominence was first given to the rising power of global markets (Ohmae 1990), the emphasis quickly shifted to the continuing role of the state in economic policy, if not at the national, then at the regional and international levels (Hirst and Thompson 1996). A third approach denies a priori assumptions about the relative importance of states and markets in the process of globalisation by considering their relationship as closely integrated (Mittelman 1996; Gill 1997; Germain 1999; Held *et al.* 1999). As the role of non-state actors across borders has become a matter of public debate as their influence has grown, a fourth strand of globalisation studies has sought to broaden the scope of enquiry to include new patterns and agents of change beyond states and firms (Strange 1996; Cutler *et al.* 1999; Hibou 1999; Higgott *et al.* 1999; Braithwaite and Drahos 2000; Ronit and Schneider 2000; Haufler 2001; Hall and Biersteker 2002; Cutler 2003; Sassen 2003; Bayart 2004; Djelic and Sahlin-Andersson 2006; Sassen 2006).

This book shares the assumption that the logic of action and the potential of change embodied by non-state actors has become a core feature of new forms of authority in the global realm. By exploring what we call *transnational private governance*, the book provides theoretical and empirical insights into the ability of non-state actors to cooperate across borders in order to establish rules and standards of behaviour accepted as legitimate by agents not involved in their definition. Non-state actors not only formulate norms, but often also have a key role in their enforcement. Accordingly, the current privatisation of rule making and enforcement goes much further than traditional lobbying in allowing private actors an active role in regulation itself. Domains concerned lie far beyond inter-governmental organisations, conventional non-governmental organisations (NGOs) and multinational enterprises. In this respect, the book covers a wide range of situations, from highly formal systems of power devolution to lax and informal platforms of interaction between private actors.

Existing research on transnational private governance is in its infancy. A decade after the first set of studies that brought the topic to general attention, it is high time to review a process that is evolving extremely rapidly and provides us with sufficient empirical evidence to develop some theoretical propositions. We still lack comprehensive concepts ordering the different types of private governance. Similarly, we do not yet know under which conditions actors 'obey' norms that are not defined by states. There is also insufficient evidence of which sectors and which organisational formats are most likely to rely on transnational private governance. Finally, it is unclear how we could reconcile these forms of governance with established concepts of democratic legitimacy.

This chapter outlines a research agenda on transnational private governance. It first presents two distinct scholarly traditions that in many respects stand as the most important contributions to our understanding of this phenomenon: on the one hand, approaches in comparative political economy (CPE) focus on institutional arrangements and coordinating logics of economic actors across nations; on the other, studies in global political economy (GPE) try to identify constitutive patterns of authority mediating between the political and the economic spheres of a transnational space. Although this distinction may be over-simplified, it may explain why GPE approaches give prime attention to channels of structural power across national economies, while CPE approaches examine how such transnational constraints require new forms of coordination among nations. Despite mutual indifference between them, we claim that important avenues of cross-fertilisation remain. We contend that three distinct issues are of particular relevance to overcome the divide between CPE and GPE approaches on transnational private governance: (i) providing *conceptual clarification* in order to define the social reality referred to as transnational private governance, (ii) identifying *framework conditions* that make transnational private governance possible and (iii) discussing *normative implications* that commonly raise many concerns. In our attempt to overcome the divide between CPE and GPE, we propose a framework of analysis, whose categories are delineated so as to offer a more systematic, yet flexible approach to understanding the conceptual, empirical and normative aspects of transnational private governance. The various contributors to this volume do not share a single theoretical perspective. They concur, however, on a political economy approach in which the interplay of structural constraints and actor-based processes drive the evolution of transnational private governance with significant normative implications. The remaining chapters of the present volume deal with various aspects of this analytical framework, each in their own way.

The core contention of the book is that transnational private governance is subject to important limits. While conventional analyses tend to highlight the newness and the innovative character of these forms of governance, we unambiguously question this view in emphasising limitations in three regards. The limits to transnational private governance refer first to the degree to which this phenomenon is really private, transnationalised and confined to governance *per se*. Second, the empirical framework conditions required for transnational private governance to be effective are circumscribed and can be for the most part systematically identified. Third, the normative shortcomings of transnational private governance clearly hinder its ability to embody procedural innovation in policy processes and to solve large socioeconomic concerns. The conceptual, analytical and normative underpinnings of this argument have emerged in concert with the project of this book. The key themes were included in the call for the ECPR 4-day workshop on the topic and served as guidelines in the extremely fruitful discussions we had on that occasion. The more detailed categories were developed subsequently so as to provide additional coherence in the process of revision. We gave each contributor a grid with core questions, themes and the more specific categories presented in Table 1.1 (hereafter p. 9) as a support to keep focus and coherence in this collective attempt to revisit transnational private governance. As the concluding chapter examines in detail, it appears that all contributors substantially share the overall argument on conceptual, analytical and normative limits to transnational private governance.

The CPE debate: when do firms obey norms that are not set by states?

The point of departure for the CPE debate is the perception that governments alone cannot solve all problems of transnational economic regulation. This appears to be particularly true for the regulation of business, while the macroissues of trade and currencies still clearly fall into the realm of intergovernmental cooperation. While the public character of currency and trade issues forces a certain degree of intergovernmental cooperation, this element is absent from business regulation. Furthermore, following Stigler's (1971) early critique on the ability of business interest to capture the state in public regulation, the state command-and-control approach to regulation is considered too inflexible and too costly, therefore inclined, to be substituted by the market-based incentives of voluntary business self-regulation (Blundell and Robinson 1999).

Cooperation between companies and civil society actors in the context of concepts such as 'corporate social responsibility', 'business ethics' and 'corporate citizenship' has attracted considerable attention. Much hope has been invested in the idea that capitalist externalities such as environmental degradation and the mistreatment of workers can be severely limited by standards developed and overseen by private institutions (Braithwaite and Drahos 2000). Examples for these standards comprise *inter alia* the ISO 14000 norm on environmental management (Clapp 1998), the Coalition for Environmentally Responsible Economies (CERES) for environmentally responsible investments as well as the Forest Stewardship Council for sustainable forestry (both discussed in Pattberg 2004) or the human rights-oriented Social Accountability Standard 8000 (Braun 2001: 271).

Given the voluntary character of these institutions, CPE scholarship aims at identifying the circumstances under which private actors obey norms that are not set by states. The following factors appear to be among the most influential conditions inferred from initial empirical studies:

- *The degree of competition between the participating firms*: The adherence to environmental or social norms can be a clear disadvantage in a very competitive environment. In contrast, the existence of a monopolistic or oligopolistic structure can help in facilitating private governance: 'Rules and standards that come from industry alone, without the participation of or enforcement by third parties, tend to be difficult to sustain due to competition among firms... other types of governance must supplement it – either by government regulation, or the dominance of a single private player' (Haufler 2002: 10).
- *The type of company involved*: Not all companies appear to be equally suited for a participation in the diverse forms of codes of conduct. Since the enforcement of private norms very much depends on consumers being able 'to respond to the signals being sent to reward those companies behaving well and punish those behaving badly' (Haufler 2002: 11), big manufacturing companies with well-known brand names are particularly affected. Under certain circumstances, coordination service firms such as insurers or institutional investors can also attach importance to political, social or environmental issues as risks to be incorporated into contracts passed with key other (non-service) firms. Thus, service firms can assume a coordinating role as standard setters and third-party enforcers, especially if they are in an oligopolistic position (Nölke 2003b: 16).
- *The type of issue involved*: The success of corporate initiatives may also widely differ as a result of the nature of the problem (Kollman 2003: 34ff).

Improving social and labour practices obviously has other implications for corporate and non-corporate actors than reducing environmental externalities; it often echoes core business concerns such as efficiency, competitiveness and technological innovation.

- *The further development of post-materialist orientations*: In a classic study on the declining significance of class voting, Inglehart (1977) found evidence of post-materialist orientations in the capacity of better-educated voters to make political decisions independent of class loyalty or other socioeconomic attributes. Recent analyses make use of a similar argument in considering, for instance, that codes of conduct that rely on the support of labour unions have much less impact than those based on environmental or human rights movements (Kollman 2003: 34). Given that most social groups promoting corporate social responsibility are themselves of middle-class background with post-materialist values, private governance also depends on the socioeconomic environment of such groups. Thus, transnational private governance may be negatively affected by global economic crises (Rieth 2004: 189), but could also be supported by an expansion of the middle classes in the societies of the global South.

These issues indicate the broad range of preconditions that have to be met in order to make private norms an effective alternative to the conventional regulation of business. But even if these preconditions were met, we might still have second thoughts about such governance in view of its power effects and democratic deficit (e.g. Sundgren 1997; Wolf 2002). In the absence of the democratic institutions of the nation state, transnational private governance suffers from the fact that not all participating actors have equal power and some are not represented at all. This is particularly true for those of the wider public interest and from developing countries that are lacking the detailed knowledge that is necessary to participate meaningfully in private norm setting and enforcement. Many hopes have been vested in the ability of NGOs to compensate for these weaknesses (Haufler 2002: 8–10). NGOs can enhance legitimacy only on certain issues. Societal actors in transnational policy networks are variously represented within these networks (Nölke 2003a, 2003b). Unions and consumer groups lack influence on the transnational level (while big multinational enterprises are being favoured), and within the NGO community mainstream Northern interests almost inevitably prevail.

In spite of these critical remarks, however, one can conclude that CPE studies usually are reasonable optimistic with private governance considered to be an important option for preventing the regulatory deficit created by the absence of (inter-)state regulation of transnational business. Although existing codes may have severe shortcomings in terms of effectiveness as well as democratic legitimacy, it is the role of the academic debate to highlight these shortcomings and contribute to the identification of alternative solutions. The CPE debate has identified some of the key mechanisms of how private governance works in practice and has developed some proposals for improving them. This pragmatic approach, however, has prevented CPE scholars from focusing on the wider economic and historical context of transnational private governance, including any broad perspective of the power structures involved.

The GPE debate: transnational private governance within capitalist development

From a GPE perspective, most contributions to the CPE debate seem to be typical examples of problem-solving theories. Based on Robert Cox's (1986: 207) famous dictum 'theory is always *for* someone and *for* some purpose' (emphasis in original), GPE scholars identify those studies as attempts to make the existing capitalist system work more smoothly. From a critical standpoint, GPE approaches are concerned with how the existing order came into being and, given the manifold exploitative features of capitalism, how to conceive its potential change. The focus is to place transnational private governance in the broader historical context of capitalist development. The line that separates public from private governance is not fixed and should be understood as contingent in time and space (Cutler 1997; Haufler 2002: 2–6). For example, rules for commercial transactions across boundaries were first developed by private actors (merchants) and only later adopted by states. State ownership of the economy was widespread in earlier times, but private firms such as the East India Company had broad regulatory competences. While stricter separation between the public and the private began with the industrial revolution, it is only in the late twentieth century (and within the Organisation for Economic Co-operation and Development (OECD) world) that it has taken on the clear character it has today.

By setting these assumptions within the broader framework of capitalism, GPE scholars focus on structural forces and power relations, in particular the structural power of capital. A structural conception of power emphasises the environment in which strategic interactions take place. The rise of private authority then points towards the development of the competition state, the deterritorialisation of capital and the related process of flexible accumulation (Cerny 1990; Sassen 2003, 2006; Graz and Palan 2004). Furthermore, it is connected with the rise of neoliberalism as a political ideology and an ongoing programme of large-scale reforms that confers on the private sector an efficiency supposedly lacking in the public sector. The form and the content of regulation should therefore not be treated separately from each other. Mechanisms and forms of private governance have implications beyond functional issues of market regulation and social justice.

Besides the significance of transnational private governance for legitimising neoliberalism, GPE approaches also focus on forms often far removed from those examined in CPE studies. Coordination service firms such as rating agencies, institutional investors, trade exchanges, investment banks as well as multinational law, accounting, insurance and management consultancy firms enjoy considerable authority over others, by setting and enforcing distinct standards of acceptable behaviour. For instance, institutional investors develop and enforce codes for corporate conduct that are based on crucial elements of the neoliberal economic model, such as the predominance of shareholder value. Rating agencies shape the behaviour of market participants by limiting the range of legitimate practices for companies based on similar principles – otherwise companies risk a downgrading of their debt and, correspondingly, higher costs for refinancing. Furthermore, private norms developed by accountancy firms undermine alternatives to the neoliberal business model, e.g. the long-term perspectives of German business based on considerable hidden reserves. These and other types of coordination service firms not only further the neoliberal orthodoxy but also are supported in this function by states. The concept of transnational private governance thus presumes a form of global hybrid authority which prompts increasing concerns about the scope of this new type of influence and the opacity of the means involved (Graz 2006a).

Most GPE studies fruitfully situate the historical, political and economic context of transnational private governance and present considerable explanatory potential in terms of structural forces and power relations. They also offer a clear normative perspective and a forceful critique of such authority. Yet, GPE scholars often neglect the concrete mechanisms of transnational private governance. Although some studies – particularly on merchant law (Cutler 1997, 1999, 2003), rating agencies (Sinclair 1994, 1999), international capital adequacy frameworks (Chavagneux 2001; King and Sinclair 2003), reporting standards (Soederberg 2003) or transnational elite clubs (Gill 1990; Apeldoorn 2002; Graz 2003) – go into much detail, they do not provide a middle-range theory of transnational private governance in contemporary capitalism that could be generalised and probed on empirical grounds. These shortcomings relate by and large to the epistemological and theoretical underpinnings of GPE approaches. First, there are obvious limitations in terms of complexity reduction for holistic historicist approaches focused on non-causal explanations. As Gill points out, 'the idea is to transcend rigid theories of causality and move towards a more reflexive and dynamic form of political economy *explanation* [...], which insists upon the centrality of the interrelationship between the "subjective" and "objective" social forces in historical developments' (Gill 1993a: 26–7). Second, critical arguments remain difficult to refute on empirical grounds. From a historical materialist perspective, developments contrary to an assumed rise of neoliberal capitalism reflect the dialectic of history. Polanyi (1944) called this a 'double movement', in that society inevitably seeks to protect itself from the market's drive to commodify increasing spheres of everyday life. Third, the broad transformative posture of GPE approaches are usually not matched by more concrete proposals on how to overcome the current deficits of transnational private governance.

Overcoming the divide between CPE and GPE

A review of the two most important current debates on transnational private governance shows that, although hardly flawless on their own ground, they might lead to substantial explanatory power if taken together. GPE accounts provide a much needed historical background in explanations highlighting power relations, but still fall short of outlining a theory of private governance that could be generalised, nor do they present concrete proposals on how to use this mode of governance for a transformative agenda. CPE accounts, for their part, provide persuasive and concrete analyses of institutional mechanisms, completed by clearly identified practical proposals, but generally lack comprehensive explanatory power and normative discernment. Therefore, their picture of private governance remains descriptive and mostly inductive.

Yet, on conceptual grounds, both approaches focus on the transnational underpinning of contemporary politics in contrast to state-centred analyses. By highlighting the importance of private governance, both argue that the conventional state-centric accounts are unable to cover important forms of cross-border collective action. Similarly, on empirical grounds, both strands of analysis would have much to gain in searching to complement each other. While GPE scholarship has accumulated a wealth of knowledge about some of the critical capitalist infrastructures such as finance, law and technical standards, CPE enquiries have explored concrete attempts to tackle some of the worst effects of capitalism in the depletion of the environment and the mistreatment of workers' rights. Finally, in their normative orientation, CPE and GPE studies have more in common than often assumed, despite their different terminologies and difficulties in finding a common ground for dialogue. Both sides worry about the outcome of an unfettered capitalist expansion; both worry over the democratic legitimacy of transnational private governance; and both sides search for ways on how to overcome this sorry state of affairs. Further convergence would therefore not undermine their aspirations to transform – although probably on different planes – the current neoliberal capitalist model.

As can be inferred from the above discussion, three distinct issues are particularly relevant in overcoming the divide between CPE and GPE approaches on transnational private governance. First, conceptual clarification is crucial to better define and circumscribe the social reality referred to as transnational private governance. Second, the explanation of the social action taking place within this distinct reality requires more detailed identification of the framework conditions that make transnational private governance possible. Third, as social action is inherently based on a set of shared or conflicting principles, the phenomenon of transnational private governance ultimately calls for a more elaborate account of its normative implications. Emphasising these three issues will allow examination of transnational private governance from a comprehensive, yet differentiated perspective that embraces conceptual, analytical and normative levels of analysis (see Table 1.1).

Definition and concepts

The significance of the interrelationships between subjective and objective aspects of reality in social sciences makes the definition of concepts a crucial

Table 1.1 The meaning of transnational private governance: an analytical framework

Conceptual clarification	Transnational	Functional scope Spatial scope
	Private	Range of private actors State recognition
	Governance	Logic of power Logic of action
Framework conditions	Structural	Social system of production Forms of competition International institutional embeddedness Policy type
	Actor-based	Resources Value homogeneity
Normative implications	Socioeconomic concerns	Problem-solving capacity Neoliberalism
	Procedural issues	Sovereignty Legitimacy

stage in understanding how existing order and potential historical change come about. As compared to experimental sciences, the object of any social science can never be treated as separate from the subject producing some knowledge about it. Inversely, the analyst cannot avoid the fact that he/she is part of the social world observed. His/her subjectivity reflects upon early assumptions, research questions, privileged theories and dataset examined. As concepts are essential, yet never self-evident tools of social enquiry, clarity is all the more necessary in referring to transnational private governance for the exploration of what seems to be a major shift in contemporary historical structures.

That may sound fine in principle, yet the question of definition raises particular problems for a collective volume bringing together theoretically pluralistic contributions. It would be all too easy to merely point out that it is up to each author to provide, on his/her own terms, a satisfactory definition of transnational private governance. While transnational private governance may, and certainly does, mean different things to different authors, the shared understanding of what it implies for the analysis of ongoing transformations of the contemporary world should not be underestimated. Referring to one concept instead of any other among existing studies places a distinct set of social phenomena at centre stage. It produces a particular view of social phenomena. In other words, the attempt to bring together a range of scholarship under the umbrella of a single concept is to look at CPE and GPE issues in a particular way. The key question, then, is: what analytical relevance does the concept of transnational private governance offer to the social sciences in general, and to CPE and GPE in particular? As the following account should make clear, each term of the concept highlights a major change in the material and symbolic organisation of our societies. The notion of transnational – rather than international – assumes foundational realignments in social spaces transcending national borders. The term private in itself stresses a substantial tilt in the relations between public and private realms. Finally, to dwell on governance instead of government supposes a profound reconfiguration of the role of the state in international affairs. This said, a central tenet of the book is that transnational private governance is something of an abuse of language as is it neither fully transnational, nor entirely private or excluding governments in its logic of action and power. This section explicates this contention on conceptual terms; the subsequent ones discuss how to probe the argument in analytical and normative terms.

Transnational

As Anderson (1991) and many others have pointed out, the assumed spatial correlation between the nation and the state has never existed, neither have distinct spaces separating discrete domestic national economies. The notion of transnational should therefore be situated beyond a mere inside/outside dichotomy. In this sense, it might be relevant to disaggregate further the notion between the function and spatial scope involved in current reconfigurations of the political space.

First, the *functional scope* of the practices concerned cuts across the territorial basis of political institutions with a propensity to merge subnational, national, international and supranational arenas. What is significant in the spatial implication of transnational governance is less the deterritorialisation of state sovereignty as such as that the deterritorialisation process brings to light a reorganisation of the logic at work in the production of space that encroaches upon the conflicting sources of authority on a transnational basis. As Saskia Sassen repeatedly emphasises in her comprehensive study on the 'denationalisation' of state agendas and the privatisation of norm making, 'the rise of private authority is not simply an external force that constraints the state. It is partly endogenous to the state' (Sassen 2006: 223). Thus, a core question to empirical research is the extent to which transnational private authority implies a shift to functional forms of governance and, by the same token, the degree of territorial basis it inflexibly retains.

Second, we should look at the *spatial scope* of the transfers of authority resulting from transnational private governance. The term transnational supposes the projection of an action beyond the territorial basis of state sovereignty, which involves social relations both *between* and *across* states. Yet this does not affect the whole world in the same way. We can expect differences according to the size of the geographic scale observed, whether global, regional or bilateral. Moreover, the spatial scope affected by such transnational processes is also likely to follow the main lines of fractures and hierarchies of contemporary capitalism. The transnational dimension of this type of governance is structured along an inclusive/exclusive line of demarcation, with clear differentiation in North–South relations and centre–periphery dynamics. As Duffield (2001) has pointed out, this may have deep implications on our understanding of the development-security nexus, insofar as such sophisticated forms of governance increasingly encounter non-liberal political complexes at their margins affected by so-called new wars. Thus, paraphrasing Lipschutz and Rowe (2005), we should be reminded that there is little, if any, global regulation for the rest of us. Brand (2005: 171) coined the concept of 'fragmented hegemony' in the same vein to emphasise that what could be observed in the centre, could not be in North–South relations.

Private

Many analyses have emphasised that governance refers to a new way to seek arrangements by systematically involving private actors, whether in the domestic or international arena (Murphy 2000; Pierre and Peters 2000). Yet from a historical perspective, this is not so new. The state, as we now know it, related to a given territory, controlling a closely defined population whose sovereignty is allegedly embodied in it, centralising monetary emission in conjunction with private agents –all this is a creation of the last third of the nineteenth century in the Western world. As Halliday (2001) points out, 'all that appears to be non-state is not so independent of the state, just as all that is new may not be as novel'. What is new with the involvement of private actors in transnational governance issues is not so much the extent and intensity of their influence as how some of them have managed to develop a new relationship with the polity. Two issues are at stake here: the range of private actors concerned and the support of the state.

As regards the first issue, a better understanding of the *range of private actors* involved in transnational governance practices undoubtedly depends on how we define the private/public distinction. While accounts may vary on how the development of capitalism, the modern state and civil society have shaped social relations along a separation between a private and a public sphere, scholarship in both GPE and CPE has emphasised how both spheres should be analysed as closely related, reflecting two faces of the same coin. For the purpose of the present analysis, the distinction can be understood as between a public sphere, which confers inclusive and universalistic rights of citizenship, and a private sphere, which brings into play such rights in order to provide exclusive and bounded contractual rights. From this perspective, the range of actors in the private sphere is larger than firms – what we refer to as the 'private sector' in narrow economic terms – and individuals from a similarly narrow behaviourist social theory. Trade unions, activists, class or gender organisations, professional associations, cadres and experts organised in ad hoc bodies, advocacy or policy networks, elite clubs, religious groups and guerrillas are all part of the private sphere. This implies that the 'private' potentially includes any collective actor organised through formal or informal contractual relations within the ambit of civil society. As Colàs (2002: 26) argues, civil society should not be conceived in a crude dichotomy with the modern state, but rather as 'an arena of social life differentiated from the state while simultaneously revealing its complex interaction with the state ... [which] reveals a number of international factors in its genesis and development'. The question for empirical research, then, is which private actors are most prominently involved in transnational private governance – can we assume that it involves all types of private actors, or only a chosen few?

This brings us to our second point. While the private dimension of governance refers to a process involving actors other than states, it also relies on an explicit or implicit *state recognition*. Recent scholarship shares the assumption that the state remains a central feature in understanding the governance functions undertaken by private actors in both domestic and international affairs. Explanations may differ according to competing theoretical approaches. For instance, scholars with a background in neocorporatist studies would emphasise the 'shadow of hierarchy' required for effective self-regulation (see e.g. Héritier 2002a, 2002b or Smismans in this volume), whilst transnational historical materialists would explain how private actors and the state should be understood as two different expressions of a larger configuration of social forces (see e.g. Gill 1993b or Holman in this volume). While there may be sharp disagreements as to the sense attributed to state recognition, there is little disagreement concerning the overall complementary and subsidiary role taken by private actors in regard to state functions.

Governance

It is widely acknowledged that the notion of governance has gained currency since the 1970s in order to appraise various forms of political reorganisation at a distance from traditional governmental and intergovernmental decision making. This is what the catchphrase 'governance without government' supposedly conveys. The notion of governance is also associated with the new institutional forms being explored with the demise of Fordism, where the state was pivotal in securing a fair distribution of high productivity gains between capital and labour so as to ensure a relatively stable growth rate of the domestic economy. The concept of governance has thus achieved prominence both as a normative compass for change claimed to be closer to the people (good governance) and as an analytical tool to explore a supposed retreat of the state and the emergence of a new form of polity (multilevel governance). Speaking of *governance* thus requires specifying the type of power relations and the scope of regulatory practices concerned. Here again, two closely related issues are involved: on the one hand, the definition of the *logic of power* involved in governance impacts upon the scope of regulatory practices under investigation; on the other, the *logic of action* implemented according to distinct procedures within the framework of such power relations.

As far as the *logic of power* is concerned, most analytical accounts of governance rely on a definition focused on consensual arrangements, intentionally agreed upon by state and non-state actors directly involved in setting and enforcing rules. Such an understanding replicates a relational view on power, which explores the ability of A to get B to do what he wants. Analysing actual decision making, its processes, procedures and potential biases from an actor-centred perspective, it mostly ignores, however, the structural underpinning of power relations, in which social forces can durably modify the environment of their practices in their own favour. As a number of contributors in this volume emphasise, governance should therefore be situated at the juncture of consensual and coercive power, involving intentional agreement as well as unintentional domination. Such an understanding of the notion of governance calls to mind Stephen Lukes' seminal conceptualisation of power, involving not only observable overt and covert conflicts, but also latent conflicts resulting from more deeper and structural contradictions in existing power relations (see Lukes 1974 and Fuchs in this volume). Just as Lukes' conceptualisation of power was inspired by the writings of Antonio Gramsci on the state, the logic of power at stake in governance can be considered as closely related to the Gramscian concept of hegemony. Hegemony is understood as a form of social domination in which one group exercises leadership and imposes its projects through the explicit or tacit consent of all those drawn into the coalition of social forces identifying their particular interest as the general interest. Recognising the logic of power in governance issues as an ongoing combination of consensus and coercion, reflecting intentional and unintentional domination alike, leads us to enlarge the scope of regulatory practices concerned. Governance in this respect encompasses both the narrow sense of regulation, deregulation or re-regulation on specific issue areas and the institutional framework embedding such rules, and the larger sense of self-reproducing unintentional domination through which a structure of thought and action can be so internalised that they appear as natural and inevitable.

Within the framework of such power relations, our second point relates to the *logic of action* implemented according to distinct procedures. Specifying the logic of action is all the more important in governance studies as they often regard the type of procedures involved as the most important feature of this new way of organising our societies. A shared assumption in the literature is that informal and non-hierarchical forms of governance are increasingly replacing command-and-control hierarchical and formal types of state regulation. Non-hierarchical 'steering modes' based on private–public partnerships are, for instance, a central feature in the debate on the legitimacy of this type of governance (Risse 2006). In a different vein, the World Economic Forum can be viewed as a critical case of the potential authority exercised on a global scale by informal and weakly institutionalised non-state actors such as transnational elite clubs. Yet, even in such a case, there are intrinsic limits in loosely informal arrangements divorced from the legitimate institutions of public life (Graz 2003). Similarly, non-hierarchical procedures such as those analysed by principal agent approaches or those implemented in private–public partnerships often need the 'shadow of hierarchy' to be effective. It makes little sense to view the logic of action underpinning governance as distinctively informal and non-hierarchical. Governance more accurately sets in motion a logic of action inventing new channels in the relations between formal and informal procedures, as well as hierarchical and non-hierarchical mechanisms of social action.

Framework conditions

Whilst the preceding discussion should contribute to better conceptualise transnational private governance, we still should explain in more detail the framework conditions that make transnational private governance possible. The core task here is to identify the circumstances under which private actors obey norms that are not initiated or set by states. Our goal is to explore the significance of a number of empirical scope conditions that appear to be essential for initiating, implementing, and sustaining transnational private governance. While there is an extensive literature on the various aspects related to governance as a new mode of policy processes and power relations, especially in the context of the European integration (Majone 1996; Héritier 2002), very few attempts so far exist in reviewing on a systematic basis its both private and transnational underpinnings.

Approaches in terms of international private authority initiated the agenda by stressing that at least three conditions should be met for such new forms of governance to be effective: (i) an explicit or implicit recognition by the state, (ii) the consent of actors subject to the rules without having been involved in their making and (iii) a high degree of compliance to the rules so as to be able to clearly differentiate between private power or influence in general and the more specific category of private governance (Cutler *et al.* 1999b: 19). Yet, despite the development of a typology of private authority along six types of cooperative arrangements from loosely informal industry norms and practices to formal private regimes governing rules in a distinct issue area, the analysis remains unclear on the compliance issue, which precisely determines whether we are to refer to this particular phenomenon. Moreover, as the analysis focuses exclusively on cooperative arrangements between firms, it remains unclear how it could be extended to arrangements including other types of non-state actors. In their attempt to broaden the understanding of private authority in international affairs, Hall and Biersteker (2002) considerably extend the types of actors potentially concerned by including not-for-profit bodies and illicit organisations. In doing so, they distinguish between 'market authority' exercised through cooperative arrangements among firms, 'moral authority' expected from NGOs or religious movements and 'illicit authority' exercised by organised crime or mercenaries. While this approach is successful in exploring the authoritative dimensions of private non-state actors other than firms in the contemporary system, the typology is misleading. Moral claims underpin market authorities, banking for instance on corporate social responsibility, just as growth and monetary concerns pervade moral authorities claimed by NGOs and new social movements. Moreover, the notion of illicit authority tends to confound authority and power, neglecting that only the former can claim to a power recognised as legitimate. As Hall and Biersteker themselves note, 'authority thus requires both recognition by and the consent of those governed by that authority' (ibid.: 204). Illicit practices can indeed be consensual as part of a resistance movement aiming for a radical change in society and manoeuvring in the covert world; yet illicit activities also often involve extortion, brute force and the rule of fear that can hardly qualify as consent. The following analytical framework tries to overcome these shortcomings in order to reach a more comprehensive, yet differentiated understanding of the core conditions into play in initiating, implementing and sustaining transnational private governance. The framework reflects an approach which presumes a profound interrelationship between ideal and material conditions, as well as structural and more actor-centred forms of explanations.

Structural conditions

The broadest structural feature defining the empirical scope of transnational private governance relates to a distinct *social system of production*. As discussed above with regard to the emergence of the notion of governance itself, transnational private governance should be situated in a particular phase of development of modern capitalism. Various accounts have provided insightful analyses of how a new social system of production, sometimes called post-Fordism, has undermined the role priorly detained by the state in the distribution of productivity gains between capital and labour on a national basis (Hollingsworth and Boyer 1997). Such a restructuring of the economic and political spheres across borders is also known as neoliberalism. No single criteria could on its own sum up what neoliberalism is. It nonetheless reflects the intellectual climate, the material reality and political project behind a form of globalisation, which sets individual freedom and ownership as supreme rights by reinforcing the domination of capital over labour, especially the power of finance, throughout a world economy expected to be free from state-imposed restrictions. As Murphy (2002) points out, 'the social forces that have continued to back the neoliberal agenda are truly transnational, which implies that to understand contemporary global governance we need to develop a class analysis that transcend national boundaries'. At the same time, it appears that the social system of production underpinning transnational private governance is prone to involve stakeholders more broadly defined than in traditional class-based tripartism between labour, capital and the state. The wide range of diverse actors involved in the proliferation of codes of conduct is for instance significant of this shift away from the central role of the state in the Fordist era.

Distinct *forms of competition* also enhance the rise of transnational private governance. While CPE and GPE approaches may be familiar with the argument, they often lack detailed analysis of the issues at stake. Various studies have none the less analysed how transformations in the organisation of markets can reinforce the ability of private actors to play a more direct role in rule setting and enforcement. From a regulation theory perspective, Petit and others contend that changes in forms of competition on an international basis are even so significant that they now tend to play the central role that the wage-labour nexus used to play in the domestic arena under Fordism (Petit 1999; Coriat *et al.* 2006; Dannreuther and Petit 2006). Drawing upon economic sociology and business studies on alliance capitalism (Dunning 1997), Portnoy (1999) also argues that strategic alliances among MNCs not only reshape the competitive environment by expanding industrial networks beyond national borders in establishing the so-called transnational industrial orders, but also promote new forms of political management in which internationally organised industries are heavily involved. As mentioned above, the type of company matters, with big manufacturing companies with well-known brand names expected to be more involved in transnational private governance than others. Besides the degree and the type of competition, as well as the types and size of firms involved, a market organised along global value chains supposing an extreme disaggregation of the production process and its relations to the consumer requires heavy coordination mechanisms. In this respect, forms of competition also relate to the coherence provided by coordination service firms. Hence, in order to understand which form of competition is most likely to enhance transnational private governance, we should look not only at the structure of the market, but also at the size and types of firms involved. The chapters that follow will fully illustrate that, contrary to what is often assumed, regulatory innovation in transnational private governance is far from echoing highly competitive markets. Rather it takes place in an oligopolistic environment, characterised by limited competition and dominated by big firms active in coordination services and highly dependent on global value chains.

International institutional embeddedness. The distinct role that institutional constraints can play on political economy issues has now been extensively explored in historical institutionalist approaches on varieties of capitalism, with strong national trajectories and regulatory sequences between the domestic and international spheres (Hall and Soskice 2001). In contrast to domestic forms of governance analysed from an international basis, such means of creating order and setting rules are conventionally considered as weakly institutionalised when projected on a transnational spectrum – apart from some specialised issues areas. This assumption is unmistakably reinforced when *private* forms of governance are involved. An extreme illustration of this view is to identify the European Union (EU) governance system as a 'multi-level, non-hierarchical, deliberative and apolitical governance, via a complex web of public/private networks and quasi autonomous executive agencies' (Hix 1998: 54). Yet, just as many studies have highlighted that the EU governance systems is backed up by a large set of institutional constraints, the question is not so much whether transnational private governance is embedded in international institutions, but rather in which institutions, at which level, granted with what kind of enforcement power and authority. In this respect, a core task in analysing transnational private governance is to identify in more detail the degree along which it is institutionally embedded on an international plane. As the following chapters show in detail, the picture is indeed quite different according to whether we are looking at transnational private governance within the ambit of the EU governance system of Internet domain names or accounting standards for listed companies, or at the UN framework on food labelling or workers rights, not to mention global banking regulation and supervision under the umbrella of the Bank for International Settlements.

Policy types. An aspect that lies at the juncture of structural conditions and explanations focused on the action of those involved in transnational private governance is the type of policy concerned. The effect that the specific problem at hand may have on the ability of policy networks to influence domestic politics was pointed out a long time ago (Lowi 1972). In this perspective, redistributive policies are far less likely to be dealt with by these networks because of their high degree of politisation. In the same vein, scholarship on transnational policy assumes that economic policies perceived as redistributive lead to intergovernmental rather than transgovernmental relations. Social groups that feel disadvantaged would mobilise against these policies and therefore shift decision making from the technical and bureaucratic transgovernmental to the more political intergovernmental level (Keohane and Nye 1974: 129; Risse-Kappen 1995: 8). Conversely, regulatory policies would be more conducive to transnational governance as they are considered to incur heavy resource dependency between actors who regulate and are regulated – the former needing, for instance, information from the latter, and the latter needing formal recognition from the former in order to pursue their interests. This scholarship, however, remains focused on public policies and public agencies. An important avenue of reasoning then is to explore how distinct policy types are decisive in the privatisation of transnational governance. While the following chapters will make clear that transnational private governance is more likely to occur with regulatory than redistributive policies, they will also emphasise that the distinction is to some extent misleading as redistributive concerns can never be totally kept out of regulatory issues. Different types of regulatory issues may also affect with great variance the ability of transnational private governance to become effective.

Actor-based conditions

Besides the four groups of factors identified above according to the degree of structural constraints exercised on the rise of transnational private governance, at least two additional, more actor-based characteristics should be included among the sets of preconditions to be met in order to make transnational private governance an effective alternative to the more conventional regulation of capitalism across borders. The first relates to the distinct set of resources at hand and the second to the homogeneous values among the agents directly involved in the process.

Resources mobilised by agents into a specific logic of action are a central issue in analysing policy processes. Financial capabilities, the use of force, loyalty, information, prestige and the like all belong to various explanations aimed at identifying a distinct set of resources reinforcing the ability of actors to define outcomes in particular issue areas. In contrast to conventional approaches in international relations, resource dependency theories on transnational policy networks give considerable space to the activity of private actors, yet they stop short of private self-regulation mechanisms and do not specifically address political economy issues (Nölke 1995, 2000). In the same vein, sociological approaches on resource dependencies in interorganisational networks help to analyse the exchange of material and immaterial resources between mutually and often asymmetrically dependent organisations, especially large firms. As the outcome of resource exchanges usually transcends the corporate actors on which those approaches concentrate, it may as well correspond to a precondition for the development of transnational private governance. Typical resources exchanged in policy networks include finance, information and legitimacy. In contrast to the domestic policy process, transnational private governance would therefore more likely be driven by resources predominantly available by private actors, involving consensual rather than coercive action, and implementing a functional scope across borders. While this assumption is closely related to conventional accounts of the inability of the state to undertake the complex tasks involved in governance and its reliance on the expertise of private actors and the knowledge of professional organisations to deal satisfactorily with such policies, the following chapters will show that, for private actors, building a consensus on complex issues across borders also depends upon resources other than knowledge and expertise, including reputation or credibility among the immaterial resources, financial capabilities and leverage power in the domain of material resources.

Homogeneity of values. Both CPE and GPE scholarship have stressed how a wide range of policies related to what we call globalisation reflect an increased homogeneity of values among the relatively circumscribed group of actors able to positively identify themselves to the process. As mentioned above, comparative studies have drawn lessons from constructivist approaches as to how the privatisation of governance mirrors middle-class preferences towards post-materialist orientations. They would also stress that 'quite naturally, intergovernmental groups prefer delegating functions to well known and reliable partners' (Ronit 2001: 570). GPE scholars, for their part, place the homogeneity of values in the larger picture of the achievement of hegemony. According to some of them, the type of power exercise through transnational private governance echoes how 'private councils [such as the Trilateral Commission or the Wold Economic Forum] are part of a much wider international process of elite familiarisation and fraternisation, mutual education and, broadly speaking, networking' (Gill 1990: 122). In respect of the strong institutional and state embeddedness of transnational private governance, shared values are not restricted to private actors but impinge upon actors more closely related to the public sphere. Among the factors fostering cooperative agreements in the complex committee work undertaken in European governance, Eichner and Majone for instance coined the notion of *copinage technocratique* (sic) in order to explain why 'actors on the technical level share more common interests than political actors' (quoted in Egan 2001: 162). More generally, as Djelic and Sahlin-Andersson (2006: 23) underscore in a recent volume on the institutional dynamics of regulation in transnational governance, there are 'powerful institutional forces that altogether constitute a transnational culture or meaning system'. Among such forces, contributors to that volume borrow to the world society perspective and the Bourdieusian field approach to pay special attention to the processes of scientisation, marketisation, formal organising, moral rationalisation and reinvented democratisation. Ultimately, the argument that a high degree of homogeneity of values is likely to be a precondition in transnational private governance takes us back to the sociology of elites (Scott 1990). Classical studies by Pareto, Mosca, Michels or Mills considered that the power of a 'governing elite', a 'political class', an 'oligarchy' or a 'power élite' depended upon a distinct organisational feature, in particular the shared consciousness of being a group with distinct interests, institutional positions enabling the achievement of such interests and a capacity for coordination facilitating greater unity of action through planning. This so-called Machiavellian tradition of elite analysis emphasises the concept of *control* over the means of production in contrast to *ownership* in the orthodox Marxian class analysis, just as transnational cadre analyses rely on a comprehensive concept of control to understand the key role professionals play in present times (Pijl 2004).

Unmistakably, a broad range of preconditions must be met in one way or another in order to make transnational private governance an effective alternative to the conventional regulation of business. Even if these preconditions were met, we might still have second thoughts about this type of governance which raises important normative concerns. This is what we want to examine in the following section.

Normative implications

Transnational private governance not only requires conceptual clarification and a detailed analytical framework, but also an examination of its normative implications to better understand the current shift in the organisation of the political economy of contemporary capitalism. The notion is indeed often used to support the participation of new actors in the policy process, assuming that they would better tackle complex sectoral issues. If left to market self-regulation or plain state regulation, the argument goes, the stakes would remain unstable at best, if not unable to deliver social justice. In this respect, transnational private governance is identified as a procedural innovation in policy processes suited to solve distinct socioeconomic concerns on a cross-border basis. The conditions under which such a claim can be sustained have gained the utmost importance in the governance debate. Yet, unsurprisingly, scholars remain deeply divided in their conclusions. For instance, Haufler (2001: 4) states: 'Voluntary standard setting by firms is a logical response to the ambiguities and uncertainties of the current global system. It responds to societal pressure, while avoiding rigid government interference. It is voluntary and therefore can be applied in a flexible manner. It is potentially global in scope, and if adopted widely, would reduce costs, increase efficiency, and prevent other corporations from gaining competitive advantage'. In contrast, Picciotto (2000: 162) reminds us that 'the growth of international regulatory or governance networks does not constitute the reduction of the scope of international politics, but rather its pursuits by other means. Certainly, it may entail an attempt to "depoliticise" issues, by deploying scientific, managerial or professional techniques and basing their solution on universalising discourses'. In order to shed light on such conflicting arguments, the following discussion attempts to explain the normative implications of transnational private governance in conjunction with two interrelated issues: the substantial socioeconomic concerns on the one hand, and procedural innovation in the polity on the other.

Socioeconomic concerns

The issue on which the CPE and GPE approaches outlined above most profoundly disagree is the normative assessment of the socioeconomic consequences of transnational private governance. While CPE scholars usually praise the problem-solving outcome of transnational private governance in distinct areas, GPE approaches lay emphasis on how it contributes to stabilising a neoliberal socioeconomic order considered as inherently unjust. The detailed empirical studies brought together in this volume should help to probe in some respects the persuasiveness of each perspective. Whilst different research agendas can benefit from each other's analytical insights and empirical evidence, distinct ontological, epistemological and theoretical underpinnings will of course remain. As Cox reminds us, problem-solving approaches are 'useful for correcting dysfunctions and maintaining order in the whole. [Yet,] a different kind of knowledge is required in order to understand how historical change has come about and how change can be brought' (Cox 2002: xxii). We should thus first clarify the more specific claims of each perspective.

Problem-solving capacity. For researchers working on the environment, labour standards or human rights, transnational private governance is frequently seen as the most realistic option to improve the state of affairs in non-OECD countries. Given the unwillingness of governments and the inability of intergovernmental organisations to provide satisfactory responses, private governance based on corporate social responsibility schemes is thought to be a pragmatic remedy for some of the most pressing concerns (Haufler 2001). In a slightly different perspective, transnational private governance is also perceived as an important contribution for the provision of problem-solving mechanisms in situations where governments or intergovernmental organisations are seen as too inflexible to provide for effective regulation. This is particularly true for fast-moving sectors such as in ICT (Salter 1999) or finance (Sinclair 2005). Yet, more often than not, these regulatory practices remain ambivalent. A core question addressed by the contributors of this volume is whether transnational private governance is really able to solve large societal problems such as environmental degradation, human rights abuses or systemic risks in finance.

Institutionalisation or transformation of neoliberalism. Even if transnational private governance could be considered as successful according to the criteria outlined above, there is still a larger problem, namely its potentially stabilising role for the current order of neoliberal capitalism. The focus of the critique here explicitly targets the reasons for which transnational private governance would be praised as an efficient problem-solving policy, i.e. the substitution of private regulation for public national or intergovernmental policy. Against this background, transnational private governance reflects an attempt to permanently fix the current weak role of public international regulation of business, in the same vein as other forms of contemporary global governance (Gill 1998; Picciotto 2000; Bayart 2004; Overbeek 2004). Having transnational private governance in place legitimises the retreat of the state or at least its unwillingness to tackle certain issues by intergovernmental regulation. This, in turn, works as a shield against popular calls for business re-regulation in case of major discontent with economic globalisation. Thus, private governance is supposed to make it more difficult for labour unions and social movements to mobilise, whereas business' preference for the existing socioeconomic order is being privileged. Correspondingly, our empirical studies will examine whether private governance prevents public regulation, and whether the substance of regulation is particularly in line with the preferences of business.

Procedural issues

Both the scholarly and public debates are concerned by the lack of democratic legitimacy of transnational private governance. Governance is usually not primarily conceived for its ability to democratise policy making, but rather as a solution to functional problems on specific issues requiring collective action. Yet, as legal scholars would put it, the new phenomenon of transnational governance must not make us forget our old questions, such as who bears the responsibility for governance without a government (Joerges *et al.* 2004)? In a recent volume, Benz and Papadopoulos (2006) precisely aim at exploring the relationship between democracy and governance from a cross-level analysis involving intranational, European and international arenas. They draw important lessons in assuming that the potential for improving the democratic legitimacy of governance lies in agreeing on the proper length and components of the chain of delegation in which the relationship between representatives and represented takes place. They also remind us that the inclusion of private actors, such as those from civil society or the expert communities, does not imply *per se* more democratic legitimacy of governance. In conclusion, they highlight how flawed governance can be when lacking linkages to democratic institutions (ibid.: 290–2). These accounts will undoubtedly help further research focused on policy-making implications of governance practices in democratic systems. Yet, they stop short of political economy considerations as such. Transnational private governance and the globalisation of capitalism are two inseparable aspects of the contemporary world. Normative considerations on the significance of the former also refer to the transformation of the latter. An adequate understanding of concerns raised by large segments of population affected in their everyday life in such a context is crucial to evaluate the normative constraints and opportunities presented by transnational private governance for a progressive change in the contemporary world. To this end, we need to clarify the closely related issues of sovereignty and legitimacy.

Sovereignty. Can public authorities always control the activities of transnational private governance or reverse the allocation of governance tasks to private actors? Most accounts of transnational private governance clearly challenge the traditional Weberian legal–rational view of state bureaucracies organised along distinct functional tasks. They emphasise the lack of clear distinction between an authority founded on scientific knowledge, technical expertise, and market power, on the one hand, and an authority built upon a formal mandate setting procedures for delegating the sovereign power of political subjects on the other. Even those sceptical of the assumption that business interests find ways to 'capture the state' in such a context examine the question of industry influence (Majone 2001; Jordana and Levi-Faur 2005). As Egan (2001: 33) points out, although regulatory studies 'are concerned with effective mechanisms to control bureaucratic discretion, the same questions have not yet been addressed with regard to self-regulatory mechanisms and private governance'. The following chapters highlight how the hybrid reconfiguration of the relationship between the public and the private spheres underway in transnational private governance may have important implications.

Democratic legitimacy. If political capture is defined more broadly than effects on outcomes, the infringement of transnational private governance on sovereign rights of citizens more structurally refers to a private control on resources and to the capacity of private actors to durably modify the environment of their practices in their own favour. For example, in the domain of technical specifications, consumers or labour representatives are at pains to compete with business interests regarding the time, money and expert knowledge required to fully take part at the global level in the procedures defined for setting and assessing technical standards such as those of the ISO. In many ways, the delegation of sovereign citizens' rights to non-elected bodies corresponds to a reinvention of corporatism: private interest groups and other private organisations are gaining public status and direct access to the political system in order to supposedly secure a stronger consensus. As many critics have argued, the theory of corporatism fails to capture the full nature of the framework of power in which these practices take place. As Ottaway (2001: 266) points out, 'it is doubtful that close cooperation between essentially unrepresentative organisations [...] will do much to ensure better protection for, and better representation of, the interests of populations affected by global politics'. Although institutional arrangements – such as the Global Compact on corporate responsibility, or the newly assigned role to the International Accounting Standards Committee (IASC)/International Accounting Standards Board (IASB) in accounting standards – can be understood as providing innovative solutions for new problems, they also encompass a more defensive aspect by neutralising potential critique through cooptation of its most moderate elements. Inclusion and exclusion appear as two faces of the same coin. As Hermet (2005: 21) emphasises, governance may thus well reflect the 'most recent reconfiguration of the imprescriptible aporia of real democracy, one that will always shy away from the sovereign rights of actors excluded from the cooptation at the top'. Whilst such a delegation of sovereign rights may have certain advantages in terms of output legitimacy, it also alters the character of governance by raising problems of accountability and input legitimacy.

Contents of the book: probing the limits of transnational private governance

The core argument of this book – reflected in its title – is that transnational private governance in the contemporary world faces tough limits on conceptual, analytical and normative issues. There are limits on definition, as each term of the concept should be understood in a dialectical perspective involving the continuing existence of the territorial basis of politics, of the state and of the structural power of governments and markets beyond various forms of governance. There are limits on framework conditions, as transnational private governance does not work in all situations. Finally, there are normative limits, as a number of implications remain highly questionable. By shedding light on such limitations, the book provides a critical account of transnational private governance taking its distance from studies emphasising the newness and innovative character of various forms of governance. The contributions put together in the volume offer a unique opportunity for constructing a theoretically coherent and empirically systematic examination of transnational private governance.

The book is organised in such a way as to probe the limits of transnational private governance in four distinct empirical domains. Part I addresses the already well-developed and perhaps less contested trend towards self-regulation in the financial sector. Part II deals with the rapidly growing but still largely contested area of corporate involvement in regulatory issues previously closely related to the state and its legal environment; it seeks to shed light on the increasingly overlapping roles of states and firms through voluntary codes in prominent areas such as labour, ecological and consumers' concerns. Part III provides a closer look on cases which reflect leading-edge developments in transnational private governance: the regulation of the cyberspace and Internet has pioneered extreme privatisation and demonstrated how in such contexts states and intergovernmental cooperation re-enter by the backdoor. Finally, Part IV explores a new, but rapidly spreading phenomenon, namely the interplay between regional integration schemes and transnational private governance. While the new generation of free-trade agreements initiated by the North

American Free-Trade Agreement (Nafta) pioneered this trend, the EU has now experienced the most forward-looking political embeddedness of private governance across nations on a regional basis.

In Part I, the chapters cover the most important segments of global *finance*, such as banking regulation, credit rating, derivatives trading, accounting and auditing. By comparing Eurobond underwriting, auditing and trading services for listed derivatives, Daniel Mügge presents several related arguments on the importance of oligopolistic market structures in the emergence of transnational private governance. For his part, Sebastian Botzem puts accounting regulation into a diachronic perspective. Drawing upon scholarship in sociology of the professions, he underlines the importance of professional experts for private governance and argues that a power shift is currently taking place, as national professional associations are loosing ground to globally operating auditing firms. Finally, the chapter by Eleni Tsingou explores one of the most famous cases of involvement of private actors in transnational governance by looking at global banking standards and regulation on capital adequacy, the so-called Basel II framework. Here again, she emphasises the important role of large financial firms and of technical expertise.

Part II provides a detailed account of the powerful role played by business in transnational private governance on core issues such as *labour, ecological and consumers' concerns*. In her chapter, Doris Fuchs presents a theoretical framework that captures the instrumental, structural and discursive power of business in global environmental governance. She emphasises that the power of business in transnational private governance should not be viewed only in the narrow sense of rule setting and self-regulation, but also in a broader sense encompassing the ability of business to influence the demand for and design of private and public governance institutions. The chapters of Frans van Waarden and Thomas Conzelmann/Klaus Dieter Wolf examine this issue in more detail. Van Waarden focuses on the significance of output legitimacy in regulatory measures aiming at controlling risks with a special focus on food labelling. In exploring options for a democratic control of this type of governance, he suggests substituting a functional legitimacy for a mere territorial understanding of this notion and, thus, defining the 'demos' as those affected by certain threats. Conzelmann and Wolf share a similar research interest and examine, for their part, more specifically the framework conditions for implementing input legitimacy in transnational private governance. They then discuss potential avenues for generalising this type of governance by combining input and output legitimacy. Finally, Jeroen Merk's chapter broadens our normative understanding by taking a political economy perspective on the private regulation of business. He analyses transnational private governance as a site of contention between different social and economic forces and discusses how compromises resulting from such processes can have an emancipatory effect for workers and civil society. Put together, these chapters cover all major issues that have been raised regarding the private regulation of transnational business, namely ecology, labour rights and consumers' concerns such as food quality.

Due to its close connection with highly dynamical technological developments, its inherently border-spanning character and, more broadly, as one of the most striking icon of globalisation, the Internet represent in many respects an *avant-garde case* of transnational private governance. While the different aspects of Internet governance examined in Part III shed light on these assumptions, they also emphasise limitations, regarding both the scope of a strictly private regulation and the normative implications of these developments. The chapter of Sven Bislev and Mikkel Flyverbom highlights the complexity of Internet governance, in particular the intermingling of public and private forms of regulation. In doing so, it offers a much-needed complement to the usual macroperspective on transnational private governance with a study on the role of individual firms such as Cisco and H-P at the core of the infrastructure of Internet governance. Subsequently, Josep Ibanez presents a detailed analytical framework to examine the specific set of power relations and structures of the emerging regime of e-commerce. Finally, George Christou and Seamus Simpson investigate a recent initiative involving complex relations between public authorities and private actors; their chapter analyses how the EU has taken an increasingly active role in Internet governance by setting up a private regulatory body in charge of the registry of the dot eu top-level domain. As a result, we see a clear tension between the liberal demands of the Internet community and the more 'paternalistic' claims of EU governance. Together, these three contributions cover the most important issues of private governance of the Internet, namely domain names, e-commerce and ICT infrastructure.

The last part of the volume explores how the EU increasingly makes use of transnational private governance as a method of economic regulation. While Simpson and Christou have emphasised this trend in their chapter on Internet governance, Otto Holman puts this recent development into a broader political economy perspective by arguing that EU-sponsored public–private partnerships not only suffer from a severe lack of democratic accountability, but also contribute to an erosion of European welfare states. Similar concerns are articulated in Stijn Smismans' contribution on industrial relations, which remains one of the classical cases of private governance. In contrast to the domestic context, the EU level is lacking major preconditions for self-regulatory autonomy in industrial relations, and, therefore, more control by public authorities is clearly needed. In a more pragmatic perspective, Karsten Ronit's chapter on the EU's initiative to create an out-of-court complaints network for financial services demonstrates that transnational private governance can contribute to problem solving, in particular if it is controlled by public authority or active social groups. The EU is not the only regional grouping that is a driving force behind the increasing importance of transnational private governance. Naomi Gal-Or's chapter provides evidence of parallel developments in the regionalisation process underway in the Western Hemisphere. By combing legal and international relation scholarship, she sets to explain the normative transformations affecting universal access to justice when private dispute resolution mechanisms are included in international trade and investment law, with a specific focus on the negotiations of the Free-Trade Area of the Americas Agreement.

In conclusion, this book not only reviews a process that is evolving extremely rapidly, provides ways for theoretical innovation, and broadens our empirical understanding of transnational private governance. It also highlights the limits of transnational private governance. These limits can be pinned down in the various facets of the three core issues – conceptual clarification, framework conditions and normative implications – explored in this introductory chapter and analysed in more detail by each author. The conclusion of the volume provides a thorough review of the findings of each chapter according to the categories set up in this introduction and to which our contributors were explicitly asked to respond in the early stage of the revising process. It is in this regard that the book is conceived as a timely attempt in stimulating a fruitful dialogue among researchers fragmented across a wide array of a research fields.

Part I

(Self-)regulation in the financial sector

2 Keeping competitors out

Industry structure and transnational private governance in global finance

Daniel Mügge

Introduction[1]

The literature on private actors in transnational politics, reassessed by Graz and Nölke in the opening chapter of this volume, has identified many important factors determining the scope and form of their influence. This chapter argues that in the field of regulation, a crucial one has been largely ignored: the pattern of inter-firm competition. It claims that it is central to explaining why transnational private regulation is sometimes effected through private institutions, and sometimes through public ones. The reasoning is as follows: in principle, producers of goods and services prefer self-regulation to rule setting through a public body. Thus, they avoid interference by other stakeholders and can tame competition. This should also apply transnationally. However, producers may call on 'the state' to intervene when other firms use transnational private regulation to the formers' competitive disadvantage. The result is a relocation of regulation to the public domain. Rule setting becomes a matter of inter-state politics. Dominant producers, according to the hypothesis, support transnational private regulation unless it threatens their competitive positions.

That seems to say little about public actors' willingness to acquiesce to such demands. Regulation is normally seen as a public task, exercised in the name of the public good. But politico-economic reality often looks different. Producers regularly 'capture' regulators and infuse policy with their own preferences (Stigler 1971), particularly in industries with high economies of scale and a tendency towards concentration. In addition, the complexity of regulatory questions frequently leaves room for producers to provide 'technical input' and mould regulation in their own favour. Under these conditions, producers' regulatory preferences, including those regarding institutional form, are likely to carry considerable weight.

Drawing on these ideas, the central argument of the corporate competition approach presented here can be summarised as follows: whether regulation of transnationally integrated market spaces is located in the private or the public domain depends on the intensity of competitive struggles among major firms in the segment concerned. If competitive struggles have been resolved and the population of firms has stabilised, transnational private regulation is likely. If such struggles remain unresolved, public regulation is likely. For this mechanism to operate, one central condition needs to be fulfilled: producer firms must exert strong influence on regulation in the sector in question. Otherwise, their preferences for private or public regulation may be overshadowed by other stakeholders' concerns.

Business and financial services are well suited to illustrate this mechanism. The second half of this article presents three cases from this realm – Eurobond underwriting, international auditing standards and derivatives trading and clearing – complemented by evidence from a study by Tony Porter (1999). These three plus one cases capture variation on the variables central to the argument: the stability or instability of producer populations and the private or public nature of transnational regulation. Even though these cases cannot 'prove' the argument, not least because 'isolating variables' is difficult in complex issues like transnational regulation, they illustrate the hypothesis and lend it support.

A theoretical framework

Early studies of American business regulation convincingly argued that producers would systematically beat other stakeholders at influencing regulation (Stigler 1971, Becker 1983, Peltzman 1989). Their relatively low numbers facilitated coordinated lobbying and high individual stakes induced higher investment into such activities compared to consumers, for example.

A socioeconomic perspective reinforces the case for producer dominance. The central pillar of 'market-making' is not the *introduction* of competition, but its *avoidance* (Fligstein 1996).

> Much of the market-making project is to find ways to stabilize and routinize competition. Much of the history of the largest corporations can be read as attempts to stabilize market for these firms in the face of ruinous competition and economic downturns. [...] Finding ways to compete that do not revolve around price competition alone has proved pivotal to producing stability for firms in all advanced industrial societies.
>
> (Fligstein 2001: 5)

Such market stability – understood as the stability of populations of producers – needs to be provided through social institutions such as monopoly and patent rights, tariffs against foreign producers, business regulation that locks in market positions, ownership structures that ameliorate competition or the formation of business associations.

Two classes of social institutions are particularly relevant here – rules of exchange and conceptions of control. 'Rules of exchange' define who can undertake which business transactions under which conditions. Most business regulation falls into this category. 'Conceptions of control' refer to the general acceptance of the way a particular market is structured. This includes 'market boundaries' – whether, for example, a bank can sell travel insurance or not – but also which firms dominate a market segment. In stable times, the 'market incumbents' live in a form of 'truce'. A conception of control prevails when the current market order, both in terms of market boundaries and the hierarchy among firms, is not seriously challenged, and the formal and informal limits to 'admissible competition' are respected. Because neither the population of incumbents nor the prevailing conception of control can change *over longer periods of time* without the other changing as well, they will henceforth be treated as two sides of the same coin.

Private preferences and public consent

In stable times, rules of exchange reproduce the hierarchy of producer firms inscribed in the prevailing conception of control. These rules can be both formal or informal, and public or private. Rule setting through private institutions ('private regulation') figures at least as prominently in history as regulation through the 'state' (Braithwaite and Drahos 2000). Producers prefer such self-regulation to rule setting through public bodies. It inhibits other stakeholders' pushing for their own preferences (transparency, lower prices, better quality, stable employment opportunities, etc.). A collective preference for self-regulation obviously depends on consensus among incumbents. Such consensus is unlikely if they face unresolved competitive struggles. Firms feeling disadvantaged will call on public actors to protect them. A stable conception of control is therefore vital for the emergence of private governance.

As the commonness of self-regulation demonstrates, public actors often abide it. This willingness grows with the complexity of the regulatory issues involved. The less policy goals or policy instruments are self-evident, the more room producers find to set the regulatory agenda and suggest 'solutions' to problems they themselves helped define. In addition, design, monitoring and enforcement of regulation for complex areas are costly. If an industry promises to address regulatory problems appearing on the political agenda through self-regulation, public actors will often be happy to agree.

Regulatory policy networks are normally fairly circumscribed. Indeed, in both public and private governance, a prime motive of 'insiders' to institutionalise access to policy is to keep 'outsiders' at bay. In contrast to 'normal' times, a policy domain can enter the political limelight in times of crisis – a market scandal, for example – punctuating the prevailing policy equilibrium (True *et al.* 1999). Politicians from outside the policy network get involved. They start initiatives under the banner of 'tightening' regulation to prevent future malfeasance. In such instances, the formal democratic accountability of public actors allows stakeholders other than producers and the population at large to leave their imprint on regulation.

Alas, such instances are the exception rather than the rule. Even when a wider audience becomes involved, producers normally do their best to 'keep the state out' and other potential stakeholders with it. One institutional solution is to leave rule setting in the private domain but to add a layer of public oversight as to provide public actors with an 'emergency brake'. In effect, such public 'oversight' often remains lax. It is of secondary importance for the argument developed here because it leaves the producers' capacity to manage intra-industry competition through rule setting intact. In the cases discussed below, this has happened with auditing firms and underwriters of Eurobonds.

Regulating the transnational domain

Transnational private governance is hardly new. Studying international (in the parlance adopted here: transnational) patent regimes, Porter (1999) documents how British textile manufacturers in the nineteenth century and US automobile producers in the twentieth century used their dominance in the respective transnational market segments to install private patent regimes and thereby reproduce their grip on markets. His cases – discussed in more detail below – supported the notion that the population of producers in the cross-border market space must be sufficiently consolidated for a transnational conception of control to have emerged. Put differently, a group of cross-border market incumbents must have found ways to stabilise their market. Not that they have stopped competing with each other. Rather, they have found means – here through private rule setting – to keep potential challengers at bay.

Porter has placed his case material in the context of 'hegemonic decline'. Translated into the criteria employed here, this meant that market incumbents were all rooted in a single (hegemonic) jurisdiction where a conception of control had previously emerged domestically. Transnational private regulation emerged because competitive struggles had already been solved at home. However, there is no reason why firms controlling or struggling over a market segment need to come from a single national background, 'hegemonic' or not. It is equally possible that incumbents are rooted in multiple jurisdictions. Then, a conception of control has to emerge in the transnational market place itself for transnational private regulation to become likely. In such cases, transnational trade associations serve a double purpose. They stabilise the population of producers through enabling cooperation on contentious issues and provide a forum for de facto self-regulation. To underscore that firms' dominance in transnational markets is not necessarily wedded to a 'hegemonic order', the case studies presented below explicitly cover situations where incumbents come from single as well as multiple jurisdictions.

Bringing in public governance

So when should we expect transnational *public* regulation? Assuming that corporations tend to disapprove of public governance and that public actors tend to heed this preference, much of the content and intensity of public regulation depends on producers' supporting it. In domestic contexts, the accountability of democratic governments to stakeholders other than producers may temper the latter's dominance, particularly in severe crises. Then, a third option arises in addition to either private or public regulation – what we might call private regulation with public oversight, discussed below.

Regulation's impact on stakeholders other than producers is often less direct in cross-border contexts than in domestic ones. That weakens public actors' accountability to the public at large and makes them even more beholden to producer interests. The trade policy-like aspects of regulation reinforce this tendency. Corporate actors will back public governance of cross-border exchange when competitive struggles have remained unresolved and corporations feel their very survival is threatened unless public authorities 'take over'. This is the standard situation when transnational market development is still in its early phases. Therefore, transnational private governance is only likely when transnational markets are either underdeveloped – and therefore such governance poses no threat to national producers – or are sufficiently developed for a stable group of incumbents to have emerged. The progressive transnationalisation of many market segments associated with globalisation thus adds a clear time dimension to the emergence of transnational private governance: it becomes more likely as such segments 'mature' in the sense that competitive issues are eventually settled and private forms of governance therefore become possible.

Incumbents in an integrated market place face a trade-off when considering to call for public governance. On the one hand, it may keep potential competitors at bay. On the other hand, relocating regulation to the public domain erodes the privilege of an industry's effective self-governance. Therefore, the threshold for calls for public regulation is relatively high and rises with further market integration. Again, two scenarios can be distinguished. First, market incumbents that hitherto 'managed' a cross-border market without public 'help' may see their positions erode. Second, dominant firms may contest the established conception of control themselves and thereby create competitive struggles. Again, firms feeling 'challenged' are likely to call on governments to create a transnational public regime where none existed before.

Both scenarios are reminiscent of protectionism in classic trade politics. Yet they exhibit a central difference: traditional protectionism aims to inhibit market access for foreign competitors. Protectionism combats transnational market integration. In calls for transnational public regulation, in contrast, private actors *support* such integration, but want to secure 'voice' in the rule setting.

The parallels with classic international regimes also extend to the varied degree to which territorial aspects still matter. Effective transnational private governance depends on the implicit support of the core countries of the global economy, those that could 'veto' such governance by refusing to accept private standards. Most clearly, no transnational private governance is thinkable in a field where American firms are significant but reject it. Needless to say, this mechanism leads to a marginal, if any, role in transnational private governance for actors from the 'global South', with the exception of a few resource-extraction industries.

The corporate competition approach suggests that a market segment should move from public to private governance when the population of firms stabilises.

A number of scenarios are thinkable: Markets could become 'deregulated', transferring oversight to market participants themselves. Also, industry incumbents might develop 'voluntary' transnational standards that are more demanding than public ones. If such standards were adopted, private actors would de facto define the rules of exchange. This second mechanism has played an important role in transnational auditing standards, discussed below.

What about the third variant, 'private regulation with public oversight', in a transnational setting? It is unlikely that it can at the same time be effective enough to make it recognisably different from 'purely' private regulation and viable, that is survive over time. In contrast to its domestic counterpart, 'public oversight' in a transnational setting would by definition involve *several* public actors *from different countries*. It would assume that the policy concerns of these actors are strong enough to warrant meaningful oversight but that at the same time they are sufficiently unified to retain collective trust in private rule setting. Unless there was unanimity among the members of a public oversight body, core disputes and de facto rule setting would shift away from private actors towards these public ones. Put differently, unless the public policy concerns warranting oversight were similar in all countries involved and their interests were harmonious and non-conflicting, public oversight over private regulation would not be viable. Such a scenario is implausible, however, if these public concerns are more than a formal cover to legitimise continued private regulation – in which case 'public oversight' would be more or less meaningless for our purposes.

Central hypothesis

The central hypothesis of the corporate competition approach to transnational regulation is that *rules for cross-border exchange will be set through transnational private regulation if dominating firms (incumbents) have managed to stabilise their population and a stable conception of control has emerged.* In contrast, if the population and the conception of control are unstable or become destabilised, transnational *public* regulation is likely. The following three empirical cases illustrate the logic of the argument and how its constituent mechanisms 'work'.

Three case studies

The presented argument consists of two components – incumbents' preference for private governance once their population has stabilised and for public governance when competitive threats emerge. The second half of the article will illustrate both mechanisms in different scenarios. Three cases are discussed at length.

For the sake of comparison in this preceding overview, they will be complemented by Porter's studies of British textile and American automobile industries. At the height of their global dominance in the nineteenth and twentieth centuries respectively producers established and enforced private rules regulating patents:

> In each case leading firms were initially able to exercise authority with respect to international markets with the help of a set of private social institutions centralized in the hegemon's territory.
>
> (Porter 1999: 258)

Only with the onset of relative decline did British and US producers pressure their governments to formalise these rules through international regimes:

> In the first [step], states were called upon by private actors to regulate the international flow of knowledge by the construction of a patent regime. Formalized, explicit rules provided by states therefore replaced the regulation of knowledge flows by informal procedures and by the effects of cultural and geographic distances. In the second step, following World War I, these new rules were used by private actors to construct powerful, multinational, and often very formal forms of private international organization – the cartels [...].
>
> (Porter 1999: 264)

Producers' changing stance *vis-à-vis* public intervention was indebted to competitive decline. Porter's cases are therefore evidence of how market incumbents from a single jurisdiction push transnational regulation into the public domain in the face of competitive struggles. Table 2.1 contrasts it with derivatives listings where competitive struggles leading to public intervention emerged among firms from different national backgrounds. At the same time, firms sustaining control over a transnational market can come both from a single jurisdiction (auditing) as well as from different national backgrounds (Eurobond underwriting).

The cases' properties are summarised in Table 2.2. Note the correlation between the stability or otherwise of the incumbents' population, the presence or not of a stable conception of control and the domain of transnational rule setting (private/public).

The regime for Eurobond underwriting – private resistance to public intervention

Eurobond underwriting has seen a stable 'conception of control' emerge in a transnational market setting. With such a conception of control in place, top firms organised to fend off threats of public governance. Instead, they launched a new trade association to continue effective self-regulation.

'Underwriters' are financial institutions (often investment banks) that prepare the issuance of bonds, fill order books with interested buyers and eventually sell the bonds. The population of firms dominating the segment has remained

Table 2.1 Corporate competition in global finance and preference for private governance: overview of the cases

		Domain of transnational regulation	
		Private rule setting	*Public rule setting/regime*
Background of top firms in market segment	Single jurisdiction	Auditing	Porter cases (formerly private)
	Multiple jurisdictions	Eurobond underwriting	Derivatives listings

extremely stable for a business considered exemplary of free-wheeling capitalism. Of the top ten firms in the Eurobond market in 1985, all but two were among the top ten in the 2003 league table for underwriting of what is now technically called 'international bonds' (Walter 1988: 93, Thomson Financial 2003). These firms' market share was more than 60 per cent, up from a little more than 50 per cent in the mid-1980s. Even though the issuance and trading of Eurobonds has traditionally been concentrated in London, this market space has been as transnational as one could imagine. Crucially for the issue at hand, the British government had long turned a regulatory blind eye on Eurobond operations.

From the early days of the Eurobond market, the handful of firms dominating the market were eager to keep regulation private and settle conflicts among themselves. In 1969, the top firms set up a trade body, the Association of International Bond Dealers (AIBD). Until the mid-1980s, Eurobond markets stood as a prime example of transnational private regulation, with rules set informally through the AIBD.

Initially, the AIBD covered both primary and secondary markets – the issuance of bonds and the consecutive buying and selling of them, respectively. Technological innovations had lowered the barriers to entry for the secondary market. AIBD membership reached several hundred firms in the mid-1980s. The primary market, however, continued to be dominated by a few dozen institutions commanding the capital and expertise to arrange billion dollar sales of bonds. Consequently, the AIBD became less and less suitable for coordination among the top firms in the primary markets and their effective self-regulation.

By 1985, the primary and secondary markets had grown apart sufficiently for the main underwriters (all members of the AIBD) to set up another trade body – the International Primary Market Association (IPMA). Here, membership was confined to firms who had lead managed six bond issues in the previous 2 years or nine in the previous 3 years. Forty-four investment banks passed the test. Twenty years later, the IPMA had 51 members, a net addition of only seven firms. Through the IPMA, incumbents in Eurobond underwriting regained exclusive control of rule setting that growing AIBD membership had diluted.

At the same time, the IPMA formed a pre-emptive response to looming public oversight of the Eurobond markets. In the mid-1980s, the Financial

Table 2.2 Corporate competition in global finance and preference for private governance: summary of case properties

	Eurobond underwriting	*Auditing*	*Derivatives listing*	*Porter cases*
Time span referred to	Mid-1980s to present	Mid-1980s to present	Mid-1980s to present	Late eighteenth to mid-nineteenth century (UK), early twentieth century to post-war period (US)
Population of market incumbents	Stable	Stable	Unsettled by competitive challenges	Unsettled by competitive challenges
Conception of control	Emerged transnationally, cemented through trade associations	Emerged domestically (US)	Dissolved since Eurex' challenge of US firms	Dissolved since economic decline of former incumbents
Transnational rule setting	Private (with indirect public oversight)	Private (with indirect public oversight)	Public (no formal regime before the challenge)	Public (private before the challenge)

Services Act was about to be finalised in the UK. One way or the other, Euromarkets would be integrated into the British future regulatory architecture. As volumes continued to grow, some of Wall Street's rogue practices associated with the 1980s began to find their ways in London's markets. Industry officials advertised IPMA as a trade association to tackle such problems, decreasing the case for public governance. John Sanders, IPMA chairman at the time, promised the organisation would confront 'sloppy legal and documentation work and potentially harmful market practices' (Urry 1985).

Through their new trade body, firms fought anything smacking of public oversight. The eventual solution of negotiations with the government was about as favourable to incumbents as the situation permitted. The AIBD would become an international securities self-regulatory organisation and a designated investment exchange allowed to set its own rules. It paid for this privilege with supervisory obligations *vis-à-vis* the British government. IPMA, in contrast, got the best of both worlds. It set its own rules, too, but submitted them to the AIBD charged with 'overseeing' them. That way, it escaped legal obligations. Attempts by smaller players to get public actors more involved – for example the legal challenge mounted of Swiss banks against 'unfair pricing practices' of the 'underwriting cartel' – did little to change that (London 1991).

In Eurobond underwriting, a conception of control emerged that has remained stable over the last two decades. Once the incumbents' population had stabilised, these banded together to fend off public governance. Indeed, they maintain private regulation for Eurobond underwriting. This reproduction of transnational private regulation depended on producers' presenting a 'common front' to initiatives by public and smaller private actors to introduce public governance.

Auditing standards – the transnational extension of domestic dominance

The central difference between the auditing and Eurobond underwriting cases is that firms dominating auditing all have the US as their home market, whereas the top Eurobond underwriters come from a range of countries. At present, auditing of large companies' accounts is controlled by four companies that all have the US as their home market – the Big Four accounting firms, KPMG, Ernst & Young, Deloitte Touche Tohmatsu and PriceWaterhouseCoopers. They are the product of mergers between the eight dominating in the mid-1980s, minus Arthur Andersen which imploded after the Enron scandal. The Big Four are unrivalled market incumbents. Second tier companies (e.g. Grant Thornton and BDO International) earn less than a quarter in fees of what each of the Big Four makes annually. This concentration is widely believed to be the limit of what public authorities (in the US in particular) will tolerate before radical public oversight becomes established. Therefore, the Big Four have a stake in each other's survival. Reproduction of the status quo, not fierce competition, is the order of the day.

From the perspective of the corporate competition approach, it is not surprising that the cross-border regime for auditing standards – the International Standards on Auditing – was drawn up by a private body: the International Auditing and Assurance Standards Board (IAASB), part of the International Federation of Accountants (IFAC). In auditing, however, attempts by the Big Four to control transnational auditing standards and keep public actors out go further. The IFAC has national accountancy associations as members, not individual firms. While the Big Four wield significant influence, the membership-through-national-associations leaves smaller firms considerable say in IFAC's affairs. As with Eurobond underwriting, top firms have felt compelled to organise on a more selective basis once public sector threats to their self-regulation emerged.

In auditing, this challenge came with the single European market that was bound to include a pan-European auditing regime. Rather than working through the Federation of European Accountants or IFAC, the top eight auditing firms established the European Contact Group (ECG) in 1993 to lobby the European Commission for continuing self-regulation (Kelly 1996). The Commission presented its Green Paper on Auditing Standards in November 1996; the ECG tabled its own proposal simultaneously (The Accountant 1997). In a pre-emptive move, the latter outlined all steps the ECG felt needed to be taken to craft an effective auditing regime for Europe without serious public oversight. Its plan carried the day. In May 1998, the Commission published its decision to opt for 'monitored self-regulation' of the industry rather than a legal detailed framework for auditing in Europe (European Accounting Bulletin 1998).

Less than 2 years later, the same firms behind the ECG set up a new body, called the Global Steering Committee (GSC), within the framework of the IFAC (Accountancy 2000). Again, the idea was to establish a body representing the top firms' interests in response to what in industry parlance are called 'regulatory challenges'. The GSC created the so-called Forum of Firms within the IFAC – a company-based platform meant to sidestep IFAC's 'bias' in favour of national associations rather than individual firms. Nesting committees and forums one into the other, the Forum of Firms finally founded the Transnational Auditors Committee (TAC); it also nominates its members. This TAC sets out to identify 'issues' in audit practice and acts as a 'formal conduit among transnational firms and international regulators and financial institutions'.[2] And indeed, The Financial Stability Forum – the body created by the G7 to collect financial sector 'Standards and Codes' – lists the TAC as one of the bodies through which the auditing industry is drawing up standards serving as global templates.

The creation of the Public Interest Oversight Board (PIOB) in February 2005 has introduced elements of transnational public regulation in international auditing standards. The PIOB comprises members of international (regulatory) organisations and its task is to ensure that private standard setting bodies – the IAASB and the TAC – take the 'public interest' into account. Its establishment follows high-profile corporate scandals in which auditing irregularities or even fraud figured prominently (Parmalat, Ahold, etc.). It has also followed the creation of the Public Company Accounting Oversight Board (PCAOB) in the US. In addition, the Federation of European Accountants had pressured the European Commission to set up a similar body itself. Thereby, it hoped, European auditing firms might escape the PCAOB's registration requirement (Parker 2003). Given their recent nature, these developments lend themselves to conflicting interpretations. Clearly, high-profile scandals lifted auditing standards onto the political agenda. Transnationally, the PIOB will oversee IFAC's work. But because PIOB's members are international (regulatory) organisations, rather than national or EU representatives, smaller auditing firms will have difficulties tilting transnational regulation in their favour through increased public oversight. At any rate, this oversight will not impair market incumbents' ability to use rule setting in their own interest.

Auditing standards constitute a prime example of transnational private regulation dominated by few market incumbents. The latter have used private associations not only to reproduce, but also to extend their grip on transnational rule making as developments up to 2002 demonstrate. Recent market scandals appeared to have discredited self-regulation of the auditing profession. Public oversight of private rule setting – through both the PIOB and the PCAOB-EU cooperation – emerged as a consequence. On the one hand, this has brought to an end purely private governance dominated by the Big Four, although this was not prompted by actions of competitors. On the other hand, increased public oversight has put the creation of transnational harmonised auditing standards high on public actors' agenda. What incumbent auditors have lost in independence (but not necessarily influence) may be more than compensated through further integration of the transnational market place that they are certain to dominate.

Derivatives trading – calling in the state to fend off competition

In contrast to Eurobond underwriting and auditing, no transnational private regulation has emerged in the market for derivatives listings. Riven by competitive struggles that challenged the hitherto prevailing conception of control, major exchanges have dragged the issue into the public domain. The case illustrates how firms use public governance to address competitive threats in transnational marketplaces.

Modern derivatives trading has its home base in Chicago. More than hundred years ago exchanges were established to trade future contracts for agricultural products. This legacy survives in the names of today's US incumbents, the Chicago Board of Trade (CBOT) and the Chicago Mercantile Exchange (CME). In June 1972, the CME introduced exchange-traded financial derivatives in reaction to the disintegration of the Bretton Woods system.

Derivatives exchanges sprang up globally in the years that followed. Their products allow investors to 'insure' themselves (hedge, in the jargon) against volatile exchange and interest rates. Until the 1990s, these exchanges' products referred to their home countries' currency, domestic bonds or stocks listed on domestic exchanges. In countries with several exchanges (as the US), products were de facto divided between them. Exchanges expected and accepted non-intrusion on each others' turfs. Effectively, derivatives exchanges enjoyed quasi-monopolies. Owing to the prominence of American markets and the US dollar, the CBOT and the CME held 75 per cent of global futures trading as late as 1985.

Even though derivatives trading was a global industry, the service providers – the exchanges themselves – had a firmly established conception of control: Contracts would be traded in their 'home country'. The one exception was London's LIFFE exchange that dominated European government bond futures in the first half of the 1990s. By introducing new technology in 1997, its German counterpart, the Deutsche Terminbörse, repatriated Bund futures trading within months. To date, this is the only example of a derivatives exchange dealing a crushing defeat to another one through a cross-border battle.

Competitive pressures built up in the background, however, as the European exchanges consolidated – for example when the Swiss Soffex joined forces with the Deutsche Terminbörse to form Eurex. Euronext, the result of a merger of the Dutch, French and Belgian stock markets, in turn bought London's LIFFE in 2002. Only two big players were left, both with sufficient size to assault the US futures market, still controlled by the CME and the CBOT.

Through arrangements reminiscent of those described by Porter in textile and auto production, exchanges had cemented the mutual acceptance of each other's positions through technology sharing, for example in trading software. Eurex entered such an arrangement with the CBOT in late 1998, with an inbuilt expiration date of January 2004. The cosy coexistence of derivatives exchanges collapsed, however, when in 2003 the CBOT rejected an extension of its link with Eurex and switched to Euronext.Liffe instead. While disappointed, Eurex had planned for such a move: it opened the battle for global derivatives trading by announcing that it would open its own exchange in Chicago (Wagner 2003).

Thus far, neither transnational public nor transnational private governance had emerged. The competition was sufficiently tamed by a conception of control that attributed products to their 'national' exchanges. Once Eurex announced its intention to intrude on the CBOT's turf, this crumbled. The CBOT and the CME started lobbying US Congress to fend off the competition or find ways to delay Eurex' entry so they could prepare themselves (Boland 2003). In an initial compromise, the US regulator of the futures industry, the Commodities and Futures Trading Commission (CFTC), allowed Eurex US to start operations, but without Eurex' trump card, the so-called transatlantic clearing link with large cost-saving potential. Accordingly, Eurex US failed to win substantial market share from the CBOT in 2004 (it captured 5 per cent of the top CBOT's contract's trading, at best).

At the behest of the European exchanges and particularly Eurex, the EU's public body for securities markets, the Committee of European Securities Regulators (CESR) (2004), pleaded with US authorities. The issue of who could operate what kind of a market where was thus dragged into the public domain. After CESR's intervention, the CFTC allowed Eurex US to use the transatlantic clearing link in October 2004. On the very same day, the CFTC and CESR announced cooperation on an 'Action Plan' to address cross-border issues (Committee of European Securities Regulators 2004). This transatlantic cooperation was cemented in February 2005.

While the publicly negotiated solution that was found to the Eurex issue as such still had an ad hoc character, US and EU authorities immediately set out to develop a more comprehensive regime. The CFTC–CESR dialogue has been further institutionalised with the aim of harmonising rules where possible and desirable. In addition to this cooperation, transatlantic derivatives business has been integrated into a wider EU–US Financial Markets Regulatory Dialogue. This dialogue has the aim of finding common 'regulatory solutions' – and one of the long-term priorities identified is 'competition in trading venues' (HM Treasury 2005).

Where a 'truce' had reigned, rising cross-border competition between derivatives exchanges pushed transnational regulation firmly into the public domain – which of course did not mean that 'the public's' concerns were heeded more than before. American incumbents had used political clout and convinced regulators and Washington politicians to amend rules in their favour. European firms in turn lobbied public EU actors to raise the issue with US authorities.

Conclusions

This chapter has asked why transnational regulation is effected through private institutions in some cases and public ones in others. Transnational private regulation is likely to emerge, it has argued, in transnational markets where a stable conception of control has emerged among producers. Then producers will try to fend off public oversight in order to 'keep other stakeholders out' and smaller competitors at bay.

How widely through different sectors should this argument be applicable? Producers' demand for private or public regulation is a general phenomenon. More tricky is the question under which conditions public actors will abide private demands. This seems to be strongest in sectors with a fairly low 'visibility' (lowering the political salience – contrast derivatives with ecological disasters), high economies of scale and a high complexity of regulatory issues. It will be left for further research to test these factors' importance and further improve our understanding of transnational politics.

From a normative perspective, the 'keeping-other-stakeholders-out' element of transnational private regulation is worrying. In a nutshell, accountable rule setting would mean that all those affected by practices covered by a particular set of rules are also somehow involved in setting or at least overseeing them. Transnational private regulation works in precisely the other direction. In the case of finance, the general damage done by recurrent crises in the markets dramatically illustrate just how wide the stakeholder base of financial market governance is. The lack of accountability goes further, however. In a wider sense, markets themselves – and certainly financial markets – are a form of governance, a mechanism for allocating values throughout society. This function of 'markets as governance' makes a wider accountability of rule setting even more pertinent and transnational private regulation even more disturbing.

Notes

1 This chapter is a revised and shortened version of an article that had earlier appeared as D. Mügge, 'Private-Public Puzzles: Inter-firm Competition and Transnational Private Regulation', *New Political Economy*, June 2006, vol. 11(2), pp. 177–200.

2 Online. Available at: www.ifac.org/TransnationalAuditors/index.tmpl, accessed on 15 March 2005.

3 Transnational expert-driven standardisation

Accountancy governance from a professional point of view

Sebastian Botzem

Introduction[1]

Private standardisation is on the rise in a globalising economy. For a long time, private standards have complemented national rules and regulations. In some cases such as accounting, transnational standardisation is going quite far, potentially replacing national standards. These developments connected to economic and political globalisation challenge corporations, stakeholders, and nation states. Evolving transnational accounting standardisation not only challenges established national actor constellations. It also leads to a harmonisation of accounting rules and practices bringing about conformity. This way, effective transnational standardisation can contribute to the establishment of a capital market-oriented global economic order.

These developments raise questions regarding the legitimacy of transnational governance arrangements and open discussions on the nature of participation and democratic accountability. This becomes more important as accounting and auditing[2] are viewed critically in relation to recent corporate scandals. These scandals are not directly connected to the application of a certain set of standards, but they reflect pressure to present positive figures to impress investors and analysts. Even if the corporate scandals of Enron, a US energy trading company, Parmalat, the Italian dairy producer, or Japanese cosmetics giant Kanebo are extreme cases, they indicate the problems arising for the credibility of corporations, auditors, and national supervisory agencies. Accounting standards are not only technical rules for financial reporting, but the foundations for the distribution of corporate surplus to shareholders and stakeholders. This makes accounting rules in general and the transnationalisation of standards and standard setting in particular a contested element of the global economy, especially as listed companies increasingly strive to please investors and financial analysts.

The most frequently heard argument in favour of harmonising accounting standards refers to reduced transaction costs on capital markets due to improved information flows of global standards. Such a functionalist perspective, however, neglects varying national socioeconomic contexts, sectoral differences, and corporation-specific developments. Therefore, the debate on harmonising accounting standards largely disregards the trade-off between universally comparable standards on the one hand and local requirements of companies, industries, or specific stakeholder groups on the other.

This chapter lays out the historical developments of private transnational standardisation in order to come to a better understanding of the characteristics of transnational governance in accounting standardisation. After a brief theoretical introduction, particularities of accounting professionalism are highlighted and key elements are assessed to explain how transnational governance structures were implemented and developed. In this perspective, governance is understood as both the structural conditions for agency and the actions exercised by participating individuals and organisations. This points to the importance of actor constellations in transnational governance and allows insights into how transnational self-regulation has been established, legitimised, and transformed.

After describing and interpreting the case of accounting standardisation, the chapter concludes with two contributions to the debate on transnational private governance. First, it shows that agency is distributed between private and public actors. Despite the importance of private actors, transnational standardisation still relies on public authority. In fact, transnational governance has to be seen as an ongoing process characterised by an interaction of private and public actors. Second, over time, power shifts within the realm of private actors, i.e. national professional associations, are losing ground to globally operating auditing firms.

Global standards and self-regulation

Standards are key instruments of cross-border regulation in a variety of settings. Their contend-specific character makes them suitable alongside existing national rules (Braithwaite and Drahos 2000, Brunsson and Jacobsson 2000). While standards may range from voluntary rules to obligatory prescriptions, their contribution to interface management is widely acknowledged (David and Greenstein 1990). Even though participants of standard-setting procedures often consider standards to be of rather technical nature, studies have shown that social and political dimensions are central to understanding standardisation processes (Schmidt and Werle 1998, Tamm Hallström 2004). As in accounting, the standards' effectiveness and acceptance by private and public actors greatly contribute to their proliferation.

While the debate on non-state actors in global affairs stresses alternative sources of authority to explain transnational institution building (Cutler *et al.* 1999, Porter 2005), particular studies of standardisation regimes point to multilevel interdependencies as a core feature of governance arrangements. Mattli (2003: 217ff.) describes the interrelatedness of public and private governance structures as 'joint standards governance'. In addition to public agencies, private actors such as corporations and associations are particularly fit for spanning national borders.

Community-building processes provide additional means of organising as cross-border interaction of experts contributes to transnational governance in different ways. While the concept of epistemic communities (Haas 1992) emphasises the role of experts in agenda-setting processes, van Warden and Drahos (2002) point to convergence effects of epistemic communities serving as channels for information exchange. A similar notion is found in Brunsson's normative communities (Brunsson 2000: 28f.). Rule shaping through argumentation is underlined by concepts such as transnational discourse communities (Bislev *et al.* 2002). Djelic and Sahlin-Andersson (2006) have coined the term transnational communities of interests, highlighting the transnational nature of these groups as expansive networks diffusing regulatory projects. Communities play an important role in the case of accounting standardisation. Their disposal over professional values and the common goal of global standard setting makes them particularly suitable to establish transnational governance structures.

Professional self-regulation

The contribution of professionals and their associations in modern societies is a core idea in the sociology of professions' literature (Abbott 1988). At the centre are selected groups of actors that display a high degree of autonomy and capacity for self-organisation, such as lawyers, engineers, doctors, consultants, or accountants. Different professional groups vary according to their knowledge base, organisational form, and power strategy (Reed 1996). These three dimensions are applied to categorise the governance contributions of professionals in the field of accounting.

The knowledge base comprises central elements of professional identity and directs individuals' actions. Its genesis has been influenced by both academia and practitioners. Practical knowledge focuses on problem solving and has been influenced by the necessities of business, investors, and public authorities. The common knowledge base is constructed via academic curricula and professional interpretations of general principles. This construction is restated through the application of rules in the processes of accounting and auditing. It is therefore a central element of professional self-organisation to maintain control of its abstract system of knowledge in order to claim professional stature (Abbott 1988: 8ff.) However, national variations between different knowledge bases exist. In continental Europe, the contribution of academics is considered to be more important, whereas in Anglo-Saxon countries, the knowledge base is characterised much more by practical considerations in a case-oriented and more localised system of knowledge generation (Nobes and Parker 2004).

Organisational forms provide a second category to assess professional influence on governance. Traditionally, associations are central to (self-)regulation. They are organised as collegiate bodies with clearly defined tasks which tightly control entry barriers via education and the issuance of certificates (Ramirez 2001). Prestige and credibility are important to ensure the status of accountants and auditors, particularly in order to secure their influence in national rule-setting processes. In countries with developed capital markets like the UK and the US, enterprises depend on transparent and investor-oriented accounting practices to secure access to capital markets. Professionals and their associations are not only important in doing accounts and bringing about reports, they also contribute to the legitimacy of rules and procedures (Covaleski *et al.* 2003: 327). Over time, experts have acquired a quasi-public role of auditors, viewing themselves as independent treasurers auditing corporations (Willmott *et al.* 2000).

Especially in the transnational realm, a second type of organisational form has gained importance. Global auditing firms have emerged as particularly powerful organisations. After a drastic process of concentration, only four of these firms remain at the global level. Their central role makes them boundary spanners mediating between differing national and organisational contexts (Ansell and Weber 1999). Their audits have become seals of professionalism and are important for attracting internationally mobile capital. The oligopolistic market structure and a diversification of their services to consulting, tax, and legal advisory has improved their position *vis-à-vis* big corporations. In addition, their global scope challenges the national logics of associational organisations (Greenwood *et al.* 2002: 64ff.). Today, global services firms exercise their influence more aggressively which poses a threat to the nationally organised professions (Macdonald 1995: 203).

A third important category to understand the impact of professionals is the power strategy used to acquire authority. Of particular importance is the establishment of clearly limited jurisdictions in which professional dominance is exercised. Jurisdictional limits define formal control over key definitions of professional activities. This is reflected in the language used in describing the techniques and the actual conduct of work performed by practitioners (Abbott 1988: 62). Due to their semi-public status, formal control is particularly relevant. This status needs to be balanced out with other actors, amongst which are the state, other occupations, educational institutions, and customers (Macdonald 1995: 189). A particular professional power strategy is aiming at the monopolisation of its competences, knowledge, and responsibilities. Social closure is achieved via education, membership control, and professional norms and values (Macdonald 2000). However, control needs to be re-established over time, making the contestation over jurisdictional competences a continual endeavour.

> Such formal control provides power, but as soon as a professional field is fully translated into the rules and programs or becomes codified, the profession's power disappears. Therefore, it is necessary for a profession to continually re-generate its abstract system of knowledge, thereby extending its jurisdiction to possible encroach upon that of adjacent professions.
>
> (Covaleski *et al.* 2003: 325)

Transnationalisation of accounting standardisation raises questions regarding the knowledge base, organisational forms, and power strategies of national professional associations. Furthermore, harmonising standards and standardisation procedures affects a multiplicity of actors, some of whom engage in cross-border standardisation. Experts bring in their national backgrounds, which leads to a renegotiation and recombination of knowledge, values, and power when a transnational private governance structure is taking shape.

The empirical case: cross-border standardisation in accounting

Differing national traditions and diverging practices are starting points for transnational harmonisation of accounting rules. One of the central motives to accounting standardisation is to overcome information gaps that stem from national differences in accounting principles and standard application. Initiatives of harmonisation aim at fostering comparability, thus easing cross-border mobility of capital. The global proliferation of capital market principles dominant in Anglo-Saxon countries in particular challenges countries and corporations taking different approaches to accounting regulation. Especially in continental Europe and Japan, a more conservative, long-term approach dominated, smoothing income declaration to protect creditors and to lower the base for taxation. Nobes and Parker (2004) have proposed a classification of accounting systems, differentiating countries according to accounting systems and regulatory styles. This antipodal scheme groups countries following Anglo-Saxon accounting principles on the one hand (US, UK, Canada, Australia, and the Netherlands among others) and countries following a continental European approach on the other hand (Germany, France, Belgium, and Italy). Lately, this approach has been renewed, categorising countries according to the importance of private equity into strong or weak equity classes (Nobes and Parker 2004: 69). In both perspectives, Anglo-Saxon countries resemble one cluster, continental European countries the other.

Central differences between countries can be seen in accounting rules, rule development, and the regulatory arrangements. Variances are reflected in the construction and embeddedness of, as well as the control over, the knowledge base. Generally speaking, in Anglo-Saxon countries, accounting rules are developed incrementally and resemble a common-law understanding. The rules are investor oriented and put emphasis on the representation of a true and fair view, identifying the companies' current situation and applying period-specific accounting. Self-regulation and associational freedom are key characteristics of Anglo-Saxon accounting professions. Over the years however, governmental regulatory agencies both in the US and in the UK have imposed stricter surveillance requirements for professional self-organisation. Above all, recent corporate failures such as Enron have weakened self-regulation and in fact led to forceful public re-regulation, most notably in the US with the Sarbanes-Oxley Act of 2002 tightening the oversight of corporations and auditors.

In contrast, accounting in continental Europe has traditionally followed different logics resembling a diverse socioeconomic configuration. Accounting is tied into a principle-based understanding of law where the role of the state is more direct. Linking accounting to taxation favours a conservative, long-term approach in financial reporting, allowing companies to smooth income, giving more room to manoeuvre in a largely credit-based financing system. The role of professions also differs. They are more closely connected to academia applying a principle-based understanding of accounting standards. Government involvement is also stronger in overseeing the professions, establishing chambers of accountants with mandatory membership.

Establishing transnational standardisation in accounting

Transnational standard setting has been going on for more than three decades. The debate on harmonising accounting standards, however, originated much earlier. Since the late nineteenth century, experts gathered in international congresses to exchange ideas about accounting and auditing across national borders (Mueller 1979: 2). After the Second World War, accountancy became an issue of intergovernmental activities, first debated under the auspices of the United Nations (Samuels and Piper 1985). Later, the OECD engaged in developing approaches for public accounts as well as in outlining accounting requirements for multinational enterprises. Within Europe, steps to standardise accounting for the internal market were taken by the European Commission as early as 1964 (Nobes 1985). However, the accession of the UK, Ireland, and Denmark to the European Community led to an orientation towards capital market principles which were also considered in the accounting directives of 1978 and 1983.[3]

Global standard setting started in 1973 when the International Accounting Standards Committee (IASC) was established. The aim was to develop International Accounting Standards (IAS), facilitating cross-border convergence of accounting rules and practices. The organisation emerged out of a tripartite study group of British, Canadian, and US-American accounting practitioners (Thomas 1970: 60). In 1973, the organisation was founded by professional accounting associations from the three Anglo-Saxon countries as well as by associations from Australia, France, Germany, Japan, the Netherlands, and Mexico. The intention behind setting up the IASC was to 'produce basic standards that would be capable of rapid acceptance and implementation worldwide' (Samuels and Piper 1985: 70). The professional project driving IASC can be seen as a power strategy to counterbalance emerging European regulation in accounting. British professional associations in particular feared that legalistic European regulatory attempts could threaten their domain of professional self-regulation (Hopwood 1994).

Since 2001, the IASC's successor, the International Accounting Standards Board (IASB), is the centre of the transnational network in accounting regulation (Braithwaite and Drahos 2000: 121). During the last 30 years, the organisation has undergone substantial changes both in its structural configurations and in its standardisation procedures (IASC 1998, Botzem and Quack 2006). The developments can be divided into three phases. The early years were dominated by establishing the IASC as a standard-setting arena building up links with other important actors (1970s and 1980s). Later, the consolidation of IASC was pushed forward on the basis of bringing accounting standards in line with capital market requirements and acquiring legitimacy from regulatory actors (late 1980s and 1990s). The most recent events have seen an encompassing organisational reconfiguration aiming at securing the implementation of standards in national contexts (since 2000).

Internally, the IASC's development is characterised by integrating and co-opting powerful actors into its different organisational bodies (Martinez-Diaz 2005). In particular, the central decision-making organ, the IASC Board, saw a number of changes throughout the last decades. At the beginning, it was comprised of delegates from national professional associations with voting rights who could bring in non-voting technical assistants. Over time, the organisation's constitution was amended, and new national associations were integrated, widening the scope of representation. Representational characteristics changed over time, when seats were granted to additional private organisations with an interest in financial accounting, such as International Coordinating Committee of Financial Analysts (in 1986), the Federation of Swiss Holding Companies (1995), and the Association of Financial Executives (1996). These changes facilitated the reach-out to experts beyond the accounting profession and helped to secure legitimacy from preparers and users of financial reports. Adapting its organisational form proved to be a prerequisite for proliferating transnational standards.

Even though some associations from southern countries were included, there was a clear dominance of actors from developed economies (Hopwood 1994: 252). At no point was the voting majority of Anglo-Saxon actors threatened. The capital market orientation was further strengthened through the close cooperation of the four global auditing firms. They contributed highly to IASC by sending staff to work on practical issues. During their secondment to the organisation, the personnel remained on the payroll of auditing firms.

From 1977 to 2000, the formal oversight of IASC was undertaken by the International Federation of Accountants (IFAC), a worldwide representation of national professional associations. Officially, it administrated the selection of IASC Board members, but in practice, the organisation remained weak. Its main task was to provide funding for IASC and to foster the worldwide proliferation of IAS through influencing national standard setters (Haller 1993: 1297).

The IASC also diversified its internal structures to link up with important players for cross-border accounting regulation. To secure funding and to establish links with international organisations, the Consultative Group was formed in 1981 to advise IASC on projects and priorities. It established links to organisations, such as the Basle Committee on Banking Supervision, the International Chamber of Commerce, or the World Bank. In 1995, the Advisory Council was created to foster reputation and provide alternative sources of funding (Kleekämper 1995: 420). Setting up these additional bodies increased the reputation of IASC, secured funding, and paved the way for the recognition of its standards (Martinez-Diaz 2005).

IASC also engaged in cooperation with national standard setters, public regulatory agencies, and oversight authorities to further improve its position.

Political recognition was a key goal during the 1980s and 1990s. In order to seek support form both sides of the Atlantic, IASC integrated US-American and European representatives. It opened its board to the US-American accounting standard setter, the Financial Accounting Standards Board (FASB) in 1988, and to the European Union (EU) in 1990, granting both entities an observer status. Furthermore, IASC not only established ties to governmental agencies, but also aimed at convincing stock market oversight agencies to accept their standards. The aim was to encourage national exchanges and their regulatory agencies to allow international standards in addition to national ones. To foster standard recognition, IASC engaged in cooperation with the international organisation of securities markets. During the 1990s, the International Organization of Securities Commissions (IOSCO) became a vital actor to accept and legitimise IAS for the purpose of cross-border listings for publicly traded companies.

IOSCO exercised its power by refusing to recommend the acceptance of IAS to its members until certain requirements would be fulfilled. In the beginning, IOSCO did not accept international standards and started a comparability and improvement projects together with IASC in 1988 to introduce a clear capital market orientation into IAS. This cooperation ensured that IAS were taking a clear capital market orientation, bringing about fair value accounting (FVA) as a core characteristic of transnational standardisation (Perry and Noelke 2005). The cooperation of IASC and IOSCO proved to be difficult. It took more than 10 years until IOSCO finally recommended the use of IAS to its national stock markets in 2000 (IOSCO 2000). Of all members, the US-American Securities and Exchange Commission (SEC) was the most important adversary. While most European members were in favour of endorsing the 14 standards as early as 1993, the SEC refused endorsement of IAS until a complete set of core standards had been developed. Until today, the US remain one of the few counties that has not accepted IAS as an alternative to national accounting standards. Because of the size of its capital market, the US succeeded in insisting on the adoption of national standards for all companies listing on US stock exchanges.

In other countries, stock exchanges allowed the use of IAS for foreign listed companies before 2000 in addition to national standards. While some exchanges encouraged the use of IAS, Germany's 'Neuer Markt' even required reporting based on non-national GAAP (generally accepted accounting principles) from 1997 onward. German companies listed in this segment had to report using either IAS or US-GAAP. This way, the exchange wanted to compete with other stock markets, drawing companies looking for foreign capital but not wanting to list in the US. The recognition of IAS by private actors, such as stock markets, contributed to legitimising international standards and supported the quest of IASC to become a globally recognised standard setter. In countries such as Germany, the acceptance of capital market-oriented IAS has contributed to the de-legitimisation of long-term-oriented national standards that traditionally had favoured a long-term approach and did not primarily address capital market requirements.

In addition to private-sector interests, governmental actors played a critical role in accepting IASC and its standards. During the 1990s, the European

Community actively engaged in the field of accounting standardisation. After abandoning plans to establish a unique European standard setter, IASC was backed by the European Commission, thus paving the way for the global proliferation of IAS (Martinez-Diaz 2005). In 1995, the Commission officially endorsed IAS because European corporations increasingly turned to US accounting standards in order to be listed at the New York Exchange. In its 'New Strategy *vis-à-vis* International Harmonisation' (European Commission 1995a, 1995b), the EU laid out the reasons behind its decisions, arguing that the increased use of US accounting rules by European corporations leads to a lack of control over corporations since US GAAP are developed without European input.

Following the decision to back IAS, the EU took further steps to secure its adoption. At the Lisbon Summit in 2000, the political leaders agreed to require IAS for all group accounts of listed companies in Europe. The regulation adopted in 2002 made the use of IAS obligatory starting in 2005, giving the national governments leeway to go beyond the requirements.[4] In addition to implementing IAS in Europe, the EU set up an array of advisory and consultative bodies concerned with the application of IAS. The EU has reserved the right to assess and decide upon each individual standard before making them mandatory within Europe. This way public authority re-entered the standardisation process. Even though the vast majority of decisions of the international standard setter is respected, the EU has opted to apply some standards only partially. The so-called carve-out of detailed rules is an indication that – within the frame of capital market-oriented international standards – the EU claims direct authority in the standard-setting process.

While the development and application of standards is dominated by private actors, their recognition and implementation depends to a large part on public actors in the US and Europe. Institutionally re-embedding transnational standard setting and linking it to US and European authorities is one central feature of transnational private governance in the area of accounting. These developments were complemented by gaining legitimacy through internal reforms concerning procedures of standard setting and financing the operations (Tamm Hallström 2004). However, after IASC had acquired the central position in global standard setting, organisational reforms were needed in order to increase its functionality and to counter criticism of intransparent procedures and overlapping responsibilities.

Reconfiguring transnational regulation

Up until 2000, IASC experienced recognition from a variety of actor groups, amongst other intergovernmental international organisations such as the International Monetary Fund and the World Bank. Especially in the aftermath of the 1997/1998 Asian financial crisis, IASC could position itself as a credible standard setter, offering capital market-oriented standards allowing global comparability (Martinez-Diaz 2005). To ensure a better control over the application of its standards, IASC launched a profound re-structuration. In 1997, a Strategy

Working Group was assembled to lead the process of organisational renewal (IASC 1998). After 4 years of discussion, the new constitution went into effect in 2001. The new organisational principles were laid out, and the name was changed to IASB. All standards issued since that time are called IFRS (International Financial Reporting Standards) rather than IAS.

The reconfiguration led to an unbundling of activities in which the formal oversight of the IFAC was removed. Instead, the international federation of national professions was redirected to deal with global matters concerned with auditing financial reports. The twin structure was disaggregated because financial resources were not sufficient anymore, and a potential conflict of interests between accounting and auditing needed to be avoided.

As part of the remodelling process, IASB streamlined its operations internally and established firm links to national standard-setting bodies and the EU. Changing its set-up proved important to increase its influence. Since 2001, the organisation is officially overseen by a foundation run by trustees. Those are individuals with high reputation in the international financial community. One of their main tasks is to ensure funding and to recruit new IASB members. The 2001 reform also brought about drastic changes in the board's composition. The organisation's new structure needed to be suitable to 'bring about convergence between national accounting standards and practices and high-quality global accounting standards' (IASC 1998: 3). Instead of having delegates from national professional associations, IASB abandoned territorial representation but granted special relationships to important national standard setters guaranteeing them representation. The seven economically most powerful industrialised countries were privileged (US, UK, CD, AU/NZ, JP, FR, and DE), perpetuating the Anglo-Saxon hegemony in transnational standardisation. In total, the number of board members was limited to 14. Despite claiming a global scope, the IASB is clearly dominated by industrialised countries. In fact, no southern representative is included at this point, except for a delegate that stems from a South African-based international mining corporation. New elements of social closure can be seen in the selection criteria of the IASB. Its official language is English and for recruitment of Board members, a 'foremost qualification for membership of the IASB shall be a technical expertise' (IASCF 2002b: section 20).

The constitutional revision has strengthened private actors, reserving 5 of the 14 board seats to auditors. They have become key players in setting transnational accounting standards. As the constitution states to 'achieve a balance of perspectives and experience, a minimum of five members of the IASB shall have a background as practicing auditors, a minimum of three a background in the preparation of financial statements, a minimum of three a background as users of financial statements, and at least one an academic background' (IASCF 2002b: section 22). Currently, all the practicing auditors are recruited from the four big globally operating auditing firms, and many of the other board members have experience as auditors in some point of their business career. After the Enron scandal which led to the liquidation of Arthur Anderson, only four global auditing firms remain. They provide the largest part of IASB's finances (roughly

30 per cent). Furthermore, auditing firms are the single most important type of organisation in which practical knowledge and expertise are gathered.

As a consequence of the reconfiguration of IASB, a shift within the private sector can be observed. At the outset, national professional associations were the most important organisations setting up transnational standardisation. After the internal reforms and the recognition during the 1980s and 1990s, additional actors such as stock exchanges and financial analysts have gained importance. The most drastic shift, however, took place with the constitutional revision in 2001. As Table 3.1 indicates, the changes strengthened global auditing firms, which are exercising influence on transnational accounting governance in a number of ways.

In the meantime, further changes are underway due to another revision of the constitution.

Characteristics of transnational private governance in accounting

Summing up the development of transnational private governance in the field of accounting of the last 30 years, a number of features are visible. First, developments have been dynamic, with changing actor constellations over time. While standard setting is clearly dominated by accountants and auditors, linking up with other organisations and high-profile individuals of the financial community has been important to acquire reputation. At a later stage, public actors re-entered the scene, becoming important in recognising standards and securing their implementation thereby legitimising transnational accounting standardisation. The continuous interaction also fosters the emergence of a transnational standardisation community with shared norms and values that potentially bring about social closure.

Second, accounting standardisation remains to be exercised in a professional context. However, changes can be identified in all the three dimensions. While professional norms and values remain important, the professional knowledge base is oriented towards corporations' and capital markets' needs. Globally operating auditing firms appear to be the superior organisational form of transnational standardisation. In fact, professional associations have lost power to private auditing firms when they were being eliminated from the IASB. The power of auditing firms stems not only from the knowledge they embody. Due to their global scope, they are in a unique position to market their knowledge when providing professional services.

Third, standardisation is characterised by technical debates out of which capital-market logics have emerged as a core feature of IFRS. One of the key elements in explaining the effectiveness of the standards is the procedural set-up. Introducing transparent proceedings and welcoming the participation of the interested public is at the centre of the due process which has evolved over time (Botzem and Quack 2006). This semi-open approach contributes to the recognition and legitimacy of IASB. In practice, however, participation is confined to

Table 3.1 Organisational characteristics of transnational standard-setters

Name	*International Accounting Standards Committee (IASC)* (as of 2000)	*International Accounting Standards Board (IASB)* (as of 2005)
Founding year	1973	2001
Objective	Formulate and publish accounting standards; improve harmonisation	Develop, promote, and diffuse global accounting standards
Membership	National professional associations; same as International Federation of Accountants (IFAC)	No membership
Oversight function executed through	IFAC	International Accounting Standards Committee Foundation (IASCF), 19 Trustees
Board members	Up to 17 member organisations (delegated by national organisations or co-opted by the board itself), in practice up to 70 individuals (members and technical advisors) present	14 members (12 full time, 2 part time)
Pattern of board representation	Territorial, functional	Functional, expertise-based, special representation of liaison countries
Funding by	– Direct funding by members (associations) – Indirect funding by private business through delegation of members and technical personal – Publications	– Funding organised by Foundation (money from auditing firms and private corporations) – Publications
Amount of funding	2 Mio, £UK	11 Mio. £UK
Employees	21	67
Influence of global auditing firms	Indirect financial support (delegating members) Indirect rule making via delegation of professions	Direct financial support (4 Mio. US$) Direct rule-making authority through reservation of a minimum of 5 out of 14 board seats

Sources: Official documents of IASC (1978) and IASCF (1998; 2002a; 2006).

experts because of the highly abstract and technical nature of decisions. Nevertheless, procedures' and standards' contents are objects of differing interests. The professional identity of participating actors contributes a large part to the integration of conflict which is also mediated via the due process.

In the last three decades, IASB has become the centre of the network spanning organisational, sectoral, and national boundaries in accounting standardisation in which a focus on capital markets clearly dominates (Perry and Noelke 2005). Most remarkable perhaps is the success of IASB outside of Anglo-Saxon countries. Its impact on continental Europe and non-industrialised countries is far-reaching. The IASB has managed to diffuse the idea of capital market-oriented accounting via its standards into a number of jurisdictions with formally different traditions. It would be going too far, however, to suggest IASB forcefully introduced its standards in these contexts. Rather, powerful actors within these national settings were striving for increased capital market orientation and took advantage of the transnational developments.

Conclusion: governance under the conditions of distributed agency and dispersed authority

As the article has shown, in accounting standardisation, private actors play a central role. However, in terms of agency and authority, both private and public actors remain important. Transnational private governance is being shaped by powerful private actors that have dominated the establishment of a private standard-setting body and the development of standards. However, when it comes to the application and enforcement of standards, public actors also play a key role. They allow, enable, or facilitate voluntary standardisation and legitimise standards when they are turned into mandatory rules. Therefore, transnational governance is not characterised by a privatisation of rule making, but by a reconfiguration of private–public interaction. Agency is distributed over a wide array of actors and needs to be pooled for successful transnational governance.

In the transnational realm, not only agency, but also authority is spread. Different national and international public actors are important in securing reputation and legitimising transnational governance structures and their outcome. At an early stage, private actors are central sources of authority, engaging in and contributing to private standardisation. Later, public actors are vital in providing recognition and legitimacy. They grant authority via the sovereignty rested upon them and secure the proliferation of standard. As the example of the EU carve-out indicates, however, public authority is coming in at a rather late stage in the transnational governance limiting the proactive influence of public authority.

The case of accounting standardisation underlines the problem-solving capacity of transnational governance settings. Arguing for the reduction of transaction costs in global financial markets, IASB has managed to provide a solution considered important by actors prone to capital market logics. This orientation has supported a shift amongst private actors. At the transnational level, auditing firms are better situated to organise and market knowledge than national professional associations. This enforces the position of global auditing firms as they advocate a capital market orientation.

In more general terms, the case of accounting standardisation offers some insights concerning the possibilities and limits of transnational governance. It underlines the interrelatedness of private and public actors but also indicates the dynamic character of governance arrangements. A historical perspective shows the evolvement over time, particularly when focusing on the disposal over knowledge which serves as a resource but can also promote social closure. In combination with a capital market orientation, such a normative base has the potential to serve as a foundation for a transnational community driving regulatory processes. Particularly when backed by an oligopolistic structure of professional services firms, the influence of experts can be far-reaching. On the other hand, the resistance of the US regulatory agencies points towards the restrictions such actor constellations have to deal with.

Interpreting the transnational interaction of private and public actors as successive steps – in which the impulses come form private actors and are later recognised and legitimised by public authorities – indicates a transnational governance cycle. Such a perspective points to differing sequences of developing, applying, recognising, and enforcing standards. While private actors dominate earlier phases, public ones are coming in at later stages. One explanation for the relative position of private and public actors in these governance structures derives from the disposal over knowledge. In the case of accounting standardisation, such a division of labour in the governance cycle facilitates cross-border-oriented capital market interests. This is supported by a high degree of abstraction and a technically dominated discourse in standard setting which effectively shield transnational governance processes against societal claims. As transnationalisation progresses, democratic control of the global expert community becomes increasingly complicated. For citizens and affected stakeholders, it is not only difficult to engage in transnational standardisation, but it is also unlikely to be heard.

Notes

1 Special thanks go to the editors of this volume for their helpful comments. I would also like to thank the participants of the 2005 ECPR Workshop 'Transnational Private Governance in the Global Political Economy'.
2 Accounting and auditing are related, but different tasks. Financial accounting is concerned with preparing the companies' books and issuing a financial report at the end of the reporting period. Auditing on the other hand aims at examining and testifying financial reports. To certify a company's report, independent auditors are hired who are checking if accounts have been prepared in accordance with laws and professional rules.
3 See respectively: Fourth Council Directive 78/660/EEC of 25 July 1978 based on Article 54(3)(g) of the Treaty on the annual accounts of certain types of companies; Seventh Council Directive 83/349/EEC of 13 June 1983 based on the Article 54(3)(g) of the Treaty on consolidated accounts.
4 Regulation (EC) No. 1606/2002 of the European Parliament and the Council of 19 July 2002 on the application of IAS.

4 Transnational private governance and the Basel process

Banking regulation and supervision, private interests and Basel II

Eleni Tsingou

Recent developments in liberalisation and innovation have altered the operation of financial markets and consequently, fundamentally changed global financial governance, notably by posing significant constraints on the traditionally public functions of regulation and supervision. State actors are no longer capable of adequately guiding and overseeing financial activities that transcend national regulatory and legal boundaries. At the same time, they appear unwilling to reverse this pattern, for fear of harming their competitiveness.[1] Transnationalisation and financial complexity have not, however, relieved pubic authorities of their regulatory and supervisory responsibilities. Instead, the challenge is to promote market efficiency and stability while sharing authority with a growing number of actors, including the private sector. The focus has shifted from regulation to supervision, and much of the emphasis is placed on systemic stability, i.e. the prevention of crises. This has left financial institutions in charge of making their own rules, or rather creating their own flexible standards, and public authorities in charge of market-based supervision, increasingly reliant on private sector know-how and transparent practices.

Industry actors, and in particular large global financial conglomerates, are participating in the formulation and implementation of both regulation and supervision. The two are interlinked but distinct functions; regulation relates to the 'establishment of specific rules of behaviour' and supervision to the 'more general oversight of financial firms' behaviour' (Goodhart *et al.* 1998: xvii). Self-regulatory practices have, to varied degrees, long been established in the financial markets. This is especially true of the securities industry, but there have also been various cases of authority sharing among public and private actors in the banking industry. Self-regulatory traditions exist in many systems where 'regulation is, characteristically, a public function done by private interests' (Moran 1991: 14). The trend has accelerated in recent years as best practice standards formulated and promoted by private groups have been widely accepted by public officials. Market-based or self-supervision, on the other hand, is a more novel step. Market discipline has long accompanied official efforts; however, market-based arrangements have been put at the centre of the supervisory process.

This chapter is organised into four parts. The first section explores the development of transnational private governance processes by examining the role of the private sector in supervisory arrangements relating to official procedures in the context of the Basel Committee on Banking Supervision (Basel Committee) accord. The second section assesses the policy role of the private sector and examines its implications for efficiency and stability. The third section evaluates the consequences of market-based supervision for our understanding of preference formulation and global financial governance and explains how the private sector has entered the policy community. Finally, the article examines ensuing questions of legitimacy and accountability in current financial governance arrangements. The principal argument of this chapter is that private-sector preferences have been internalised in financial policy processes; this has not necessarily happened as a result of a conscious and deliberate strategy of capture but rather, as the consequence of formal and informal practices of public–private interaction and agreement among an increasingly coherent and transnational policy community. As a result, a small, elite group of private actors have become an integral part of the policy community and in the context of Basel II, have acquired semi-institutionalised functions in the making of global rules. This indicates that (i) transnational private governance is an explicit mode of governance in global finance and (ii) private preferences and interests are defining policy debates and restricting policy options and alternatives.

Regulatory and supervisory practices: 'markets are an ally in the system of supervision'[2]

Official recommendations and disclosure practices – bringing private actors in

As part of their supervision functions, public authorities require access to relevant information but due to expertise and sheer volume constraints on their authority, they are also keen to promote transparency and market discipline among market actors. Speaking on behalf of the Federal Reserve Board, former Governor Laurence Meyer (2000) summarised official US supervisory positions as follows: 'we have limited public policy choices for large and complex organisations. Choice 1: we can accept systemic risk as a cost of having large, global organisations in the marketplace. Choice 2: in order to limit systemic risk, we can adopt very detailed regulation and supervision programmes that include a growing list of prohibitions. Choice 3: we can rely more on market discipline to supplement capital reforms and can maintain a level of supervision similar to the one we have today. Given the choices, we simply must try market discipline'. Similarly, William McDonough (2002), former president of the Federal Reserve Bank of New York, has argued that the principal elements of supervision in the twenty-first century are 'effective bank-level management; market discipline; and, official supervision'.

For public officials, market-based mechanisms such as discipline, transparency, increased disclosure and the understanding of risks have come to represent key elements in the supervision of financial institutions. The Basel process, the principal arena for standard setting in global banking regulation and supervision, has been instrumental in promoting market-based supervision by producing frequent reports on disclosure. In a consistent effort to strengthen and improve transparency as a supervisory mechanism, its recent studies have concentrated on the right balance between quantitative and qualitative disclosures, consistency in risk assessment and disclosure methods and the regular release of information. These recommendations do not stand alone but are complemented by comprehensive regular surveys of industry practices (Basel Committee on Banking Supervision 1998, 2002; Multidisciplinary Working Group 2001). Most importantly, however, the central role of private self-supervision is evident in the New Capital Accord, the ultimate banking rules on capital adequacy. The revised accord, known as Basel II, was developed on the basis of a three-pillar framework and with the understanding that banking rules must reflect the needs and sophistication of financial institutions. The pillars, minimum capital requirements, supervisory review and market discipline aim to deliver an accord more suitable to financial practices (Basel Committee on Banking Supervision 2004).

Pillar 1 on minimum capital requirements allows banks, with the approval of their supervisors, to self-assess these requirements on the basis of the complexity of their activities and the status of their internal risk-management systems. In this context, global conglomerates, those most exposed to risk, are subject to market-based regulatory arrangements which institutionalise private-sector practices and relieve financial institutions from additional costly regulatory requirements. Pillar 2 focuses on the supervisory review process, proposing practices that would allow supervisors to evaluate banks' risk-management techniques and internal procedures and encouraging continuous dialogue between the private and the public sectors. For the most part, however, Pillar 2 provides a structure that formalises market-based supervision and encourages bank-by-bank risk analysis instead of broad supervisory principles and direction. Finally, Pillar 3 puts forward disclosure requirements and recommendations which can strengthen market discipline by allowing market participants to have access to information on risk-management and measurement, and hence on the capital adequacy of the institution.

In their reform of the capital accord, it appears that banking regulators and supervisors had three goals. First, the Basel Committee designed a capital requirements framework that reflects institutions' risk-management systems for identifying and measuring exposure to risk, acknowledging that different firms require different treatment. Second, it set up a framework for active supervision of banks' internal practices. Third, it encouraged the efficacy of market discipline, by providing guidelines for improved disclosure and transparency. Throughout the process, the private sector was extensively consulted, both formally and privately, and the final document is a product of these consultations.[3] The shift to a system of regulation and supervision which has the interests of transnational financial institutions at its core appears accomplished. Indeed,

Basel II can be interpreted as the perfect example of regulatory and supervisory capture: it benefits big players, does not include tough regulation and its complex approaches are a clear market entry barrier.

Explaining Basel II: transnational private (financial) governance at work

The development of the Basel Committee as an influential actor in global financial governance and the articulation of respective state interests have been well documented (Kapstein 1991; Wood 2005). This analysis offers additional insights by focusing on the role of private actors in shaping these interests as well as the agenda guiding the reform of the accord. In particular, this study explains that private actors are now an integral part of the policy community and that their role has evolved from one of influence to writing the policy script.

In the run-up to the reform of the accord, the Group of Thirty (G-30), a private organisation that brings together 30 senior public- and private-sector officials in a part-think tank, part-interest group and part-club setting, produced a report with a series of guidelines for the design of an enhanced regulatory and supervisory framework (Group of Thirty 1997). The report called for global institutions to 'take the lead in developing a global framework for comprehensive and effective management controls, in cooperation with supervisors and as a continuing exercise', a proposal that highlighted the importance of sound internal risk-management structures and underlined the value of technical expertise. The group also produced instructions on dialogue between public officials and industry practitioners, adapted remuneration schemes for supervisors in order to ensure up-to-date skills, coordination of supervision and incentives offered to financial institutions, such as differentiating between good and bad performers. The report's authors were, in their views, representative of the financial policy community at large, exhibiting a high comfort level with the principle that the private sector needs to be more involved in its supervision and that traditional supervisors should no longer have the lead.

The G-30 did not embark on this project independently. A few months prior to the publication of the G-30 study, the Institute of International Finance (IIF), a global banking association that concentrates its efforts on international agreements such as Basel II, issued its *Report of the Task Force on Conglomerate Supervision* which advocated developments in supervision along the same lines as the G-30 (Institute of International Finance 1997). The IIF's recommendations included a focus on *globally active financial institutions*, transition to supervisory practices based on risk analysis, coordination among supervisors and upgrading of their technical ability and increased use of disclosure, both in confidential and in regulatory reporting. In the late 1990s, the transnational financial policy community as a whole appeared to be favouring increased private-sector involvement and were identifying possible policy proposals to that effect; indeed, it is widely acknowledged that the G-30 report was an exercise in testing the waters and a useful start to the revision of the Basel accord.[4]

These rather informal private-sector exercises led to intensified and arguably institutionalised policy functions for private actors in the development of the accord, as exemplified most strikingly through the influence of the IIF: indeed, the organisation played an active consultative role in the drafting, revision and final version of Basel II. As part of an extensive consultation process, the IIF, along with a plethora of other actors (public and private), was regularly sounded out and offered consistent feedback, including providing expertise on highly technical issues, throughout the process; it also, more informally, provided an up-to-date and uniform review of private-sector preferences and reactions. The end result has been that IIF preferences for market-generated standards and market-based oversight solutions have been internalised in the Basel process, and that consequently, large sophisticated banks are the best placed and best suited to the ensuing proposals.

The IIF represents a wide variety of institutions (in terms of both size and geographical scope), but in essence, its positions, especially on questions relating to the Basel process, reflect those of the big financial players. The predominance of the interests of those players is manifest in the final text of Basel II. But the consultative process itself is indicative of the growing policy role of the IIF: the interaction had no typical pattern but took the form of standard responses to official documents and press releases, private letters, as well as face-to-face meetings. These informal meetings in particular allowed for an exchange of views with senior Basel Committee people and proved consistently fruitful in moving the accord forward. It is also widely acknowledged that such informal procedures, including consultation about what constitutes best practice, while not formally documented, are an essential part of the process.[5]

These findings are 'conventional' in the context of current financial governance arrangements: in essence, industry comments were listened to and adapted in the Basel II accord. A close examination of financial market activities and their governance reveals a significant degree of transnationalisation as well as a significant place for private-sector interests and concerns in the prevailing arrangements. Large global financial institutions have increasingly more in common with each other across borders than with the more domestically oriented financial entities of their home markets. Similarly, their regulators and supervisors cooperate on an international basis to develop regulatory and monitoring frameworks that, as is the case with the work of the Basel Committee, become predominant; they do not always enjoy the same level of agreement over sets of priorities with other public-sector officials in their home jurisdictions. At the same time, a well-established engagement with neoliberal economic practice (which has also become progressively more transnational) has brought private-sector concerns to the forefront of policy making. This also helps to explain the apparent 'US Paradox' in the development of Basel II. Indeed, during the final stages of the drafting of the accord, US regulators announced a reduced applicability of the accord in the US, with only the largest institutions expected to adopt the relevant requirements and practices. Arguably, this came about as a result of sharp divisions among the US regulatory community where, at a technical level, the emphasis is on safety and soundness, whereas at the political level, the focus shifts to competition. This brought about concerns about competitive advantages, especially among European financial institutions, which are to be bound by the adoption of Basel II in the form of a Capital Adequacy Directive. While most of these concerns have subsided, the relative unease with the final US position illustrates some of the contradictions that exist within national contexts, as well as the considerable extent of shared understanding at the transnational level.

A global policy role for the private sector

Private authority is not a novel phenomenon in financial governance. There has long existed a pattern of dialogue and interaction between the public and private sectors, and a tradition of self-regulation in the securities and banking industries. Nevertheless, the crash of 1929 and the consequent depression brought about strong public agencies and, despite private-sector involvement, for most of the twentieth century, there was some clarity with regard to public and private functions, with regulation and supervision firmly in the hands of public authorities. The above analysis shows that the balance has shifted and that the private sector has acquired not only a formal regulatory role but also a supervisory one.

But is this new policy role accompanied by a corresponding degree of responsibility? In economic terms, market discipline amounts to much more than transparency and disclosure: 'transparency of risk and capital positions; incentives to process information; formulation of unbiased estimates of the probability of default reflected in appropriate price and quantity sanctions; and bank responses to increase in price and/or reduction in quantity by reducing exposure or increasing capital'.[6] This means that not only must there be adequate information available to market participants but also that these participants must be at risk of loss and that a negative market view of a financial institution must have significant effects. It becomes apparent that Basel II does not deal with most of these issues. There are, indeed, significant limits to market discipline, such as the existence of safety nets and deposit insurance, and the central bank function of lender of last resort, especially for institutions that are *too-big-to-fail*. 'If there were no implicit or explicit guarantee, such as deposit insurance or a lender of last resort, the bank supervisors could let Pillar 3, market discipline, do their job entirely. That is, or should be, the ultimate goal towards which this framework is moving'.[7] Whether this could be a politically acceptable solution in the long run can be extensively debated; what is clear is that at this moment, strong political considerations maintain the responsibility status quo and thus provide a considerable level of security to private-sector actors.

Concerns remain, therefore, as to how responsibly the private sector takes its policy role, as well as with regard to the safeguards that are in place should something go wrong. The probability of failure for a financial institution cannot and should not be driven to zero, but in the current financial environment, the private sector enjoys a great degree of autonomy without assuming a corresponding level of responsibility; the public sector is (or would be in the event of a crisis) left with the task of picking up the pieces when private-sector decisions prove detrimental to the stability of the financial system. Private actors are therefore contributing towards and sometimes defining the emerging structure of the financial system, but currently, they are taking advantage of their position without making themselves fully accountable. Along with improved disclosure, the issue of clearer patterns of responsibility and that of a more open and visible policy role for the private sector need to be urgently addressed.

Understanding transnational private governance in global finance

The influence and authority of the private sector over its regulation and supervision have affected the wider context of global financial governance. Private institutions, individually or through membership of various industry associations and other private groupings, help shape policy preferences because they are now part of the policy community. Members of the community appear to have common goals and similar beliefs and present a unified front; whereas some debate may indeed be taking place about the public–private balance within the community, no one is openly questioning the general benefits of the interaction, nor indeed, the main policy orientations that it entails. As a result, the level of controversy that is often associated with important and potentially explosive financial issues is not fully reflected in the making of policy. In this context, the influence of the private-sector participation is seen as legitimate. Legitimacy stems from the situation of *revolving doors* among financial sector employees; eventually, those in charge of regulation and supervision and those representing the financial institutions being regulated and supervised are the same group of people. Most importantly, however, the complexity and speed of financial innovation has put banks in a privileged position as knowledge holders. Public authorities lag behind in terms of technical capabilities and expertise. If regulators and supervisors cannot keep up (and cannot afford to keep up) with the development of financial products that are complex, often tailor-made and used by a variety of institutions and firms, they cannot regulate nor supervise effectively. As a result, private initiatives gradually take over important functions and promote standards based on private practice. This transfer of authority is further assisted by the reputation of global finance as complicated and technical. Financial issues attract limited attention as evidenced by the 'low domestic visibility of the issue of financial liberalisation among politicians and the general public' (Helleiner 1994: 14). This has helped to de-politicise global financial matters and to account for public–private dynamics in the making of policy in technical terms (Picciotto and Haines 1999).

But why is there such underlying agreement among public- and private-sector officials on transparency and market-based supervision? This conformity is based on public- and private-sector representatives belonging to the same financial policy community; public officials and practitioners have common educational and professional backgrounds and regularly meet and network in their professional capacity (Gill 1990; van der Pijl 1998). In Cerny's analysis, 'both formal and informal private organisations and relationships, which themselves are organised more and more around international competition and transnational linkages, come to set standards and to shape practices (including 'best practice' and 'benchmarking') which are then transmitted in a feedback process at domestic, transnational and international levels through both private and state action operating in mutually reinforcing ways' (Cerny 2002: 202). Moreover, 'transnational policy communities of experts and professionals that share their expertise and information and form common patterns of understanding regarding policy through regular interaction, [bring about] policy convergence' (Stone 2001: 6). Contact can be formal, as in the case of the Basel Committee, semi-formal, in the context of private association meetings, or informal, based on personal relations and unofficial interaction. This concentration of specialist policy makers facilitates agreement among the members of the policy community but also acts as an exclusion zone for alternative points of view, or indeed for discussion of the consequences of commonly agreed approaches based on private-sector preferences and interests for the allocation of wealth but also for market competition and financial stability.

What does this mean for our understanding of financial governance? Public and private actors advance market structures, which promote private interests and moreover, move policy-making procedures to the transnational level, leading to policy harmonisation. In this context, going beyond sterile distinctions of public and private enhances our understanding of global financial governance and reveals that public and private are working together to get markets to operate in a certain manner and that their combined decisions have an impact on the relative balance of public and private in the proceedings. In turn, this suggests that those same actors and the policy community could express preference for alternative market structures and a different degree of private-sector influence. The market is a policy tool (Pauly 2002), and the transnational policy community is made up of both public and private actors; it is thus possible to conceive of the balance shifting again and of state actors reasserting authority (Weiss 2003).

Bringing the politics back in? Legitimacy and accountability

When examining the legitimacy of global financial governance arrangements, we also need to look at the legitimacy of policy priorities, actors and the structure as a whole. The analysis of this chapter shows that the policies that make up global financial governance are accepted as legitimate primarily as a result of the high level of expertise involved in the policy process. But does this make policy priorities legitimate? The transnational policy community focuses on efficiency and stability over social or distributive justice, which is also a public good (Kapstein 1999). In practice, this means a shift of economic policies and a phasing-out of the welfare role of the state in favour of support of the private sector

(Prakash and Hart 1999). These conflicts are not new: Polanyi (1944) provided an account of nineteenth-century finance which highlighted tensions and attempts to reconcile laissez-faire economics and an active social role for the state.

Inevitably, these policy priorities produce winners and losers. In other aspects of economic governance, policy outcomes in terms of winners and losers are easily apparent; Sell's (2003) analysis on the influence of private actors over the regime of intellectual property protection shows a clear impact on the ability of states in the developing world to tackle health issues and the HIV/AIDS crisis in particular. The identification of losers in the politics of banking supervision is subtler; the failure of regulation and supervision can impact workers who become unemployed as a result of a currency crisis or taxpayers who have to bail out insolvent financial institutions (Porter 2001). More generally, Cutler *et al.* argue that private actor authority leads to decisions about 'who gets to play, what are the limits on play, and often who wins' (Cutler *et al.* 1999: 369).

The legitimacy of actors in the current arrangements is equally problematic. Authority is linked to legitimacy (Friedman 1990). Hurd (1999: 388) argues that the 'operative process in legitimation is the internalisation by the actor of an external standard', a standard other than self-interest. In global financial governance, external standards tend to revolve around stability and efficiency and, thus, are too closely linked to private-sector interests. This also has consequences for the legitimacy of public actors: 'when states delegate effective authority to actors in private markets, both the act of delegation and the future performance of those actors have implications for their own continued legitimacy' (Pauly 1997: 18). The state's relations with its non-financial constituencies are thus compromised.

Finally, what is the legitimacy of the structure of global financial governance? Germain (2004) proposes the principles of inclusion and globalising accountability as a way to enhance legitimacy. While it is the case that the institutional framework became more inclusive in the aftermath of the Asian financial crisis, core governance arrangements are, however, still inhabited by a relatively small number of financial institutions and public authorities with a strong North American and European bias.

The legitimacy of non-state actor influence and authority becomes more problematic when we examine accountability patterns relating to the activities of these actors. This is particularly true in global finance, where policy making remains 'esoteric' and leads to a 'limited democracy' (Coleman 1996: 10). Against this background, the 'power of the vote in shaping public policy decreases' while at the same time, the private actors that hold authority are not part of a mechanism that assigns appropriate responsibility (Reinicke 1997: 3). 'Market actors are neither elected nor politically accountable' (Cohen 1999: 135). In this context, who, or what, are policy makers (public and private) accountable to? It would be tempting to answer that the main accountability mechanism is the *market*. Nevertheless, when losses happen, or crises occur, market mechanisms do not always take over by inflicting punishment or discipline. Instead, the public sector does act to remedy problems, and its interference affects a wider set of actors in ways that are not explicitly recognised by the governance framework. This is further evidence that *who* exercises authority matters and that in the current financial governance arrangements, under the pretext of market efficiency, private interests have been internalised by the transnational policy community.

Conclusions

This chapter has provided an overview of trends and practices in the supervision of financial markets and has shown that the policy process is increasingly shaped by private-sector preferences, as evidenced in the promotion of market-based arrangements in Basel II. In particular, the analysis has shown how a small group of elite and sophisticated financial institutions have used their strong market position, expertise and networks to position themselves at the core of a global rule-making policy community. This significant development in transnational private governance is based on an understanding of transnational policy communities of public and private actors that transcends traditional distinctions of public and private and which is a product of consensual interaction between official public actors and the private sector against a background of a neoliberal political and economic framework.

In identifying the market mechanisms favoured by this policy community, the chapter also comes to the conclusion that despite the overwhelming tendency towards thinking about banking supervision in technical and economic terms, as well as theorising about the de-politicisation of global finance, politics and private interest coincide to produce a supervisory set-up that is far from the ideal of market discipline and efficiency. The existence of safety nets and lender of last resort functions of central banks removes the prospect of efficient market discipline, yet there is little evidence of serious proposals that would limit safety nets or reduce insured deposits. Moreover, principles of corporate governance, despite the recent plethora of examples of bad practice from the corporate, world have yet to be included in policy discussions on the banking industry. We thus need to clearly distinguish between neoliberal economic principles and the politics of neoliberalism and focus on the efficiency and accountability of transnational private governance arrangements. These shortcomings, coupled with the legitimacy and distribution issues addressed, make the question 'who benefits?' all the more pertinent and indicate that we need to think further about the capture of the policy process.

Notes

1 For a comprehensive discussion of these issues, see Strange 1996 and Cerny 1993.
2 Remark made by the Governor of the Bank of Spain and Chairman of the Basel Committee in a speech at the Conference on Market Discipline, cosponsored by the Bank for International Settlements and the Federal Reserve Bank of Chicago, Chicago, USA, 1 November 2003.

3 For more information on the consultative process, see www.bis.org. The informal aspect of the consultation process was also confirmed in interviews with Basel Secretariat and Institute of International Finance officials.
4 This point is made in the introduction to the G-30 report but has been further corroborated through a series of interviews with relevant public- and private-sector officials.
5 This is widely acknowledged not only by IIF officials but also by officials in the Basel Committee and its secretariat. National banking associations also expressed strong views on IIF privileged access in the context of interviews.
6 Remarks made by Richard Herring at the Conference on Market Discipline, cosponsored by the Bank for International Settlements and the Federal Reserve Bank of Chicago, Chicago, USA, 31 October 2003.
7 Idem.

Part II

Transnational corporations facing labour, ecological, and consumers' concerns

5 The power of TNCs in transnational environmental private governance

Doris Fuchs, with Jörg Vogelmann

Introduction

Today's increasing relevance of transnational private governance (TPG) can be positioned in a framework of broader developments in business political power. Indeed, if one adopts a power-theoretic perspective on TPG, the political implications of the growing extent of TPG become much more visible. Moreover, such an approach reveals developments in business political role that are frequently not considered in analyses of TPG but are crucial parallel and interactive trends in business participation in governance. These trends need to be included in analyses of TPG, if one wants to understand fully its meaning, processes and implications.

The present chapter adopts such a power-theoretic focus on TPG in the environmental field (TEPG). From this perspective, the chapter highlights the need to consider rule- and agenda-setting as well as discursive activities by business as elements of TPG. It is the interaction and interdependence between these elements that has promoted the increasing societal acceptance and therefore growth in TPG. Moreover, the power-theoretic focus highlights that the control over economic, technological and organisational resources and networks in interaction with the dominance of neoliberal norms and ideas are fundamental driving forces behind the ability of business actors to exercise political power via TPG institutions. In consequence, the analysis suggests that TPG externally reflects an increase in the relative political power of TNCs *vis-à-vis* the state and civil society, and internally in the power of TNCs *vis-à-vis* small- and medium-sized firms. Likewise, the power-theoretic focus reveals the particular relevance of TPG in oligopolistic forms of competition since hypercompetitive markets or branches of business characterised by turbulent, open change render economic power relations more complex.

In pursuit of its objectives, the chapter follows the conceptualisation of TPG adopted by the editors and other contributing authors to this book. It understands TPG to refer to functional, in this case environmental, transborder governance arrangements. The spatial scope of the analysis will include national, as well as regional and global initiatives.[1] Moreover, we understand TPG to refer to institutions in which private actors play a dominant role, although public actors need not necessarily be excluded. In other words, we consider public–private partnerships examples of TPG. The relevant private actors can include TNCs, small- and medium-sized firms as well as civil society organisations. As pointed out above, TNCs play a particularly prominent role, however, and therefore provide the focus of our analysis. In addition, we understand governance to include a range of logics of power and action, reaching from consensual to coercive, formal to informal and hierarchical to non-hierarchical (though within our focus, we find mainly formally non-hierarchical) institutions. Consensus and force co-determine the existence of TEPG.

In its power-theoretic approach to TEPG, the chapter develops a framework that captures the instrumental, structural and discursive facets of the political power of TNCs. With the help of this conceptual lens, it then explores developments in TEPG in the narrow sense, i.e. rule-setting activities by business, as well as in TEPG in the broader sense, i.e. including developments in business agenda-setting and discursive activities. It highlights, in particular, that TNCs have obtained increasing rule-setting power by taking on an active role in TEPG through self-regulation and participation in public–private and private–private partnerships (PPPs). In addition, the analysis shows discursive governance by business, i.e. the shaping of its image as a political actor as well as the active participation in public debates on the (re-)definition of environmental problems and solutions as a crucial and stabilising element of TEPG.

Assessing power

A systematic and comprehensive power-theoretic framework has to integrate different levels of analysis and consider material and ideational, as well as actor-specific, structural and systemic sources of power. Accordingly, the present analysis explores various sources of business capability to pursue political objectives by employing a power-theoretic framework that distinguishes between the instrumental, structural and discursive facets of business political power.[2] These facets of power have different sources, intervene at different points in the political process and face similarly differing potentials and constraints.

The instrumental power of business actors is captured in assessments of its influence on political/policy output. It appears in analyses of business influence on politicians via lobbying and campaign/party finance, for instance. This is the form of power that power-theoretic concepts emphasising the notion of 'A's power over B' and assuming the existence of a functional, unilinear causality, of individual voluntary action and instrumental causality will point out (e.g. Dahl 1957). It is a form of power, moreover, which can be traced back to actor-specific resources, such as financial, organisational or human resources, as well as access to decision makers. In political science, instrumental power has been at the centre of analyses of pluralism and interest group politics. Instrumentalist approaches to power can also be found in traditional power theories in international relations, where scholars focus on the use of power by states in pursuit of national interests (Morgenthau 1948). An instrumentalist perspective on power reveals important ways in which TNCs pursue their objectives in the political process. However, such a perspective neglects structural sources of power that predetermine behavioural options, as it assumes the autonomy of actors' choices of actions.

In consequence, a structuralist perspective on power needs to be added to the framework to capture additional channels through which TNCs exert political influence. Such a perspective emphasises the importance of the input side of the political process and of business influence on the choice set of political decision makers by existing material structures that allocate direct and indirect decision-making power. A structuralist perspective on power points out, for instance, why some issues never reach the agenda and some proposals are never made (Bachrach and Baratz 1962). Thus, critical approaches in International Political Economy highlight governmental dependence on business investment, employment and tax revenue (Cox 1987). In environmental policy analyses, the structural power argument has led to a controversial debate on the existence of pollution havens, i.e. the need of governments to attract investment via a race to the bottom in environmental (and social) standards.

Existing material structures can not only provide actors with agenda-setting power, however. They also may place them in the position to make decisions themselves, i.e. replace those holding the formal decision-making power. In today's globalised world, economic and institutional structures, processes and interdependencies mean that actors in control of economic and technological networks and resources have the capacity to adopt, implement and enforce rules with an obligatory quality and distributional consequences for other actors as well. Thus, the traditional notion of structural power needs to be extended for analyses of business power in global environmental governance. Rather than merely providing indirect agenda-setting power, structural contexts may also endow business actors with direct rule-setting power. This acquisition of rule-setting power by business is most clearly reflected in TPG in the narrow sense, i.e. self-regulation, PPPs and the emergence of 'private authority'.

Next to an actor's instrumental and structural power, a comprehensive analysis needs to pay attention to his discursive power. This 'third face' of power rests in norms and ideas and is reflected in communicative practices and cultural values and institutions. In today's mediatised world, discursive contests play an increasingly important role in the political process. Actors compete in offering frames and definitions for political problems and solutions, linking them to specific fundamental norms and values. Accordingly, scholars highlight the importance of shifts in core dimensions of policy issues and of symbols, story lines and the provision of 'effective' evidence and compelling arguments in the public debate (Hajer 1997).

Two major implications arise from a discursive perspective on power. First, power does not simply pursue interests but creates them and thus intervenes in the political process in the broadest sense (Lukes 1974). It allows the framing of policies, actors and broader societal norms and ideas. In consequence, such an analysis would pay attention to business media and public relation efforts.

Second, discursive power is closely tied to legitimacy. After all, discursive power relies on the willingness of recipients of messages to place a least some trust in the validity of the contents of the message. Political legitimacy, can derive from a variety of sources. Public actors draw this legitimacy from electoral processes and the formal authority associated with political office. Business actors today tend to be able to count on the perception of political (output-)legitimacy due to the increasing trust the public as well as regulators place in their expertise and capacity to provide desired outcomes (Scharpf 1998).

A comprehensive analysis of the political power of business, then, would need to pay attention to all of the dimensions of power discussed. With respect to TEPG, however, the structural and discursive dimensions of this power are the most relevant. Accordingly, the following section will provide empirical illustrations of business exercise of structural and discursive power in environmental governance today.

Business power and TEPG

Business power and TEPG in the narrow sense

The most relevant development in business political power reflected by TEPG is its increasing acquisition and exercise of rule-setting power. Structural economic resources and networks allow business actors, in particular TNCs, today to actively design and implement rules through participation in self-regulatory institutions and PPPs in a wide range of policy areas including environmental issues. As pointed out above, business actors cannot just influence the policy choice set of governments anymore, but also the standard choice set of private actors. This applies to TNCs, in particular, which via supply chain management exercise considerable influence on standard adoption by their suppliers.

Self-regulatory institutions today are the most visible embodiments of business active rule-setting power in the environmental field. They exist at the company level in the form of environmental codes of conduct, at the sectoral level such as the Responsible Care Program of the chemical industry and at the global level such as the ISO 14000 environmental management system. The ISO 14000 standard, for instance, delineates principles for environmental management systems that individual business actors can adopt and be certified for in order to improve and communicate their environmental conduct. The standard is highly popular with more than 90,000 facilities in 127 countries having been ISO 14000 certified by 2004.

Evaluations of ISO 14000's effectiveness in actually improving the environmental conduct of business actors, however, are ambivalent. Some scholars perceive the standard as definitely providing incentives to business to improve its environmental conduct by fostering communication and awareness (Kollman 2003).[3] Moreover, scholars argue that improving the environmental conduct of business actors at the global level faces difficulties, even in the best of circumstances. Complex interactions between the national and international economic and political levels frequently have delayed and prevented the development of public law in this regard.

To many critical observers, however, the voluntary nature and lack of public influence on the contents of the standard and its application often mean that the standard is missing the teeth required to actually achieve the desired goals. They point out that ISO 14000 certification does not entail actual environmental performance requirements beyond compliance with local laws.[4] In addition, scholars report that the participation in the development of the standard has not been distributed 'democratically' but dominated by large firms from industrialised countries and their interests. Clapp (2001: 19) even argues that ISO 14000 standards have 'tended to reinforce, rather than reduce, the gap in regulations on hazardous waste and production processes between rich and poor countries'. In sum, many empirical studies demonstrate that business actors may often use codes primarily as superficial window-dressing measures in order to secure and increase profits, as well as avoid public regulation.

Due to the considerable criticism civil-society actors levelled at self-regulation for the reasons cited above, more recent generations of TPG in the environmental and social field have been based on cooperation between business actors and civil society in PPPs (Nadvi and Wältring 2002). A highly noted example of such a partnership is the Forest Stewardship Council (FSC), which aims to improve the sustainability of forest management through the creation of a certification system for businesses along the timber product chain on the basis of environmental, social and economic criteria. The FSC has achieved much acclaim as a TEPG institution due to its rather stringent environmental (and social) standards. At the same time, however, the FSC has also become a prime example of the threat of TEPG failure. Perceiving the FSC standard as too stringent, timber industries in several countries have created weaker, competing labels, which has led to a marginalisation of the FSC standard in the market (Fuchs 2006a). Clearly, then, the active role business plays in the setting of rules and regulations via codes and standards has both advantages and disadvantages. Studies identify both 'green' and 'greenwashing' motives in the development and adoption of voluntary environmental commitments, and the same applies to social ones (Arts 2003; Fluck and Schmitt 1998).

Three reasons exist as to why the expansion in TEPG in the narrow sense matters from a power-theoretic perspective. First, the design and implementation of these rules tend to be dominated by corporate actors, while medium- and small-sized firms as well as firms from developing countries frequently are underrepresented but have to bear the costs of the rules and standards as well. This is the case even with voluntary standards, where the costs of non-adoption may involve a loss in sales. Second, the distributional consequences of business set rules also affect employees and consumers and therefore societies (not necessarily negatively, of course). Third, and perhaps most important, TEPG may prevent or undermine (more stringent and effective) rule setting by public actors. Indeed, some self-regulatory institutions such as the Responsible Care

Program of the chemical industry have been created after major scandals like Bhopal or Seveso and a rising perception that public regulation would be forthcoming. In other cases, such threats of public regulation have been more diffuse, with self-regulation being a reaction of TNCs to 'weak signals', in Ansoff's (1981) words. They hereby arise from the presence of public skepticism regarding corporations in general rather than the foreshadowing of concrete plans for public regulation of business. Moreover, some scholars have found evidence that governments are starting to lift public regulation in the presence of private self-regulation. Thus, Clapp (2001) reports that governments have in some instances softened environmental regulatory requirements for ISO 14000 certified plants.[5]

In sum, the potential regulatory and distributional consequences of TEPG in the narrow sense suggest that it deserves our attention from a power-theoretic perspective. In this context, the increasing level of control and autonomy business is gaining in self-regulation and PPPs is worth noticing. Clearly, there are significant differences among self-regulatory institutions with respect to the relative power of business actors. Some self-regulatory institutions, for instance, exist in the shadow of hierarchy. Increasingly, however, self-regulatory arrangements develop without input from and control by public authorities (Brühl *et al.* 2001, 2004; Haufler 2001). The necessary public authority for this shadow of hierarchy, moreover, does not exist in a similar manner at the global level, and changes in practices there frequently induce corresponding changes at the national level.

Business power and TEPG in the broader sense

Business structural power in its agenda-setting form also plays a role in TEPG. First, business can influence governmental support for and adoption of previously private standards similar to its influence on other policy choice sets. In this context, it is important to note that the agenda-setting power of business arising from capital mobility has grown considerably in the globalised world as the number of states (and sub-national units) competing for investment in the international system has increased, highly mobile finance capital makes up an even larger share of global capital flows and production processes and their capital bases have changed to provide companies with even more flexibility[6] (Altvater and Mahnkopf 1996; Brand *et al.* 2000; Strange 1998). These arguments are supported by empirical studies linking the general decline in corporate tax levels in OECD countries to global competition for investment (Ganghof 2005).

Second, specific business actors, most notably rating agencies and financial actors, are in a particularly powerful position with respect to TEPG. They can exercise a kind of quasi-regulation located between agenda- and rule-setting power by determining the acceptability of public environmental policies, a development which has provided new momentum to the pollution havens debate. Although environmental costs clearly are not the only factors influencing investment decisions, they are high in some industries and environmental standards and charges frequently are linked to competitiveness concerns in political debates (as for example, in the context of national allocation plans for CO_2 emission certificates in Europe recently).

Moreover, financial actors can influence the diffusion of private environmental standards through the ranking of companies and the tying of credit to environmental standards and assessments. As Schaper (2005) delineates, both public and private financial actors can exercise substantial leverage that way, which he considers to provide a positive impetus for improvements in business environmental conduct. Again, however, critical observers will point out that such environmental assessments by private financial actors frequently lack depth and aim to reduce the liability and risk of scandal for the financial actors themselves rather than pursue environmental objectives.

An important part of TEPG in the broader sense is the discursive facet of such governance efforts. This discursive facet is frequently overlooked in research on private governance. Yet, TEPG would not exist in its present form, were it not for the interaction between rule-setting activities by TNCs and their discursive power. Business discursive power contributes to TEPG in two ways. First, business discursive power allows it to maintain and improve its legitimacy as a political actor and therefore as a rule setter. Second, business discursive power allows it to participate in the public framing of policy problems as well as the definition of the public and the private realm, and thereby influencing the demand for private (and public) governance. While growing, business discursive power is not uncontested, however, which implies a certain degree of fragility for TEPG. Still, business material resources and structural interdependence with the (private) media allows it to maintain a preponderant influence in the contest over its legitimacy as a political actor at this point.

One of the most important characteristics of TEPG is its reliance on the perception that business is a legitimate political actor, especially in cases in which TEPG takes place in areas traditionally not considered core activities of business such as environmental and social regulation. Business legitimacy as a political actor, in turn, results from the dominance of neoliberal norms and ideas and the increasing emphasis societies have placed on efficiency, competitiveness and growth in the last three decades of the twentieth century. This political focus has turned business into *the* politico-economic expert, the primary actor considered able to provide and guarantee the provision of the desired goods, and thereby providing it with output legitimacy. Due to a perception of the possession of superior information and expertise by business, in combination with the view that complex and fast-changing technological and economic environments require decentralised governance and flexibility in reaction, business has come to be perceived as the better regulator (Reinicke 1998).

This legitimacy business has acquired is potentially unstable, however, as the public may trust business ability to provide certain outcomes but not its willingness to do so. In order to be trusted as a (self-)regulator on environmental issues, therefore, business needs to have a certain degree of moral legitimacy, and it is here that business discursive power plays a pivotal rule. The exercise of discursive power by business actors allows them to shape their own identity as 'good corporate citizens'. Accordingly, business actors, in particular corporations and business associations, increasingly have been engaging in and promoting new discourses such as the 'greening of industry', 'green and competitive', 'ecological modernisation', 'sustainable design' or 'corporate environmental responsibility'. These perspectives have by now been expanded to the notion of 'corporate citizenship' in general, thus combining social and environmental aspects.[7]

Likewise, TNCs have fundamentally reshaped their image from car companies to mobility providers or oil companies to 'beyond petroleum' energy providers. Similarly, the World Business Council on Sustainable Development, for instance, promotes environmental success stories of its member corporations, thereby advancing 'the notion of sustainable development as an environmental gloss on corporate business as usual' (Dryzek 1999: 43). Finally, communication on the 'success' and 'effectiveness' of TEPG is also of crucial importance here. In this respect, the proliferation of business conferences on private standards, corporate social responsibility, and so on, is noteworthy. These conferences are characterised by the presentation of best practices and success stories, and, at the same time, by such high conference fees that the participation of critical NGOs can be prevented.

Philanthropic activities by corporations also contribute to such efforts to improve one's image. Daimler Chrysler, for instance, supports a variety of environmental projects. It defines environmental protection as a major corporate objective and reports to have spent 1.6 billion Euros in 2004 for this purpose.[8] It has contributed to the establishment of the Greater Limpopo Transfrontier Park, for example, by donating financial resources to WWF South Africa and the South African Peace Parks Foundation. With the company's support, the project was able to link sanctuaries in the border triangle South Africa, Zimbabwe and Mozambique, thereby creating a conservation area or 'Peace Park' almost as big as the Netherlands, which enables the free movement of animals. Such philanthropic investments may well improve the public perception of Daimler Chrysler as a governance actor providing transnational environmental goods.[9]

Philanthropic, discursive and economic objectives may go hand-in-hand in such cases, of course. A clear example of such linkages is the cheap vegetable oil cooker 'Protos', which had been developed by the university of Hohenheim as a technological solution for the more than 2.5 billion people on earth cooking their daily meals on open fireplaces – with 1.6 million people dying each year of the consequences of this indoor air pollution (apart from severe deforestation problems), according to the WHO. Bosch and Siemens Hausgeräte GmbH bought the patent and offered a job to its innovative engineer in 2003 and – in collaboration with partners – invested in efforts to achieve series production readiness. Next to the good cause of providing people in developing countries with healthier cooking options, the huge potential of demand means that the break-even-point may soon be reached. Moreover, the fact that Bosch/Siemens cookers may be standing in millions of kitchens in developing countries in the future means a massive image gain and increase in brand recognition in many of the important markets of tomorrow.

Next to business exercise of discursive power in efforts to shape its own identity, such public opinion efforts can also aim at the framing of other actors. Critical observers stress that business has fostered the diffusion of images of government and politicians as incompetent if not capricious (Smith 2000). Thus, trust in government is declining parallel to the rise of faith in business actors (Ledgerwood and Broadhurst 2000). Likewise, studies show that business campaigns have challenged IGOs as undemocratic, costly and inefficient actors (Ong and Glantz 2000).

Besides business investments in the framing of actors' identities, its discursive power is also of fundamental importance in TEPG insofar as the participation in public discourse allows business to influence the framing of political problems and solutions as well as the definition of the public and private realm, thereby influencing the demand for private (as well as public) governance. Levy and Newell (2002) delineate the Global Climate Coalition's advertising and education campaigns, which emphasised scientific uncertainty and images of attacks on the American values of freedom and prosperity in the context of the climate change negotiations. As part of this campaign, business actors established NGOs, such as the 'Information Council for the Environment', which ran media campaigns specifically targeted at selected sectors of society, produced newsletters such as the 'World Climate Review' (mailed to all members of the *Society of Environmental Journalists*), produced the video *The Greening of Planet Earth*. In addition, the Global Climate Coalition commissioned studies and created expert groups with scientists supporting its interests and claims.

Similarly, Dryzek (1999) illustrates the competition between two different frames on sustainable development in public discourse. He points out that business actors such as the World Business Council on Sustainable Development have framed sustainable development in terms of continued growth. Thereby, they have been able to impose the norms and ideas of market liberalism on the concept and pushed the sustainability discourse in a pro-business direction.

At the most fundamental level, discursive contests in the public arena target the question of the border between public and private. The answer to this question has implications for the definition of what is a political problem. Where does governance need to take place and where not? In this context, we have seen an emphasis of prominent business voices on the desirability of market mechanisms rather than governance institutions.[10]

Finally, business discursive activities at the broadest level also affect environmental governance via societal self-definition. After all, advertising and commercial entertainment emphasise notions of consumer society and materialism. From an environmental perspective, that means that ideas of sustainable consumption are overpowered by opposing messages in everyday life. It is not surprising therefore that sustainable consumption policies that go beyond improving the efficiency of products and processes have rarely been adopted even by state actors to date (Fuchs and Lorek 2005). They certainly have not been the focus of demands for TEPG.

Business discursive power, however, is not invulnerable, as its legitimacy as a political actor is contested. Numerous books in the popular literature lamenting the power of corporate actors have appeared in recent years (Balanya *et al.* 2000; Cox 2006; Klein 2000; Korten 1995). Likewise, global surveys reveal high levels of suspicion of and aversion to corporations (Gallup 1999). Thus, while providing normative support for TEPG, business discursive power may also turn out to be its stumbling stone in the long run. A decline or disappearance of business political legitimacy would not only lead to a dramatic reduction in its discursive power, but cause challenges to its rule-setting power as well. If business loses its legitimacy as a political actor in the eyes of the public, self-regulation will become very difficult to justify.

Business legitimacy as a political actor may face challenges on two accounts. First, the political legitimacy of business in general and TNCs in particular is vulnerable to scandals arising from the exposure of illegal behaviour, or environmental or social misconduct, which in turn can render NGOs powerful enemies especially in times of worldwide mass media. Thus, the exposure of black sheep in the media, highly visible law suits as well as the creation of pressure and negative publicity in shareholder meetings have become important tools of NGOs in targeting the legitimacy of business. National and transnational NGOs such as Corporate Watch, Multinational Monitor, AccountAbility or Corporate Europe Observatory have made it their task to monitor corporate conduct and threaten exposure and scandals.[11]

Second, business political legitimacy and discursive power is vulnerable to changes in dominant societal norms and ideas.[12] Today's discursive power of business cannot be understood without the global diffusion of neoliberal ideas. Some scholars argue that the dominance of neoliberal ideas in global politics is an episode that is drawing towards its close, however, as they perceive social justice norms and frames to be becoming increasingly important (Florio 2002). Thus, current trends may be both 'empowering' and 'enfeebling' TNCs (Prakash 2002).

In the discursive contest regarding its legitimacy as a political actor, business currently is operating from an advantageous position, however. While discursive power does not necessarily and certainly not solely depend on material power, in the age of the (private) mass media and an increasing relevance of private funding in academic research, material resources can facilitate its exercise. In fact, some scholars argue that the power of resource rich interests, such as corporate actors, in the political process primarily originates in their ability to create and repeatedly send messages shaping the public debate (West and Loomis 1999).

In sum, TEPG in the broader sense entails agenda setting and discursive power of TNCs. The latter also provides a pivotal foundation for TEPG in the narrow sense, i.e. rule setting by business actors. Analyses of TEPG thus need to pay attention to the different facets of business power in TEPG and their interaction and interdependence.

Conclusion

This chapter has analysed the nature and foundations of TEPG. In its analysis, it has adopted a power-theoretic focus based on a differentiation between especially the structural and discursive facets of the political power of TNCs. Thereby, the analysis has been able to show that TEPG in the narrow sense reflects increasing rule-setting power by TNCs carried out in the form of self-regulation or participation in PPPs. Moreover, the chapter has demonstrated that one needs to consider TEPG in a broader sense, i.e. in the form of business ability to influence the demand for and design of private and public governance institutions via its agenda-setting and discursive power. Finally, the analysis has linked TEPG in the narrow sense to business discursive power, showing that the latter provides a pivotal foundation for the public acceptance of business rule-setting activities.

In its analysis of TEPG, the chapter has provided insights allowing a better understanding of its empirical scope conditions and normative implications. Thus, the chapter has emphasised the extent to which neoliberal norms and ideas provide a necessary setting for TEPG. Likewise, the strong link between the structural and discursive power of business actors (both *vis-à-vis* other business actors and *vis-à-vis* civil society and the state) and TEPG underlines the relevance of oligopolistic markets and concentrations in economic as well as political power. In other words, TEPG is firmly embedded in the international institutional structures of global market mechanisms and a (neo-)liberal world order. In addition, TEPG to a considerable extent is based on structural resources held by TNCs, access to and control over economic networks as well as technological and organisational knowledge resources. Finally, the existence of TEPG results from a certain homogeneity in values among at least the largest, Western TNCs, which is a function of the public pressure imposed on the latter's environmental conduct. Importantly, however, this homogeneity in values is not a sufficient condition for success of TEPG in terms of its effectiveness in improving environmental conditions, as both greening and greenwashing objectives can be noted.[13]

This last point ties the question of the empirical scope of TEPG to its normative implications. Most fundamentally, it has to be noted that TEPG's capacity to solve environmental problems is limited. There appears to be a clear preference by business actors for weak standards that communicate environmental intentions but do not impose high costs in terms of actual behavioural changes.

Similarly, TEPG functions mainly as a stabiliser of the current status quo in terms of the neoliberal world order due to the combination of business rule-setting and discursive powers. TEPG thus does not imply a move away from a market-centred approach to societal organisation or a new concerted effort to regulate markets. Changes in dominant societal norms could follow if the widespread failure of TEPG became apparent. However, given the discursive power of business and the associated ability to frame the evaluation of TEPG, such changes are not particularly likely at this point.

Finally, the chapter has shown that the interdependence between rule-setting and discursive activities by business actors has serious implications for democratic processes and legitimacy, which the reinforcement of neoliberal ideas and norms provided by TEPG tends to hide. TEPG clearly has the potential to constrain state sovereignty, limit public control over private actors and undermine governments' policy choices. As noted above, it can prevent the development of public regulation and has been tied to relief from public regulation. In other words, private actors may replace public actors and private standards may undermine public standards. While state recognition thus is not necessary for the existence of TEPG, such state recognition certainly can render it more powerful.

Most fundamentally, however, TEPG tends to be characterised by limited transparency and asymmetries in participation, both within the business community and externally. While generally based on consensual agreements among large (Western) TNCs, it involves coercive dynamics towards small- and medium-sized firms as well as business actors from the South. Similarly, TEPG frequently takes place without public or civil society participation, and even in the cases in which civil society actors are invited to participate, business is in the position to choose between more or less demanding NGOs as well as opt for self-regulation in the case of a demand for stringent standards by NGOs. These characteristics are all the more troubling, as TEPG has implications for the distribution of environmental and economic costs and benefits both for economic actors and for civil society, even if the explicit objective is regulatory in nature. The spread of private governance institutions in environmental policy and politics thus entails pivotal normative questions for democratic legitimacy.

Notes

1 The term global here should not disguise the fact that the TPG institutions we talk about frequently are dominated by actors from industrialised rather than developing countries.

2 For a more elaborate discussion of such a framework, see Arts 2003; Fuchs 2005; Levy and Egan 2000.

3 Benefits of private governance discussed in the literature also include the need for decentralised, flexible governance mechanisms caused by complex, fast-changing economic and technological conditions. In this respect, TPG fits with Ashby's (1958) law of requisite variety.

4 Similarly, scholars have documented that there is no evidence of a positive influence of the Responsible Care Program on the rate of environmental improvement among its members, while at the same time dirtier firms are actually more likely to participate in the program (King and Lenox 2000).

5 In this context, it is noteworthy that the ISO 14000 standard was on the horizon when in 1994 the Technical Barriers to Trade (TBT) agreement was being developed under the GATT and is therefore considered as legitimate and confirming with global trade rules by the agreement (Clapp 2001). Similar standards with more stringent performance requirements, however, would invite challenges under the TBT.

6 This ability is strongly demanded by contemporary management theory like Ghemawat and del Sol's flexible commitments, Beinhocker's populations of multiple strategies or Teece's dynamic capabilities (Zahn and Foschiani 2000).

7 The discussion of such activities as exercises of discursive power is not meant to

imply that business engages in them only with the intent of improving its image and moral legitimacy, of course. Whatever the intentions, however, such investments will influence business perceived legitimacy. Therefore, business discursive power and respective activities have to be taken into account when assessing the nature of TPEG.

8 DaimlerChrysler Umweltbericht 2005: p. 3 (see www.daimlerchrysler.com).

9 A TNC's return on such investments is also a function of the perceived legitimacy of the respective activity as such, which in turn depends on civil society participation among other factors. In the case of the Peace Parks project, this perceived legitimacy is high as NGOs like the German Euronatur or the WWF, and state officials and individuals with high perceived transnational legitimacy like Nelson Mandela (as a founding patron of the Peace Parks Foundation) are also involved in the tripartite project.

10 Similarly, the question of the border line between public and private has implications for the political options of civil society. In the environmental field, this aspect becomes clear in the context of access to information. As long as information on the environmental performance of business, i.e. emissions, effluents, etc., is considered private, NGOs have difficulties in targeting poor environmental performers.

11 In this context, business benefits from the lack of resources and difficulties and costs of gathering the necessary information by NGOs, moreover. If TNCs find it difficult to be informed about the production processes and practices of their suppliers, NGOs face even larger hurdles. Due to these difficulties and costs, the ability of NGOs to continuously, thoroughly and comprehensively monitor business conduct should not be overestimated. Furthermore, this ability tends to be limited to the largest and most visible business actors to begin with. Finally, information overflow, the public's short attention span and its general getting used to scandals constrain the ability of NGOs to successfully use publicity as a tool to challenge the legitimacy of business actors.

12 Such change could be brought about by major scandals, of course, but it can also derive from other sources such as political, economic or societal innovations or crises.

13 For a more elaborate analysis of the effectiveness of TPG in the environmental and social field, see Fuchs 2006b.

6 Where to find a 'demos' for controlling global risk regulators?

From private to public regulation and back

Franz van Waarden

From private to public regulation of risks and uncertainties

The state has always been in the 'business' of reducing risks and uncertainties for its citizens. Much of its public goods do just that. This holds first for the primary – Hobbesian – task of the state: the protection of its citizens against threats to their life, liberty, and property, be they from domestic or 'foreign' origin. In the old days, Hadrian's, the Chinese, and medieval city walls created visible borders around – and thereby defined – the 'group' to be protected; and watch towers, castles, and soldiers kept threats, varying from wandering dogs to foreign enemies, out. Nowadays, institutions such as the coast guard, the customs, airport security checks, and satellites do in principle the same. Other public goods regulate the 'grid', the relations within the demarcated 'group' (Douglas and Wildavsky 1982). They protect against internal threats: the police against thieves and murderers; hospitals against infectious diseases; and environmental inspectors against unsafe water or unpleasant odours.

Other institutions protect citizens from unexpected and 'uncivilised' action by the protectors themselves. The rule of law, constitutionalism, the judiciary, Committees of Public Accounts, and other institutions 'check and balance' state power and reduce the risks and uncertainties of possible arbitrary action of rule makers and rule enforcers.

Civil society also produced its own means for reducing the risks and uncertainties of life. First, through the division of labour, trade, and other forms of economic action. These provide essential securities as shelter, food, and reproduction. However, division of labour and markets are no spontaneous social orders. Unregulated markets pose such great uncertainties – information asymmetries allow for fraud and deception – that transactions are not likely in the absence of risk- and uncertainty-reducing institutions.

Again, civil society has produced its own transaction facilitating institutions: detectives check the reputation partners in the transaction; commercial rating agencies rate their financial reliability; accountants audit their books in the interest of clients and investors; advertisers pretend to help ameliorate information asymmetries; lawyers draw up and monitor contracts; gangs, strong-armed bandits, and the mafia aid in enforcing contracts; insurance companies insure calculable risks; technical standards increase market transparency and allow for interconnectivity; educational institutions certify labour and in particular specialised skills such as those for doctors, lawyers, or accountants; trade unions reduce the insecurities of workers in the labour market; guilds or trade associations regulate the quality and reputation of products and their producers, keep moonlighters from the market, or provide bodies for commercial arbitration, etc. (van Waarden 2002).

However, here too, the state has a task, as many private solutions to the risks and uncertainties of the market turned out to have problems of their own, and/or to become new sources of risk and uncertainty themselves. Detectives and other reputation rating agencies threaten the privacy of economic actors; the mafia and other gangs became themselves threats to life, liberty, and property, not infrequently of the very transactional partners that had engaged them in the first place; lawyers cannot do much without a legal framework; advertising agencies do not exactly have an image of neutrality and objectivity; insurers can go broke, and this threat limits the trust of consumers to insure risks with them; associations suffer from the threat of free riders and find it difficult to enforce self-regulation; competition between educational institutions for students can produce diploma-inflation; and a proliferation of competing private technical and administrative standards can become self-defeating as they may obfuscate markets rather than make them more transparent.

Such problems have led the state to support private risk- and uncertainty-reducing institutions: 'law and order'; a legal infrastructure; uniform statutory standards for weights and measures; product and labour quality (diplomas) norms; regulation and supervision of accountants and insurance companies; and recognition, privileged access, and statutory powers for associations. In the end the state added its own regulations.

All these state-produced 'public goods' aim to reduce risk and uncertainty and to increase public 'trust' in public space (streets and cities), private space (planes, trains, taxis, factories, offices, and houses), goods and services, and labour (especially in risky occupations such as doctors, butchers, and lawyers).

These activities provide legitimacy to the state, and justification for taxation. Any perceived failure and any perceived increase in risk and uncertainty threaten the legitimacy of the state, *in casu* of the ruling parties. Unemployment, inflation, rising crime, contagious diseases in humans (aids and SARS) or animals (bovine spongiform encephalopathy (BSE) and chicken pest), waiting lists for health care, and corruption have been often causes for small revolutions in politics.

Crises and scandals fuelling more and stricter regulation

The long-term historical trend has been one of ever more state regulation, notwithstanding repeated attempts at deregulation. This process has been fuelled by incidents. State aid to, oversight over, or replacement of private regulation increased often after scandals, crises, fraud, and other sudden threats to security.

The recent accountancy scandals are a case in point. Not long ago, several governments, among them the Dutch, took steps to 'deregulate' the accountancy profession. One of the measures contemplated was the abolition of the 'fences' between the professions of law, consultancy, and accountancy. These divisions had been built up because these professions were considered to be guided by conflicting motives: consultants advice business firms, lawyers defend their interests; but accountants control their activities in the interests of investors and the general public. However, under pressure from large 'commercial service'-providing firms, like Ernst and Young, Arthur Andersen, and others, who integrated these different activities, governments were about to tear down these fences . . . until, the bookkeeping scandals of Enron and Worldcom hit the headlines of the world-press. It turned out that the scandals were in large part traceable to accountants being at the same time consultants. Those who should have exposed illegal bookkeeping practices were the same ones who invented and advised these practices. In no time came proposals to remove the abolition of these fences from the political agenda. Instead many countries scrambled to solve the credibility and trust problem by raising rather than lowering standards for auditing, accountancy, and corporate governance.

History abounds with scandals and crises driving social and economic regulation. Modern labour law was boosted by the revolutionary threats at the end of the First World War; the economic crisis of the 1930s led to an extensive elaboration of agricultural, economic and social regulation in Europe, and to the New Deal in the US. More recently, the 1963 softenon (thalodamide) scandal set the stage for the worldwide regulation of the admission of pharmaceuticals to the market; a dozen senior citizens dying from eating peeled shrimp in the Netherlands led to an overhaul of consumer protection regulation; while the various animal epidemics (BSE, foot and mouth disease, and pig and chicken pests) since the 1990s have led to a tightening of veterinary inspections, animal fodder standards, and food regulation general.

Two further developments have enhanced this historical trend. First, a revolution of rising expectations by ever more assertive citizens in democratic societies – both as voters and litigants in court. They hold states responsible for providing solutions to ever more risks and uncertainties: Workers want compensation for headaches because of the weather; horticulturalists for broken greenhouse glass because of the same weather. Second, advances in science and diffusion of information have made citizens aware of risks they were formerly unaware of (e.g. the consequences of asbestos or suspected carcinogens).

Globalisation: external sources of risk and uncertainty

Curiously enough, modern states threaten to get squeezed between rising expectations of citizens for risk and uncertainty reduction against decreasing capacity to do so. With globalisation, more and more sources of risk and uncertainty are beyond the direct control of the nation-state. Many emanate from outside its territory.

Globalisation means first of all an increase in international division of labour and international trade, thus an increase in global interdependencies. This is most visible in the products we consume. They come from everywhere: apples from Australia, beef from Argentina, cortisone from China, cars from Ireland, and cod from Iceland. It has been estimated that an average product has travelled 5000 miles before it reaches its final consumer. More and more goods are composite ones. A simple cellphone incorporates hundreds of patents held by companies across the globe. Globalisation is not only visible in assembly, but also in process industries. Manure from Chile may have been transformed into US corn; that into Belgian cows and milk and that into Dutch cheese. A leftover, whey powder, is turned into French calves and bonemeal, that into British beef, ad infinitum. It is difficult to follow ingredients in these ever longer food chains.

Not only goods are increasingly mobile due to the modern technologies of transportation, telecommunication, and conservation, so are waste products, services, people, capital, ideas, and information. This mobility can entail a great diversity of risks and uncertainties for nation-states.

Contaminated food or unsafe chemicals or pharmaceuticals may spread quickly, and may be difficult to trace. Live produce may spread pests and infectious diseases fast, in particular to the dense population concentrations typical of the bioindustry. This entails even risks of moving to – also frequently dense – areas of human population. The recent international animal and human epidemics of BSE, pig and chicken pests, AIDS, and SARS are cases in point.

Similarly, people on the move can also spread diseases. (Illegal) migrants also bring risks of unemployment, crime, and social unrest, or at least as many citizens believe. Others spread risks of terrorism. The mobility of capital can undermine economies, lead to speculations against currencies, create great volatility in financial markets, and bring major companies to bankruptcy and mass lay-offs, with the attendant risks of loss of trust among investors, consumers, and employees alike.

Technological developments are another external source of risk and uncertainty, difficult for nation-states to control. Every day new chemical substances, with yet unknown properties and risks, are being developed. 'Weapons of mass destruction' become easier to produce and to deliver. The list is endless. Science has also provided greater knowledge about various threats and risks, which we were formerly unaware of.

All this enhances citizens' expectations towards the state: they expect politicians to act, and to use all available knowledge, resources, and powers to ward off imminent threats. This is reinforced by instant diffusion of information through the mass media about threats from far away (SARS in China, nuclear arms in Korea) and about the demands of citizens elsewhere. A veritable 'race of rising expectations' results.

Old and new responses to 'foreign' risks and uncertainties

The traditional response of states to threats from abroad has been to try to keep them out: by erecting, maintaining, and enforcing borders – the very essence of a *territorial* state; and by controlling the 'import' or intrusion of 'foreign' goods, people, soldiers, criminals, diseases, ideas, and information considered 'harmful' to their citizens (and the political power holders). This strategy of building 'fortresses' becomes increasingly difficult in a globalising world. Citizens demand goods available elsewhere, illegal immigration is rampant, states punish each other for protectionism, terrorists are invisible, and polities that tried to keep seditious ideas out (the DDR, China) have failed dramatically.

This creates incentives for states to try to extend control beyond their own territory, by exporting their standards, imposing them on others, entering in international negotiations on harmonisation of regulatory standards to increasingly higher levels, or other forms of regulatory cooperation. As in the past, this 'race-to-the-top' is found at any point in time foremost on issues where citizens feel their security acutely threatened by crises or scandals, such as, currently, the insecurities of investment (accountancy scandals), of food and health (animal and human epidemics), and of life (terrorism). But as crises and scandals follow each other in quick succession and emerge in quite different policy areas, regulatory 'races-to-the-top' are spreading.

Shifts in Governance I: centralisation of regulations

These demands on the state to reduce new risks and uncertainties produce 'shifts in governance' (van Kersbergen and van Waarden 2001, 2004) and shifts in power to those levels and actors of whom it is believed that they can most effectively deal with the problems. Often, this implies *centralisation*. It did so earlier in the process of state formation. Now it is behind the pressures for formation of and regulation by supranational institutions.

What to centralise? Obviously, the regulation of the production, handling and quality of mobile goods, services, and people, that cross borders, and particularly those that may affect the security and health of citizens: foodstuffs, drugs, their ingredients such as plants and animals, animal fodder, veterinary medicine, fertiliser, etc. Here great controversies between nations have arisen: over genetically modified organisms, or hormones in beef (Princen 2002). The list is however longer: qualifications of doctors, veterinarians, or butchers; hygiene and safety of hospital equipment; immigration and travel of potential terrorists (i.e. in principle everybody); airplane security; privacy issues and exchange of information; and the safety of investments elsewhere and information about those (accountancy standards).

It may seem less likely that also standards for less mobile products, services, activities, or people will experience pressures for central harmonisation. Building codes, housing standards, and traffic safety rules differ between countries. Yet, past explosions of factories processing dangerous materials (Flixborough in Britain and Seveso in Italy) have led to supranational regulation of factory security, e.g. the European Seveso directives (Versluis 2003).

How do countries try to influence regulatory standards elsewhere? Economically or politically powerful nations can and do impose their standards on other nations, through trade relations (the 'California effect', Vogel 1995), or by political, diplomatic, or military pressures (the 'war on terrorism'). Recent new cases of the California effect have appeared: the US SEC exporting its accountancy standards as condition for listing on American stock exchanges and airplane security standards as condition for landing rights in the US.

More frequently used are less asymmetric forms: international regulatory cooperation and negotiation, and harmonisation in arenas of longer established supranational organisations, such as the European Union (EU), the WTO, the ITU, or the WHO.

The importance of enforcement and compliance

Mere export, harmonisation, or convergence of regulations on paper does not suffice. What counts is whether and how these 'rules-in-the-books' are translated to 'rules-in-action'. Enforcement and compliance are the Achilles heel of any regulation.

Standards one country wants to 'impose' on others, or internationally agreed regulations, have to be applied and enforced on street level, shop floors, harbours, airfields in other countries, if not 'the world', by local food and labour inspectors, airport security marshals, or auditors and accountants elsewhere. Product and people standards can still be checked for when they enter a country, but this is not possible for process standards or product standards that can no longer be identified in the product, e.g. whether a tomato is genetically modified. In such cases, countries have to *trust* the certificates and licenses that street-level bureaucrats in other countries have issued: the Thai inspector who controls the hygiene of shrimp peeling and the Guatamaltecan one who certifies that the bananas are not genetically modified.

Mutual trust between countries in their enforcement practices and value of certificates is complicated because the discretionary authority of street-level bureaucrats and their enforcement styles differ significantly between countries (Vogel 1986). American enforcement officers have limited discretion and apply regulations in an indiscriminating way, making the full force of the law fall equally on all subjects of the regulations, without much concern for individual circumstances. This practice is often experienced by citizens and firms as 'regulatory unreasonableness', but serves the maintenance of universalistic values: all citizens/firms are equal before the law (Bardach and Kagan 1982; Kagan 2001). British, Dutch, or Italian rule enforcers have more discretionary authority and can take account of individual circumstances. They can give (temporary) exemptions, bargain with the subjects of regulation, and be flexible in sanctioning. The price of flexibility is uncertainty and possible inequality (Bakker and van Waarden 1999; van Waarden 1999a, 1999b).

Given these differences in regulatory styles, countries and agencies that maintain stricter enforcement procedures will hesitate to trust others that are known for having less strict ones. Instead, they will try to control foreign controllers. By sending their own controllers and inspectors for double-checks; or by having international organisations with a strong reputation send out inspectors Yet external controllers of local controllers have the disadvantage that they are less familiar with local circumstances, customs, people, reputations, and networks. Sooner or later, they will have to collaborate with local informants.

Shifts in Governance II: back from public to private – from national public to international private regulation and enforcement

Many national governments have long and good experience with private interest associations, NGOs, standardisation bodies, patent offices, foundations, and even business in regulation and its implementation. Now that they hit upon the limits of their legal jurisdictions with more threats to domestic risk and uncertainties coming from abroad, there is an inclination to again engage private organisations in regulation and enforcement, or, where international private self-regulation spontaneously emerges, to tolerate, recognise, or even support and sanction it Private organisations rely less on a legal system to regulate their environment, and are hence less bound by territorial jurisdictions than nation-states. They can easily and more legitimately extend their activities abroad. And they have already been involved in informal or formal networks with organisations in other countries, sometimes under the umbrella of international corporations. Thus, they have become interesting partners for nation-states that want to extend their regulatory influence beyond their borders.

This often starts from already existing public–private partnerships at the national level. The international contacts and activities of private partners can gradually get integrated and instrumentalised in domestic regulations. They can assist in developing, setting, and extending standards and may aid in enforcing them through their international relations or foreign supply chains. Some examples may elucidate this.

One case is the developing international chain of standards and controls for animal feed. Animal feed is a major input at the beginning of the food supply chain, and problems with its quality (dioxin and ground up bones) have caused recent scandals and crises (BSE and chicken pest). 'Safe feed = safe food' is the industry's slogan. Thus, national governments have quite a stake in this product, but much animal feed comes from far away, is being shipped back and forth, and gets mixed in all kinds of combinations of fodder.

In the Netherlands, animal feed is regulated and inspected by the Ministry of Agriculture and a statutory trade association PDV (a trade association with a public law status and statutory powers: compulsory membership for the relevant industry, powers to tax and regulate the industry) – all under the umbrella of European agricultural and food regulation. The PDV recognises certification, inspection, and monitoring bodies that in turn certify production and trade and transport firms throughout the production chain from raw materials to transport and livestock breeding. Their monitoring bodies employ private control and auditing organisations to carry out quality inspections throughout the chain. To this end, it employs GMP (good manufacturing practices) and HACCP (hazard analysis and critical control points) standards and an early warning and response system, which is linked to the EU rapid alert system for food and feed. These standards have been developed in international public–private cooperation, in which the Codex Alimentarius, the European Commission, and the European Feed Manufacturers Federation and its daughter associations in the other European member states cooperate. The European Feed Manufacturers Federation has also affiliated members from non-EU states and has an observer status at the Codex Alimentarius. That is, the sector is enmeshed in an international network of safety standards and both public and private certification and control organisations (Brkulic 2001; den Hartog 2003; Freeriks 2004; van Waarden 2006).

Animal feed safety standards concern product quality, which can be inspected at the border, though the products often enter countries as mixtures whose origin is difficult to trace. Hence, international cooperation in controlling the whole production chain is advisable to avert surprises. More difficult is *process* quality control. How can animal-friendly consumers be sure that imported eggs really come from free range chickens? How can enlightened coffee drinkers be sure that the growers of their coffee really get a fair share of the price? To ensure this requires controls all along the production and trade chain, including faraway countries. Therefore, national associations (like the Dutch Max Havelaar) have formed the Fair Trade Labeling Organisations International (FLO), which sets standards for fair social and economic development, concerning both production and process methods, management systems, and supply chain relationships. It engages in certification and employs a network of national organisations and independent auditors and inspectors that monitor compliance by producers, traders, and retailers. The FLO is in turn a member of the International Social and Environmental Accreditation and Labelling (ISEAL) alliance, to which also organisations such as the Forest Stewardship Council, the Rainforest Alliance, and Social Accountability International belong. The ISEAL has a Code of Good Practice for Setting Social and Environmental Standards, which is both a benchmark for, and a control on, the control by organisations such as the FLO. It in turn draws on semi-public standards such as the ISO/IEC Guide 59 Code of Good Practice for Standardisation, the WTO Sanitary and Phytosanitary Measures (SPS), and the WTO Technical Barriers to Trade (TBT) Agreements Annex 3 Code of Good Practice for the preparation, adoption, and application of standards. ISEAL does not only set standards for standards, but it also aids members in capacity building to meet standards. Though these are mostly private initiatives, they get support from national governments and international organisations such as the FAO.

A third channel of private international organisations that aid in public control are multinational corporations, such as large supermarket chains. They have to abide by food quality standards in the consuming countries and nurture their reputations among consumers, leading them to adopt even standards that are not statutory. The supermarket chain Sainsbury, for instance, decided voluntarily to ban GMO products from its shelves. In this way, they impose national standards onto foreign suppliers, and they often do have the organisational capacity for careful monitoring and control along the supply chain (Havinga 2003).

In regulating sustainable fishing practices, again many international private organisations work together: functionally specialised organisations like the Marine Stewardship Council, public interest associations (the World Wildlife Fund), multinationals such as Unilever and supermarket chains; all recognised, encouraged, and supported by nation-states and the EU, advised by the International Council for the Exploration of the Sea.

Thus, whereas first the long-term historical trend was one of public authorities coming to aid private regulation in civil society; in the era of globalisation, private actors come to the aid of public authorities. Such private and semi-private international organisations help solve governability problems for national governments; but their involvement and responsibilities add to or create new problems of legitimacy and democratic accountability.

In these complex networks of national and international organisations, the identities and boundaries of public and private organisations are no longer so clear. The distinctions get blurred. Public dissolves and blends into private and vice versa. Is a foundation created and governed by a state agency public or private? And what about an (international) association of national public agencies? Is an international public interest association like the FLO really only private even though it performs public tasks? What about the Codex Alimentarius or the ISEAL? The traditional legal distinctions are less useful if organisations cannot link their identity to jurisdiction over a certain territory. Characteristic of a public organisation is that it can be held politically accountable by a 'demos'.

Shifts in Governance III: increasing influence of expert epistemic policy communities

The pressures for international regulatory cooperation produce shifts in governance and hence in the distribution of political power. We know from organisation studies that those parts of an organisation that are best able to ward off threats from the environment gain in importance and power within the organisation.

This also holds for the risks and uncertainties that give rise to pressures for international regulatory cooperation. At issue are often highly technical matters. Scientific and technical knowledge is required to estimate the risks involved in feeding animals bonemeal, or the effectiveness of an emergency management plan. This gives experts and specialists power in political decision making. Think of the potential influence of the expert weapon inspectors in Iraq. However, one should not only think of natural scientists, engineers, veterinarians, medical personnel, or ICT experts, but also of economists, financial experts, immigration, competition and food law lawyers, accountants, military specialists, secret servicemen, airplane security specialists, etc.

Such experts meet with experts of other nations. They do so first in the processes of negotiation, attempted imposition, cooperation, and development of common standards. However, given the importance of implementation and enforcement, experts of one country will contact street-level controllers in other countries, often also experts in their field. US secret servicemen seek the collaboration of local agents in Kurdistan and Baghdad; WHO-authorities in Europe contact doctors in Hong Kong who deal with SARS. Thus, the expert networks that develop are not only 'horizontal' but also 'diagonal' between standard setters in one country and implementers in others.

These experts tend to form technically specialised policy or epistemic communities. They include not only experts employed by the state or by international organisations such as the WHO, the World Bank, the WTO, ITU, European regulatory agencies, or the ISO; but also privately employed experts: consultants, rating agencies, and multinationals involved in the production and distribution of risk-sensitive products (food and drug or aircraft manufacturers) which have often larger scientific and information resources than public agencies.

Thus, extensive networks of regulators and enforcers develop, which can be highly specific for certain risks, products, or policy areas. The Seveso II directive, which we studied in detail in Utrecht (Versluis 2003) produced such a specialised network: those charged with enforcement meet regularly, either individually or at joint meetings and conferences, where they exchange experiences and information.

A third phase in the development of democracy

These international epistemic and regulatory communities represent a challenge to a possible third wave of democratisation, but a different one than Majone (2002) distinguishes, following Dahl (1989). According to him, the first wave was the introduction of *direct democracy* in the Athenian city state, in which the demos, the people (at least a part of it), directly participated in the formulation, but also implementation of public decisions, the 'policy'. The second wave was the introduction of *indirect or representative democracy*, the indirect participation of the demos in policy making, through democratically elected representatives. This made it possible to extend the democratic idea to larger social groups, usually territorially defined. Majone sees the formation of supranational organisations like the EU as a third stage of democratisation. I wonder if it is not much more the introduction of these international expert policy making, standard-setting and monitoring communities. While the second stage entailed citizens electing representatives who formulate and administer policies, the third one is a form of *second-level indirect representative democracy*: citizens elect representatives who control and supervise 'technicians' who formulate and administer policies, even beyond their borders.

The constitutionalisation of international expert communities

This third phase of democracy has also surfaced at the level of the nation-state with the growth in size of the public administration and the increasingly technical nature of policy formulation and implementation. At this level, political oversight of technical agencies operationalising, administering, and enforcing regulations is already difficult. How much greater will the problems then not be in even longer principal–agent chains of implementation of international or supranational regulations?

If international expert communities exercise de facto more and more power, then the question becomes urgent to whom these communities are accountable, what the checks and balances on their power are. History teaches that whenever and wherever such checks are absent, sooner or later those in positions of power will abuse their prerogatives and privileges. Without such checks and balances, public trust in such officials will wane. What is needed is *constitutionalisation of international networks of technocrats*. We need checks on the powers of secret servicemen, food inspectors, immigration officers, diploma certifiers, risk assessors, accountants; in short, expert bureaucrats, acting in international networks, including NGOs, where the control of national politicians is severely limited. I can do no more than offer some suggestions for such checks and balances.

- Can the old and well-tried idea of the Trias Politica be a source of inspiration?
  - Judicial review of decisions of international and supranational institutions, placed at the nuclei of expert networks, e.g. by an international court for administrative law, following the example of the recently created international criminal court? That is, possibilities of appeal against decisions of the WTO or the World Bank, or of foreign/international controllers of local controllers?
  - A balance of power between networks and their institutions representing different disciplines, or policy areas, i.e. a functional division of powers, following the already existing functional balance (or more frequently de facto imbalance) of powers between different ministries at the level of the nation-state
- To what extent can the market model be a source of inspiration?
  - *Peer review and competitive markets of enforcement ideas*. Of course experts provide first and foremost 'checks and balances' on each other. There is peer review, more or less public exchange of arguments, and within many disciplines there are rival theoretical and paradigmatic schools. They may vie for domination, but as long as no one succeeds in acquiring a dominating position there is some form of mutual control. This seems to work well in science, but should not the formulation and implementation of risk and uncertainty regulation be more publicly accountable?
  - *A competition authority* for expert networks. Does not the danger of monopolisation of certain schools of law, economics, food safety, etc. require some regulation itself? Do we perhaps need 'competition authorities' for these epistemic communities? Should there be some form of 'affirmative action' for disadvantaged schools and approaches? Or guarantees for 'market entry' for new approaches?

- Associational self-regulation
  - At the national level, professions regulate themselves in associations with statutory powers. Can we envision something like that at the international level? For example, an *international disciplinary tribunal* for accountants, or food inspectors, or NGOs?
- Publicity, the reputation mechanism, the press
  - At the national level, major checks on abuse of political power come from a critical press, from publicity affecting reputations, and from actors caring for their reputations. Could this also be used for networks of powerful experts? This would of course require press interest, and that in turn requires interest of its readership. Such interest is likely to come from crises and scandals. A BSE or SARS crisis should be good enough to point the attention of the press to the wheeling and dealings of the relevant expert community. It does already occasionally. But what is missing is knowledge and insights of the press in the existence of, power of, and functioning of such international expert networks. Would a *specialised journalist school* and a specialised international association of journalists be a solution?

Constitutional democracy for which 'demos'?

Majone (2002) bases the legitimation for regulatory intervention – that is, the ideal regulatory jurisdiction – on a *territorially* circumscribed *demos*, which derives its identity from a certain homogeneity. He writes: '...the primacy of the territorial state has the same origin as the idea of democracy. Cleisthenes, ... the founder of Athenian democracy ... brought the territorial principle to triumph over the kinship principle of social organisation ... Democratic theory presupposes a territorially based 'demos', and 'the democratic process presupposes the existence of a fairly homogeneous polity'.

But what if regulation by supposedly homogeneous nation-states is no longer effective and regulation at higher levels of aggregation is required? And what if the logical connection between legitimacy–democracy–demos–territory–homogeneity is not so convincing any more in an age of globalisation? Why and whence did territory become a defining unit for a 'demos'? Homogeneity is the answer of Majone. But homogeneity of what? Interests? Cultural norms and values? Are nation-states really so homogeneous as is often (including by Majone) argued? Are they really such 'tight' communities? The *criteria* by which homogeneity should be measured are not so clear.

If we take language, religion, or culture as a criterion, many nation-states are or were not so homogeneous as Majone implies. Many supposedly 'homogeneous' European nation-states were split along religious, language, or class lines, which found expression in political ideologies, movements, civil society organisations, and political philosophies (socialism, communism, Christian democracy, and liberalism). Furthermore, many West-European countries are becoming even more 'multi-cultural'. They harbour immigrant minorities which are quickly growing in size, coming in part from former colonies, in part from neighbouring – Mediterranean or East European – countries.

A functional as opposed to a territorially defined demos?

If a territorially defined 'demos' is not so homogeneous, what kind of legitimacy does it provide for regulatory jurisdictions? Merely because that is the turn history took? Are there no alternatives? What about a *functional* as opposed to a *territorial* definition of a 'demos'?

I have argued in this article that most regulations by *public actors*, like states, have a functional foundation: they are public goods that reduce risk and uncertainty for the citizens that have created these public actors. From this functional criterion, one could also derive a functional criterion for delineating the demos: those affected by certain threats; or, in other words, sharing a *common fate*.

That is also what usually happened in history. The demos of existing nation-states were originally no demos at all. Any unity that may exist now is the result of a shared fate, usually a common enemy, which gave rise to state formation. The Swiss state began forming with the mythical oath of the Grütli in 1291 among the three 'forest' cantons around Lake Lucerne that saw their freedom threatened by the Habsburg Rudolf I, the then Holy Roman Emperor. Three centuries later, seven protestant Dutch provinces united in the Treaty of Utrecht (1579) and revolted against the Catholic authoritarian Spanish Habsburgs. Again, about two centuries later, thirteen, then quite heterogeneous, American colonies of Britain signed a Declaration of Independence (1776) against the Georgian monarchy. A short war with France eventually completed German unification in 1871, and Italian Risorgimento was completed amongst others in wars with the Papal States and France. Paraphrasing Tilly (1975), 'war made the states, and the states made war'. These states then forced the peoples within their borders – with different degrees of success – to become one people, a demos for the later democratic governments. There is nothing 'natural', mythological, or metaphysical about European peoples. What created territorially defined peoples was ambition by certain monarchs, war, bad, or good luck on the battlefields, and, because of all that, shared fates.

With the new transport and communication technologies and the resultant mobility of 'citizens', territory may become less of a criterion for 'shared fates', identity, and interests. Territory may be replaced by function. We may live more and more in different 'states' at the same time for different functions.

The Dutch have done so already for some time. They have a long history of functionally defined and differentiated 'state' institutions that reduced different risk and uncertainties for groups with a shared fate. As elsewhere, the oldest shared threats were territorial: from enemies outside the local (feudal autarchic) community (roaming bands, vagrants, highwaymen, and 'foreign' armies), and from criminals within the community. These threats gave rise to standard state organisations. However, the inhabitants of the marshes and peat bogs at the mouths of the Rhine, Meuse, and Scheldt had to withstand another threat – the water. Sea and rivers were sources of frequent flooding. To counter this threat, the peat boggers formed, from the eleventh century on, functionally specific 'state' institutions, the *waterschappen* (hydraulic boards). They organised the construction and maintenance of an ideal typical public good: dykes, waterways, sluices, and later mills, which kept the feet of local inhabitants dry, and later on even draining parts of the delta.

Originally, it was a form of Dahl's direct democracy: all the inhabitants of the territory owning real estate decided on common policies and carried them out. Individuals were responsible for the maintenance of specific pieces of a dyke, dams, or sluice. They collectively organised a system of control and enforcement, and sloppy members – who risked the lives of others – were severely punished. Later, this system developed into one of indirect democracy that still exists.

Other forms of functional governance and democracy developed in the middle ages: the guilds that regulated economic life. Originally, this was still tied to territory: the guild had jurisdiction in a clearly demarcated territory, the walled city. In the twentieth century guilds got successors without such ties to territory: statutory trade associations that organised economic actors from across the country, whose shared fate was that they were involved in a similar economic activity, diffused in space. The statutory trade associations still in existence have – similar to the corporatist Chambers in Germany, Switzerland, and Austria – state-like powers: membership is compulsory, the government is democratically elected, and they have powers to tax and to regulate.

Globalisation will and does reinforce this trend. Our shared fates are less and less territorial, and more and more functional: worldwide risks and uncertainties of terrorism, food poisoning, contagious diseases, and global warming. Consequently, we live increasingly under regulatory regimes of functionally specialised international agencies, who perform state-like tasks: they help reduce such risks and uncertainties. At the European level, functionally specific institutions or forms of inter-state cooperation (involving different EU member states) have arisen: the European Commission, the European Monetary Union, and the Schengen Treaty. At the global level, institutions like the WTO, WHO, World Criminal Court, World Bank, IMF, UNDO, ISO, ITU, etc. have been formed, all for functionally specific tasks. And also private governance institutions such as in food safety or fair trade are functionally specialised. Any democratic control of such organisations goes so far via the nation-states. But what about direct democratic representation by functionally defined demos, i.e. those in whose interests such organisations try to reduce risks and uncertainties? It may not be easy to perceive exactly along which lines and with what institutions (electoral systems, eligibility for passive and active voting rights, etc). Such functionally defined demos should form to provide checks and balances on the power of functionally defined expert communities. But it is an idea worthy of further development.

7 The potential and limits of governance by private codes of conduct

Thomas Conzelmann and Klaus Dieter Wolf

Introduction[1]

The effective and legitimate governance of global affairs faces considerable challenges. The traditional mode of interstate accords developed in order to deal with collective problems at the global level seems increasingly incapable of producing reliable and sustainable solutions to global problems. Two of the main hurdles are the limited territorial and functional reach of national regulation and the burdensome process of producing global agreements under the conditions of unanimity and interstate consensus (Zürn 1998). Against this background, the increasing emergence of voluntary private self-regulation has been seen as a possible way of filling at least some of those regulatory gaps. The common aspiration of these initiatives is to express commitments of the participating companies towards ecological, social, and other standards and thus 'to influence or control behaviour for the benefit of the organization itself and for the communities in which it operates' (Gordon and Miyake 2000: 3).

Due to the fact that accession and compliance with the codes is voluntary, they have been criticized as being of mainly symbolic nature. Opponents point out that voluntary measures allow business to 'greenwash' themselves, but are of little significance in improving the environmental and social performance of firms. Furthermore, some NGO actors and other critics argue that codes take off the pressure from governments to put in place an effective and powerful regulation and thus to improve business conduct (cf. Kerkow *et al.* 2003). Proponents of the codes take issue with these statements for two reasons: First, they doubt the viability of state- or interstate-sponsored regulation of business activity, symbolized by the dissolution of the United Nations Centre for Transnational Corporations in 1992. Second, they point out potential beneficial effects of voluntary private codes. Due to the non-binding nature of the codes, the hurdles for accession to the code may be lower for individual firms. Once a business has become party to the code, however, there is the potential that both an internal process of adapting to the code and an external process of the individual firm being subject to peer pressure or NGO scrutiny are set into motion. While it is conceivable that businesses are pressured to comply with even the more demanding parts of the regulations through such processes, another possible effect is the beginning of learning and reorientation processes within the individual firm that may increasingly question its behaviour, this in turn inducing the firm into wishing to become a member of the community of 'well-managed' and 'ecologically sound' firms. Seen from this perspective, voluntary private codes may take on an important role in either supplementing or preceding public regulation or even making public regulation unnecessary (Gunningham 1995; Gordon 2000; Webb 2004).

Against this background, the present chapter aims at discussing the governance potential of codes of conduct for business. In order to maintain that private codes of conduct may provide meaningful contributions to transnational governance, the following second section will suggest a number of normative criteria of *input* legitimacy against which the governance potential of private codes of conduct can be measured. How far and through which mechanisms private codes of conduct can fulfil these criteria will be illustrated with reference to the United Nations Global Compact, the Forest Stewardship Council (FSC), and the chemical industry's Responsible Care (RC) initiative. On the basis of this normative assessment, the third section will introduce and discuss competing theoretical accounts for the explanation of accession to and compliance with private codes of conduct in order to find out how far this mode of transnational governance can be generalized and to what extent expectations as to its output legitimacy, i.e. effectiveness, are justified. In the final fourth section, we will discuss potential avenues for combining public and private regulation. The basic argument will be that the more effectiveness we can attribute to business self-regulation, the more interesting these governance arrangements become as alternatives or supplements to public regulation under the conditions of denationalization.

Why bother? The normative potential of voluntary self-regulation

Criteria for the input legitimacy of private self-regulation

Normative objections to the involvement of private actors in governance processes usually stem from the argument that these actors have certain characteristics that disqualify them. Firms usually are organized in a hierarchical and non-democratic fashion, and unlike governments, they are not obliged to act with the public interest in mind. Furthermore, they cannot be held responsible by the institutional checks and balances of a democratic political system. Therefore, while it may make sense to include private actors in order to profit from the technical expertise they can bring into regulation or in order to overcome their potential political opposition in the preparation and perhaps also the implementation stages of the governance process, they should be kept out of decision making itself.

In principle, these objections seem to be applicable both to national and to transnational forms of governance. As soon as we enter the sphere of governance beyond state boundaries, however, nation-states and non-state actors become more and more alike with respect to these objections. First, not only non-state actors fail to fulfil the criterion of being a democratic institutional structure, but so do most of the nation-states involved in global governance. The democratic control by parliaments and the critical public is blocked where intergovernmental negotiations are shielded from public attention and where the knowledge and resources to critically follow the conduct of governments at the international level is missing. Second, individual nation-states do not any longer represent actors that are oriented towards the 'public' interest at the global level. Whereas states may be public in form at the international level, they become 'private' in purpose insofar as they pursue national (or even their own institutional) interests rather than the common good.

While this argument de-emphasizes the differences between the normative quality of public and private actors at the international level, it does not answer the question as to how the inclusion of private actors into global governance can be positively legitimized. First, if we subscribe to the view (see Wolf 1999) that international agreements themselves suffer from a severe 'democratic deficit' in the sense of a lack of input legitimacy, then acquiring authority through intergovernmental agreements would only pass on the democratic deficit of the latter to the governance competencies granted to private actors. Second, there is no supranational authority that could delegate some of its power to private actors and oversee the functioning of private self-regulation. Global governance does of course involve governments, but it is and always has been *governance without government* (Rosenau and Czempiel 1992). Therefore, it is hard to conceive of an effective public oversight of private self-regulation at the global level.

In order to overcome this dead end, we suggest to leave behind the notion that self-governance is 'a favour handed down by public authorities', and to conceive it as 'an inherent societal quality that greatly contributes to the governability of modern societies' (Kooiman 2002: 83). This change of perspective also brings to the fore sources of input legitimacy that are not tied to formal delegation of competencies by the state or by interstate agreements. In order to identify them, one may distinguish between input legitimization through *formal* (inter-) governmental *authorization* (a criterion which highlights the quality of delegation procedures) and substantial *authority*, which stresses the qualities of the participants themselves (see Cutler *et al.* 1999b: 18). In other words, an actor may (or may not) have substantial *authority* independent of formal authorization. His or her claim to being involved in governance may be based, for instance, on a credible commitment to basic norms or to the general welfare, or on the recognition of his expertise and problem-solving resources. The quality of input legitimacy to be derived from this kind of authority depends on whether private actors commit to follow generally accepted norms, and whether these commitments are consistent with their conduct.

Nevertheless, this actor-based conceptualization of the input legitimacy of private actors needs to be complemented by some institutional safeguards, which, however, should be compatible with the specific milieu in which governance beyond the state takes place. Such criteria are, first, *responsiveness*: How can it be assured that private self-regulation is regardful of people's demands and that action deemed necessary by the public is taken? The voluntary nature of private self-regulation implies that it cannot be obliged to deal with a certain issue. Private actors may decide to self-regulate, but they may also opt for non-regulation. Second, the criterion of *self-determination* means that there is congruence between those who can take part in the decision making and those who are affected by it. 'Self-regulation' by its very nature seems to be capable of fulfilling this requirement, but a closer look is necessary. Third, some measure of *control of power* needs to be in place. This is important since – much as in public regulation – an authoritative allocation of values (Easton) may occur through mechanisms of private self-regulation. As regards possible sanctioning mechanisms, it seems plausible that private actors could be called to account for their governance activities in a number of ways. Formal entitlement may be withdrawn, legal action may be taken against them, the credibility of their moral and professional authority may be lost, and subsequently their public acceptance, financial support, or reputation and success on the market may suffer.

Criteria applied: the United Nations Global Compact, the FSC, and the RC

We will illustrate our argument that the actor-based and institutional criteria discussed above are relevant and can principally be met by applying them to three prominent cases of voluntary self-regulation, namely the United Nations Global Compact, the FSC as a multi-stakeholder initiative, and RC as a predominantly private form of self-regulation. These differences in the actor constellation of the initiatives are expected to be relevant as regards the legitimacy criteria developed above. The Global Compact (GC) came into being at the initiative of the United Nations and is not engaged in standard setting but seeks to improve the implementation of already existing and worldwide accepted normative standards. In contrast, RC and the FSC operate without any nation-state involvement and fill standard setting and implementation gaps left open by governance through nation-states. The FSC, however, makes a clearer reference to internationally developed norms and standards. For constraints of space, we can only give a very cursory account of the normative and factual authority of the participating actors and the extent to which the respective institutional designs correspond with normative demands of self-determination, control of power, and responsiveness.[2]

The Global Compact was established after an address of United Nations' Secretary General Kofi Annan to the World Economic Forum in Davos on 31 January 1999. In this address, M. Annan invited leaders of the private sector to join a voluntary corporate citizenship initiative by supporting nine (now ten) universal principles in the fields of human rights, labour standards, environment, and anti-corruption. The initiative has grown rapidly since then, with now over

3,000 participants, of which around 2,800 are businesses. After expressing its support to the ten principles, a company is expected to make them part of its business strategies, to publicly advocate the principles, and to describe in its 'Communication on Progress' in what way it implements them. In addition, companies are invited to take part in the 'Global Compact Learning Forum' where participants share their experiences of good practices on the basis of short descriptions of practical actions they have taken with regard to the GC's principles ('examples' and 'case studies'). Non-business participants can get involved as equal partners. For instance, annual 'policy dialogues' are open to all GC stakeholders and serve the function of identifying innovative and practical solutions. In addition, there are a great number of national GC networks. Their key task at the national level is to provide an internal forum for national GC participants for the exchange of experiences and to promote the GC within their countries. Networks are also expected to assist companies in the implementation of the principles and to report to the GC Office at New York about country-specific activities of the GC and implementation models that could be replicated globally.[3]

In sum, the institutional design of the GC aims at committing the private sector – in partnership with other social actors – to deliberative processes through which experiences and good practices can be shared. This inclusive, consensual, and partnership-oriented approach to governance complies with the criterion of *self-determination* because at least in principle, it offers all groups of stakeholders the opportunity to take part in the dialogue. The *control of power* is not achieved by sanctions, but mainly relies on the transparency of the exchange of good practices (and the observable refusal to take part in it). These relatively weak mechanisms may be rectified because as a non-regulatory instrument, the GC is unlikely to produce negative externalities. The companies participating in the GC do not produce standards themselves, but simply refer to and implement those international norms that are institutionalized in the UN context. There is a medium degree of *responsiveness* in the GC: On the one hand, the GC seeks to react to the less-than-satisfactory implementation of international human rights and social norms by states through voluntary action by companies. On the other hand, the normative guidelines manifested in the ten principles of the GC are extremely vague and leave companies wide room for interpretation. GC member companies are completely free in deciding *how* they want to address environmental standards, anti-corruption, and social and human rights norms. As explained above, the GC does not assess the overall performance of companies nor does it seek to prescribe a certain standard of behaviour. Companies do not have to fear any sanctions if they choose to promote the goals of the GC selectively in one area of their activities, but violate them in other areas about which they do not have to report.

The Forest Stewardship Council represents an independent worldwide non-profit initiative bringing together a broad set of different stakeholders, including environmental NGOs, the timber industry, traders, indigenous peoples' organizations, and forest product certification organizations. The FSC's mission statement identifies sustainable commercial forestry as the prime objective of the initiative. The main regulatory instrument in attaining this goal is a voluntary code of conduct based on ten 'principles' and 56 more concrete 'criteria' for the forestry sector. In substance, these have been derived from Agenda 21 and other internationally recognized standards such as CITES, ILO core labour conventions, and the International Tropical Timber Agreement.[4] The criteria may be adapted and interpreted at the national and regional level in order to give more precision to them, but also to satisfy local needs and in order to engage more stakeholders with the FSC principles. The dissemination of FSC standards works via a certification system for sustainably managed forests. Since 1996, the FSC has issued about 4,500 'forest management certificates' for the forestry sector as well as 'chain-of-custody-certificates' for the timber industry. In January 2006 there was 68.13 million hectares of woodland certified according to FSC standards, encompassing 775 certified sites in 66 countries. However, around 82 per cent of these certified forests are in Europe and North America and more than 87 per cent are boreal or temperate forests. Tropical forests in which ecological and social problems are possibly the most severe thus play only a relatively minor role in the FSC.[5]

The governance structure of the FSC is unique and highly institutionalized. The General Assembly, the FSC's highest decision-making body, consists of three membership chambers – economic, environmental, and social – the representatives of which have equal voting rights. The purpose of this tripartite construction is to safeguard an equal balance of power between the relevant ecological, social, and economic stakeholders. In order to balance interests not only along potential sectoral, but also along geographical divides, representatives of the North and the South have the same voting rights in each chamber. The transnational FSC bodies are underpinned by a number of national initiatives that report back to FSC International. Their task is to adapt and implement the global standards at national level, to develop national certification standards, and to promote the FSC in their countries. Voting rights in the formulation of the national standards to be approved by FSC International follow the same principle of equal stakeholder participation. In practice, this decision-making structure is an institutional invitation to consensual decision making.

In terms of the actor-based criteria for input legitimacy, the FSC combines normative and factual *authority*: Notwithstanding their different motives, all participating parties declare their support to generally accepted international principles and norms. As a multi-stakeholder initiative, the FSC also consists of members who can all contribute specific problem-solving resources. The institutional design complies with the demands of *self-determination* in that the equal participation of all groups of stakeholders provides the necessary congruence between those who take the decisions and those who are affected by them. This is enhanced by the provisions governing the certification process and the adaptation of standards that include the mandatory consultation of local stakeholders. *Control of power* is taken care of through horizontal checks and balances within the three-chamber structure of the FSC decision-making system. These are complemented by additional vertical links between transnational, national, and local decision making, coordination, and implementation (see Kern 2004). The allocation of certification and monitoring tasks to independent third-party auditors enhances the balance of power. As far as the criterion of *responsiveness* is concerned, the definition of national standards and the inclusion of all relevant stakeholders seek to ensure that the political process is close to people's demands. It may even be argued that in many countries, the participatory rights granted to non-state actors within the sectoral reach of the FSC exceed the rights that exist under national legislation.

Responsible Care is an initiative that encompasses both a base code and an environmental management system. Firms that subscribe to RC are obliged to comply with ten 'Guiding Principles' that cover issues such as minimizing safety hazards and accidents, the decrease of pollution and the diminution of negative environmental impact, the responsiveness to citizen concerns, and the prompt reporting of health and environmental hazards. Firms that subscribe to the RC principles are obliged to report their performance on several indicators to the national associations that publish these data in an aggregated format. RC nowadays spans 52 countries, including all major industrial nations. The main agents with regard to implementation are the national chemical associations that report to the world federation named International Council of Chemical Associations (ICCA). The national associations are largely free in adapting the base code to national circumstances, thus making for an enormous diversity in the implementation and stringency of the principles across countries. This heterogeneity is addressed by the recently launched Responsible Care Global Charter (RCGC) that seeks to streamline RC across the globe and also introduces new principles such as product stewardship and sustainable development into the RC programme. All requirements laid down in the codes were originally developed by the industry itself with no external consultation. Concerning the amendment and development of the principles, however, some associations set up a so-called National Advisory Panel that is made up of independent scientists and environment and labour advocates. These aim at providing 'a vehicle through which the public may play an integral role in shaping the Responsible Care initiative' (Gunningham 1995: 62).

Regarding the *authority* of the actors participating in the RC programme, it is important to note that the initiative is solely implemented by national associations and their member companies. On the one hand, these are the actors that avail of the necessary expertise in developing and implementing environmental and safety standards at the company level. On the other hand, apart from a relatively abstract reference to the norm of sustainable development, there is little acknowledgement of publicly accepted norms. The assessment regarding *self-determination* and *control of power* is mixed at best. While some chemical associations (such as the Canadian and the US initiatives) seek to extend their reach to civil society actors through consultation in stakeholder forums, these forums invariably have a merely consultative mission, and the selection of members remains in the hands of the national associations. Furthermore, because the performance indicators are published at national and not at company level, it is almost impossible to publicly identify (and call to order) individual firms that violate RC standards. However, *within* associations, a transgression of standards by individual members can very well be identified and that mechanism of peer pressure seems to be among the more powerful tools of RC (see chapter 3 below). RC also is a relatively weak initiative with respect to the criterion of *responsiveness*: While civil society input into the development of RC standards is possible in many countries, the national associations are free in deciding what inputs they want to listen to and which proposed changes to the standards will be implemented. For example, while the recent adoption of the principles of sustainable development and product stewardship in the RCGC are presented as reactions to popular concerns,[6] the way in which they are implemented will be under the almost exclusive control of the industry.

Conclusion

The examples sketched above demonstrate that there are a number of different routes in fulfilling the normative demands of input legitimacy. One important result is that multi-stakeholder models (such as the FSC) may have an advantage in that their institutional design is more likely to fulfil the criterion of congruence between decision makers and those affected by the decisions. Initiatives sponsored by public actors (such as the GC) also have distinctive strengths due to their strong reference to publicly accepted norms, but also because they usually build upon broad consultation exercises with civil society and the business world (as does the FSC). While the latter is also true for RC, one important drawback of this initiative is its strong focus on business interests and the weak connection to public concerns. On the other hand, RC may have important advantages because it is more likely to be accepted by the chemical industry.

The most important finding of this section is, however, that judged from a normative point of view, there are no insurmountable flaws to private voluntary self-regulation. Hence, it is worthwhile to take a more detailed look at the regulatory potential of this mode of governance. Table 7.1 gives an overview of the main results so far.

Why do corporations enter into and comply with voluntary codes of conduct? Competing hypotheses and empirical illustrations

Conceptual outline

If it is true that the governance potential of private self-regulation is not necessarily inferior to public regulation from a normative point of view, then it becomes interesting to know more about the empirical conditions under which private actors will enter into voluntary agreements and will comply with the respective obligations. Answers to these questions can in principle be given both

Table 7.1 Criteria of input legitimacy in three self-regulatory initiatives

Initiative / *Criterion*	*Global compact*	*Forest Stewardship Council*	*Responsible care*
Authority	*high* (broad stakeholder participation, reference to commonly shared norms)	*medium to high* (inclusion of all relevant stakeholders, reference to a commonly shared norm of sustainable development)	*medium* (firms are crucial in developing and implementing environmental and safety standards, reference to sustainable development, although relatively abstract and not yet implemented)
Self-rule	*high* (inclusive participatory model, no entry barriers)	*high* (inclusive participatory model, no entry barriers, equal voting rights for delegates from 'North' and 'South')	*low* (selective consultation with a limited number of stakeholders)
Control of power	*medium* (relatively transparent for outsiders, but no sanctions within GC, extent of 'learning' unclear)	*high* (checks and balances, tripartite system)	*low to medium* (relatively transparent for outsiders, although conduct of individual companies hard to identify, no sanctions, unclear significance of, 'peer pressure')
Responsiveness	*medium* (learning forums are open to civil society input, but implementation of GC principles completely up to individual companies)	*high* (broad stakeholder participation in setting and implementation of norms)	*low* (strong discretion of national associations)

on the actor level and on the level of structural conditions of business action. As regards the general question of actor orientations, it is often argued that the prime motivation for business actors must be profit and survival in the marketplace. Therefore, one may posit an inherent contradiction between economic rationality and potentially costly ecological and social commitments. If this was generally the case, it would not be worthwhile to go any further, since voluntary self-regulatory commitments of business would under no circumstances be capable of reining in this logic of action. Voluntary commitments could be discarded as PR instruments that would be used to give a friendly image to an otherwise impervious business practice.

One prime criticism of this approach is that the business environment is much more complex than it is depicted in pure economic accounts. This environment is made up of civil society and critical consumers that heed certain normative expectations as regards business conduct, an emerging norm of 'business ethics' among at least parts of the international business community, and – last but not least – public actors that may resort to binding regulation at the national level. In consequence, business actors will take account of this environment when deciding about the way in which they conduct their business. They may decide that the long-term viability of their business strategy is contingent upon the observance of certain environmental and social standards. For example, membership in the GC or the FSC may open up new business opportunities and may improve the reputation of individual firms *vis-à-vis* their customers and business partners. A more 'constructivist' interpretation would go even further and point out that changing societal expectations regarding business conduct will be reflected in a changed definition of identity and interests of firms. Virginia Haufler in particular has argued that we currently witness the emergence of a global epistemic community made up of like-minded corporate leaders, scientists, and public regulators, which has defined certain standards of appropriate behaviour for firms (Haufler 1999: 215). King and Lenox (2000: 701) also mention the possibility that the formation of codes of conduct can codify certain values and standards within an industry sector and lead to a value change among business leaders. In consequence, firms would voluntarily comply with certain environmental and social standards out of a perception that they are morally 'doing the right thing' (KPMG 2005: 2).

Against this background, business codes of conduct become important in several ways. First, they serve to operationalize the more diffuse standards of appropriateness that are floating around in society or within the business community and help to implement them on firm level. Second, they serve to communicate the commitment to certain standards to the outside world and – in cases where the observance of standards is certified independently or where there is a regular monitoring and reporting of performance – to produce common knowledge on the rate of compliance with standards. Third, the institutional aspect is important since standards also produce a platform for business actors where best practice can be exchanged, performance can be monitored, and where processes of persuasion and 'socialization' (Checkel 2002; Schimmelfennig

2003) can be organized. The following discussion therefore focuses on two aspects, namely (1) the *emergence* of codes of conduct – what social and economic forces can explain their creation – and (2) the *institutional design* of the initiatives through which operationalization, communication, and socialization in the sense outlined above can take place.

Empirical illustrations

Kofi Annan's initiative to invite business leaders to join the United Nations Global Compact and the readiness of almost 2,000 companies to participate cannot be attributed to forthcoming public regulation. The incentive which the world of states provided for voluntary self-regulation was not binding regulation, but rather its failure to implement the ten principles at the national and international level. There are also no discernible individual incidents of civil society protest or consumer boycotts. However, civil society had a latent influence by providing a general horizon of normative expectations which also proliferated to relevant segments of stakeholders, such as consumers, shareholders, and investors, with which corporations have to interact. There are very few indications that participation in the GC is motivated by the expectation of improving one's position in the market. According to a McKinsey study commissioned by the GC Office, to 'improve market access' ranges last among business motivations to participate in the GC (McKinsey&Company 2004: 5). Much more important are the willingness to gain know-how in implementing corporate social responsibility (CSR) principles and to deal with civil society expectations in a proactive manner (ibid.). In that sense, the prime advantage of the GC may be that it is the best-known initiative in the field and that membership in the GC may increasingly become a signal of 'good' business practice. According to reflectivist explanations, the GC's power rests almost exclusively on the power of learning in a process of exchanging and diffusing good practices. The discursive philosophy underlying the GC becomes manifest in the Global Compact Learning Forums and in the annual multi-stakeholder dialogues. However, learning is not a precondition for entering into self-regulation, but is intended as a consequence of GC membership. Empirically, however, it is very hard to assess the extent to which such 'learning' and identity changes actually materialize in the GC initiative, and although the McKinsey study seems to indicate the willingness of participants to 'learn' and modify their behaviour, its actual occurrence remains unclear. Participation in the GC remains geographically uneven. Of the around 2,800 business participants, there are 126 coming from African countries and 524 from Asia (mostly located in NICs), while the figures for Europe are 1,363. Participants from the Americas total 806, with an astonishingly low number (126) located in the United States and Canada. There is a 60:40 distribution between larger companies and small- and medium-sized enterprises (SMEs) (smaller than 250 employees) and a relatively even spread of participants across sectors.[7]

Because of its weak compliance system, the GC suffers from poor credibility in the eyes of many non-governmental organizations and public observers (cf. Unmüßig 2005). There is no regular assessment of the substantial performance of companies in the light of the ten principles. Members of the GC network may, however, direct the attention of the GC office towards perceived 'systematic and egregious violations' of the principles by member companies. The GC office will then 'assist the participant in aligning its actions with the commitments it has undertaken with regard to the Global Compact'. Only in the case that the company concerned refuses to engage in a dialogue, it may be exposed as being 'inactive' on the GC website and may ultimately be removed from the membership. The same sanctions are possible if a company fails to submit the required description of how it is translating the principles into practice.[8]

Although these measures may be essential in defending the credibility of the initiative, observers have pointed out that the GC enters a potentially detrimental route here. The more companies have to fear sanctions once they enter the GC, the less willing they may be to voluntarily engage in the free exchange of good practice. Nowrot, for example, argues that we are witnessing the GC's transformation 'from an experimental dialogue forum and learning network for the improvement of corporate social responsibility into a normatively relevant transnational regulatory regime for the promotion and protection of global public goods' (2005: 5). While the GC office continues to put much emphasis on the fact that the GC is 'not designed, nor does it have the mandate or resources, to monitor or measure participants' performance',[9] the institutionalization of the potentially contradictory mechanisms of learning and public shaming may in the end impact negatively on the effectiveness of both instruments.

Similar to the GC, the FSC was a result of the failure of interstate initiatives to define and implement appropriate standards for sustainable forest management at the national and intergovernmental level. This time, however, the initiative to overcome this failure did not originate from another public actor, i.e. the United Nations, but from civil society. As early as 1989, environmental NGOs, such as the World Wide Fund for Nature, Friends of the Earth, Greenpeace, and consumer organizations, had articulated not only their criticism of existing intergovernmental initiatives such as the International Tropical Timber Organization, but also the results of the United Nations Conference on Environment and Development (UNCED) in 1992. The strength of these potent non-governmental organizations as well as the public awareness of the environmental damage done to forests worldwide and its potential negative impact on the greenhouse effect were mutually enforcing conditions for the successful establishment of the FSC.

The approach taken by the FSC is to improve the economic viability of sustainable forestry by making 'good forestry practice' known to customers in a transparent and comprehensible manner. Certification codes and the FSC logo (other than the GC logo) can be printed on goods produced by certified FSC companies. The effectiveness of this approach, however, hinges on the existence of demand for such products and the public visibility and acceptance of the FSC logo. The decision by the former German red-green coalition government to allow only FSC-certified wood in bids for public tender still is an exemption to the rule. Starting from the spearhead '95+ Group' of wood buyers and traders in the UK, there is also an increasing number of 'Wood' or 'Buyer Groups' under the auspices of the WWF, Greenpeace, or the Friends of the Earth. These groups bring together major retailers and wood users in national networks that publicly pledge to use solely certified (in practice: FSC) wood in their business.[10] Still, the market share of FSC-certified wood remains relatively low until now.[11] Further engagement mechanisms of the FSC are the manifold local, national, and transnational stakeholder forums that are active in the definition and dissemination of standards. It may be hypothesized that participation in these forums may create additional intrinsic motives for compliance. A purely rhetorical subscription to the FSC principles is unlikely since accreditation is costly and performance is monitored regularly and in a comprehensive manner.

If one looks at the great number of (less demanding) certification systems that have come into existence besides the FSC, it becomes clear that the ultimate success of the FSC is dependent upon its ability to establish itself as the major and also the 'cutting-edge' wood certification scheme. One major danger of voluntary self-regulation in general seems to be the proliferation of different and competing standards and the potentially lacking transparency of what compliance with one particular standard actually signifies. Again, the dilemma here is between the visibility of standards (that can best be reached by a large number of participating firms) and the credibility of the initiative. The latter can probably best be safeguarded by stringent rules and monitoring and costly sanctions, which however may deter some potential participants and may act as a barrier to a large membership.

Observers have pointed out that the emergence of the RC initiative was a reaction to the series of major chemical disasters in the 1970s and 1980s (such as the Bhopal and Seveso incidents and the Sandoz leakage of chemicals into the Rhine, cf. Gunningham 1995: 58–60; Moffet *et al.* 2004: 177–80). The prime aim of the initiative, as explained in a 1993 statement of the United States Chemical Manufacturers Association, was to 'promote continuous improvement in member company environmental, health, and safety performance in response to public concerns and to assist members' demonstration of their improvements to critical public audiences' (quoted in King and Lenox 2000: 699).

As mentioned above, the conditions for accession to the RC initiative, its contents, and its implementation differ widely across countries. Some national associations make subscription to RC obligatory for all their members, a move that can be explained by the fact that the public is unlikely to differentiate between RC members and non-members when assessing the trustworthiness of the entire industry (Prakash 2000). In cases where RC membership is voluntary, a mixture of economic considerations and peer pressure may work in bringing the membership rates of firms (as a ratio of the total number of firms organized in the respective association) up to 70 per cent (Argentina, Denmark, Uruguay; cf. CEFIC and ICCA 2005). When measured as percentage of total chemical production in any given country, the ratio of chemical industry turnover covered by RC can be as high as 80–95 per cent (Australia, France, Mexico, Slovak

Republic, Sweden, Switzerland, and USA), while other countries report figures of about 45–50 per cent (Austria and Italy). Although this is significantly higher than, for example, the market share of FSC-certified wood, it has to be mentioned that not all member associations publish these figures so that they are likely to be lower in other countries.

The implementation of RC standards is overseen by national associations and to some limited extent by the public to which aggregated performance data are reported. The prime mechanism in raising the standard of business conduct, however, is peer pressure. The yearly performance data of a company have to be signed by the CEO and then submitted to a peer review panel under the auspices of the national association. The process is reported to cause considerable embarrassment among CEOs of firms that are found to be lagging behind (King and Lenox 2000: 701; Moffet *et al.* 2004: 195–6). Although there is the possibility of sanctions for continued poor performance (in particular the expulsion from the national association in the Australian and US cases), the prime focus is upon a system of exchange of best practices and technology as well as mutual learning (Gunningham 1995: 69).

Several writers (King and Lenox 2000; Moffet *et al.* 2004) point out that RC has become a largely consensual standard within the chemical industry worldwide precisely because of its authorship by the industry: It may therefore constitute a more influential standard of appropriateness for firms than externally defined norms and criteria. As concerns the actual impact of the RC programme, assessments differ widely. While some observers claim a whole range of beneficial impacts of the initiative (e.g. onto industry–community relations, environmental performance, and public perception of the trustworthiness of the industry, cf. Moffet *et al.* 2004; SustainAbility 2004), others argue that RC members do not systematically outperform non-members of RC as regards the emission of toxic substances, a finding explained by the 'assurance effect' of RC membership against critical scrutiny by the public (King and Lenox 2000: 708). While it is beyond the scope of this article to take sides in this debate, there seem to be a number of interesting effects concerning the relation between the RC initiative and public regulation: First, RC as a de facto standard of appropriate conduct for the chemical industry is increasingly recognized by public courts that seek to concretize abstract principles like 'due diligence' and 'best-available technology' that are often used in public regulations. Second, at least in the Canadian case, some RC procedures have taken over the task of defining acceptable emission levels for certain substances, thus effectively replacing public regulation by the voluntary RC standard (Moffet *et al.* 2004: 189–90). Third, the chemical industry seeks to get the global RC programme acknowledged as an important contribution to the global movement towards sustainability, most markedly in connection with the launch of the RCGC at the recent UNEP-sponsored Dubai conference for a 'Strategic Approach to International Chemicals Management'.[12]

Lessons learned: the governance potential of private self-regulation

The capability of private actors to take binding decisions and to enforce rules is frequently questioned with the argument that business lacks the necessary legal authority. However, this objection ignores that – on a legal basis – national governments cannot use this instrument either in the context of international governance. If they want to constrain the behaviour of other governments or of any other national or transnational actors outside their own territorially limited jurisdiction, they depend on the sense of obligation created by the norms and rules on which they are based, or from actors' rational calculation of the gains they can expect from rule compliance, rather than on subordination by the threat or use of (unauthorized) force. In principle, non-state actors do have these instruments at their disposal as well when they want to alter the behaviour of others (cf. Gordon 2000). They can try to persuade with normative or utilitarian arguments, exert moral pressure, mobilize public opinion, or instrumentalize market forces against firms *and* governments. The effectiveness of these options depends, however, on the extent to which these instruments can be brought into play with respect to the specific sensitivity and vulnerability of their addressees. Only brands are susceptible to shaming or consumer boycotts. In addition, boycotts can only be effective if consumers or business partners can afford the 'luxury' of a good conscience when choosing which products they want to buy. As far as monitoring rule compliance is concerned, numerous independent private inspections systems have worked quite successfully in many fields. But again, there are limits to successful private monitoring: the norm of 'partnership' prevalent in many voluntary initiatives may prevent open conflict, and the limited financial and personal resources of NGOs may be overstretched if used for the supervision of increasingly complex regulatory commitments. In addition, private self-monitoring as in the case of RC suffers from serious credibility problems.

Just like intergovernmental negotiating processes, negotiations within networks in which private actors are involved can orientate themselves to the self-interest of those participating or may be geared towards the general interest (see also Haufler 1993: 99–105). Interestingly enough, in the fields with regard to which there is a broad discussion about general norms to be observed by corporate private actors – labour and the environment – the generally accepted normative standards have emerged from cooperative efforts of public *and* private actors in international forums. In both the ILO and the UNCED, formal and informal participation of private actors was essential for the emergence and general acceptance of the respective normative frameworks. RC, which started out as a private rule making exercise by business in the meantime, has given various stakeholders a voice (although not necessarily a say) through the civil society advisory panels mentioned above.

Still, it becomes clear from the preceding discussion that 'privatization requires a public framework' (see also Hummel 2001: 26). If 'private regimes' produce negative externalities that cannot be accounted for within networks, there is a need for coordination that requires more than 'single issue' competences. Most importantly, however, private actors are incapable of providing and protecting the regulatory framework within which self-regulation can take place: they are, in other words, incapable of 'meta-governance' (Kooiman 2002: 170–89). As there is no relative balance of power between private actors in world society, public sector actors are called upon to counterbalance and effectively regulate business power in order to protect the rule of law and to guarantee procedural fairness. Public rules are also required for establishing and protecting functioning markets, and for guaranteeing an open access to public discourses. Thus, self-regulation by private codes of conduct can mobilize additional sources of legitimacy and may alleviate the burdens and difficulties in governing a complex world society. But in fulfilling these functions, it needs to be grounded in a functional division of labour between private and public actors. In such arrangements, the part to be played by the public sector is less *substantial* policy making, but rather the provision of certain meta-governance functions. In a nutshell, these functions are:

- the provision and guarantee of the constitutional legal framework for private self-regulation, the functioning of markets, and an open access to the public arena,
- the shaping of the normative environment of private self-regulation which can lend legitimacy to the goals of private actors and keep self-regulation geared towards the general good,
- the facilitation and encouragement of voluntary self-regulation through the maintenance of a credible 'shadow of hierarchy',
- to support the monitoring of self-regulation,
- to avoid negative externalities by linking the different sectoral self-regulation efforts between them.

In the light of these meta-governance functions, which only the public sector can fulfil, private self-regulation will always have to be *embedded self-regulation*, in which public actors, private corporations, and civil society are involved in different arenas and functions.

Notes

1 The authors thank Nina Bressel for her intellectual and technical support in the preparation of this chapter.
2 For a more extensive treatment see Conzelmann and Wolf 2006.
3 See www.unglobalcompact.org/NetworksAroundTheWorld/index.html (accessed 2 August 2006) for more information.
4 See www.fsc.org/en/about/policy_standards/princ_criteria/ (accessed 2 August 2006).
5 Data from the website www.certified-forests.org/global.htm (accessed 2 August 2006).
6 Interview with RC official, 6 April 2006.

7 Data taken from the GC online database at www.unglobalcompact.org/ParticipantsAndStakeholders/search_participant.html (accessed 2 August 2006).

8 See www.unglobalcompact.org/AboutTheGC/integrity.html (accessed 2 August 2006) for further explanations.

9 *Global Compact* Note on Integrity Measures: www.unglobalcompact.org/AboutTheGC/gc_integrity_mesures.pdf (accessed 2 August 2006).

10 See Synnott 2005: 33–8 for a description of the emergence of Buyer Groups. Also see www.wwf.de/imperia/md/content/pdf/waelder/nutzungneu/HG_wood_group_240504.pdf, www.wwf.us/about_wwf/what_we_do/forests/what_you_can_do/architect_builder/wwf_95_group/index.cfm (accessed 2 August 2006).

11 FSC does not collect data on market shares, but some national initiatives do. The Dutch initiative reports a market share of 11 per cent in the Netherlands for the year 2005 (up from 4 per cent in 1999), see www.fscnl.org/faq.htm#11 (accessed 2 August 2006). The members of the 95+ Group are reported to have a market share of around 20 per cent in the UK wood market, see footnote 8. These are probably among the higher figures worldwide.

12 See 'International Council of Chemical Associations Welcomes Approval of SAICM', Press statement, 9 February 2006, Online: www.icca-at-dubai.org/dbfiles/1854%20ICCA%20SAICM%2009%2002%2006.pdf (accessed 2 August 2006).

8 The private regulation of labour standards

The case of the apparel and footwear industries

Jeroen Merk

Introduction

The failure of governmental and intergovernmental institutions to implement effective labour legislation in the course of the last decade has resulted in a rich variety of private (or non-governmental) regulatory initiatives that seek to address labour standards and enforcement in a wide range of global product chains. Such regulation is not least aimed at deflecting anti-sweatshop campaigns attacking the substandard working conditions in the factories at the far ends of global commodity chains, which threaten to turn feel-good logos of the large corporations running them into symbols of exploitation and human degradation. However, I will argue that the non-governmental regulatory systems that have emerged in the process represent not only terrains of struggle but also nodes of collaboration between different social and economic forces that could potentially have an emancipatory impact for workers and civil society.

I will start with contextualising transnational private governance as embedded in and structurally related to transnational structures of accumulation. I will argue that non-market relations of planning, coordination, cooperation and governance are necessary for the functional integration of dispersed productive activities. They are testimony to a deeper process of socialisation of labour (Vergesellschaftung), which creates the spaces in which codes of conduct, and regulation generally, have emerged. This will be illustrated by assessing the development of regulatory practices in the apparel and footwear industry, and by identifying four phases of political struggle surrounding these regulatory practices. In the final section, I briefly discuss how the aggregate effort by individual companies to adopt codes of conduct impinges on the competitive universe of private capital and adds new opportunities to further regulation.

Global production networks

Almost all sportswear and apparel brands have cut themselves free from actual production and have transformed themselves into so-called 'manufacturers without factories', e.g. manufacturers that separate the physical production of goods from the design and marketing stages of the production (Gereffi 1994; Dicken 1998). The International Labour Organisation (ILO) typifies the apparel and footwear industry as a 'one-world employer' in which the 'geographical distribution of world employment is affected by the rapid changes in production and trade' (2000: 4). The companies that dominate this industry have formed, as one scholar puts it, 'global flagship networks' using their brand as flag and controlling a global fleet of suppliers (Ernst 2003: 3).

The 'flagship' metaphor rightly suggests that a system of internationalised production needs regulation to coordinate and manage the various integral processes and companies involved. According to neo-liberal theory, such regulation should be provided by the self-regulatory market. Since the market is understood as a spontaneous and superior allocation mechanism for the distribution of scarce resources, social order is the result of profit-maximising activity under the rule of law. International trade is accordingly seen as the 'result of endowments, technology, taste difference and product differentiation at an abstract level' (Raikes *et al.* 2000: 4). Organisational linkages tend to be qualified as 'rigidities' or 'market imperfections'.

In the global commodity or value chain approach (e.g. respectively, Gereffi 1994; Kaplinsky 2000), on the other hand, the emphasis is on the various non-market linkages that are necessary for the functional integration and coordination of dispersed productive activities. These include the coordination of the linkages within the value chain (input–output structure), the monitoring of quality, price and delivery (QPD) reliability and procedures in appearance and packaging. Humphrey and Schmitz argue that the concept of regulation, or governance, implies that 'some firms in the chain set and/or enforce the parameters under which others in the chain operate. A chain without governance would just be a string of market relations' (2001: 20). Power therefore plays a crucial role. Instead of a spontaneous order, trade between corporations develops under 'the discipline imposed by complex webs of contracts and sub-contracts dominated by key agents' (Raikes *et al.* 2000: 5).

The concept of socialisation of labour (from the German Vergesellschaftung), which identifies the processes of coordination and cooperation by which divided labour is reunified to cohere in a single effort, takes this argument one step further. Along with the widening and deepening of commodification by which goods, social relations and people, and nature itself, are turned into marketable items, socialisation develops as 'capital utilises planning at increasingly higher levels of the productive process—from simple cooperation to manufacture and to large scale industry—in order to strengthen and extend its command over labour-power and obtain larger access to it' (Panzieri 1976: 7). Or, in the words of Stephen Hymer (1975: 37–8), with the growth of capital, 'business enterprises needed a more complex administrative structure to coordinate its activities and a larger brain to plan for its survival and growth'.

So whilst the production of a single commodity takes place through an ever-larger sequence of input–output activities that encompasses an entire range of firms, sectors and countries connected with each other through exchange relations, the consciously organised labour process increases as well. As an objective process internal to capital accumulation but potentially driving beyond it, the socialisation of labour cannot be suspended, only regulated one way or another.

Socialisation of labour and standardisation processes

As a result of socialisation of labour, any company that seeks to enter the world market must abide by rules of coordination of an industry, state and, ultimately, world society (Low and Gleeson 2000). Thus, while commodity fetishism obscures information about the direct objectives or intentions of others, efforts are undertaken to overcome this alienation through the creation of institutions that provide information (Marx 1939: 161).

Standardisation and certification here play a particularly important role in this process. Although standards remain largely invisible in daily life for consumers, corporations – who buy and supply products to each other – rely crucially on standards or processes covering quality, safety, reliability, efficiency and interchangeability. As 'external points of reference' (Hawkins 1995, cited in Nadvi and Wätring 2002), standards facilitate the international exchange of goods and services and widen the social division of labour (Elam 1990).

A number of scholars have pointed out how service coordination firms, such as law firms, management consultancy firms, debt-rating agencies, insurance companies, accountancy firms, financial clearinghouses and so on coordinate the behaviour of other firms (Cutler *et al.* 1999b). These firms play an important infrastructural role by reducing uncertainty, acting as gatekeeper, promoting parallel practices or coordinating and facilitating the flow logic of global production chains. In other words, these companies promote 'the narrowing of the expectations of the different social elements of capital to a shared, transparent set', which is crucial in enabling market exchange between distant parties (Sinclair 1999: 184).

One type of coordination service firm that greatly benefit from the fragmentation of production across borders and the expansion of world trade are companies specialised in inspecting, testing and certification services. The largest three global companies in this business are Intertek, SGS and Bureau Veritas. Each of these employs tens of thousands of people and operates offices and laboratories on a global basis. They provide services to coordinate and supervise fragmented production processes by carrying out inspections of consumer products during manufacture and before shipment. They seek to ensure that manufacturers comply with the buyer's specifications related to quantity, quality, colour, packaging, labelling and so on. In addition, these companies certify products, systems or management processes. A certification provides evidence to customers of a factory's compliance with regard to a set of requirements or standards set by governments, standardisation bodies or buyers themselves. Such certificates are often a prerequisite for local companies to entering global circuits of capital. With already more than 360,000 organisations certified to an ISO 9000 or ISO 14000 standards, certification itself has grown into a big business.

The importance of standardisation and certification also indicate that today – under neo-liberalism – the institutional forms that support these activities are increasingly of a private, non-state, nature. Various scholars have pointed out that this represents a wider shift within society from a politically negotiated system of rules towards privatised systems of negotiations in which business plays a more important role (see, e.g. Cutler *et al.* 1999a; Raikes *et al.* 2000: 10; Graz 2006b). In this shift, regulatory tasks are delegated away from state bodies to private specialists, as discussed above. Market-based and private voluntary strategies are presented as an alternative or a supplement to traditional state regulation. They have created a political context highly conducive to the rise of private regulation in which reporting, standard setting, auditing, monitoring and certification have become central elements (Utting 2000: 74).

Rules, regulations, codes, standards, benchmarks, networks and a range of state institutions and other specialised agencies such as coordination service firms remain necessary for social, functional and normative reunification of fragmented productive activities (cf. van der Pijl 2004). Instead of being something alien to the liberal, capitalist economy, regulation and private governance is already an integral part of market exchange. For capital, regulation always carries the risk of eroding the core principles on which the mode of production rests (principles such as private property and free contract), and, because of this risk, corporations will not easily yield to regulations not written by themselves or backed up by authority other than their own. This is all the more so since the planning and coordination of (fragmented) productive processes is never a purely technical or organisational question faced by capital alone, but immediately a social question. This implies that labour too emerges as active force in the process. At various points in the production network, locally, nationally and internationally, a variety of groups, will, for a variety of reasons, contest the specific principles and conditions under which production and reproduction takes place. Thus, while from a structural perspective, socialisation of labour accompanies worldwide commodification processes leading to wider circles of social interdependence, from a strategic perspective this process is accompanied by social forces intersecting this process in an attempt to direct it. In other words, various actors attempt to coordinate their activities in order to shape the processes of socialisation of labour.

In what follows, I will focus on the strategic questions and assess the development of codes of conduct in apparel and athletic footwear production. Although codes of conduct are being challenged frequently, not least because they remain privatised, non-enforceable forms of regulation, the hypothesis of this chapter is that they also reflect how relations of a non-market type are (increasingly) part of a complex web of exchange upon which internationalised production relies.

Private regulation of labour standards

Transnational production has increased the discipline of capital and has led to a deterioration in labour conditions on world scale. The downward pressure on labour conditions in the apparel and sportswear industry is represented in poverty wages, the structural lack of job security, long hours and forced overtime, unhealthy working conditions, abusive management regimes and the suppression of trade union rights. The various – often legal – barriers to the right to organise only exacerbates the problem because employees are prohibited from demanding basic workers rights.

Substandard labour conditions and extreme forms of exploitation became a public issue in the early 1990s when anti-sweatshop groups started to target branded corporations over labour conditions in the factories that produced their wares. Particularly large branded corporations became targets of these campaigns, which gained momentum over the course of the decade and succeeded 'in bringing to the fore an aspect of the polarisation characteristic of capitalist globalisation – on the one hand the glitter of consumption ideology, and on the other the brutal reality of production in conditions of extreme exploitation' (Mello 2003: 27). A global network, comprised of non-governmental organisations (NGOs), student groups, labour organisations, church groups and consumer groups, has emerged and has become a social force in its own right. The central aim of these transnationally organised campaigns was to improve working conditions and, 'to bring back to the TNC level some responsibility for workers no matter in whose employment they are or in what part of the world they live' (Clean Clothes Newsletter 2000).

As a result, the 1990s have witnessed a revival of interest in 'codes of conduct' regulating the behaviour of transnational corporations (TNCs). Contrary to earlier (failed) initiatives to regulate TNCs that were driven by governmental or intergovernmental organisations, contemporary initiatives have largely been fuelled by NGOs. Together, they form a loosely organised global movement that seeks to hold corporations accountable for their actions (Bendell 2004).[1] Hereafter, I will therefore refer to them as the corporate accountability movement or simply as labour advocates.[2]

While voluntary initiatives often set out to compensate for government deficits, e.g. their failure or unwillingness to implement effective labour legislation, the emergence of these private instruments cannot be understood outside the neo-liberal framework (Bartley 2003). Voluntary initiatives like codes of conduct were seen by business interests as 'non-threatening as [they] respected the central tenets of neo-liberalism centred on FDI, export-orientation, privatisation and downsizing of the state' (Utting 2000: 4). Codes of conduct could serve different interests and agendas, 'catering to both reformist and conservative interests' (ibid.). The proliferation of codes of conduct is therefore driven by a wide range of stakeholders, which have different interests and contrasting expectations of the purpose of these instruments (Jenkins 2002: 13). Hence, it is crucial to understand the context, the history and the political processes associated with the emergence and development of these voluntary initiatives. These instruments can therefore best be understood as objects of political contestation and strategic framing between different social forces searching for ways to fill the regulatory vacuum (Bartley 2003: 437). Unlike many other private regulatory structures, the scope of these arrangements is not limited to a particular region but cover spatially dispersed production chains.

Next I will discuss four phases of political contestation through which the code of conduct debate has developed since the early 1990s. Each phase also demarcates a terrain of struggle which is absorbed into a broader field in the subsequent phase. As a result of these struggles, the opportunities for achieving transparency are much greater, as are the possibilities for connecting with established worker organisations. While I limit myself to the apparel and athletic footwear sector, many of these developments can be witnessed in other sectors as well. Indeed, a whole range of commodity chains have turned into transnational sites of social struggle, ranging from mobile phones to toys, and from the collection of plant-gene data in the tropical forests of Costa Rica to the organisation of health care.

(i) Denial

The first area of political contestation has been centred on making companies accept that they can be held responsible for working conditions in entities which they do not own. When branded companies such as Nike or Adidas were first confronted with allegations of sourcing from factories with substandard working conditions in the early 1990s, they tended to reject the assumption that they had any association with the circumstances in which their commodities were produced.

Very few companies today maintain the principals behind this position, although some neo-liberals maintain that corporations have only a fiduciary duty to make profit for their shareholders. Instead, when it became clear that anti-sweatshop campaigns were a permanent feature of TNC's operating environment, and furthermore were actually gaining strength during the 1990s, many corporations replaced this kind of defensive posturing by a more proactive stance on corporate social responsibility (CSR). Codes of conduct represent one way of responding to pressures exerted by NGOs and trade unions (Utting 2000; Jenkins 2002). Still, by implementing CSR, companies started to recognise their responsibility for working conditions. Such recognition represented the first step by which social instructions and directives started to play a role in the planning and organisation of production.

(ii) Substance

The second phase of political contestation was to make companies or business associations – who also started to adopt codes of conduct – accept internationally recognised labour standards as set by the ILO. Many corporate codes are criticised for representing weak principles or vaguely defined guidelines. Often, code requirements only focus on those issues that are considered most sensitive to public outcry such as child labour or forced labour. In other instances, they are defined in such general terms that they amount to be 'useless as instruments that would uphold or advance workers' rights' (Kearney 1999: 210).

Trade unions and NGOs reacted to these weak codes by adopting 'model codes', the purpose of which was to set standards for standards, i.e. minimum levels which the codes themselves should reach. Model codes make an explicit reference to international labour standards and ILO jurisprudence. Trade unions use them in their negotiations with companies, while, for NGOs and activists, the adoption of a model code has been useful as a campaigning tool against companies 'highlighting the often glaring differences between codes on paper and the actual standards found in the workplace', as Ineke Zeldenrust, coordinator of the International Secretariat of the Clean Clothes Campaign (CCC) (2005), argues.[3] For the CCC, the model code made it possible for European and Asian labour advocates to speak with one voice to the companies, granting them a benchmark against which corporate codes could be measured. For campaigning objectives, these model codes turned out to be useful as a point of reference in order to push corporations into accepting higher standards, or as a way to create a public debate.

Furthermore, reference to the ILO's tripartite membership grants these core labour standards a high degree of legitimacy and raises the credibility of the instrument. As a consequence, the legitimacy (or moral authoritativeness) of these model codes is superior compared to most company codes. This is in spite of debates that have continued to crystallise around issues such as freedom of association, wages (minimum vs. living wage) and the scope of ' "non-discrimination" clauses' (O'Rourke 2002).

(iii) Implementation, monitoring and verification

No matter how stringent the criteria contained within a code are, they remain symbolic instruments for improving workplace conditions as long as they lack a programme 'to go from paper to practice'.[4] Critics soon challenged companies to demonstrate conformity to the standards they had adopted. A third moment of political contestation was therefore centred around the question of what would constitute an adequate way of implementing, monitoring and verifying compliance with codes of conduct (see for positions Yanz and Jeffcott 1997; Connor 1998; Bartley 2003). Implementation refers here to the range of concrete measures that a company carries out to give effect to a code (SOMO 2003: 5). This implies a managerial system capable of translating standards into operational practice. This is not only necessary to ensure that the structure and resources are in place to implement the code (Urminsky 2001: 34), but also to ensure that business is conducted in such a way that suppliers can meet the standards they are supposed to uphold. The latter particularly refers to the need of addressing the negative impact which purchasing practices or sourcing systems can have on code compliance.

Internal monitoring or company monitoring refers in the context of this article to the procedures and practices a company carries out in order to check that labour standards have been implemented and are continuously observed in the workplace (SOMO 2003: 5). Some companies have set up social compliance teams for these tasks, while others have extended the tasks of their quality controllers to include monitoring of labour standards. It is increasingly argued that when companies employ a commercial firm to monitor code compliance (i.e. the outsourcing of monitoring) and pass this off as external verification, this is in fact not much different from having the work done by company staff. But company-initiated procedures alone, while necessary to integrate ethical standards into business operations, remain insufficient. Neil Kearney, secretary general of the International Textile, Garment, Leather Workers Federation (ITGLWF), formulates it as follows:

> Self-assessment, no matter how well applied, will not deliver credibility. Only independent verification will confer legitimacy and credibility. In reality companies cannot police and judge themselves when they themselves are the potential offenders.
>
> (Kearny 1999: 214)

Therefore, verification is all about establishing the credibility of claims concerning actual labour practices, the observance of code provisions, or the observance of code implementation. In other words, credible verification would require rule based systems covering the selection and training of auditors as well as inspection techniques etc. This implies at least that verification is carried out by a body independent of the entity whose claim is being verified (SOMO 2003: 8).

These kinds of criticism have brought into the open the need for an overarching system for evaluating company claims and to rise above the limits of corporate self-regulation. It has stimulated the creation of a number of so-called multi-stakeholder initiatives (MSIs), which involve a variety of business interests, NGOs and/or trade unions trying to develop (more) systematic approaches to code implementation, monitoring and verification, as well as developing structures for accountability to civil society. In the apparel and (athletic) footwear industries, the most important MSIs are: Fair Labour Association, Workers Rights Consortium, Ethical Trading Initiative, Social Accountability International, and Fair Wear Foundation. These initiatives have the following in common. They:

- bring a wider range of actors into decision-making procedures
- agree upon a standardised code of conduct generally informed by ILO standards
- concur upon follow-up activities designed to put labour standards into effect

To a varying degree they might also:

- use social audits as a mechanism for monitoring/verifying codes of conduct
- authorise or accredit organisations to conduct the verification process
- certify workplaces or branded companies
- promote social dialogue and learning between different stakeholders

- facilitate the processing of complaints from workers, trade unions or NGOs as part of the monitoring/verification process
- stimulate stakeholder participation in code verification at points of production
- get financial or facilitative support from governments

At the same time, governance arrangements, standards and procedures differ significantly between these different initiatives. Also, important to note is that these systems are still in an experimental phase and subject to change.[5]

Some are more multilateral (involving several corporate actors) than genuinely multi-stakeholder (involving several stakeholders representing diverging interests). The more corporatised (or privatised) initiatives remain top-down elite structures based on voluntary or incomplete self-regulatory structures involving little serious participation of non-corporate actors. Verification, or 'independent monitoring', may also be used as a substitute for enforcement of law. Yet, some MSIs are genuinely 'attempting to build democratic, locally accountable, substantively responsive, participatory strategies of governance' (O'Rourke 2004: 31). They might provide a space where NGOs and trade unions have a voice in furthering the development of regulatory initiatives. They embody new forms of social dialogue where different stakeholders regularly meet, exchange views or devise joint projects (Faure 2001: 48). By moving the debate from corporate self-regulation to co-regulation, the credibility of these initiatives is further enhanced.

(iv) Workers' participation

MSIs succeeded in placing the topic of implementation, monitoring and verification high on the code of conduct agenda. They address some of the weaknesses associated with corporate-led attempts, particularly by recognising the core ILO conventions. In addition, they have opened up space for participation and social dialogue between different stakeholders on an international level. Nonetheless, many within the corporate accountability movement stay critical about the realisation of these standards on the ground, e.g. the real impact these standards have in the factories and workplaces around the world. For labour advocates, the critical question remains how to guarantee a meaningful role for the workers concerned, their unions and labour-related NGOs. Their main question is how to encourage labour self-organising at sites of production and/or to connect with traditional workers' struggles in today's decentralised, globalised context. The promotion of worker self-organisation and participation within (and beyond) these code-monitoring and verification systems has become a fourth area of political contestation.

Much of this criticism is directed against the dominant role social audits have started to occupy within a number of monitoring/verification initiatives. The term social audit emerged to distinguish the auditing of labour practices from financial auditing. In some cases, it refers to the entire social and environmental 'footprint' of the activities of a company, in others it refers only to social issues. Most often, these social audits are performed by global audit firms. Labour advocates have questioned whether these social audits will (a) actually empower workers; (b) accurately assess labour conditions; and (c) encourage improvements in working conditions (Esbenshade 2004; CCC 2005).

Others point at the danger of managerialism, in which a growing number of self-assigned experts (law firms, accountancy, consultants, ethics officers and so on) that have jumped on the CSR bandwagon in order to extract a 'business' out of it. While these kind of coordination services firms have become prominent channels of transmitting the codes of conduct from the branded headquarters to the workplaces around the world, some scholars worry that this has helped to 'domesticate the CSR space as a docile, auditable, and management friendly arena that is inhabited by professionals' (Sum 2005). The CCC (2005: 74–84) argues that too much focus on social audits distracts attention from other activities that labour rights advocates believe to be crucial to ensure code implementation, such as complaints mechanisms, reporting, worker training and education and changes in purchasing practices.

A mixed picture

The anti-sweatshop campaigns, as well as the codes developed in response to them, have carved out a new global space in which essentially political struggles are being fought out. The four phases discussed above represent the four most vocal criticisms and political struggles since the early 1990s.

Certainly, the overall influence of this movement must not be overstated. Global production practices continue to worsen in many places of the developing world, and governments still fail to enact or enforce labour laws. Labour movements that have won some rights in recent years, for example in Indonesia and Mexico, have witnessed the migration of industry to China. Among labour advocates, there is recognition that progress with voluntary initiatives is limited since it has not succeeded in persuading governments to put in place legislated regulatory regimes that ensure workers' rights, particularly their right to freedom of association, are respected (Miller 2003; Connor 2004). A World Bank (2003: 34) study concludes that 'systemic progress will not happen unless governments get involved more vitally'.

Yet, however minimal the results so far, the process of socialisation of labour that accompanies all capitalist development has created new spaces for emancipatory regulation. Real gains have been achieved which are circumscribing the discipline of capital. First, most corporations active in these sectors now accept responsibility for labour conditions in factories they do not own. Second, there has been a converging pattern away from firm specific standards towards the evolution of generic minimum standards along the guidelines of the ILO core labour standards. Third, the overall centre of gravity has now moved in favour of more stringent forms of code implementation and monitoring. Finally, a small number of branded and retail companies have joined one of (the various) MSIs to implement, monitor and verify labour standards. These initiatives articulate heterogeneous interest and are (more) open to democratic checks. Here, we can perhaps observe the beginnings of a trend towards a more consensual logic of power sharing which might lead to negotiated social compromises.

Anarchy in the sphere of social compliance

The dynamics of action/reaction has resulted in a myriad of diverse, non-state-driven regulatory initiatives. Estimations about the number of codes in the apparel and athletic footwear industry run from about 300 up to an astonishing 1,000 (World Bank 2003). There is a similar uncertainty about the number of social audits that annually take place; one specialist estimates that the number amounts to 30,000 (personal communication with Francois Beaujolin). Indeed, anarchy in the sphere of the market seems to have found its counterpart in the sphere of social auditing.

This proliferation of corporate and MSIs has now been widely acknowledged as confusing and inefficient. Manufacturers, who often supply several retailers or branded companies, find themselves subjected to numerous – partly overlapping, partly diverging – standards, assessments and social audits. They complain that the multitude of 'audits divert management time and resources, disrupt workflow, and challenge planning processes' (World Bank 2003: 18).

Retailers and brand-named corporations but also labour advocates increasingly recognise that the multiplication of private efforts is inefficient, expensive, time consuming and probably counterproductive. The weight of multiple audits and monitoring programmes has started to push different social forces to promote the harmonisation of compliance models and/or the exchange of social audit information. Efforts are underway to manage social audit information among corporations through the creation of global databases that would facilitate the exchange of non-competitive information on workplace conditions. Others have started dialogue on how to achieve better coordination among the various MSIs by drafting a common code of conduct. Like the four phases discussed earlier, this process of upscaling the regulatory effort is framed by different interests, agendas and political strategies. Nonetheless, they will add yet another layer to the integrative governance structures that have emerged alongside the spatial fragmentation of labour.

Conclusion

The internationalisation of productive capital has been integral to the strategic disruption of national economies, and the power of labour in that context. It has increased the discipline of capital and has led to a deterioration in labour conditions on a worldwide scale.

Yet, if socialisation of labour is understood as an objective process, which develops in conjunction with commodification, one can point to numerous processes by which it actually does demarcate space for forms of negotiation, governance, regulation and, potentially, democratisation – even if the profit-maximising logic still dominates.

In this light, we may understand why in response to the corporate accountability movement of the 1990s, voluntary codes of conduct appeared. This chapter has identified four phases of political contestation. Each phase demarcates a terrain of struggle which is absorbed into a broader field in the subsequent phase – one might call this the ratcheting up of the regulatory objective. Even though corporations are in control in most of these programmes, the capability for transcending formal ownership relations has increased. Moreover, the weight of multiple audits has pushed different social forces to promote the harmonisation of compliance models at an international level. Even if this trend remains mortgaged by failing social auditors, lack of worker participation and failing state institutions, the spiralling debate between corporations and their critics has become a possible matrix for stronger forms of transnational regulation.

Notes

1 For an anatomy of the social forces that drive this movement, see Connor 2004 or Jenkins 2002.
2 One such international coalition is the CCC, which aims at improving working conditions and at empowering workers in the global garment and sportswear industry. There are CCCs in 12 European countries; each of them represents a coalition of consumer organisations, trade unions, human rights and women rights organisations, researchers, solidarity groups and activists. Total membership is close to 300 NGOs and trade unions. While every national campaign operates autonomously, they collaborate together towards international action. In addition, the CCC works closely with network of international partners in most countries where garments are produced.
3 Personal communication with the author. 19 March 2005.
4 Ineke Zeldenrust, personal communication with the author. 19 March 2005.
5 For further details, see O'Rourke 2003; Nadvi and Wältring 2002; Wick 2003.

Part III

Prospects and limits of *avant-garde* cases

The private regulation of the cyberspace

9 Transnational private governance of the Internet

The roles of business

Sven Bislev and Mikkel Flyverbom

The Internet is more *transnational* than almost anything: from the user's perspective, borders are invisible and can largely be ignored – or at least circumvented. Internet *governance* is, to the extent there is any, situated mostly in a *private* realm. Still, this emblem of transnational private governance (TPG) has its limitations, and those limits are currently exposed and contested to an unprecedented degree. Governance initiatives involving private and public, technical and political, national and transnational participants abound. This chapter fleshes out TPG and the Internet governance process, with a focus on the roles that business corporations play in this development.

The short history of the Internet begins in the research community, a context where quite specific notions of governance exist – a culture of science, in which knowledge is the currency that regulates the course of events.[1] Originally a small-scale experiment in moving information around in a flexible way and at high speed, it grew in a culture of mutual trust and technical, rather than political concerns. As it became popularised outside the scientists' preserve, this knowledge culture was first translated into a notion of an idealistic, anarchistic universe. The Internet was seen as a playground for the progressive and the creative, and the first generation of Internet 'gurus' hailed it as a limitless world of free expression. Now, as the Internet is demonstrating its enormous potentialities, it has become too important to be left alone. While traces of idealism still exist – in user communities of different sorts – the importance of the Internet for commercial, political, and technical issues means that it has emerged as an object of governance (Kleinwächter 2004).

Most recently, discussions about Internet governance have emerged in a process initiated by the United Nations. Recent years have seen the World Summit on the Information Society (WSIS), the creation of the UN ICT Task Force, and the Working Group on Internet Governance (WGIG). Discussions and decisions in those forums have turned on key issues of governance, such as the status and responsibilities of various actors of the Internet. The process has encouraged broad-based, cross-sectoral participation and brought together actors that previously had very little contact. Among the participants are a number of large business corporations and associations which have involved themselves in both public campaigns, political discussions, policy bodies, and concrete projects pertaining to Internet governance in more or less direct ways.

As the Internet is a 'virtual' network embedded in an already regulated 'real' one (the telecommunications network), the first question that these UN processes sought to address was what is to be governed, and what methods exist for that purpose. In this way, the present interest in the politics of the Internet constitutes a *problematisation* (Dean 1999) which questions the very activity of governance, the object to be governed, and the roles and responsibilities of both those organisations involved and those seeking to become involved in the regulation and running of the Internet. From a Foucauldian perspective, Dean suggests an 'analytics' rather than a general theory of government: '... rather than starting from a global theory of the state or of power relations, an analytics of government directs us to examine the different and particular contexts in which governing is called into question, in which actors and agents of all sorts must pose the question of how to govern' (Dean 1999: 27).

This chapter provides an account of international attempts to regulate the Internet and focuses on the way corporations are drawn into the process of regulation – not as mere objects of regulation, nor as completely self-regulating, but in both these roles and also, significantly, as participants in governance networks that include political, commercial and other private participants. That focus brings a number of issues in the literature on private authority, global governance, and regulatory techniques into play and invites a discussion of the way governance has changed in recent decades.

Internet governance

The most fundamental feature of the Internet is its particular technological architecture and its reliance on 'protocols'. We adopt a definition of the Internet as 'the global data communication system formed by the interconnection of public and private telecommunication networks using the Internet protocols, such as IP, TCP and DNS' (Mathiason *et al.* 2004: 6). From this perspective, any discussion about the Internet should take into account four characteristics: (1) the Internet revolves around open and non-proprietary standards that can be 'freely' adopted by anyone; (2) private, commercial companies own much of infrastructural cable and wireless connections, so that services and interconnections are coordinated on commercial premises; (3) it is based on the 'End-to-End Principle', which separates the transmission part, the Internet *per se*, from the 'ends', the inputs and outputs of the Internet. Most of the information carried, and most questions of responsibility, are located outside the transmission, in one or another end of the Internet. Accordingly, the transmission is 'designed to provide a neutral, transparent channel' (idem); (4) the global or non-territorial character of the Internet means that all the technical protocols, the routing structure, and the distribution of costs are all independent of distances as well as of jurisdictions.

Three core governance functions in relation to the Internet result from these technical and institutional features. First, *technical standards* replace government regulation to a large degree. The determination of those standards, accordingly, is of prime importance. Any change in them may endanger the function of the Internet, and the weight of interests attached to its workings is growing. Second, the *allocation of resources* is a significant issue – institutional resources, rather than financial and physical ones. The assignment of rights and identities, crucial to the function of the Internet, must be centrally controlled. In other policy areas, such distribution of specific rights and allocation of scarce, non-marketable resources[2] would have become the domain of government regulation. Third, a number of *public policy* issues remain – a policing function that prevents service providers from interfering with each others' rights, limits the impact of harmful communications, and ensures a stable function of the transmission systems. While the end-to-end principle implies that 'content' problems like harmful communication are not generic Internet problems, the Internet intervenes in existing legal systems and undermines their working in a way that calls for solutions (Baird *et al.* 2004).

While these particular characteristics are important to keep in mind, it is also relevant to stress that the Internet works through the international telecommunications network – the cables and other communications lines connecting the whole world. In both technical and regulatory terms, the Internet is part of the larger complex of information and communication technology (ICT) and associated policy and regulatory issues (Braithwaite and Drahos 2000; Siochrú and Girard 2002). It is significant that within the UN context, Internet governance has been conceived as essentially different from any other ICT.

In the mid-1990s, earlier attempts to build a multilateral governance system were based on the International Telecommunications Union (ITU). Yet, at the same time, the US government – the leading force in the invention of the Internet – opted for an almost complete self-regulation by the technical community and the private sector. The technical side of the Internet was left to non-state actors, and the only quasi-governmental structure was a technical system of standards and licenses.

There have also been a few, unsuccessful attempts to establish national, direct legal control of Internet contents, such as the US Communications Decency Act, which was passed in 1995, and then withdrawn in 1997 on the grounds that it violated the First Amendment's guarantee of freedom of speech. For the US, implementation of such laws would be difficult in a privatised telecommunications universe, but even for other governments, still in charge of telecommunications monopolies and less inhibited by civil rights concerns, the Internet remains technically difficult to regulate. For instance, the Chinese government regularly closes down access to particular sites that are deemed unhealthy for Chinese nationals (Deinert 2003; Mengin 2004), with not much results, though, on the ongoing battle between government controllers and Internet users. A number of states have pushed the content-providing industry to develop codes of conduct, standards, and other self-regulatory tools for content considered harmful, risky, or offensive (Price and Verhulst 2000: 57).

The Internet as an object of global governance

Three kinds of political concerns have set off the recent problematisation of the governance of the Internet within the UN context. First, the core resources of the Internet lack intergovernmental control, as it is the Internet Corporation for the Assignment of Names and Numbers (ICANN) that has been in charge of them since 1998. This private organisation oversees technical aspects of the Internet's domain name system, on the basis of a 'memorandum of understanding' (MoU) made with the US Department of Commerce. While it considers itself as independent, international, and inclusive – also for governments – contending views claim that in fact the US is in control and does not allow for meaningful (inter)governmental participation. This, and the lack of a link to international organisations, provoked controversy and fostered several attempts to influence its operations or establish alternative structures. The second concern relates to the 'digital divide': the enormous difference between the ubiquitous access to ICT facilities in the rich world and the absence of even elementary communication systems in the poorest places. As ICT grew in economic and societal importance, the poor nations were being even more excluded from largely agreed development objectives. Finally, some governments wanted to control Internet contents. While the US government (hesitatingly) accepted the principle of free speech on the Internet, others, like the Indian, Brazilian, Chinese, and South African governments, felt a strong urge to control contents – a difference still remaining (Kleinwächter 2004).

In the late 1990s, initiatives were taken that led the UN and the ITU to hold the WSIS in 2003–2005 (Klein 2003). The purpose was to establish some form of international umbrella for the Internet, but the issues proved difficult (MacLean 2004). In 2004–2005, a number of meetings were held: the Workshop on Internet Governance held by ITU on 26–27 February 2004, an ICANN Meeting on 2–6 March 2004, the Global Forum on Internet Governance, held by UN ICT Task Force on 25–26 March 2004, and two phases of the WSIS, the last in Tunis in November 2005. In both parts of WSIS, negotiations on Internet governance have been stalemated, despite a very shallow consensus on the need for further discussions among all stakeholders – conventionally listed as four groups: states, business, NGOs, and international organisations.

There were expectations that a new regulatory framework would be concerned with the coordination or oversight of existing governance mechanisms – a sort of 'metagovernance' function (Jessop 2003). Other developments pointed to the possibility of changes, especially the fact that the MoU between ICANN and the US was set to expire in 2006. ICANN stated in its 2004 Strategic Plan that it intended to cut all ties to the US government and function as a separate private entity in the future (www.icann.org/strategic-plan/strategic-plan-16nov04.pdf). Since then, however, the US government has renewed the concession of ICANN to oversee the domain name system, thereby foreclosing any significant role of international, intergovernmental bodies. So far, the institutional outcome of the WSIS efforts is the formation of the International Governance Forum (IGF) (www.intgovforum.org), which has no regulatory 'teeth' but allows for multi-stakeholder dialogue.

The business point of view has been to see Internet governance as a matter of technical coordination – what ICANN has referred to as 'plumbing' (ITU meeting on Internet governance) – while governments have seen it as a form of policy making with wide-ranging consequences. The struggle was won by the plumbers, leaving the field open to market forces and business self-regulation schemes. But nevertheless, the process has resulted in the construction and stabilisation of the Internet as an object of global governance, a field open to 'soft' regulation.

Government and governance

In the case of the Internet and its regulation, governmental interest has arrived at a late stage. And the *governance* arrangements involved do not resemble the classical ideal of *government*: they lack sovereignty, territoriality, legal regulation, and private/public distinctions.

In technical, scientific, and infrastructural issue areas, this is not an entirely novel occurrence. Most major scientific and technical innovations have been driven by professionals and the entrepreneurs, and governmental oversight has arrived late in the process. It is, however, significant that a major and important area of modern society remains outside the confines of the nation-states.

The acceptance of such conditions can be seen from another angle, as part of a general movement from 'government' towards 'governance' (Rhodes 1997; Kooiman 2003). The idea is that *networked* governance arrangements, in which state agencies and political offices participate along with commercial and professional groups, seem to be replacing arrangements that at least in principle were hierarchical, with the state as the sovereign power. In the case of the Internet, its governance system began in a network of scientists, and lately, participants in the system have been state agencies, as well as businesses, professional groups, NGOs, and international organisations. No power holder has been sovereign or hegemonic.

Apart from being networked, contemporary governance is *discursive* (Barry *et al.* 1996; Fuchs 2005) in the sense that it employs a specific language, expressing a particular logic, a rationality of governance, or 'governmentality'. That logic constitutes a certain perspective on the issues in question – it 'naturalises' its existence as an issue, suggests its causality, and frames the way the issue can be addressed or the problem solved. In the Internet case, there is obviously a plurality of different rationalities at play. The crucial contradiction between 'plumbing' and 'policy' and the different ideas about 'governance' and 'government' are responsible for the existence of several different ways of posing the problem of Internet governance.

Contemporary governance, furthermore, works with power that is *dispersed* among numerous power holders (Burchell *et al.* 1991; Dean 1999). In a Foucauldian sense, power equals resources – like money, knowledge, numbers, and authority. Whoever has relevant resources is able to influence the conduct of things, and thus has some sort of power, which is located, produced, and employed in numerous places. Governance, therefore, operates in a configuration without a sovereign, where a number of holders of different sorts of power interact. Out of the problematisation of Internet governance has emerged a notion of 'multi-stakeholder participation' as a key governance technique. This mode of governance not only allows for dialogue among adversaries, but also allows for the emergence of an entanglement of types of authorities that challenge traditional perspectives (Bislev and Flyverbom, forthcoming).

These three aspects of the shift from government to governance provide us with a distinct understanding of the increasingly blurred distinction between *public and private* spheres. In Max Weber's ideal typical model of the modern state, separating the private sphere from the public was one essential aspect. It is a distinction never entirely sharp in any realm of practice or discourse (Weintraub 1997), but liberal governmentality remains organised around the ideal of public man vs. private man (Sennett 1978). Lately, however, the two spheres are penetrating each other again – public concerns are being pressed on private lives (Dean 1999, and private sector rationalities are penetrating the public sphere (Hansen *et al.* 2000; Pollitt and Bouckaert 2000; Christensen and Lægreid 2001). The Internet is simultaneously public and private. It is the first dialogical mass medium – a powerful means of communication and of direct intervention in public affairs, useable by anyone disregarding status and authority. Private citizens can publicise their lives on the net. All governments are using the system and relying on its operations, but also accepting, more or less, that they take part in it on an equal footing with private organisations and companies.

Business and public responsibility

What we observe in the discourse of ICT businesses on Internet governance is a hesitation to assume direct responsibility for governance functions. Businesses wish to preserve what they call their 'freedom' to act as they see fit, but do not want to prescribe directly what others can do, or what is allowable in general.

A notion of communal responsibility, of being a good citizen, or of playing a societal or social role, however, is not foreign to businesses. Social issues were always discussed by idealistic business people (Carroll 1996). In the early twentieth century, notions of corporations replacing the state in the provision of social benefits gained some prominence, although never with any large effect (Esping-Andersen 1985). The ascendancy of the welfare state seemed to invest the state with general responsibility for societal affairs and reduce business to a status of merely economic action. Milton Friedman, arguing against not only the social engineering of the welfare state, but also the idea of any social responsibilities of business (Friedman 1970), seemed to emphasise that. It was Friedman, however, that became the guru for the conservative reaction of the 1980s wanting to roll back the state and let society be ruled by markets and morals (Savoie 1994).

As the untenability of this position became clear to more people in the 1990s, the discussion of the societal role for business was re-actualised – framed now as 'business ethics', 'corporate citizenship', and 'corporate social responsibility' (CSR). Quite logically, the present period of unprecedented power for business has become the era of questioning its conduct, and today, few large corporations or business associations dare neglect the expectation that they embrace CSR notions and act accordingly in one way or another (Garriga and Melée 2004; Werhane and Freeman 2005).

All the most important ICT corporations have CSR policies of one kind or another, and a number of them are taking part in the discussions about Internet governance. In their capacity as major actors in relation to the Internet, they possess huge powers and responsibilities, and they have to try to use those possibilities at the same time as they must demonstrate social responsibility and prove that they are not thinking solely in terms of private interest and profits. For some of them, the participation in the governance process is portrayed in the same light as the attention to social responsibilities: it is all done philanthropically, as a duty of citizenship, and not as part of striving for profits and position.

In the rest of the chapter, we sketch how two ICT companies, Hewlett-Packard and Cisco Systems, and a business association, the International Chamber of Commerce (ICC), contribute to the acceptance of TPG of the Internet. While it is outside our reach to prove business influence, we can provide examples of the strategies and actions of business representatives and attempt to evaluate the intentions acted upon and perhaps some of their effects.

Hewlett-Packard, the giant computer corporation, provides a good case for studying the opportunities and ambiguities involved in business and Internet governance. H-P has an extensive CSR agenda, including several philanthropic projects to further the acquisition of computer literacy and the development of adequate ICT infrastructures. On top of that, H-P is also actively involved in ICT regulation, including the emerging governance mechanisms for the Internet (Smith 2002).

Cisco Systems, the largest provider of ICT infrastructure services and equipment, such as routers and other Internet backbone technology, is heavily involved in Internet governance and ICT policies more broadly. Cisco ties its CSR activities closely to its governance efforts, participates in a number of policy networks, and participates actively in UN efforts at rethinking the area of Internet governance. The ICC, the global business association, advocates business views on the importance of trade and investment, open markets, and the free flow of capital to governments and intergovernmental bodies. In relation to Internet governance, the ICC is very active and publishes lengthy reports, participates in all relevant policy dialogues, and functions as the main business coordinator and partner in UN summits and in relation to the various UN agencies (www.iccwbo.org/home/menu_what_is_icc.asp).

The strategies employed by business in the ongoing 'problematisation' of Internet governance take multiple forms; below, they are exemplified according to the three above-mentioned key aspects which distinguish governance strategies from government practices: discursive strategies, networking strategies, and partnership strategies.

Discursive strategies

This strategy revolves around disseminating statements, positions, and commentaries on developments within Internet governance, both in very public contexts and in more limited circles.

Both Cisco and H-P present their CSR activities in the area of ICTs in great detail and stress the importance of these not only for those at the receiving end, but also as sources of inspiration for policy makers and regulatory bodies in need of best practice cases, learning experiences, and partnerships that will help them find the most suitable policy solutions and approaches.

> H-P has defined a set of ethics and governance practices that it claims to follow in this area, using phrases like: 'Creating value to customers without compromising the health of the planet'; 'encourage employees to engage in communities'; and 'close the gap between technology-empowered and technology-excluded communities'; 'engaging in partnerships with both public and private entities'.
>
> (www.hp.com/hpinfo/globalcitisenship/commitment.html)

With those claims, H-P wants to be visible as a CSR-conscious actor, addressing most of the known issue areas, using most of the available discourses and managerial techniques, and focusing primarily on the North–South issue. Such statements are to some extent 'speech acts'. The company will expose itself to severe public criticism, if it is seen not to follow those intentions. Thus, we can expect HP to 'contribute' in some of the stated ways. To have any material effect, however, internally or externally, the declarations need to come closer to 'hard' matters like rules and resources. Most of them are not binding, policy declarations; they do not constitute internal rules, nor necessarily involve resource allocations, nor commit to existing or future agreements.

But CSR is more than serving the community. First, H-P signals that the CSR goals go together with economic goals: 'we hope to speed sustainable economic development and create new markets for HP and our partners. . . .' (ibid). Second, H-P seems to be turning its philanthropic and corporate citizenship activities into *strategic* attempts at setting political agendas through a pro-active, 'naturalising', and holistic approach. Rather than drawing a clear demarcation line between philanthropy, marketing, and government relations, H-P seems to be pursuing an integrated approach to positioning itself at the centre of concrete problem-solving and long-term solution development.

A close familiarity between CSR and political participation is thus suggested: a qualitatively different relation between politics and business as 'collaborative' and 'hands-on', and where government should suspend its regulatory role and become advisor and *partner* instead (Policymaking in the Internet Age, speech by Fiorina). It is not a consistent point, however. Then H-P CEO, C. Fiorina, did not hesitate to express at the same time a traditional liberal view on the division of labour between business and state: 'we like to encourage policy-makers to focus their sights on policy making, … on … the minimally acceptable set of standards'.

Similarly, Cisco has developed a comprehensive discursive strategy promoting its CSR and digital divide activities, with lengthy reports, various programs, and activities. Representatives from Cisco intervene repeatedly in policy dialogues such as those initiated by the UN ICT Task Force and the WGIG – sometimes as representatives of the company, sometimes as representatives for ICC, and sometimes as vice-chairman of the UN ICT Task Force. In these contexts, Cisco steadfastly promotes the 'plumbing' rationality. Cisco publishes a quarterly journal, the *Internet Protocol Journal*, purporting to be an informational and educational resource on technical issues pertaining to the Internet. In an online discussion forum on Internet governance hosted by UNDP's Asia Pacific Development Information Program, the editor of the journal notably stated that 'The technical stuff that makes the Internet work OPERATIONALLY is called COORDINATION, and it is specifically different from governance in that it depends on collaborative processes rather than mandates, laws and rules … the Internet … operates just fine without any governance' (http://lists.apdip.net/pipermail/igovap/ Week-of-Mon-20050110/000058.html).

It is worth noting the extent to which Cisco supports the view of Internet governance as merely technical coordination by arguing against the very term governance, which they associate with governmental, top-down, and rule-based forms of regulation (Flyverbom 2005). If the governance problem, thus, is merely technical coordination, politicians and administrators simply need to be educated, so that they will realise the dangers of regulating the Internet. It is all a question of learning the correct, the only logical rationality.

The ICC, on its part, has published a number of reports on Internet governance; it has also been heavily involved in all the major events related to this issue under the umbrella of the UN. In this context, the ICC consistently argues that technical coordination must be clearly distinguished from public policy issues; like Cisco, it assumes that the very concept of Internet governance as misleading, as it allegedly implies that 'a single entity controls the Internet' (MacLean 2004: 170). Existing private organisations carrying out technical coordination should remain in control. ICC seeks influence through discursive means by presenting its material as a 'helping hand' to those seeking to understand the Internet and its surrounding technologies, and as 'roadmaps' and 'matrices' for the kinds of political (non-)decisions that will ensure the future growth and smooth operation of the Internet.

The strategy presented in this section is discursive in nature. It intends, through the creation and dissemination of meanings, to shape the activities subsumed under the heading of Internet governance as well as influence the more general view of the roles and responsibilities of business in social and political life. It does so by identifying and naming problems and solutions, bringing important resources into the field – such as knowledge, access, and status – that are relevant to the problematisation taking place and that enable the participants to be heard in this situation.

Multi-stakeholder participation as networking

The ICC and Cisco argue against governmental interventions in the management of the Internet, but not to the extent that they reject cooperation with governments. While assigning distinct roles and responsibilities to the different sectors involved in the Internet, they support the notion that all sectors must take part in carrying out concerted action. Such actions, however, must be voluntary and based on learning and persuasion, not rules and coercion. The WSIS process adopted the notion of multi-stakeholder participation, which was not only widely accepted and applauded, but has since been posited as the key characteristic and raison d'être of the Internet Governance Forum. When we talk about authority in the area of Internet governance, this kind of international institutional embeddedness is crucial (cf. conclusions of this volume).

All three actors investigated in this article have a high level of visibility in all the relevant policy bodies, summits, and dialogues, often with high-level representation by CEOs (although in practice, there is an extensive reliance on alternates).

The ICC chairs the Coordinating Committee of Business Interlocutors of the WSIS and thus functions as the primary coordinator of business input into the summit. The ICC's Commission on E-Business, IT, and Telecoms has created an advisory committee to address the issue of Internet governance directly. In this context, the ICC presents its rationale for engaging in the UN problematisations of Internet governance and the ICT domain in the following way: 'It is only by leveraging the entrepreneurial spirit of business, harnessing private sector resources – and putting them to work in partnership with others – that we will truly realise the full potential of an information society' (Cattaui, Secretary General ICC, Chair of that Committee, http://businessatwsis.net/mainpages/position/introduction/index.php?PHPSESSID=7e7bdc3fd3e4e6d9234cba40c8b9ba02). H-P is involved in the work of the UN ICT Task Force, and an H-P vice president chairs the working group on 'business enterprise and entrepreneurship'. H-P was very visible during the WSIS and had one of the larger stands in a prime location of the ICT4D platform where ICT companies, international organisations, aid initiatives, and others involved in ICT activities could showcase projects, products, and 'best practice'. When asked why H-P is involved in UN policy dialogues, such as WSIS and the UN ICT Task Force, Kristin Hughes, Federal and International Public Policy Manager alternate for Fiorina and CSR manager Dunn in most UN meetings, replied that rather than affecting government policies directly, these policy dialogues play an important role 'from a process or educational point of view' as they help governments and policy makers understand that 'the ways in which their policies affect companies' efforts at bridging the digital divide', at increasing connectivity and at 'creating opportunities' in what she calls 'emerging market countries'.[3]

Cisco is involved in the UN ICT Task Force, the Global Knowledge Partnership, and the Coordinating Committee of Business Interlocutors of WSIS, and also actively participates in the consultations and activities of the Working Group of Internet Governance. Partnerships such as the UN ICT Task Force, in which governmental representatives take part and in which business actors like H-P, Cisco, and ICC play a significant role, work towards the development of business-friendly ICT policies. Under the heading of an 'enabling environment', the UN ICT Task Force deals with a complex of issues listed as the 'promotion of regulatory regimes conducive to elimination of barriers for competition and to encouraging investments in communications infrastructure, support for the development of comprehensive and sustainable ICT-for-development policies and national e-strategies' (www.unicttaskforce.org/perl/showdoc.pl?area=enab).

H-P and Cisco have spent considerable resources on initiating operational partnerships aiming to bridge the digital divide. H-P has initiated a number of spectacular projects, most notably 'e-Inclusion' in 2001, a program spending 1 billion dollars on increasing access to ICTs in developing countries. These social investment programs presently focus on broadening access, employing ICTs in education and in community projects.

In the case of Cisco, the launch of 'Networking Academies' in 1997 with a number of education institutions has provided technical training in the design, maintenance, and building of ICT networks. According to the latest figures, Cisco has almost 10,000 academies around the world, providing 260,000 students with technical ICT training (www.cisco.com/en/US/learning/netacad/academy/About.html).

Such CSR activities, aimed at narrowing the digital divide and providing ICT education, serve numerous ends for companies like H-P and Cisco. They help position themselves as pioneers in the area of CSR; yet, as selected CSR issues are close to their business concerns, they also help building future markets. With respect to TPG, this strategy is employed by business to show governments the importance of, and the kind of, policies needed to encourage ICT-driven economic development. Concrete projects are models and opportunities through which business can influence policy makers through learning, providing expertise, and showcasing 'best practice'.

Business, partnerships, and political authority

Partnership is an endearing term, evoking notions and feelings of cooperation, construction, equality, and reciprocity. It is also an imprecise term. In a governance context, it shrouds the elements of power and influence in a discourse of cooperation and shared responsibility. In an emerging, cross-national field like Internet governance, partnership serves to permit experiments and to let the strong and the knowledgeable be involved in governance without giving up their cherished autonomy.

For business, the discourse of 'partnership' is employed to normalise a form of Internet governance where businesses are deeply involved. Other participants

– officials, organisations, media, and individuals – come to perceive their activity as authoritative, as the way the technology is regulated. This sort of patched-together authority is not undisputed (Kleinwächter 2004), but after a hegemonic struggle it seems that the mixed governance arrangements emerge victorious on the scene.

The business actors we have looked at support an interpretation of Internet governance as technical coordination. This interpretation, however, has not won general acceptance. Challenged by civil society organisations and researchers (APC 2004, Mueller *et al*, in MacLean 2004), it did not gain hegemony in the WGIG. Rather than simple technical coordination, most of what a body like ICANN does is known to have broad ramifications for the public, therefore being a form of governance subject to political processes.

The strategies pursued in this context help establishing business as a source of expertise and inspiration for governments and intergovernmental organisations involved in Internet governance. This may be described as a learning approach – as opposed to a lobbying approach – to political influence, where business exemplifies the merits of particular policy approaches and shows its expertise, rather than demanding concessions from governments and regulatory bodies. Increasingly, business works through *involvement*: it informs government officials about the possibilities and needs of the ICT sectors and convinces them about the willingness of companies such as H-P, Cisco, and ICC to provide relevant resources. Together – as partners – they develop a discourse about the way things can and must be done in the field. One powerful technique is the use of a demonstration effect: H-P and Cisco establish spectacular ICT projects in developing countries as an efficient way of demonstrating the positive role and contribution of the corporation (Smith 2002).

Conclusion

For a superficial view, the Internet is not subject to 'private governance': states and international organisations are significantly involved. The special status of states, however – their sovereignty – which is what makes them states, is not so important when they take part in Internet governance. While states and international organisations remain significantly involved in some aspects of Internet governance, the interaction among a wider range of participants tends to empower a new network of private partners – partners that all have rights to participate and, at times, to veto decisions despite their unequal power. To facilitate this interaction, multi-stakeholder participation plays a key role as a governance technique that allows hitherto dispersed, even antagonistic, groups to collaborate.

Manoeuvring in such different rationalities represents a challenge for business. Corporations like Cisco and H-P seem to be bringing together not only philanthropic and profit objectives, but also political/policy objectives, via the partnership principle. The partnership approach to gain political influence emphasises consensus over conflict, aims at values rather than regulations, employs qualitative rather than quantifiable resources, and values entrepreneurship over philanthropy. It involves, incites and invites, centres on convergence of interest, responds to local demands and needs, and is culturally and contextually sensitive. In a Foucauldian perspective, it is both a discursive development, where the discourse of partnership and empowerment gains ground and normalises the role of corporations, and, clearly, a form of 'productive power', where the power of a corporation consists of its ability to do things, to build, and to develop institutions and competence.

In the context of a late-liberal, post-welfare society, partnership is a distinctive form of an emergent governmentality, which puts little emphasis on the public–private divide and gives rise to new conceptions of democracy (Dean 1999; Miller and Rose 1992). Instead of ideas of popular representation and participation, democracy – or legitimate political authority – is understood to be built on professionalism and pluralism – a form of global elitism. In this new rationality, business comes to the forefront, not only with tools used in new public management and the acceptance of corporations as ethical and responsible citizens seen in CSR, but also as an increasingly important player in global politics. In the area of Internet governance explored in this chapter, business corporations and business associations are clearly influential in setting agendas, proposing policies, and participating in decision processes.

Notes

1 Technical standards have historically been produced through a decision-making process, where participants are not elected or representative, nor authorised by a sovereign state – but operate according to expectations of openness, transparency, and professionalism (Frankel, 2004, p. 93).

2 Interestingly, this anarchistic and unregulated area has not seen the emergence of competing standards and institutions otherwise predicted by neo-liberal institutional theory. No alternative protocols have been tried or suggested, no private server networks with exclusive access launched as alternatives to the open, quasi-public ones. Only recently has the idea of a Business Class Internet – particularly high bandwidth, speed, and reliability for paying users – been launched with some force.

3 Personal interview conducted with H-P representative, at WSIS I, Geneva, December 2003.

10 Who governs the Internet?

The emerging regime of e-commerce

Josep Ibáñez

Transnational private governance (TPG) has become a prominent phenomenon in the history of cyberspace. The growth of the Internet and of electronic commerce has been successfully managed and promoted by various forms of TPG. But, the resulting patterns of power and order also show the limits of private actors in governing social relations at the transnational level. The analysis of such patterns will illustrate how important the role played by private authorities has been in the control of electronic markets in the Internet. The power of private actors in this domain has clearly exceeded the power of public authorities, and very often such power has been backed by some legitimacy, by some acknowledgement that those private actors were authorised to exercise it. When power is vested with authority and when it is exercised by private authorities, then it is an act of private authority (Strange 1996; Cutler 1999). In electronic markets, private authorities have been decisive in the emergence of an e-commerce regime.

Since the beginning of the commercial activities in cyberspace, some American corporations have been in a privileged position to be able to control the structures of power and to determine what users and consumers can and cannot do. Such control has been exercised through a combination of resources and instruments shaping the emerging e-commerce regime. Thus, order has been increasingly established and assured in the electronic markets, but very often according to the preferences of the private sector, in the interest of business, and at the expense of public interests. In order to balance this situation, public authorities have a fundamental role to play and should be expected to fulfil their responsibilities for the sake of social justice. The argument of the chapter unfolds in three sections. The first provides a brief description of the structural nature of power on the Internet and in electronic markets. The second presents the analytical framework and examines the core features of the e-commerce regime. The third considers normative implications of the emergence and limits of TPG in cyberspace.

Conceptual clarification: structural power in electronic markets

The nature of power in information and communication technologies (ICTs), as in any other field of activity in international relations, is both relational and structural. The same statement applies to the Internet and to the electronic markets created in cyberspace. The development and expansion of the Internet is part of broader developments in various areas of the ICTs – telecommunications, microelectronics, and computing. This is why similar patterns of power might be expected in cyberspace when compared with other ICT areas. However, the structural dimension of power and the privileged position of private actors are specific features of the Internet, at least for two reasons. First, at the technical level, the Internet protocols and the architecture of the Internet allow for decentralised communications and lack of central control, which affects some structural elements of cyberspace without much interference by public actors. Second, at the social level, the plurality of actors and factors contributing to the emergence and present shaping of the Internet underlines the private character of the Internet and the minor relative weight of public involvement in the process (Rosenzweig 1998).

In terms of power patterns, e-commerce on the Internet is not substantially different from other activities taking place in cyberspace. A broad definition of e-commerce comprises all activities entailing an exchange of value between economic agents through electronic means. Older forms of e-commerce, such as transactions with EDI (electronic data interchange) and EFT (electronic fund transfer) systems, were important tools for business and markets. But the economic use of the Internet since the beginning of the 1990s represented a revolution for e-commerce and transformed electronic markets into open and accessible economic spaces. Business to business (B2B) has become the leading economic form of e-commerce on the Internet, but other activities such as business to consumer (B2C), business to government (B2G), and government to consumer (G2C) have also flourished in less than a decade. All these activities have shaped electronic markets on the Internet. Since cyberspace provides electronic markets with physical infrastructures, software code, and digital content, power patterns on the Internet will necessarily coincide with power patterns in e-commerce.

In electronic markets, power is the ability of actors both to influence other actors and to create the framework of economic relations taking place on the Internet. In international relations, powerful actors are highly interested in the existence of order, and they provide for such order. In cyberspace, there is also order – a pattern of behaviour among the stakeholders oriented to the maintenance and expansion of benefits and profits arising from economic activities on the Internet. As the next section will describe, the sources and instruments of control assuring such order have reached a high stage of development and they constitute an emerging regime of e-commerce.

This regime, as any other regime, benefits mainly those actors involved in its creation and maintenance – the most powerful actors. Some of them are public authorities, like the US government and agencies, the European governments and EU institutions, the governments of some Organisation for Economic Co-operation and Development (OECD) countries, and the agencies of some inter-governmental organisations – World Intellectual Property Organisation (WIPO), International Telecommunications Union (ITU), World Trade Organisation (WTO), United Nations Commission on International Trade Law (UNCITRAL), and so on. Some other powerful players are private technical agencies, such as the Internet Corporation for Assigned Names and Numbers (ICANN), the Internet Society (ISOC), or the World Wide Web Consortium (W3C). And sometimes private organisations with more social and political consciousness – even organisations linked to hackerism – have played significant roles, such as the Free Software Foundation, the Open Source movement and Linux, the Electronic Frontier Foundation, or the Hacker's Defence Foundation. But since the commercialisation of the Internet at the beginning of the 1990s, the most powerful actors have been private companies with business interests on the Internet. They have imposed their preferences and conditions in cyberspace, and quite often with state acceptance and recognition. Tensions between public authorities as opposed to private actors and authorities have sometimes arisen, but overall private interests of big companies have tended to prevail without much resistance by public authorities.

Despite the above-mentioned dual dimension of power in electronic markets, the structural dimension is particularly decisive in order to determine the conditions of markets in cyberspace. Following Susan Strange (1988), we can affirm that the structure of power in e-commerce is formed by the mix of institutions, norms, values, and beliefs governing the electronic markets. It is the result of stakeholders' preferences, but likewise it shapes the framework of relationships where these preferences are defined and it constraints the action of governments, companies, and international organisations, both governmental and non-governmental. The resources allowing for those structures to be in place are very diverse. As Strange would have put it, several power structures converge in electronic markets. First, there is the trade structure determining what goods and services are exchanged in cyberspace, how, in which conditions, and by whom. Second, the financial structure partly determines the availability of credit necessary for those commercial operations through electronic transactions, how can they be made, in which conditions, and by whom. Third, the production structure determines what is produced in the ICT sector, with what technology, in which conditions, and by what companies. Last but not least, there is the knowledge structure, which determines what technology and knowledge are acquired, how they are kept, who diffuse it, through what means, to whom, and in what conditions. Closely related to the knowledge structure would be the culture structure, although the borders between these two power domains are rather fuzzy and hardly discernible. The political economy of e-commerce shows how interlinked the trade structure, the production structure, and the knowledge structure are, and how changes in any of these structures are transferred to the others. Knowledge is the critical resource in any of these changes. The historical importance of the information revolution lies in the transformation of the traditional ways of producing and transmitting knowledge, and cyberspace and e-commerce are outcomes of such historic transformation.

The governance of the issues and risks arising from these outcomes have been managed by the most powerful actors according to their interests and preferences. The actions of major players have been directed at controlling uncertainties in the electronic markets of cyberspace. But governing the Internet, generating governance mechanisms, or contributing to create a new international regime were not their aims. The emergence of an e-commerce regime is a collateral or unintentional result of the structural power exercised by the major players in electronic markets. Their logic behind their action leads very often to informal sources and instruments of control, and these governance mechanisms tend to work without strong hierarchical structures or institutional support. In the business environment and in industry and business associations, TPG certainly works. But in broader social and political contexts, the limits of such private governance mechanisms are also very obvious; issues related to social concerns, economic inequalities, political legitimacy, and so on go well beyond the technical or economic functions fulfilled by those private actors at the transnational level.

Analytical framework: the control of the Internet

The power structure governing electronic markets determines the conditions of exchanges of goods and services in cyberspace. The business sector has mostly been interested in the development of those markets and has pushed private interests so that they prevail over public interests in negotiations affecting the shape of electronic markets. Inter-firm cooperation has made it possible for the private sector to influence governments more effectively so that private demands are assumed, and the US government has been particularly receptive to them. Overall, the major claim put forward by companies has been (private) self-regulation of electronic markets, and this principle has been broadly acknowledged by the US government, the EU institutions, and by all OECD countries. Big companies with some interest in e-commerce have led the self-regulation processes establishing normative frameworks and technical configurations allowing them to expand their business with a wide margin of manoeuvre.

American and European public authorities promoted the self-regulatory approach and helped it in at least four ways. First, they monitored the effective implementation of private instruments of control and used public means for the sake of such implementation – economic resources, governmental bodies, courts, and so on. Second, they adopted public instruments of control when private authorities especially requested them, as the intellectual property regime clearly shows. Third, when necessary, they cooperated through intergovernmental organisations in order to assure the harmonisation of electronic markets at a transnational level. Fourth, they denied public incentives to private initiatives of minor players – free source and open source promoters, hackers, start-ups, and so on – and, by so doing, public authorities contributed to the strengthening of rules and regulations imposed by big players in the electronic markets.

American corporations control the Internet

The power structure of e-commerce is inevitably interlinked with the power structure in the production of all the necessary infrastructure, software, and contents required by e-commerce. Telecommunication operators, hardware companies, software firms, and big content producers (mainly entertainment content) establish the conditions for the production of the material and digital basis of electronic markets. In the three layers of the production structure, the environment of each industry and the nature of companies do differ, but similar forms of competition have developed, with strong concentration processes and oligopolistic structures in most of the industries and markets involved. The activities of some of these industries and markets have historically been tightly controlled by public authorities, but the processes of economic globalisation, the ICT revolution, and the widespread adoption of neoliberal policies have tended to alleviate such control.

During the 1990s, the liberalisation of telecommunications put many state monopolies in a difficult situation; these public companies lost state protection, but at the same time they were helped to enter broader international markets in extremely favourable conditions of competition. Some of the new players in the liberalised international markets were remarkably benefited, whereas other players went through mergers or acquisitions which transformed the markets and industries in fundamental ways. In any case, liberalisation processes reduced the power of public authorities in the telecommunication markets.

In the computer industry, since the arrival of the first PCs, public control has been almost non-existent. A few hardware companies have controlled the world production of computers in the best suitable conditions that they established for themselves. The antitrust case against IBM, closed down by the US government in 1982, did not prevent this company from keeping its leading role in the computer industry, although the environment was certainly more competitive with the participation of other giants like HP-Compaq, Sun Microsystems, and Dell. Since the mid-1990s, the patterns of business concentration have intensified and a greatly reduced number of manufacturers control every single segment of the industry, while the restructuring or diversification of Internet activities has helped these big manufacturers to now enter the Internet service business. Regarding computer chips, the oligopoly is even more acute, with Intel prevailing over all other players, despite the fierce competition having arisen for the last decade from Asian manufacturers – initially Japanese, later Korean, and Taiwanese. Combined with Microsoft's power in the software industry, this prevalence gave rise to Wintelism, a huge reflection of power in the production structure of the computer sector (Borrus and Zyzman 1997; Hart and Sangbae 2002). With the spreading of Internet and the worldwide web at the beginning of the 1990s, software production patterns shifted in a significant manner. Nevertheless, if there is one company with structural power in the digital economy, this company is still Microsoft.

Companies producing content for electronic markets have not only eluded the control of public authorities, but they have also received public help in the liberalisation of information flows through copyright protection laws. The production structure of Internet content is greatly determined by the big corporations, most of them American, controlling the mass media – Time-Warner, Disney, Bertelsmann, Viacom, News Corporation, Universal, NBC, TCI, Philips, Polygram, Sony, and so on. During the last decade, in order to deliver their services and products, they have intensified their cooperation with big telecommunication companies, hardware manufacturers, and software producers.

In the domain of Internet content, the production structure of global political economy meets the knowledge structure and feeds 'cultural power' – the ability to shape the knowledge processes in a society, the ability to directly or indirectly shape concept systems (Comor 1999: 118–19). As two US government advisors bluntly stated: 'This new political and technological landscape is ready-made for the United States to capitalise on its formidable tools of soft power, to project the appeal of its ideals, ideology, culture, economic model, and social and political institutions, and to take advantage of its international business and telecommunications networks'. In terms of soft power, the result has been clear: 'American leadership in the information revolution has generally increased global awareness of and openness to American ideas and values' (Nye and Owens 1996: 29). This sort of soft power, as well as the historical wave of neoliberalism developed since the beginning of the 1980s and translated into the policies of the Washington Consensus, has undoubtedly contributed to spread homogeneity of values in TPG practices for electronic markets.

US public authorities have a rather limited control over the knowledge structure, whose power patterns are established by the big American ICT companies. It is not necessarily accurate to identify US business interests and US national interest, and not only because of the imprecise and doubtful content of the 'national interest', but also because the welfare of American citizens is not improved more by profits of the companies' affiliates abroad than by profits from foreign companies' affiliates in the United States (Reich 1991).

Order on the Internet: sources and instruments of control in e-commerce

Large ICT companies, most of them American, control the power structures of world e-commerce. The international (or transnational) regime of e-commerce is the result of such control and has been brought about by cooperation and bargaining between firms, as well as between public and private authorities. As in other social spaces, order in cyberspace serves mainly the interests of those who establish the rules, principles, norms, and values of such order. And this represents the main limit of TPG in electronic markets. Broader socioeconomic

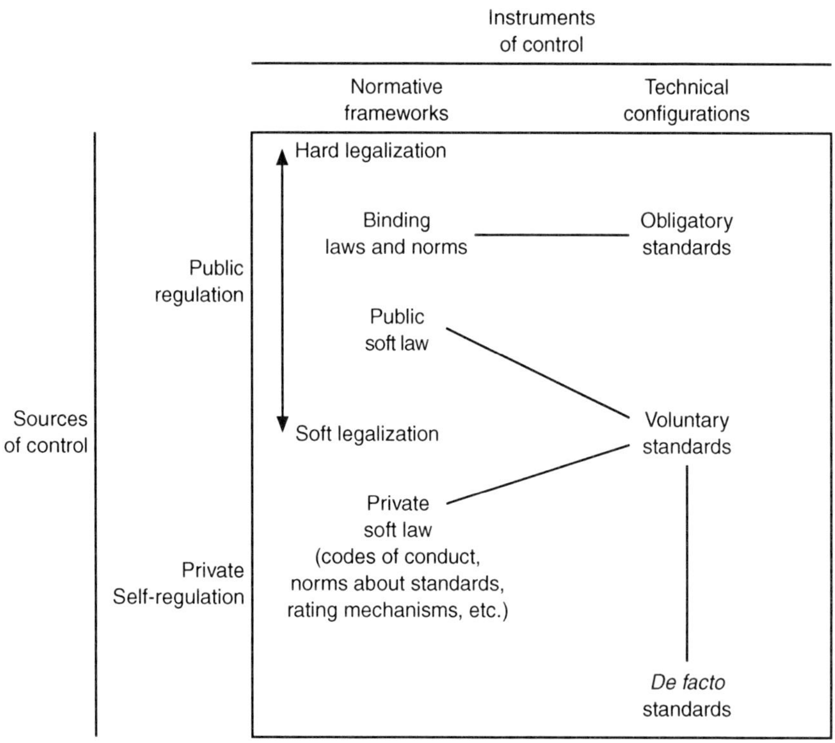

Figure 10.1 Sources and instruments of control in e-commerce regime

concerns and interests are not necessarily embedded in the order promoted by major players in cyberspace.

Order on the Internet lies between the structural dimension of power and each of the major players' actions to promote their interests in electronic markets. Also between structural- and actor-biased perspectives lies our analytical framework, which identifies the main sources and instruments of control at the basis of the e-commerce regime. A simple model integrates these two sets of means for the control of electronic markets, and this combination is represented in Figure 10.1.

On the one hand, the two fundamental sources of control are public regulation and private self-regulation. Public regulation refers to public instruments of control, normally regulatory frameworks that establish rules for the functioning of electronic markets, either through binding laws or through soft law. Occasionally, public authorities contribute to the creation of obligatory technical standards, although technical configurations are usually determined by market operators. Private regulation or self-regulation refers to private instruments of control, both regulatory frameworks and technical configurations. Quite interestingly, the transnational nature of electronic markets brings these sources of control to the transnational level, and the traditional state-based debate between regulation and self-regulation has been transferred to the global arena. Electronic markets are not national markets, and any private or public framework addressed at governing them must also have a transnational or global character. In any case, the types of policies emerging from public and private sources are mainly of regulatory nature, not redistributive.

On the other hand, two fundamental instruments of control are the normative or regulatory frameworks, and the technical configurations of electronic markets. Regulatory frameworks from public sources refer to legal norms and soft law (in any degree of legalisation), as well as to the public acknowledgement of standards being used by market operators and users. Regulatory frameworks from private sources refer to private norms and standards effectively regulating how businesses operate on the Internet – codes of conduct, formal and informal adoption of technical standards, rating mechanisms, and so on. Technical configurations refer to the technology necessary for the functioning of electronic markets, and this is determined mainly by private sources of control, since market operators produce and diffuse the technology that becomes standard in the market. These technical standards often emerge from competition between companies to become de facto standards, but many times technical standards are established with the help of regulatory frameworks, either norms of soft law (voluntary standards) or norms of hard law (obligatory standards).

The e-commerce regime

One of the main questions being addressed here is whether the normative frameworks regulating e-commerce constitute a regime or not. From a formal perspective, in line with the generally accepted definition of international regime, the existence of an e-commerce regime is clear. Electronic markets are governed by 'principles, norms, rules, and decision-making procedures around which actors' expectations converge in a given area of international relations' (Krasner 1983: 2). A decade after the beginning of commercial activities on the Internet, the institutions governing e-commerce appear to have reached a certain level of development: the domain name system, the protection of intellectual property, the legal security of digital contracts and signatures, the acknowledgement of secure means of payment, or the tax regime for electronic transactions on the Internet are some of the core issues of e-commerce already addressed by the emerging international regime.

But are we really considering one international regime or a series of international regimes? From a theoretical perspective, Friedrich Kratochwil tackled some of the difficulties arising from the imprecise limits of international regimes – or the connections between some of them (Kratochwil 1993). According to his view, the material specificity of a regime is a necessary condition for its existence, though an insufficient one, since the specific issue should also be highly consensual. Certainly, institutions controlling e-commerce do not refer to a specific issue area, rather to a number of different and sometimes connected areas.

These are not always precisely bounded, and their consensual character is sometimes strong, sometimes weak.

When considering the existence of an e-commerce regime in electronic markets, as in any issue area, these difficulties might be avoided by distinguishing between categories. In turn, this would allow the creation of a basic typology of regimes partly based on Kratochwil's work. He distinguished between explicit and implicit regimes, public and secret regimes, and formal and informal regimes (1993: 84–92). Taking into consideration some of the categories used in Figure 10.1 (sources of control and instruments of control), here we introduce a series of criteria and distinctions regarding:

1 Development. Institutions forming a regime may be at a low or embryonic stage of development, or they may be well established, at a higher stage. The degree of development depends on the density, soundness, and consistency of norms, and not on how long they have been developing, although older regimes tend to include a higher number and more consistent norms.
2 Structure. Institutions forming a regime may be specific to an issue area or they may belong to connected but different issue areas. In the former case, the regime would be simple, while in the latter, the regime would have a complex structure.
3 Density. The number of norms and the degree of connection between them will determine whether the regime is very dense or not. There is a correlation between the degree of density and the stage of development because the former is a function of the latter, although they refer to different features of a regime.
4 Legalisation. Depending on how institutionalised the norms of a regime are, a basic distinction must be made between 'hard' legalisation and 'soft' legalisation (Abbott *et al.* 2000). This criterium refers to instruments of control identified in Figure 10.1 as normative frameworks, and in particular to those established by public regulation as the source of control in electronic markets.
5 Authority. When considering the source of authority from which the regime emerges, there is a basic distinction between public regimes, private regimes, and, if both forms combine, hybrid or mixed regimes – in any such hybrid regime, there will always be a predominance of either public regulation or private self-regulation.

This criterium corresponds to the sources of control defined in Figure 10.1 (public regulation vs. self-regulation).

According to these categories, a characterisation of the e-commerce regime easily emerges. First, in order to evaluate the degree of development, it is necessary to bear in mind the fundamental feature distinguishing electronic markets from traditional markets, i.e. e-commerce activities take place (at least partly) on the Internet, not in the 'real' world. Thus, whether an e-commerce regime exists or not will to some extent depend on the existence of an Internet regime. Marcus

Franda has extensively dealt with this question, and, in his view, the Internet regime is embryonic and incomplete (Franda 2001: 213). In the same vein, Milton Mueller considers that the ICANN and other important technical non-governmental bodies are part of a nascent international regime (Mueller 2002: 212). Although the e-commerce regime is fed with norms from other well-established regimes, Internet governance is still at an embryonic and less developed stage, and the regime of electronic markets is still in formation.

Second, e-commerce is not really a specific issue area, but a combination of diverse issue areas from traditional and electronic markets. The e-commerce regime is formed by the mix of norms from different regimes regulating commercial activities on the Internet: international trade, intellectual property, foreign investment, international contracts, personal data protection, to name but a few. Each of these regimes has its own features of development, structure, density, legalisation, and authority. Thus, the convergence in the e-commerce regime of norms from other very diverse regimes makes its structure particularly complex. And such complexity stresses the difficulty to articulate norms from international regimes which operate rather autonomously in traditional markets, but which are inextricably linked with each other in electronic markets. This is the case of the relationship between privacy protection and the global agreement on trade in services (GATS), between the trade-related aspects of intellectual property rights (TRIPS) and the World Intellectual Property Organisation (WIPO) treaties, or between GATS and the protection of computer systems.

Third, the e-commerce regime is very dense because its high number of norms and the connections between them. Obviously, the complex structure of the regime adds to its density and difficulty of articulation: norms against harmful contents obstruct freedom of expression; privacy protection norms may conflict with those trying to maximise security; or norms assuring freedom of expression may interfere with these protecting intellectual property. Therefore, a choice of values and priorities will be critical to determine which norms or which regime will prevail in each of these conflicts (Ibáñez 2005).

Fourth, in the normative frameworks of e-commerce, soft law clearly prevails over other more institutionalised legal forms. Thus, electronic markets are characterised by soft legalisation. Although binding and non-binding norms coexist, the e-commerce regime is hardly not legalised.

Fifth, as regards sources of authority, private authorities play a leading role in some core issues of the e-commerce regime. However, this is not a private regime, since public authorities have also contributed highly to its creation and coordination. After all, states have fulfilled some critical functions: they have endorsed and promoted private self-regulation; they have guaranteed the implementation of private norms through public means; and they have legalised soft law norms (public and private) when such norms were insufficient for the protection of business interests – intellectual property rights – or public interests – consumer rights. This combination of public regulation and private self-regulation confers the e-commerce regime its hybrid character, to a far greater extent than in other international regimes.

According to the features above, the regime of e-commerce is a regime at an embryonic stage, structurally complex, with a high density of norms, with a low degree of legalisation, and hybrid in terms of sources of authority, although with prevailing private governance mechanisms. In terms of international institutional embeddedness, in the emerging regime of e-commerce, TPG has escaped the control of public authorities and, in particular, it has been kept out of the reach of intergovernmental organisations. This has been clearly illustrated by the two phases of the World Summit on the Information Society (WSIS), held in Geneva (2003) and in Tunis (2005), which resulted in political declarations and plans of action, but with little effective involvement of public authorities in the Internet governance.

Graphically, the characterisation of the e-commerce regime can be represented with a combination of development, structure, density, legalisation, and authority that would vary from one international regime to another. Figure 10.2 represents such characterisation of the e-commerce regime and also of the Internet regime. Both representations are quite similar, although the resulting polygons also show some differences.

The graph assigns different values for each criterium using five levels: very high, high, medium, low, and very low. For the criterium referred to authority,

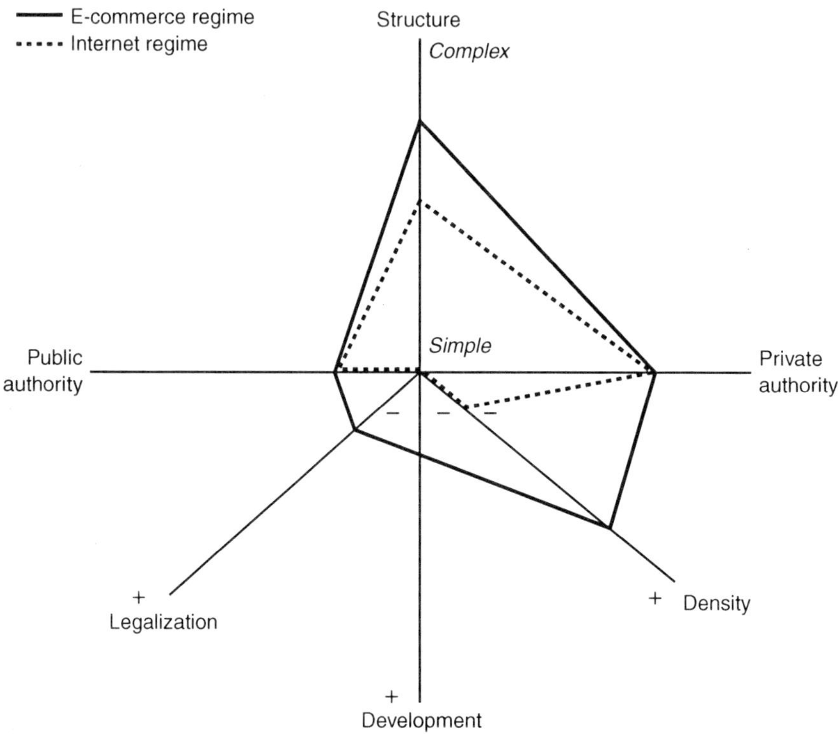

Figure 10.2 Graphic representation of the e-commerce and Internet regimes

the scale is applied separately to both public and private authority. The value level for each criterium has been determined after the examination of the most important activities of control by both public authorities – US government, EU institutions, and international governmental organisations – and private authorities – ICT companies, technical bodies, non-governmental organisations, and hacker groups (Ibáñez 2005). In the analysis of the e-commerce regime, the assigned value levels have been: high for the structure; low for public authority; low for legalisation; low for development; high for density; and high for private authority. In other words, the e-commerce regime has a highly complex structure, low public authority, low legalisation, low development, high density, and high private authority. For the Internet regime, the assigned value levels have been: middle for structure, low for public authority, very low for legalisation, low for development, low for density, and high for private authority. In other words, the Internet regime has a half-complex structure, low public authority, very low legalisation, low development, low density, and high private authority.

The graph is not intended to offer a mathematical model, but only a graphic representation of differences between international regimes in a comparative way. Thus, the graphic characterisation of each international regime will result in polygons with different surfaces and locations. The assignment of value levels to each dimension might slightly vary according to the evaluation of the observer, but such variation should not be fundamental and would not alter the basic patterns of surface and location for each polygon.

Normative implications: public interests in cyberspace

The resulting order of power structures in electronic markets benefits mainly those with most power in e-commerce. Big ICT companies have been the main beneficiaries of these commercial activities and of the control exercised over the risks threatening them. Public authorities have undoubtedly affected the power structures of electronic markets, but the preferences of major private actors and authorities have prevailed over the preferences of less powerful players. Thus, private preferences have determined the agenda and the TPG patterns of the e-commerce regime. On the one hand, the agenda of e-commerce has included a series of issues and risks, which have been managed according to the priorities of big companies in the electronic markets. On the other hand, the management of issues and risks in the agenda has been addressed mainly through private self-regulation, which has prevailed over public regulation.

One of the main problems of these TPG patterns is the democratic deficit generated by the lack of accountability mechanisms. Private authorities are not subject to such mechanisms (Price and Verhulst 2000: 60). The authority of some companies, business associations, and other private bodies derives from the acknowledgement of a rather small number of individuals, companies, and organisations. In democratic political systems, the legitimacy of private authorities is not comparable to the legitimacy of public authorities. Any of the forms adopted by representative democracy cannot seriously consider anything like a re-delegation of citizens' sovereignty from public authorities who are representing a community to private authorities representing nobody but themselves, and their own business interests. If this is already a problem at a local or state level, it becomes much more serious at an international or global scale. And this is what has happened with e-commerce on the Internet; big transnational companies have taken advantage of the lack of coordination amongst state policies in order to further impose their own interests and preferences. Yochai Benkler clearly stated this trend (Benkler 2000: 184–5): private actors with most structural power in electronic markets are interested in the lack of interference by public authorities – the less public authorities intervene, the better private actors and authorities will control how these markets will function. Only in the protection of intellectual property rights do private authorities demand protection by public authorities, since they cannot guarantee by themselves the implementation of these rights, nor any punishment for violations. Such practices are consistent with the rationale of neoliberalism and the diminishing role of the state in the global political economy during the last decades.

For very different reasons, until the end of the 1990s, many Internet users and hackers defended total freedom in cyberspace. The evolution of cyberspace since the mid-1990s demonstrated how harmful the retreat or lack of public intervention can be. And this for a very simple reason: private self-regulation favours the imposition of norms promoted by the most powerful actors, whose values and interests will prevail over the majority in case of any conflict. As Debora L. Spar puts it, on the Internet 'power lies with those who make the rules' (Spar 1999: 48), as in any other area of social relations. If norms are made by big companies through self-regulation, power will lie with big companies. Actually, this is where it already is. It can be even worse if the Internet is commercialised on a larger scale and if more public goods brought about by the Internet become privatised. Scholars like Saskia Sassen (1999) have pointed out the former danger, while Lawrence Lessig (1999, 2001) has brilliantly shown the loss of free spaces in the face of growing control by business. Both ideas emerge from the same evidence: the Internet is being transformed; it is ceasing to be a public, open, free, and cheap space; and it is becoming a private, closed, controlled, and expensive space.

In our view, it is absolutely necessary to reconsider the role of public authorities in cyberspace. This means neither regulation for the sake of regulation, nor total control of the Internet by the state, nor unrestricted state intervention in electronic markets. However, public authorities have a critical role to play in three directions. First, the Internet should be maintained as a public good, since its sociopolitical benefits for societies are much more valuable than the economic benefits generated by e-commerce. Second, socieconomic inequalities should be avoided in cyberspace; they are sufficiently deep in the real world and the digital divide should not add to the socioeconomic divides already existing. Third, the Internet offers huge possibilities of social, political, and economic benefits, but these should be widely spread and effectively used to improve human development all over the world – not only in some sectors of some societies, whether rich or poor. From the perspective of regulatory efficiency, TPG may have shown some successes, but also a very limited capacity to solve societal problems and to address redistribution issues.

The Internet has opened up the door for the development of new forms of political participation and organisation, but their real value will depend on their ability to improve the existing conditions of political activism. New forms of legitimacy and representation are still to appear in cyberspace, and in the meantime, it would be a huge mistake to undermine the role that public authorities could play as depositories of the citizens' will. For the moment, only these authorities have some kind of obligation to guarantee order and justice in a postinternational society characterised by the coexistence of overlapping authorities cooperating and competing for the imposition of their own values and interests (Ibáñez 2004). In cyberspace, only public authorities are expected to adopt and impose measures of distributive justice assuring the protection of human dignity in any society. Private actors and authorities are only expected to expand markets and to favour business activities, and TPG has contributed to fulfil these functions. Things being the way they are: being so, for those in need of protection and help, public authorities are not a panacea, but their retreat is much worse.

11 Limitations to transnational private governance of the Internet

The dot eu top-level domain

George Christou and Seamus Simpson

Introduction

The electronic communications sector has made both a significant direct and enabling contribution to the internationalisation of economic activity for over a century. Within the last 30 years, rapid advancements in communications technologies and services coincided with the most recent phase of economic globalisation and in the process have played a significant role in it. One of the outstanding breakthroughs here has been the Internet, whose underlying logic of global communications seamlessness led quickly to expectations of a new, ungovernable (and thus ungoverned) 'virtual' economic landscape which could transcend traditional barriers to free international trade. However, the strategic international political-economic significance of the Internet quickly motivated first-mover nation states to attempt to create an international Internet governance framework, in the hope of securing a stake in the emerging Internet economy.

This chapter explores one of the most well-developed aspects of the international Internet economy: the governance of the domain name system. Its particular focus is the European Union (EU), which provides an important developing example of the emergence of transnational private governance (TPG) of Internet domains, which, put simply, provide the means of securing an identity on the Internet to allow communication to occur. An arcane technical area in its own right, domain names – and specifically their governance – became increasingly important as the economic value and potential of the Internet grew from the mid-1990s. At this time, the EU, keen to promote its interests in the global economy, became aware of the opportunities that might be accrued from developing a specific European presence in the emerging virtual economy of the Internet. One of the strategies chosen to achieve this was the creation of its own top-level domain (TLD) – dot eu – which would provide a recognisable EU identity to Internet users registered thereunder.

The chapter's core argument is that the governance of the dot eu TLD provides another illustration of the diversity of, as well as the limitations to, the development of TPG in the international political economy. Though TLD governance developed at the global level – since 1999 within the Internet Corporation for Assigned Names and Numbers (ICANN) – has been undertaken by private interests, the dot eu system of governance, though transnational, is only partly private in nature. This outcome can be explained by the EU's approach to communications regulation, as much as the penchant for private governance of the Internet through self-regulation.

In its analysis, the chapter aims to provide a contribution to the four key lines of enquiry highlighted in chapter 1 of the volume. First, it provides strong evidence that the Internet economy can be added to the list of sectors which are likely to draw on TPG. Second, the EU, as an 'organisational format' grappling with issues of economic globalisation appears likely to employ TPG, albeit far from the 'ideal type'. Third, the chapter explains the form of TPG for dot eu through extending and applying the concept regulatory agencies to our case. In the process, it aims to add to the list of those concepts which can be used to order TPG. The consequent public–private governance model which the EU has created for dot eu also illustrates the importance of regional embeddedness, yielding scope for diversity to develop in areas which are governed at the global level. Fourth, its form aside, like other cases examined in this volume, the dot eu governance system raises the key issue of the extent to which the presence of the EU – in the form of the European Commission – in dot eu's governance will deliver the transparency and accountability which critics of private governance often find wanting in such arrangements, something which is examined in the conclusions of the chapter.

Private interest governance, the Internet and the EU

The limitations of TPG in the case of the dot eu TLD cannot be understood fully without grasping the extent to which regulatory patterns in the electronic communications sector have come to be embedded within the EU institutional structure, where the Internet is forming an increasingly important concern. Here, the broader governance context is the transition from traditional hands-on public state control of communications across the EU's Member State to 'regulatory' state (Seidman and Gilmour 1986, Moran 2002) action in which there has been an emphasis on proceduralism rather than politics, and the provision of legally based 'riding instructions' to be implemented and enforced through the creation of public regulatory authorities at the national level coordinated to a considerable extent by the European Commission. This has been very clearly evident in the telecommunications sector (Thatcher 1999).

The decisions taken by EU Member States gradually over more than a 20-year period which amounted to a wholesale reform of the governance of their telecommunications sectors can be regarded as a collective response to pressures of economic globalisation which questioned deeply the traditional way in which telecommunications were governed. To create a new system of governance at the EU level required a considerable investment of regulatory responsibility, despite the fact that the lion's share of regulatory control remained at the national level, though exercised in a (then) new regulatory state form (see Humphreys and Simpson 2005). Thatcher (2001) has argued that this pattern of change in telecommunications can be characterised in terms of the principal agent model where EU Member States, as principals, delegated considerable responsibility to the European Commission, their agent, in the administration of the new telecommunications regulatory package required to effect the desired changes, as well as a series of national level regulatory authorities. Elsewhere, Majone (2000), citing the telecommunications sector as a prominent example, has examined the increasingly important role played by the European Commission and is critical, highlighting a 'credibility' crisis in which a poorly resourced Commission, *inter alia*, is unable to ensure the optimal discharging of its duties. As a consequence, the idea of creating European level-independent public agencies delegated to undertake such work is advocated, though these are defined very broadly. The decision to delegate responsibility in regulation can be based on a number of factors, not least the desire to make regulation more efficacious by delegating to an agent with technical expertise of some kind (see Pollack 1997) something clearly recognisable in the case of dot eu.

The creation of new types of governance in response to changes in the global political economy is something which the EU has shown considerable interest in pursuing in recent years, prominent amongst which has been self-regulation (Eberlein and Kerwer 2004: 22, Héritier 2002a: 3). Here, however, the EU has been keen to place its own interpretation on what this should entail arguing for the inclusion of a public authority role, creating what it describes as co-regulation, which '…may be more flexible, adaptable and effective than straight forward regulation and legislation' but which, importantly, 'implies an appropriate level of involvement by the public authorities [and]… consists of cooperation between public authorities, industry and the other interested parties' (European Commission 2004c: 6).

New global economic phenomena, such as the Internet, epitomise the kind of public policy challenges which have faced the EU and motivated efforts such as these The Internet community, originating primarily from the USA, espoused a preference for private, self-managed governance which largely excluded state influence, something subsequently manifest in the working structures of ICANN's governance of the TLD system (see Christou and Simpson 2006) with which any EU TLD would have to comply. The original core principles for Internet governance neither emerged from the pressures of globalisation (even though they evolved within the ideological context of globalisation), nor embedded norms within national and European political-economic domains. The commercialisation of the Internet – bringing in the interests of industry, business and governments – meant this 'post-governmental' form of governance could not be preserved, though private self-regulation remained the dominant governance preference for several reasons. The technical complexity of the Internet, in the first instance, militated against government officials adequately understanding and fulfilling any required regulatory role effectively or efficiently. As in many other areas of such complexity self-management and self-regulation were the preferred regulatory forms. Second, there was a concern, in particular from the US government, to ensure that the Internet was unencumbered by strict governmental regulation of the kind that had characterised (and hindered liberalisation in) certain other parts of the electronic communications sector historically, notably telecommunications, but also broadcasting. Third, self-regulation chimed more readily with the requirements of an Internet architecture that was global and decentralised, than that of any top-down command and control state-driven regulatory regime.

The dot eu governance system provides an important example of how EU Member States have modified their approach to the regulation of electronic communications to cater for the exigencies of the Internet. Here, an extended form of the principal agent model can be utilised to explain the chosen policy approach to dot eu. Specifically, the dot eu system of governance exemplifies a novel situation in which EU Member States have delegated governance responsibility across a number of agents. This, we argue, is another stage in the process of delegation evident in the European electronic communications sector begun with the movement towards the regulatory state which commenced in the 1980s.

In the case of dot eu, the European Commission can be viewed as the direct agent of its Member States and, as a consequence, is in an interesting position. Specifically, we argue that the Commission has been given the highly challenging dual role of agent and principal in the evolving system of governance. Here, it has been delegated responsibility for ensuring compliance with a series of public policy rules (PPR) which EU Member States have created for dot eu. However, the day-to-day governance of dot eu has been in turn delegated by the European Commission (at the behest of Member States) to the European Registry of Internet Domains (Eurid), a private, not-for-profit company, to whom the Commission can be regarded as a principal. An essential problem of delegation concerns the ability of the principal to maintain control over the agent's behaviour – a reduction in this is termed 'agency loss' – whilst at the same time ensuring that the agent is given enough freedom of movement to discharge its responsibilities fully (Kassim and Menon 2005). The use of public–private 'double agency' in our case would appear to make this challenge even more complex and places the European Commission in a potentially delicate position (see below). Although private self-regulation may bring with it advantages in the form of flexibility, responsiveness and predictability of outcomes, it also raises questions as to the extent to which such a form of governance is legitimate, democratic and accountable and how (self)-regulatees can be relied on to comply if the public backstop element is not present.

The emergence of the dot eu TLD

Once the Internet became both a popular and more significantly a commercial tool, domain names (which could be generic TLDs such as .com or country code names such as .uk) took on a strategic and economic significance as they could provide industry, business and governments with a presence in the developing global 'virtual' market. The creation of the dot eu TLD can be located within the context of an increase in demand for TLDs following commercialisation. The central catalyst leading to the recommendation for the dot eu TLD, which came from the Directorate General Information Society (DGIS) of the European Commission, was the 'dot com boom'. This paralleled with, at the time, a shortage of TLD choice provided an opportunity for the EU to stamp its authority and identity in cyberspace, and simultaneously created an opportunity for European business to possess a European trademark in the global Internet market.

The governance framework for dot eu was shaped within the institutional peculiarities of the EU policy-making process, allowing the significant impregnation of embedded governance traditions, whilst simultaneously reflecting a scepticism about the efficaciousness of private governance models across the EU transnational space. The first indication of the importance placed on the EU (communications) governance tradition, and ultimately the limits on the importation of the TPG model for the Internet into Europe, came in initial deliberations on the regulatory form that the dot eu should take. Here there were clear divisions between the Internet community, broadly defined, and the European Commission's legal services. The former insisted on a fast-track 'project' approach to launching dot eu that would avoid the perceived procedural inefficiency of the EU policy-making process and thereby allow a self-managed private transnational regime to emerge. The latter, however, highlighted the need for a European 'Regulation' for dot eu in order to address critical issues of public policy. Moreover, the need for a legal framework was underpinned by concerns about accountability and, additionally, how far a private self-regulatory model outside the EU legal framework would be susceptible to capture by the industry being regulated, thus possibly precluding the involvement of wider societal interests. There was also the broader political-economic concern surrounding the extent to which a private model would raise issues in relation to the EU's stringent competition policy rules. A public element to the dot eu model would define the responsibilities and obligations of the private element of the dot eu governance framework, imbuing it, theoretically at least, with greater legitimacy and broader scope with regard to participation and social impact, as well as ensuring protection from anti-competitive behaviour. It could also reflect the generally supportive consensus position within the European Internet business community reached on dot eu (Commission Working Paper, February 2000: 8).

The consultations[1] that led to the decision to proceed with the dot eu as a traditional legal 'Regulation' were extensive amongst stakeholders in the European Internet community (see Commission Working Paper, February 2000 and Commission Report, July 2000[2]). Those relating to the design of an operational framework for dot eu were conducted within an Interim Steering Group which included European Commission officials and a prominent and influential group, the European Community Panel of Participants in Internet Organisation and Management whose members were drawn from business, government and industry (see EC-POP 2000a, 2000b). This provided an interesting example of EU regional (spatial) scope in terms of private transnational governance. It reflected the extent to which in Europe 'industry's self-image of self-regulation has a corporatist twist, that is, the public sector is accepted as a *participant* in the self-regulatory process' (*emphasis in original*, Newman and Bach 2001: 9). So although the values guiding the governance philosophies of the EU and the European Internet community could be located at two 'cultural' extremes, these were reconciled in an acceptance of 'public' (European Commission) and 'private' actors' (Internet community) participation in the policy and operational process within the dot eu governance framework (Christou and Simpson 2006). The extent to which the European Commission would, in the final analysis, exercise a public oversight and supervision role, however, was perhaps not expected by the European Registry for Domain Names (Eurid),[3] when it was selected to manage the dot eu TLD after a Call for Expressions of Interest in August 2002 made by the European Commission (European Commission 2003a). The EU's proclivity for overregulation in the PPR raised questions about the consensual nature of the dot eu governance framework, whilst also enforcing structural constraints on its operational mechanics.

Eurid was only able to project its preferred liberal, self-regulatory model, once the key decisions on governing the dot eu had been taken by the Commission and the Council's Telecommunications Committee (succeeded by the Communications Committee). The latter's inclination towards an approach of 'regulated self-regulation' (Ronit, this volume) was clearly reflected in the framework outlined in the final dot eu regulation (European Parliament and Council 2002), more so than the private delegated self-regulatory and self-management aspects. These were subject to thick procedural conditionality and a (renewable) contractual agreement between the European Commission and Eurid. Moreover, the public oversight role delegated to the Commission was reinforced through established global level protocol within ICANN's Governmental Advisory Committee, which provided that the dot eu TLD would be subject to the jurisdiction of the relevant competent authority – in this case, the EU (see Commission Working Paper, February 2000). Whilst the principles of non-interference, self-management and self-regulation were acknowledged in the dot eu governance framework, they were also domesticated to such an extent that the nature of the private element, delegated to Eurid, took on characteristic features of regulatory state practice.

The nature of the dot eu governance system

Many of the features of TPG described in the introductory chapter of this volume are evident in the arrangements in place – and at the time of writing still developing – for the dot eu TLD. Country code TLDs (ccTLDs) provide an example of the tensions that exist between the national and global levels in situations where global governance arrangements have been created to deal with issues of transnational economic importance (see Christou and Simpson 2007). The dot eu TLD did not fit neatly into either of the TLD classifications, though as noted above it was designated as a ccTLD. The transnational element of the governance system of dot eu reflects the challenges which the EU faces as an international political actor in systems of transnational governance. On the one hand, dot eu is required to comply with the rules system for ICANN whose approval the EU needed to secure to create dot eu in the first instance. Thereafter, at the point at which the policy initiative was sufficiently developed, the EU had to request that dot eu be assigned to the 'root' of the Internet's TLD classification system, agreed to by ICANN in March 2005, more than 6 years after the EU originally discussed the possibility of creating dot eu. On the other hand, the dot eu system operates transnationally across the EU and, if it is to be successful, must be accommodative of commercial and regulatory practices and conventions of a steadily expanding number of EU Member States, though in this case Internet regulation does not possess the strong regulatory traditions developed in other sectors of the economy, not least those other elements of the electronic communications sector.

The dot eu system of governance provides an interesting case of the agencification of transnational regulation. As noted earlier, the use of public regulatory agencies for governance is a well-established phenomenon of the European regulatory state. In this case, EU Member States, as principals, took the decision to delegate responsibility for the governance of dot eu to the European Commission as their agent. However, they also decided to develop a system of public–private 'dual agency' where the dot eu registry, Eurid, was designated as the private, not-for-profit company, charged with a series of tasks related to the detailed day-to-day governance of dot eu. Furthermore, within the private agency of dot eu regulation, a dispersal of responsibility for governance is evident in the roles played by private registrar companies and alternative dispute resolution providers.

The dot eu case reflects both the political-institutional nature of the EU and the core features of Internet governance developed at the global level over the last decade. Specifically, the EU has attempted to perform a delicate balancing act to accommodate relatively strong European public policy tendencies alongside the out-and-out private, liberal governance agenda of Internet commercial interests. The public element in the system of governance for dot eu is expressed in a detailed series of PPR which were agreed by EU Member States in 2004 (European Commission 2004d). The fact that these are described as 'rules' rather than 'guidelines' indicates the extent to which the private interest governance in the system for dot eu is buttressed by more traditional public policy measures. Commensurate with this, the PPR are detailed in nature and direct most of their attention to the remit given to the dot eu registry, Eurid, and the main tasks of private interest governance pertaining to dot eu. In this respect, the European Commission finds itself in the dual role of both agent of its Member States and principal of Eurid in administering and ensuring the enforcement of the PPR.

Eurid holds a, perhaps *the*, vital position in the governance of dot eu. In its core features, it is an embodiment of the regulatory principles which have grown up around the Internet. A private not-for-profit consortium, initially made up of the national ccTLD registry operators of Belgium, Italy and Sweden,[4] it plays a number of vital roles in the administration and governance of dot eu. A key aspect of Eurid's remit is its management of two of the most important elements of dot eu regulation. First, it is responsible for the accreditation of a series of profit-making registrar companies which provide registration services for parties wishing to register a name under dot eu. In doing so, Eurid was required to establish principles and procedures for accrediting registrars, as well as the terms of competition between them. It also was responsible for drafting and implementation of a registration policy for dot eu. At the time of writing, this highly competitive registration marketplace contains 1560 companies from 46 different states from within and beyond the EU. However, the vast majority, 624, are from the USA (Eurid 2006: 12).[5] By contrast, Eurid is responsible for setting up the alternative dispute resolution (ADR) procedures relating to matters arising from registration activities around dot eu. Here, in 2005, it appointed the Czech Arbitration Court, a not-for-profit organisation, to the position of administrator of ADR proceedings for dot eu.

Aside from delegating and managing these two core self-regulatory aspects of dot eu governance, Eurid is also charged with the task of maintaining the integrity of the databases containing information on dot eu registrants. This has already generated controversy. In mid-2006, it emerged that it was technically possible for dot eu registrar companies to obtain lists of names registered under dot eu, which they were not the responsible registrar for, from the dot eu registry database. Clearly an important issue of data protection, Eurid was quick to point out that this technical deficiency in the system was not abused widely by registrar companies before it came to light and that, once highlighted, it was quickly remedied.[6]

Eurid also plays a number of other roles in the governance of dot eu which might traditionally in Europe have been considered very much the remit of public bodies. For example, it was charged with the task of negotiating with relevant international bodies – in this case ICANN – to secure recognition of dot eu. It similarly plays key 'ambassadorial' roles through being required to promote dot eu in the official languages of the EU, to provide publicly available information services on dot eu, to liaise with the European Internet community and, finally, to liaise with, and participate in, relevant international organisations for Internet governance. Eurid is also involved in the kind of distributive issues associated with governance referred to in chapter 1 of this volume. Part of its remit involves making decisions on the rights of individuals to ownership of domain names under dot eu. This was clearly illustrated at the inception of dot eu with the launch of the sunrise period in which those (from both the public and private sector) claiming prior rights to domain names were given the opportunity to apply to secure such rights asserted under dot eu. During the process, Eurid appointed a private-sector company as its validation agent to decide on the legitimacy of claimants from the private sector to existing prior rights to a domain name under dot eu.[7] However, it could be argued that the process was undertaken more efficiently using private governance methods – the validation agent, PricewaterhouseCoopers, according to Eurid, was able to review as many as 1500 applications per day (Eurid 2006: 14).

Despite this wide-ranging and powerful private governance remit, Eurid's activities – and the dot eu system overall – evidence the strong public shadowing presence of the EU in the shape of the European Commission as an agent of its Members States but also a principal of Eurid. For example, the PPR, for which the Commission has been delegated responsibility, set out in great detail the procedures which Eurid must follow when appointing and managing dot eu registrant companies, down even to the order in which Eurid must ensure registrant companies forward requests for registration to it. A classic case of 'old' EU-regulatory styles interfacing with newer Internet regulatory practices is to be found in the stipulation in the PPR that Eurid must take responsibility for the creation of a code of conduct among registrant companies. However, the PPR also mandate that this code, which has not been created at the time of writing, must be first approved by the European Commission before it becomes operational (European Commission 2004d). In a similar vein, the regulated self-regulation of the dot eu governance system is evident in the stipulations of the PPR on ADR. Here, whilst Eurid has been assigned the responsibility for appointing ADR providers, key elements of the ADR procedure are laid out in the PPR in detail, such as the number of people comprising the ADR panel and down even to a specification on the means which must be employed when communication with a complainant or respondent in a dispute is conducted (European Commission 2004d: article 22, paragraphs 9 and 13). The European Commission has also been granted exclusive and irrevocable rights to the data on the dot eu database and has the authority to terminate Eurid's contract should it be deemed to have been in breach of its terms (European Commission 2004d: article 15). Thus, whilst Eurid can be viewed as a regulatory agent within the Internet domain industry undertaking or facilitating self-regulatory activity, such self-regulation is both delegated (in the first instance) and thereafter itself regulated by the EU Member States' principal, the European Commission. It has been argued that the stipulation of rules and procedures by its principals for an agency to follow provide transparent, accountable and cost-effective arrangements for delegation (Majone 2000: 293). However, the PPR, typical of the quite far-reaching and detailed approach of the European 'regulatory state', are uncharacteristic of the more laissez-faire arrangements for Internet governance at the global level in organisations like ICANN.

At the same time, however, alongside its private not-for-profit status, other aspects of Eurid are strongly reminiscent of the self-regulatory culture of the Internet, exemplified in ICANN. For example, though not at the time of writing fully constituted, its Board will contain a range of participants from European industry, European Internet Service providers, the dot eu registrar market and the Internet technical and academic and research communities. Eurid's Policy Council similarly will contain a large number of members from across the European Internet community, whose opinions Eurid must take into account.[8]

Although only operational for a short period of time, there is some evidence of the extent to which dot eu has developed. In December 2005, registration under dot eu for those, from the public and private sector, claiming prior rights in a name began as part of the aforementioned temporary sunrise period. Following this, in April 2006, the opportunity to register names under dot eu was made generally available. By the end of its first week of 'open' acceptance of domain names, with 1.5 million new registrants, dot eu had become the fourth most popular TLD in Europe and the eighth most popular globally, when generic TLDs are included. Most registrants in dot eu came from Germany, the UK, the Netherlands and Italy (Eurid 2006: 7–8). It is too early to make any judgement on the efficacy of the ADR system put in place for dot eu, since, whilst by the end of April 2006, 153 ADR complaints had been made, only one of these had been adjudicated upon (Eurid 2006: 13).

Conclusions

The case of the dot eu TLD provides insights into both the conditions under which TPG in Europe can operate functionally, whilst simultaneously demonstrating the considerable propensity for, as well as clear limitations to, the spread of TPG norms and associated practices in the global political economy of the Internet. It demonstrates in particular the intensity of the EU's embedded 'regulatory' frame of reference in the communications sector, and thus the significance of regional scope and differentiation in relation to the Internet, where global governance norms have historically evolved through private-libertarian traditions, and where public interference has often been perceived as anathema. The governance of dot eu is characterised by the use of public and private agency in a context of regulated self-regulation in which the role exerted by the European Commission will be very important, though at the time of writing it is too early to be able to determine the precise nature of the Commission's relationship with Eurid, the key private regulatory actor in the system. Some early evidence from the period of formation of the PPR for dot eu suggests that that there are broad differences of approach in the regulatory culture of each which will have to be overcome quickly if the dot eu governance system is to be successful (authors' interview, 2004). Nonetheless, it may be more important that the governance network for dot eu is characterised by the regulatory specialisms of both the European Commission and Eurid rather than their commonalities.

The extent to which strong claims can be made about functional robustness of the EU's chosen governance system for dot eu compared with purely private or public alternatives is also limited since evidence is rather sparse beyond some indicators on volume of registrations under the domain and much more limited alternative dispute resolution activity. Dot eu highlights the way in which the EU and, specifically, its Member States as principals have effectively determined the way in which TPG is delivered for the Internet in Europe through an extension of the well-developed approach of public agencification into the private realm. In the double agencification process which this has generated, Member States have delegated regulatory tasks to the European Commission for reasons of functional expertise, and the Commission, in turn, has further delegated the day-to-day management of dot eu to Eurid because of its technical expertise and knowledge of the ccTLD market. Eurid has been given expansive transnational policy latitude to govern dot eu by its principal, the Commission, albeit within the shadow of a 'thick' set of PPR, which allow for a transfer of governance away from Eurid if it (and the private actors under its guidance and management) is seen not to be fulfilling its remit in line with the public policy norms of the EU.

The conditions under which this partly private, transnational model for dot eu has emerged bring with them certain risks. Given that Eurid has potentially the central and most significant 'agency' role in the dot eu model, there exists strong scope for agency loss on the Commission's part as the operational mechanics of the system bed down and Eurid becomes more established. This in turn has implications for the control exercisable by EU Member States, as initial principals in the system. It is here that concerns over public accountability may arise, with a 'knock on' calling into question of the legitimacy of the governance system for dot eu. Furthermore, when considering the double agency approach to dot eu governance, it is also appropriate to reflect on issues of ownership and, moreover, sovereignty. Although the dot eu TLD is effectively a European cyberspace label, ownership of its central elements rests with the initial principals in its governance model, namely EU Member States. Clearly, the possibility of agency loss is increased in an arrangement like that for dot eu and has potentially serious consequences from both a functional and a public policy perspective. For these to be avoided, it is imperative that the European Commission forges the kind of working relationship with Eurid which is 'hands on' enough to ensure that the PPRs are not broken, yet is simultaneously 'hands off' enough to allow Eurid to make dot eu attractive enough to registrants, many of which expect to encounter the laissez-faire approach of the Internet community and have alternatives available to them beyond dot eu should this not be the case. Eurid's performance to date suggests that it has the experience and status within the TLD industry to monitor compliance of private agents with the regulatory parameters which it has set, which relate principally to registrar companies and those wishing to register their names under dot eu. However, when dot eu has been operational over a longer time period, more research aimed at an evaluation of the normative and practical strengths and deficiencies of this partly private, transnational model of governance should be undertaken. By that stage, it should also be possible to determine with more accuracy the possibilities for deployment of this kind of model in sectors of the international political economy other than electronic communications.

Notes

1 Initial public consultations confirmed strong support for the proposal to create a new Internet TLD for the EU. See http://europa.eu.int/ISPO/eif/InternetPoliciesSite/DotEU/WorkDocEN.html
2 See http://europa.eu.int/ISPO/eif/InternetPoliciesSite/DotEUMay2000/EN.html
3 Eurid was selected in May 2003 and was an alliance between three established national country code TLD registries: the Belgian, the Swedish and the Italian.

4 Eurid's membership has expanded since its inception in April 2003 to comprise also the ccTLD operators of the Czech Republic and Slovenia.
5 The nearest to this figure from EU Member States were the Netherlands (186 registrants), Germany (156 registrants), Italy (76 registrants) and Belgium (74 registrants).
6 Nonetheless, as many as 40 names were subject to such interrogation.
7 A series of governmental validation points were used to assess the legitimacy of claims made by public-sector actors during the dot eu sunrise period.
8 The Policy Council can issue non-binding opinions on any issue. The Chair of the Policy Council is set to become a member of the Eurid Board.

Part IV

Regional integration as a driving force towards transnational private governance

12 Public–private partnerships and transnational governance in the European Union

The case of the Lisbon Strategy

Otto Holman

Introduction

The present state of affairs in the European Union (EU) can be best described in terms of a paradox. On the one hand, there is much talk about the so-called legitimacy crisis in the EU, particularly after the French and Dutch referendums of 2005. Although the reasons, justified or not, of the French and Dutch people to vote against the Constitutional Treaty were quite mixed – ranging from the dismantlement of social welfare provisions at home to the elaboration of a superstate at the European level, and from the influx of foreign workers (notably from the member states that entered the EU through the 2004 big bang enlargement) to the future accession of Turkey – a more structural discontent with the elite-driven process of European integration seems a common trend, and not only in France and the Netherlands. On the other hand, this very elite-driven process of European free market integration, though not uncontested at the national level, is moving full speed ahead. Both at the European and at the national level, new measures are announced, almost at a daily or weekly rate, to increase European competitiveness *vis-à-vis* the outside world. The overwhelming importance of competitiveness is reflected in the so-called Lisbon Strategy, particularly after the March 2005 mid-term review and its subsequent relaunch. In this chapter, we will look at the Lisbon Strategy not as an utter failure (as so many commentators want to have it) but as integral part of the ongoing process of welfare state restructuring at the national level.

At a different level of abstraction, and turning to the central theme of this volume, the above paradox can be illustrated by two different conceptualisations of the notion of governance. First, and reflecting the 'legitimacy crisis' position, a recent study equates governance with 'the perplexing maze of order and edict, directive and regulation, and administrative law and judicial interpretation that comprises the purportedly sacred and irreversible corpus of law and administrative fiat … by which Brussels tries to rule Europe' (Gillingham 2006: 5). The diagnosis – opaque European institutions and decision-making procedures creepingly creating the image (if not the reality) of a European superstate – is intrinsically linked to the author's suggested cure: 'popular consent, the sovereignty of the nation-state, the subsidiarity principle, and competitive economies' (ibid.). Second, in its 2001 *White Paper on European Governance*, the European Commission more optimistically defines governance as 'the rules, processes and behaviour that affect the way in which powers are exercised at the European level, particularly as regards openness, participation, accountability, effectiveness and coherence' (European Commission 2001d: 8). The normative underpinnings of this definition – i.e., 'better' governance in terms of more efficient and transparent rules, processes and behaviour – resembles a common assumption in the so-called multilevel governance literature that state sovereignty is in retreat – and with it state-centric or intergovernmental interpretations of European integration – and that a new and to a certain extent unique polity is emerging which is supposed to be 'closer to the people' and better equipped to enhance democratic legitimacy and effective decision making. In this respect, the descriptive value of bringing in sub-, trans- and supranational (non-state) actors and multiple levels of government turns into an apology of recent (political) attempts to substantiate the principles of subsidiarity and proportionality (the enshrining of competences in the Constitutional Treaty can serve as an example).

This chapter attempts to move beyond these two (at first sight) mutually exclusive conceptualisations. In fact, normatively, both conceptualisations point at the same direction in terms of preferred outcomes (a multilevel polity based on the principle of subsidiarity) while at the same time hiding the real impact and meaning of what will be referred to as the system of asymmetrical regulation. The chapter discusses the so-called Lisbon Strategy – aimed at making Europe 'the most competitive and dynamic knowledge-based economy in the world' – as part and parcel of the dominant competitiveness discourse in the EU. It explores the correlation between economic and monetary integration, on the one hand, and the so-called 'modernisation' of the European Social Model, on the other, by referring to the privileged partnership of big business in the agenda-setting and policy-planning process, and to the lack of democratic accountability. From a theoretical perspective, it argues that a political economy perspective on transnational *private* governance should concentrate on the intersection of politics and economics, on the symbiosis of public and private forms of governance and on the interaction between state (or quasi-state) actors and non-state actors in the framework of public–private partnerships (PPPs). Empirically, the chapter examines an early example of such a PPP, i.e. the Competitiveness Advisory Group (CAG), which was established in the mid-1990s – as a co-initiative of the European Commission and the European Round Table of Industrialists (ERT). It then discusses the (more recent) role of PPPs in achieving the Lisbon goal. Finally, the chapter deals with some normative considerations about the effectiveness and democratic legitimacy of these PPPs, as well as about their significance for the transformation of welfare state structures in the EU.

Transnational governance and asymmetrical regulation

The fourth part of this volume deals with regional integration as a driving force towards relatively new forms of transnational governance. As the editors point out in their introductory chapter, governance has become an important feature of today's EU. In fact, it can be argued that the emergence of transnational governance structures in the EU is related to the so-called 'extended relaunch' of European integration since the early 1980s (i.e. the completion of the Single Market and the subsequent Maastricht decision to move towards Economic and Monetary Union). This raises some important questions. What is the relationship between regional integration schemes at the European level and the emergence of transnational governance practices (this basically boils down to raising the *how does the EU work* question)? Does European integration facilitate the evolution of transnational governance or is the latter a constituent part of the former? What do we mean by *transnational* governance? And how do practices of transnational *private* governance interact with formal (and to a certain extent traditional) structures of state authority? Can the EU accurately be described as an instance of 'governance without government'?

In addition to these 'how' questions, we should also address the 'why' question: why did these structures of European governance emerge and what kind of EU did they seek to promote? In short, what is the social purpose of transnational governance in the EU? One possible answer is the widespread adoption of neoliberal policies in the EU and the transfer of responsibility for service provision to the private sector (Pollack and Shaffer 2001: 18). To further elaborate this explanation, we should first look into the notion of governance more closely. In a much quoted article, Roderick Rhodes (1996) distinguishes six different ways in which the concept of governance is used (and has gained new relevance since the late 1970s and early 1980s). The first use is governance as 'the minimal state'. This is part and parcel of the large-scale privatisation schemes which have been executed in all member states of the EU over the last three decades. As a result, ownership of public services has been replaced by regulation, sometimes in the form of (partial) self-regulation. According to Rhodes, the rhetorical value of the concept of governance is that it encapsulates the ideological preference for less government. At the European level, these national privatisation schemes were to a substantial degree inspired by European re-regulation in the context of the Single Market project, notably in those sectors with traditionally strong state monopoly structures. Governance (particularly in the meanings of multilevel and good governance) has become the key term to defend 'the minimal state' at the European level, as opposed to a would-be 'federal super-state'. The second use is governance as corporate governance. Though this use is normally restricted to the enterprise level, and the way executive management is checked and balanced by, for instance, shareholders, Rhodes is right to conclude that 'the concerns of corporate governance are echoed when discussing accountability in (...) good governance' (ibid.: 654). It is interesting to note that the regulation of corporate governance has recently moved to the

European level as well. Formally as part of completing the internal market, a number of new initiatives – like the takeover directive – aim at undoing the separation between management control and shareholders' ownership, *inter alia* by removing national restrictions to foreign (hostile) takeovers. This in turn is part of a more general introduction of the so-called Anglo-Saxon 'shareholder' values into continental 'stakeholder' capitalism (see Nölke *et al.* 2003). The third use, governance as new public management, refers to the introduction of private-sector management methods in the public-sector and private-sector 'incentive structures' into public service provision. Inasmuch as the new public management is about steering and competition, transforming traditional patterns of hierarchical government in the process, it is relevant to Rhodes' discussion of governance. Below, we will see how this new public management has entered the European decision-making structures too. Fourth, governance as good governance refers to the political conditionality attached to the lending and financial aid policies of the World Bank, the EU and so on (the Cotonou agreement between the EU and more than 70 developing countries is a case in point). But it has also been used in the EU enlargement strategy towards Central and Eastern Europe and more recently in the reform of the EU decision making itself. Democratic accountability is one side of good governance, efficiency in terms of privatising public services, cutting budget deficits, slimming down bureaucracies and so on is yet another. Fifth, governance as a 'socio-cybernetic system' comes close to alternative notions like 'the centreless society', the polycentric state or indeed 'governance without government'. Next to central government, a large number of interactions take place between public and private actors, state and non-state actors (and sectors) at multiple levels. Policy outcomes are increasingly determined by (and dependent upon) these interactions beyond – and to a certain extent independent of – a single sovereign authority. The fact that complex (inter)dependencies between different actors are replacing central government is at the heart of the sixth and final way governance is used according to Rhodes: governance as self-organising, interorganisational networks. The main difference with the former one seems to relate to the self-organising capacity of these networks, which means that they are not accountable to the state. In other words, 'networks are an alternative to, not a hybrid of, markets and hierarchies and they span the boundaries of the public, private and voluntary sectors' (Rhodes 1996: 659).

In gathering the threads, we may conclude from the above that a clear shift from government to governance has occurred since the 1970s, involving different (state and non-state actors) and different levels of decision making. The rise of governance structures and practices is concomitant to the neoliberal turn during the same decades (encapsulating not only the ideological preference of less government and more market but also the concrete practice of private governance and self-regulation within civil society). The rise of governance is – at least within the EU – a fundamentally transnational phenomenon in the sense that it refers to a process that is constituted in a social space transcending national borders and takes place simultaneously in subnational, national and supranational arenas. The rise of governance is inextricably connected to the relaunch of European integration since the mid-1980s, governance and free market integration being different parts of a single totality or process and mutually reinforcing each other. But it would be wrong to conclude that the rise of governance in the context of (and in interaction with) European integration is gradually replacing government, as the 'governance without government' literature wants to have it. True, the emergence of structures and practices of *transnational* governance takes place without a concomitant strengthening of *supranational* government, but government at the *national* level is still firmly in place. In fact, it was and is national government that enabled the rise of governance at multiple levels and it is national government that is still in control (be it in the last instance) of the outcomes of multilevel governance. In order to avoid the image of the relationship between government and governance as a conflictual one (which may be certainly the case at some moments and/or places) – i.e. as some kind of zero-sum relationship – I want to argue that the analysis of transnational *private* governance – as the central theme of this volume – should concentrate on the intersection of politics and economics, on the symbiosis of public and private forms of governance and on the interaction between state (or quasi-state) actors and non-state actors in the framework of PPPs. In order to fully grasp this point, we must first turn to the notion of asymmetrical regulation.

Asymmetrical regulation in the EU

The concept of asymmetrical regulation intends to grasp a phenomenon which mainstream multilevel governance literature fails to take into account, i.e. the fact that some policy areas are moved to the supranational arena while other policy areas are strictly reserved to national authorities claiming national sovereignty. Concretely, asymmetrical regulation not only refers to the discrepancy between European economic and monetary free market regulation, on the one hand, and the lack of social regulation (or harmonisation) at the European level, on the other, but – more importantly – to the adverse impact of economic and monetary integration at the European level on social cohesion at the national level. In fact, economic and monetary regulation at the supranational level and social deregulation at the national level are two sides of the same coin (for a more detailed account, see Holman 2004). The key to this is Economic and Monetary Union. What can national governments do to correct macroeconomic imbalances? They no longer can use the mechanism of interest rate adjustment to counteract slackening growth. Indeed, recent interest rate increases by the European Central Bank clearly show the primacy of eurozone price stability over national concerns with economic growth. The same goes for government spending to steer demand. Due to the Stability and Growth Pact, this neo-Keynesian strategy is severely limited. Needless to say that competitive devaluations through the exchange rate mechanism are past history. Austerity measures, regime competition and microeconomic supply-side structural adjustment are the only policy measures left to national governments to correct macroeconomic imbalances. Part and parcel of the underlying shift from demand-side corporatism to supply-side corporatism is the full-blown labour market flexibilisation programme, which in turn is an integral part of the attempt to make Europe the most competitive economy in the world by the year 2010 (the so-called Lisbon Strategy). This argument goes against those (Third Way inspired) politicians and scholars who still believe that the present *situation* can be understood as an *outcome* of a transnational struggle between contending projects, a kind of synthesis between competitiveness and social cohesion (Rhodes and van Apeldoorn 1998: 422). I tend to look at these developments as a *process*, gradually disembedding social relations in the context of the neoliberal turn.

In my view, the correlation between economic and monetary regulation at the European, supranational level and social regulation at the national level is not an unintended consequence of previous decisions to further integrate the different European economies. In a similar way as European monetary integration has been used by Italian modernising forces to break up the post-war Italian social and political system (starting with Italy's membership of the European Monetary System – see della Sala 2004), European monetary integration has been the conscious, intended strategy of transnational business to modernise the 'rigid' social systems at the national level. As argued above, governance and government are inextricably bound up, though not necessarily at the same level of decision making. The novel, multilevel polity that emerged in the context of the so-called extended relaunch of European integration in the 1980s and early 1990s can be best described as transnational governance without supranational government. The privileged partnership between the European Commission and the ERT shows that transnational informal practices of governance have (had) an impact on formal practices at the national level. This is at the heart of what is referred to as asymmetrical regulation: supranational regulation in the context of the Single Market and Economic and Monetary Union is limiting the national capacity to act, notably in the field of social regulation. While keeping up the illusion of self-determination, it is national government that is in charge of reforming labour markets. This is the real meaning of the fashionable concept of Europeanisation, i.e. the process by which domestic policy areas become increasingly subject to European policy making. And this is the very reason why governments handed over sovereignty to supranational institutions like the European Central Bank: to compel compliance by future domestic governments and, more importantly, by domestic social forces. We will return to the normative implications of this strategy in the last section. First, and before we turn to the case study of the Lisbon Strategy, we have to say a little bit more about the notion of PPPs.

PPPs: the European Commission and transnational business

The European Commission defines PPPs as 'forms of cooperation between public authorities and the world of business which aim to ensure the funding, construction, renovation, management or maintenance of an infrastructure or the provision of a service' (European Commission 2004b: 3). It explains the development of PPPs in recent years through a variety of factors, such as budget constraints and the subsequent need to find private funding for the public sector and the desire to learn from private know-how and working methods. More generally, it associates this development with 'the change in the role of the state in the economy, moving from a role of direct operator to one of organiser, regulator and controller' (ibid.). While this account is directly related to our previous discussion on the shift from government to governance, it requires a broader understanding in order to include the informal and formal structures (or networks) where chief executive officers (CEOs) of European capital, politicians and high representatives of the European cadres meet each other. It is particularly the agenda-setting and policy-planning capacity of these networks that is of importance here. And this is as much about decision making than about non-decision making: keeping specific policy areas or topics out of the European agenda is as important as keeping the momentum of neoliberal restructuring and disembedding free market capitalism (under the banner of competitiveness).

The partnership between the European Commission and the ERT is perhaps one of the most striking (and influential) examples in this respect. The European Commission is of particular importance in its policy-planning capacity and in its role of *Guardian of the Treaties*. As far as the former task is concerned, the Commission has operated in close cooperation with organised business at least since the early 1980s. The ERT is a privileged agenda-setting and policy-planning group, privileged in its access to European institutions and member state governments and in its capacity to influence the European agenda. The relationship between the two can best be described as a 'symmetrical interdependent' one: the Commission and the ERT need each other in the realisation of their respective goals. Already in the early years of its existence, a member of the Delors cabinet referred to the ERT in the following way: 'We see this group as a very useful bunch of people. These men are very powerful and very dynamic. They seed us with ideas. And when necessary, they can ring up their own prime ministers and make their case' (quoted in Merritt 1986: 22). In other words, the Commission could (and can) use the members of the ERT in its attempt to strengthen its position *vis-à-vis* the member states, both in its policy initiating and in its innovating capacity. On the other hand, the ERT needs the Commission because of its role as executive and co-legislature at the European level. The fact that the Commission has 'a quasi-monopoly of policy initiation and innovation inside the Community' (Church and Phinnemore 1994: 271) makes it the ideal partner of transnational business in its attempt to 'modernise' the European social model through policy initiation and innovation from above, i.e. at the European level.

It is now generally acknowledged that the ERT played an important role in the relaunch of European integration in the 1980s, with respect to both the completion of the internal market and the development towards EMU (van Apeldoorn 2002). After Maastricht, the agenda-setting and policy-planning activities of the ERT shifted from a more comprehensive approach (including all the major issues of European integration) to an approach focused on the more limited competitiveness discourse. Most of the reports of the ERT published after 1991 have European competitiveness as a central theme, with a strong emphasis on deregulation and labour market flexibilisation. In the words of the former Secretary General of the ERT, Keith Richardson, 'the competitiveness of European business must be strengthened by making it possible to build an integrated free market economic system, with a maximum of flexibility and a minimum of regulation'; and more explicitly, 'jobs cannot be created by laws or by writing some new clause or chapter into the Treaty of Maastricht. What is urgently needed is the deregulation of labour markets and better education and training. New jobs will then follow from economic growth and the creation of wealth by business' (Richardson 1997: 64–5). In 1995, then, the relationship between the European Commission and the ERT was institutionalised with the creation of the CAG. As a co-initiative of the then German Commissioner for industry, Bangemann, and the ERT, the CAG would 'act as a watchdog, by subjecting policy proposals and new regulations to the test of international competitiveness' (European Round Table of Industrialist 1994: 3).

The impact of the long-standing PPP between the European Commission and the ERT can be easily underestimated. In fact, the recent sixth edition of a widely used textbook on the government and politics of the EU refers to the ERT only once, in passing, as a thinktank which produces reports that are intended 'to identify how the right conditions can be created for business to flourish' (Nugent 2006: 337). In the following section, we will use the examples of the European Employment Strategy (EES) and the more recent, all-encompassing Lisbon Strategy as examples of the way the ERT – in partnership with the European Commission – has successfully managed to put competitiveness as top priority on the agenda of today's EU.

From Luxembourg to Lisbon and beyond: the primacy of competitiveness

Following earlier attempts to create a European employment policy – notably through the 1993 Commission's White Paper on Growth, Competitiveness and Employment, and the proposals of the Essen European Council in 1994 – the Amsterdam European Council of June 1997 and, more importantly, the Luxembourg Extraordinary European Council Meeting on Employment in November 1997 for the first time introduced a coordinated strategy for employment. Four broad guidelines structured this EES:

- improving employability, *inter alia* by moving from passive to active labour market policies and promoting life-long learning. Active labour market policies include reforms of tax and social security policies (aiming at an increase of the gap between minimum wages and unemployment benefits), making it 'more attractive' for the unemployed to take up jobs;

- developing entrepreneurship by making it easier to start up and run businesses and making the taxation system more employment friendly;
- encouraging adaptability of businesses and their employees by modernising the organisation of work, including flexible working arrangements, and by incorporating into national law more adaptable types of contract;
- strengthening the policies for equal opportunities: tackling gender gaps, reconciling work and family life and facilitating reintegration into the labour market. This objective seems first and foremost directed at increasing employment rates in Europe.

These guidelines were supposed to be taken into account by the member states in their respective employment policies. Each member state should provide the Council and the Commission with an annual report, the so-called National Employment Action Programme, on the principal measures taken to implement their employment policies in the light of these guidelines. On the basis of an examination of these reports, the Council could make recommendations to member states. The European Commission was asked to distil from a best-practice comparison-specific but non-binding recommendations on the basis of the above (and equally non-binding) guidelines. In 1999, a Peer Review Programme started in order to disseminate best practices of member states in labour market policies aimed at enhancing transferability and mutual learning processes and promoting greater convergence towards the main EU goals (see online peer-review.almp.org/en/principles.html, accessed 9 January 2006). If we carefully look at the Luxembourg guidelines, it is clear what this convergence was intended to boil down to: successful attempts to break up national systems of social protection in some member states were supposed to be used as benchmarks for other member states. Benchmarking and related concepts as best practice, mutual learning and so on have since become integral parts of what is commonly referred to as the Open Method of Coordination (OMC).

It must be emphasised that the Luxembourg European Council launched the EES on the basis of previous proposals from the European Commission. The European Commission, in turn, developed these proposals in close partnership with the ERT. First, as far as the methodology is concerned, the ERT published in 1996 a report called *Benchmarking for Policy-Makers*, which clearly outlined the policy potential of this management toolkit:

> Benchmarking means scanning the world to see what is the very best that anybody else anywhere is achieving, and then finding a way to do as well or better. [It] is a simple, flexible and above all dynamic process. It helps companies and governments to compare their own performance with the best in the world, and to motivate everybody concerned to do better.
>
> (European Round Table of Industrialists 1996: 5)

Benchmarking for policy makers in the field of labour market policies then implies scanning the world (i.e. Anglo-Saxon practices of internal and external labour market flexibilisation) to motivate workers to do better by reducing social protection and enhancing individual competition.

Second, a clear resemblance between the content of the EES and the proposals of the ERT can be discerned. In a number of reports, the ERT unambiguously stressed the need for deregulation and flexibilisation of labour markets. According to the ERT analysis, the causes of structural unemployment in Europe and the weak response of employment to economic growth were mainly due to institutional rigidities and high levels of social protection. This made it mandatory to flexibilise and upgrade the supply of labour, to allow for more wage differentiation and more responsive labour markets and, where necessary, lower wages and non-wage costs. In its 1993 report on *European Labour Markets*, the ERT states that 'even painful measures should become socially acceptable, provided they contribute to a sustained improvement of the unemployment situation' (European Table of Industrialist 1993: 2). A recovery of European industry's competitiveness could only be realised through adjustments in the supply side of the European economy, because 'only a healthy, efficient and competitive private sector is able to provide sufficient jobs' (ibid.: 9). All other decisions within the EU had to be tested against this all-pervasive goal. In this context, the ERT came up with the idea of a European CAG, which was eventually established in 1995 to keep competitiveness high on the EU policy agenda.

The first CAG was chaired by Carlo Ciampi and consisted of 16 members: seven representatives of transnational business, four representatives of trade unions, four representatives from the public sector (apart from the former Italian Prime Minister Ciampi, one former central bank governor, one former finance minister and the Commission Permanent Representative Alexis Jacquemin) and one independent expert. In the years 1995–96, CAG-I published four reports, all titled *Enhancing European Competitiveness*. Headed by the former Secretary General of OECD Jean-Claude Paye, a CAG-II started in 1997. Next to Paye, 12 members were recruited from business (5), trade unions (3) and the public sector (apart from Jacquemin, a former prime minister and two former ministers, one of them being Neelie Kroes, the present commissioner for competition). Without any doubt, the composition of both CAGs was clearly in favour of free market proponents. In fact, a number of its members were directly recruited from the ERT. And this was in turn openly reflected in the subsequent reports. Between 1997 and the end of 1999, CAG-II published four new reports. The first report, called *Competitiveness for Employment*, repeatedly emphasised the need to modernise/reform social protection systems (Competitiveness Advisory Group 1997). Its first chapter straightforwardly established a negative correlation between laws to protect existing jobs and job creation, albeit an endnote mentioned the fact that the three union leaders in the CAG were 'not convinced of the evidence of this assertion on the effects of labour laws'. Overhauling social rigidities at the national level was seen as an essential part of Europe's ambition to return to the top rank of the world economy. In a final report of the CAG-II, published in September 1999, all the recurrent themes of the previous reports were summarised in a list of 20 priorities, including the reform of the 'European social model' in general and labour market flexibilisation in particular. The report concluded that the 'Commission must develop high level benchmarks, with associated targets, to monitor Europe's place in internationalisation and European competitiveness' (Competitiveness Advisory Group 1999: 20). The conclusions that can be drawn from this and other statements is that the aim of enhancing European competitiveness was not focused on increasing intra-European competition. The stakes were much higher: the ultimate goal was to increase competitiveness of European business *vis-à-vis* the outside world. This suggests that the CAG's 'operational conclusions' can be read as a blueprint for the Lisbon Strategy which was launched only half a year later.

The Lisbon Strategy as competitiveness discourse

Echoing the ambitions of the CAG, the Lisbon European Council meeting of March 2000 introduced 'a new strategic goal for the next decade: to become the most competitive and dynamic knowledge-based economy in the world capable of sustainable economic growth with more jobs and greater social cohesion'. The subsequent Lisbon Strategy attempted to reconcile supranational, economic and monetary integration with the illusion of national self-determination in 'modernising' the so-called European social model. In the words of the Lisbon European Council, 'achieving the new strategic goal will rely primarily on the private sector, as well on PPPs. It will depend on mobilising the resources available on the markets, as well on efforts by member states'. In terms of governance, however,

> A fully decentralised approach will be applied in line with the principle of subsidiarity in which the Union, the Member States, the regional and local levels, as well as the social partners and civil society, will be actively involved, using variable forms of partnership. A method of benchmarking best practices on managing change will be devised by the European Commission networking with different providers and users, namely the social partners, companies and NGOs.
>
> (Lisbon European Council 2000)

It is not the place here to evaluate the Lisbon Strategy in terms of the sectoral targets that were set. It suffices to recall that, on the eve of the planned 2005 mid-term review of the Lisbon Strategy, all the major players in Europe – be it the European Commission, transnational business or national governments – were in agreement that the delivery of the Lisbon objectives was utterly inadequate. In order to review the Lisbon process, a High-level Group on the Lisbon Strategy was established in April 2004. Chaired by the Dutch former Prime Minister (and social democrat) Wim Kok, this High-level Group was much more balanced in its composition than the previous CAGs. Three CEOs of European transnational business were joined by three (former) trade union leaders, four independent experts and three representatives of the public sector (including Wim Kok). This did not, however, prevent the High-level Group from taking a rather exceptional stand. First, it was argued that the Lisbon agenda was overloaded with objectives and conflicting priorities. Social and environmental objectives were only to be realised if, first, European competitiveness could be enhanced. Accordingly, priority should be given to the competitiveness objective. Second, national governments were to blame for the inadequate delivery of the Lisbon goals. As time was running out leaving no room for complacency, a successful relaunch of the Lisbon process would thus depend on coordinated action at the member state level, involving all the relevant 'stakeholders' (i.e. social partners) (High-level Group 2004).

On the basis of this report, the Commission submitted a number of documents to the March 2005 Spring European Council, which, *inter alia*, adopted with only minor modifications a new governance cycle based on partnership and ownership. Although it is too early to assess the impact of this new governance cycle, some preliminary conclusions can be drawn as far as the OMC is concerned. First, there seems to be much more stress on credible commitment and delivery than before. Member states and national civil societies are much more involved and – though the guidelines are still nonbinding – it seems more difficult to defect. Second, coordination between member states (through peer pressure and benchmarking) is still in place, but more emphasis is laid on coordination between the Commission and each individual member state (avoiding excessive blaming and shaming among member states) and between national and subnational public authorities and private actors. The latter is captured with the new buzzwords partnership and ownership. Third, the Commission seems to play a bigger role in the new governance cycle, not only through its direct contacts with individual member states but also through its role in setting up a 'Community Lisbon Programme' covering all actions to be undertaken in the interest of growth and employment. This last point actually gives license to subordinate important policy areas – like the EES and the EU's cohesion policy – to the all-encompassing Lisbon Growth and Employment Strategy (on the effects of the Lisbon agenda on cohesion policy, see Holman 2006).

It is still unclear whether the new governance cycle may strengthen the 'soft' OMC, which basically remains an uneasy combination of PPPs at the European level (agenda setting and policy planning) and multilevel governance (implementation). In an 'integrated market governed by fragmented sovereignty', as Wolfgang Streeck argues, 'the wielders of that sovereignty compete with one another, in part for the respect of their citizens (...) but most importantly for the allegiance of mobile production factors' (Streeck 1997: 3). The 'open method of co-ordination' is perhaps one of the best examples of this: in keeping up the illusion of the 'persistent plurality of national citizenship regimes', it introduces mechanisms of regime competition in the field of social policy. More specifically, peer pressure and recommendations from the European Commission are used to make domestic political and social relations more fluid and more adaptable to the exigencies of European capital. It is about separating employment and labour market policies from broad political accountability in order to make national governments more responsive to the discipline of market forces. The Lisbon Strategy is certainly not a supranational policy, but neither is it strictly of intergovernmental nature. The open method of co-ordination underlying this strategy is a new political style which successfully attempts to reconcile supranational, economic and monetary integration with the illusion of national self-determination in dismantling (or, in official discourse, modernising and flexibilising) post-war welfare state structures. As applied in the Lisbon Strategy, it is not only an instrument in the intentional regulation of social relationships at the national level – reflecting the rational and strategic objectives of particular interests at the European level – but also, and perhaps more importantly, an instrument in mobilising human effort. It is about the role of symbols or, to put it differently, about discourse production at the European level. And again, the partnership between European business and the European Commission has been a vital element in this process.

Conclusions

This chapter has been centred on the following key concepts: governance, asymmetrical regulation, PPPs and the OMC. It was argued that the shift from government to governance was concomitant with the neoliberal turn of the 1980s and 1990s, on the one hand, and the relaunch of European integration, on the other. At the same time, it was emphasised that the emerging structures and practices of private governance were always politically embedded, though in the case of the EU, in a rather peculiar, multilevel way. The concept of asymmetrical regulation tried to capture the political and institutional embedding of transnational governance in quasi-state structures at the supranational level, on the one hand, and in traditional structures of public authority at the national level, on the other. In fact, this multilevel embeddedness determined the extent and limits of non-state authority, notably that of organised transnational business. At the same time, it constituted the playground in which the ERT could materialise its strategic goals, *inter alia*, through its privileged partnership with the Commission, in the process circumventing practices of democratic accountability at the national level. It was further argued that the informal partnership between the ERT and the Commission got a more formal setting through the establishment of the CAG which, in the second half of the 1990s, prepared the ground for the subsequent Lisbon Strategy. In the course of the Lisbon process, and particularly after its 2005 relaunch, finally, the notion of PPP (and ownership) as well as of the OMC was redirected in order to involve (or co-opt) the social partners at the national level. In short, new practices of what we could call transnational *public–private* governance were top-down imposed on national civil societies (while at the same time, being legitimised by national governments through European Council decisions, as we should not forget) and supported by an all-encompassing competitiveness discourse.

As a result, industrial relations – for long a classical case of private governance and self-regulation at the national level –are no longer a matter of trade union and business leaders negotiating under the umbrella of elected politicians. Transnational public–private governance embeds industrial relations into much less transparent and accountable structures.

13 Transnational private governance in the EU

When social partners bargain beyond borders

Stijn Smismans[1]

Introduction

Neo-corporatism has a long history both in practice and in academic analysis. It refers to a form of socioeconomic governance in which peak associations of trade unions and employer's organisations play a central role. Neo-corporatism has been mainly linked to the European continent – although with strongly different intensity across countries, and excluding the communist countries – and often placing it in opposition to a more pluralist system of interest intermediation in the United States. The neo-corporatist reality includes both a tripartite interaction between trade unions, employer's organisations and the government on aspects of socioeconomic policy, and the recognition of an autonomous sphere in which trade unions and employers' organisations can on a bipartite basis set standards for the employment relation through collective agreements. While the natural and legal effects of collective agreements differ across the countries, one can generally argue that neo-corporatism includes this aspect of leaving certain regulatory tasks to the autonomy of the social partners. This tradition of collective bargaining and collective agreements can be considered as one of the most developed examples of private governance, although the traditional literature on the issue would not employ that concept. In fact, the neo-corporatist literature has focused more on the tripartite interaction with the government, whereas the industrial relations literature mainly describes the different national systems in a comparative perspective. Labour lawyers have been most confronted with the particular 'private–public' nature of collective agreements since they noticed on the one hand the private contract features of such agreements while recognising on the other hand a more public governance dimension to them due to their normative function. Yet, while the concept of 'private governance' is relatively young in political science, it is even less a part of the lawyers' vocabulary.

Industrial relations and the possibility of regulation through collective agreements are institutionally embedded in a national context. This relates first to the scope of such private governance, since it would not go beyond the national borders, confined to national agreements – be they of a cross-sectoral or sectoral nature – and more decentralised levels than the company level or occasionally at regional level. Moreover, natural and legal effects of collective agreements and the relation between different levels of bargaining are defined within a national institutional context. This national institutional context can be set to different degrees by the public authorities, but it can also be defined in a more autonomous way by the social partners at the national level, with public authority setting only the margins and leaving it mainly to management and labour to define themselves the institutional framework for their interactions.

However, with European integration, industrial relations transcend national borders and trade unions and employers' organisations have been able to engage into European level collective bargaining and collective agreements. One can therefore talk about transnational private governance, although both in its emergence and in its effectiveness, such transnational private governance by the European social partners strongly depends on its institutional embeddedness.

In the following sections, I will first analyse how the European social dialogue emerged and will then consider under which conditions it works or not. I will subsequently assess the scope and outcome of such transnational private governance together with its features as seen from a democratic perspective.

The emergence of European social dialogue as transnational private governance

The emergence of bargaining between the social partners at the European level is both the result of autonomous action on the one hand, and support and institution building by the Community institutions on the other.

Since the 1960s, the Commission has supported the creation of Joint Committees bringing together, at the European level, management and labour in particular sectors of the economy. The aim was 'no less than to contribute to the construction of a European system of industrial relations and foster free collective bargaining' (European Commission 1985), but the outcome fell far short of this goal. Although 26 sector-specific joint committees, informal working parties and non-structured discussion groups adopted more than 100 joint texts (European Commission 1995b), real sectoral agreements were not signed and the joint opinions remained very general and vague. Rather than being a forum for bipartite dialogue, the committees functioned, at best, as a consultative structure with regard to the European Commission (EC), especially for the Commission directorates dealing with a particular sectoral policy (e.g. agriculture). The Commission relied also on other consultation structures such as the European Economic and Social Committee (Smismans 2000) and tripartite advisory committees composed of management, labour and representatives from national administrations, and an attempt was made in the 1970s to establish tripartite concertation at the European level on the broad direction of socioeconomic policies by way of Tripartite Conferences creating direct interaction between social partners and ministers. However, bipartite action at European level between trade unions and employers' organisations remained hard to develop, not least because the European confederations of management and labour (in the sector) needed to be organisationally consolidated or even created.

The idea of bipartite dialogue between both sides of industry at the European level was revived in particular with the arrival of Jacques Delors as president of the European Commission. He strongly favoured such dialogue and argued that the Commission had a role to play here as 'facilitator'. He subsequently found backing by Member States with high social standards that saw in the European social dialogue a way to circumvent social policy stalemate in the Council (Falkner 1998: 72; Johnson 2005: 63).

The idea of European collective agreements and the role of the Commission as facilitator was formally recognised in the 1986 Single European Act (Article 118b): 'the Commission shall endeavour to develop the dialogue between management and labour at European level which could, if the two sides consider it desirable, lead to relations based on agreement'. It was not only a question of formally recognising the possibility of such transnational private governance, but the European Communities also engaged in financial support to strengthen the organisational structure and expertise of the social partners at the European level, in particular via support to the 'weaker party', namely the European Trade Union Confederation.

However, while this strengthened the dynamics for bipartite action at the European level (in particular for cross-sectoral dialogue), one has to wait until a further reinforcing of the institutional structure by the Maastricht Treaty – and in particular by the Social Agreement attached to it – to arrive at the first European collective agreements.

Today, the EC Treaty provides a detailed institutional framework for European social dialogue which builds both on the autonomy of the social partners and on the role that the European institutions may play to encourage and to give effect to such dialogue. Article 139(1) EC Treaty states clearly that 'should management and labour so desire, the dialogue between them at Community level may lead to contractual relations, including agreements'. Moreover, the Charter of Fundamental Rights of the European Union includes the right of collective bargaining – although with some limitations (see Ryan 2003: 78; Smismans 2004: 375–380). While the Treaty thus recognises the importance of such private governance, it also sees a role for public authorities in relation to it. The EC Treaty promotes social dialogue at all levels, on the one hand by identifying the promotion of such dialogue as one of the Community's social objectives (article 136) and on the other by giving the Commission the task to encourage cooperation between the Member States on this issue (article 140) and to provide balanced support for dialogue at the European level (article 138(1)). Although apparently contradictory, all of these provisions can both be read as a recognition of the autonomy of the social partners but at the same time also as a recognition of the role of public authorities in such private regulation.

The procedures provided in Articles 138–139 EC Treaty further strengthen the potential interaction between European public institutions and the European social partners, building at the same moment on the examples of national industrial relations systems with strong public intervention and those with weak public intervention. According to Articles 138–139 EC, the Commission has to consult the European social partners on all legislative initiatives in the social policy field. On such occasion, the European social partners may express their desire to deal with the issue by European collective agreement rather than by legislation. In that case, the Commission will suspend its legislative action and if the social partners reach an agreement, this solution will be preferred to legislative action. Such a European collective agreement can be implemented in two ways. In the first place – which can be called the 'regulatory route' – the European social partners ask the EC and the Council to implement their agreement by Directive, in which case the agreement will have the same effect as European legislation and be binding for all Member States, which can be sanctioned in court for non-implementation. This solution is inspired by national industrial relations systems which provide strong public intervention to give effect *erga omnes* to collective agreements. In the second place – which can be called the 'autonomous route' – the European social partners decide to implement the agreement themselves by relying on their national member organisations and the instruments of industrial relations available in the Member States. In that case, the agreement does not become part of Community law, and the possibility to sanction non-implementation through court action appears to be non-existing or very limited, although still an issue of controversy among lawyers (Treu 1996: 172; Bamber and Cordova 1993; Deinert 2003; Schiek 2005).

The European social dialogue is thus a complex reality, which allows for bipartite action[2] among the European social partners at both cross-sectoral and sectoral level.[3] While most of the dialogue has consisted of joint opinions addressed to the European institutions, gradually the European social partners have also addressed bipartite documents to their member organisations. Yet, such documents have been mainly very mild in nature, such as manuals, exchange of best practices or recommendations without particular follow-up mechanisms. Only following the Maastricht Treaty have some binding European collective agreements been adopted – using the regulatory route – whereas more recently there is a tendency to European collective agreements in which the social partners provide particular follow-up procedures they will take care of themselves – i.e. autonomous route to implementation.

A form of transnational private governance has thus emerged in which social partners bargain and set standards for employment relations beyond national borders. However, to be something more than weak declarations of intent, such transnational private governance seems to a great extent dependent on 'the shadow of hierarchy' provided by the Community institutions. Moreover, to make it work in practice, such transnational private governance has to feed back into national industrial relations systems and is thus also dependent on institutional embeddedness at the national level.

When it works and when not

Following the Maastricht Treaty, the first European collective agreements have been signed; on parental leave, part-time work and fixed term work. In the three cases, the European social partners engaged in negotiations after the Commission had consulted them on a legislative initiative. Moreover, once they had signed the agreement, the social partners asked the Commission and Council to implement the agreement by Council Directive. The three agreements provided for regulation on issues for which legislative initiatives in the Council had been blocked for years.[4] The European social dialogue could thus be seen as a particular breakthrough in European social policy due to the introduction of a private governance procedure. Yet, at the same time, this 'private' governance mechanism appeared to be very dependent on public authorities. Only following the EC's move to take legislative action, did the European social partners engage in negotiation.

In fact, European employers' organisations have no particular interest in European regulation on social issues. Management has the comfortable position that a *status quo* is to its advantage. For business, the European integration process can best be confined to a process of market building in which 'negative integration' – based on the freedom of movement and on competition – removes barriers to trade. Non-decision on social issues plays consequently into the hands of management.[5] Moreover, business has enough resources to avoid (through lobbying by individual undertakings, ad hoc coalitions and business associations) 'market-distorting' redistributive intervention or the development of welfare-state-like international institutions. The European employers' organisation UNICE is consequently only used as a weak confederation which may enter into negotiation with labour as far as social regulation concurs with market-building logic and does not induce particular economic costs.

Labour, on the other hand, is the party in the forefront of demands for further European social policy intervention, but it lacks the bargaining power to get management to the negotiating table on issues it considers important. This is partially due to the fact that 'labour at European level' is not homogeneous and that trade unions from different Member States may consider their interests to be divergent. Thus European-wide labour standards may be perceived by workers and unions in poorer countries as devices to protect their fellow workers in richer countries from investment and employment losses. In certain cases, 'national corporatist' alliances of management and labour in some Member States arise against comparable alliances from other Member States.[6] Even if national trade union leaders still develop a common 'European labour interest' within the framework of the ETUC, it is less evident that the rank and file will develop a sense of European labour solidarity (Turner 1998: 119). Both due to divergent interests and levels of scale, the basic instruments of class struggle, such as a strike, are particularly difficult to develop at a European level.

The particular imbalance between management and labour is the main problem for the European social dialogue. The basic idea of industrial relations is that management and labour are brought to agreement by social power relations, based on the classic weapons of class struggle (Kahn-Freund 1972: 134). Therefore, besides (very) soft norms that are not considered problematic by management, the European social dialogue is only likely to lead to results under the threat of legislative action. Only under the threat of binding and more constringent provisions, management will have the advantage to negotiate with labour. Bercusson has therefore talked about 'bargaining in the shadow of the law' (Bercusson 1994: 20, 1996: 541).

The first European collective agreements did not only show a certain dependence on public authorities for initiating the bargaining process, but also for the implementation of the agreements reached. In fact, the first European collective agreements have always opted for implementation by Council Directive. Most observers had – and to a great extent still have – serious doubts on whether autonomous implementation is a viable alternative. The question is to what extent the European social partners can convince their national member organisations to put the agreement into practice. Moreover, this strongly depends on national industrial relations traditions, which implies that European collective agreements would be implemented to very different degrees across Europe (Bamber and Cordova 1993; Treu 1996). If the intention of signing collective agreements at the European level is to create a minimum level of common standards and application across Europe, the only realistic option may then be to implement by Council Directive. This makes the European social dialogue obviously strongly dependent on public intervention to the extent that one can question the 'private' character of such transnational governance. In fact, the European social dialogue has been described as a regulatory technique rather than an additional level of bipartite negotiation in a multilevel collective bargaining system (Lo Faro 1999; Bernard 2000).

However, more recently, one has witnessed some more autonomous developments in the European social dialogue. Namely, the first 'autonomous' European collective agreements have now been signed on issues of telework, work-related stress and crystalline silica, a cancer-causing agent. In these agreements, the European social partners provide follow-up procedures through which they would, on a regular basis, assess the implementation of the agreement by their member organisations in practice.[7]

While this creates a new dynamic in the European social dialogue and a tendency towards more autonomy, there remain important doubts on the viability of such a dialogue out of the shadow of public intervention. First of all, the main autonomous European collective agreements signed until now, namely on telework and on stress, have still emerged in relation to initial attempts of the Commission to take action in the field. Second, there remains great uncertainty on whether these agreements will be effective and implemented. The European social partners are currently busy reporting on the implementation of the telework agreement which will clearly function as a test case. As the main UNICE negotiator for the telework agreement stated: 'if it is not properly adopted, this will be the last sort of agreement of this type' (cited by Branch 2005: 342).

The European social dialogue is likely to remain strongly dependent on its international institutional embeddedness. The more agreements would attempt at binding provisions, the more the emergence of such an agreement would depend on the threat of legislative intervention, and the more it would depend on public authorities to ensure the implementation. If joint action between the European social partners only aims at common statements, the threat of public intervention is not necessary, but the effects of such statements can be questioned. In between, there is a broad continuum of types of joint actions of the European social partners providing their own follow-up mechanisms. While we remain for the moment ignorant about the effectiveness of such follow-up procedures, practice shows that the social partners only tend to agree on the strongest follow-up procedures if the threat of Community initiative is more realistic (e.g. agreements on stress and telework), although entirely autonomous initiatives are not excluded in cases with strong common understanding between management and labour (e.g. agreement on Crystalline Silica).

This brings us to another condition – in addition to institutional embeddedness – to make the European social dialogue work, namely value homogeneity. It is often argued that the European social dialogue – in contrast to traditional industrial relations – is non-conflictual (Quintin 1998). As argued above, trade unions lack at the European level their classic instruments of class conflict. Agreement will therefore be reached only on limited issues for which, on the basis of rational argument and common interest, management and labour do not strongly differ, such as in the less conflictual area of occupational health and safety,[8] as illustrated by the autonomous agreement on Crystalline Silica. Alternatively, agreement can be reached under the threat of European legislation. However, this also implies that European collective agreements should be in line with the objectives and market-building nature of the European Union. Value homogeneity is thus not only an issue between management and labour but also one of fit with the European integration project in which Member States, although anxious about the effects of globalisation, attempt to keep control over their social and welfare systems and prefer to engage into 'open coordination'[9] of best practice rather than embarking on anything that might encourage the idea of a European welfare and industrial relations system (Kleinman 2002: 132). The transnational private governance of the European social dialogue is thus very unlikely to develop beyond the contours of a European integration project that is above all the project of building a common market.

In addition to institutional embeddedness and value homogeneity, the success of the European social dialogue also depends on the resources of the main actors of this private governance mechanism, i.e. the European social partners.

In particular, since the Delors Commission, the European Union has played an important role in supporting financially the formation and functioning of European social partners organisations. In particular, the strengthening of ETUC (*vis-à-vis* its own constituents and *vis-à-vis* the employers) was considered by the Commission to be a crucial condition to get the social dialogue off the ground (Ross 1995: 377). Therefore, it provided substantial funding to facilitate union training, research and meetings at the European level. Moreover, the Commission has provided an infrastructure for the European social partners to meet by the creation of the social dialogue committees at cross-sectoral and sectoral level. While the Commission can provide financial support for dialogue infrastructure and for the organisations, it is up to the European social partners themselves to strengthen their internal decision-making procedures in order to allow them to engage into European negotiations on behalf of their member organisations. Whereas the cross-sectoral organisations, such as European Trade Union Confederation, Union of Industrial and Employers' Confederation of Europe and European Centre of Enterprises with Public Participation, have strengthened their structures to act as representative actors in European social dialogue, at sectoral level there remain problems in certain sectors to identify representative organisations. The problem has become more acute since the last enlargement of the EU. Industrial relations systems in the former communist countries had mainly to be built up from scratch. In particular the sectoral level of bargaining is very weakly developed in these countries (Weiss 2004). This is a problem for the representativity of European level agreements as well as for their implementation. The problem is particularly acute for autonomous collective agreements. The new Member States have reformed their political institutions and have the instruments to transpose European collective agreements implemented by Council Directive. While the application on the ground of such agreements may still show difficulties given the weakness of the industrial relations infrastructure, this problem is even bigger for autonomous agreements where the implementation depends entirely on the autonomous means of the social partners. It has even been suggested that this important problem of implementation in the new Member States could explain why management has now suddenly agreed on autonomous agreements at the European level, i.e. it does not risk much by engaging into such agreements (Branch 2005).

This also shows how the European social dialogue is not only embedded in public institutions at the European level but is also strongly dependent on its embeddedness in national industrial relations systems. European social dialogue is not a form of transnational private governance which would regulate the behaviour of transnational actors that act independently of decentralised levels. The European social dialogue has not the objective to regulate the behaviour of the European social partners as such, but to regulate conditions at work. This implies that this transnational private governance has to feed back into the reality of industrial relations at a more decentralised level. To be effective, it has to rely on national industrial relations systems – either by government intervention at the national level or by means of industrial relations available within the national system. Transnational private governance will have to take into account this national diversity of industrial relations traditions. However, national diversity might also lead to European agreements being very vague in content, or to such divers implementation that one can question the added value of transnational regulation that aims for common standards across borders.

Input- and output-legitimacy of the European social dialogue[10]

Neo-corporatist systems have been criticised from a democratic point of view since they take regulatory tasks out of the parliamentary realm and leave it in the hands of a small number of peak associations of management and labour. Also at the European level, the procedures of Articles 138–139 EC Treaty provide an element of 'horizontal subsidiarity' in favour of the European social partners, since the Commission would suspend its legislative initiative if management and labour prefer to deal with the issue by collective agreement. Even where the collective agreement is implemented by Council Directive and thus will have the same value of a law, the procedure does not provide any intervention of the European Parliament and the Commission, and the Council will simply adopt the agreement drafted by the social partners without changing a single letter in it. Moreover, in addition to the lack of parliamentary involvement, the UEAPME case before the Court of First Instance of the European Communities – in which a European organisation representing associations of small and medium enterprises contested an agreement signed by the peak associations – illustrates how the neo-corporatist features of the European social dialogue are not without controversy. Although the Commission consults a large spectrum of European social partners' organisations, and negotiation is based on the principle of mutual recognition among the social partners, practice has seen a tendency for centralisation of negotiation by the main peak associations, in particular at cross-sectoral level. UEAPME, for instance, having lost its case before the Court of First Instance, preferred a collaboration with UNICE to get its opinion represented at the negotiating table – an evolution towards inter-organisational coordination and centralisation that has been welcomed by the Commission (European Commission 1998a).

Authors on neo-corporatism have mostly stressed that they were merely describing reality and did not want to make any normative proposal (Schmitter 1979: 8). Nevertheless, some normative considerations can be found in the neo-corporatist literature, in particular opposing the system to (neo-)pluralism (in particular: Schmitter 1983; Streeck and Schmitter 1985). First, it is argued that neo-corporatism allows the voice of weaker interests. As Schmitter states 'the spontaneous, voluntaristic, and episodic relations of pluralism seem freer in principle, but in practice they produce a greater inequality of access to those in power' (Schmitter 1993: 338). So one can argue that the consultation by the Commission of 57 organisations under Article 138 guarantees the participation of weaker interest groups which, in a pure pluralist setting of lobbying, would not get access to policy making. Second, whereas in a pluralist setting, interest groups lobby policy makers directly to present their particular interest without taking into account positions of other groups; a neo-corporatist setting, on the contrary, provides structures where opposed interests meet; for instance, in tripartite concertation or in bipartite negotiation. The opposing parties are confronted with each others' arguments, which causes a process of 'adjusting and adapting preferences' (Streeck and Schmitter 1985; Mansbridge 1992, 1995). Third, it is argued that in a neo-corporatist setting, the 'encompassing organisations' internally balance a wide variety of interests (Schmitter 1983: 36; Streeck and Schmitter 1985: 132) contrary to a pluralist setting of interest group competition, in which the numerous small interest groups act as rent seekers of their particular small interest (Mansbridge 1992: 47). Finally, the legitimacy of neo-corporatist systems has also been sought in the fact of State's policies being substantially egalitarian, principally through its redistributive welfare policies. The majoritarian principle is followed by virtue of the fact that the majority's economic interest is served (Schmitter 1983: 45; Cawson 1986: 146). Commentators have argued that corporatist countries tend to have above-average levels of egalitarian or welfare state income redistribution (Olson 1995: 31).

It is impossible to base the legitimacy of the European social dialogue on output in terms of substantial egalitarian and redistributive welfare policies as would be the case at the national level – if the argument is valid at all independently of the level of analysis. Resulting from our analysis above, given the market-building nature of European policy, the reluctance of the Member States to transfer policy-making powers on social issues to the European level, and the imbalance of power between management and labour also at the European level, the European social dialogue will be limited to regulatory issues rather than direct redistributive ones, such as wage bargaining or concertation on levels of public expenditure. Moreover, the limited number of European collective agreements as well as their content shows that, even as a regulatory technique, European collective bargaining provides procedural norms rather than substantive ones, and soft instruments rather than binding norms. From that perspective, concerns about the democratic weaknesses of European collective bargaining seem to be outweighted by the moderate results and problems of effectiveness.

Yet there may be a way seeing the glass half-full rather than half-empty. The European social dialogue has enabled the weaker party, namely labour, to act at the European level and has provided a forum for more balanced representation. It has led to the regulation of some social issues which had been blocked by political stalemate until then. Moreover, it has led to horizontal collaboration and awareness among trade unions across borders (and among employers' organisations) in an attempt to provide common answers to the challenges of globalisation. Compared to the importance of the challenge, the response is a weak one, and as a form of transnational 'private' governance, it depends strongly on public intervention to ensure both effectiveness and legitimacy in particular where norms are aimed to have a binding nature. And yet, whilst globalisation undermines States' ability to implement social regulation, any attempt towards transnational governance in which public–private interaction leads to more balanced representation, which can provide for such regulation, may be considered as a small step in the right direction.

Notes

1 I am grateful to the programme 'Incentivazione alla mobilità di studiosi stranieri e italiani residenti all'estero' of the Italian Ministry of Research and University for

funding the research related to this chapter. I would also like to thank my colleagues Evelyne Léonard, Pierre Tilly, Paul Marginson and Roland Erne with whom I engaged in a study on 'New structures, forms and processes of governance in European industrial relations' for the European Foundation for the Improvement of Living and Working Conditions. Some of the arguments in this chapter have profited from my participation in that project.

2 The concept of European social dialogue is sometimes used in a broader sense including also forms of consultation of the European social partners by the European institutions or forms of tripartite interaction at the European level. The European social partners expressed their preference to use the concept only to refer to their bipartite action. In this article, both the concept and the analysis are limited to such action.

3 In addition, collective bargaining can also emerge beyond borders at company level, namely within Multinational Companies with a global or European nature. The European Union has played an important role here with the Directive on European Works Councils which requires companies with enterprises in several European countries to establish a European Works Council, i.e. a consultation and information structure for the employees. While only very few of these EWCs provide the possibility to negotiate, by early 2005, about 46 joint texts had been concluded in this context in 32 companies (EWCB 2005), most of them, though, of very mild in nature. In this article, I will not further deal with the company level but focus my attention on what has traditionally been understood as 'European social dialogue', namely the cross-sectoral and the sectoral level. For transnational collective bargaining at company level and EWCs, see Marginson (2000) and Arrowsmith and Marginson (2006).

4 The first initiatives of the Commission on parental leave, for instance, date back to 1983 (Delarue 1998: 175).

5 National employers' organisations may in certain conditions plead for higher European social standards. Namely, for management in countries which already have higher standards, such European regulation would mean a (temporary) competitive advantage given that their competitors will now have to make the investments they have already made.

6 National interests of labour may seek to outcompete labour in other countries on investment, export markets and employment (economic nationalism) and to defend established national industrial relations systems (institutional nationalism) (Streeck 1996: 92).

7 It is not always easy to identify when one can talk about an autonomous collective agreement. The European social partners have not been consistent in the definition of their texts, which can be called agreements, recommendations, guidelines, codes of conduct and so on. In an attempt for conceptual clarification, the European Commission (2004b) has suggested that (autonomous) agreements are those texts to be implemented and monitored by a given date according to the process provided in the agreement, whereas recommendations entail a regular reporting and following-up over a longer period without a specific deadline by which results need to be achieved.

8 The protection of workers against accidents and diseases has become such a basic principle of the European welfare states that it has more easily constituted a common ground between labour and management than other social policy issues – although the technicalities of the sector make collective agreements not always the preferred instrument. See Smismans (2004: 93 and 398).

9 The 'open method of coordination' uses benchmarking and reporting as a policy instrument at the European level to coordinate national policies and has become a key feature of European social policy. Among the extensive literature, see Zeitlin and Pochet (2005) and De Schutter and Deakin (2005).

10 For an in-depth analysis of the argument, see Smismans (2004: 329–400).

14 Self-regulation and public regulation

Financial services and the out-of-court complaints bodies

Karsten Ronit

Introduction

In 2001, a Europe-wide out-of-court complaints network for financial services (Fin-Net) was launched by the European Commission. This initiative followed an earlier action plan relating to the financial services and rested on the formulation of a new strategy to dismantle barriers to the free operation of an international market in the area of financial services (European Commission 1996). The task of this network is to resolve disputes between service providers in the financial sector and consumers.

Thus, the Fin-Net is the first fully functioning cross-border and alternative dispute resolution (ADR) system to be established at the European level. The European Commission has taken a key interest in breathing life into new forms of governance and has put great emphasis on the self-regulatory capacities of the financial industries and the participation of civil society organisations. The institutions in the Fin-Net, and the principles guiding them, are interesting from the perspective of private transnational governance. Thus, the general public initiative is triggered largely by private national bodies that need a more encompassing – and public – framework for problem solving.

These institutional developments in the financial services also raise a number of interesting theoretical questions that will be addressed in this chapter:

- Public and private: Private transnational governance is not isolated from public authority, and there are various forms of interaction. In our particular case, a public scheme at the international level is based on experiences with private regulation at national levels and solidified through the creation of new private institutions linked to international public regulation. Indeed, there is much experimenting with mixed regulation.
- International and domestic: International governance can be institutionalised exclusively at international levels, but, in many cases, international institutions must build upon and produce domestic arrangements. However, the sequence of institution building is not simply a matter of establishing national arrangements by creating a common international framework, or an

international initiative being translated to national traditions; rather, the process comprises a complex set of procedures.

- Business and outside participation: Self-regulation can be accomplished through business alone, but there is also the possibility of outside participation by interested and affected parties. The question is whether such arrangements involving consumers are prompted by enlightened business interests or active consumer groups, or, perhaps, encouraged by public authority in domestic settings and at the European level.

In this chapter, we shall first examine the basic properties of the Fin-Net that are essential to understanding its complexity. The network is not widely known, and, to some degree, it represents a novel form of international business regulation. Having sketched the infrastructure and mechanisms of the network, we shall relate it to more recent attempts to draw on self-regulation as an alternative to traditional top-down public regulation. Thus, the emergence of the Fin-Net is not an isolated event or a unique model that fits the financial sector and that is not applicable beyond this narrow domain. The broad principles formulated in the emerging European consumer policy are also applied in our case, but the creation of the Fin-Net is in no way reducible to the implementation of a general scheme in a specific branch of industry. Having laid out these regulatory contexts, we then discuss some of the key problems in the framework – namely, the linkages between public and private authority, the role of European and national arrangements, the involvement of outside parties and the cooperation between organised business and consumer interests. Finally, a conclusion will summarise the major findings and discuss their implications for private transnational governance.

Oscillating theoretical contexts

Today's self-regulation has several historical precursors (Milgrom *et al.* 1990), but much regulatory innovation has been documented. To grapple with this sprawling regulation, a new vocabulary of self-regulatory mechanisms has emerged. Accounting for this empirical and theoretical richness is, however, beyond the scope of this chapter; instead, three aspects of the study of self-regulation demand attention. First, self-regulation unfolds in different territorial contexts and, in a period of international governance, these territorial forms must be closely linked. Second, self-regulation suggests that only private actors are involved in regulation; however, in many cases public authority is crucial if private arrangements are to work. Third, the category of private actors is a very mixed one: it not only deals with business, but also includes independent professional bodies and various countervailing forces.

Self-regulation has mainly been studied in either a domestic or an international context. Unfortunately, few studies have examined how national units are linked either to each other or to an international directive and monitoring body (Ronit 2001). Indeed, many regulatory arrangements exist independently of international developments and, international arrangements are not always building upon, and linked to, a domestic scene – but linkages are growing.

A factor contributing to this negligence is the traditional compartmentalisation between international relations and comparative politics as sub-fields of political science. In both fields, self-regulation is largely sidestepped and pushed into the periphery by state-centric views on regulation.

In the study of domestic politics, the discovery, or rather rediscovery, of alternative governance systems beyond the realms of market and state was made in the 1980s, but these exercises were largely unnoticed by scholars of international relations. As a discipline, international relations have been particularly stubborn in recognising the role of private organisations. During the last decade, however, numerous works have emphasised the contribution of these actors to international governance (Cutler *et al.* 1999a; Ronit and Schneider 2000; Hall and Biersteker 2002). Self-regulation completely run by business – or other authority holders – is practiced in a number of cases, and no one can completely rule out the possibility that business-driven arrangements can solve a range of societal problems. Research, however, has shown that self-regulation is rarely purely private. Assistance by public authority is often needed to sustain such private interest governments (Streeck and Schmitter 1985); otherwise, free-riding leads to lower standards and disqualifies private solutions. Private rule-making is not necessarily a conspiracy against society because 'regulation-for-competition' is a hallmark of public intervention and aims at providing a collective good (see Jordana and Levi-Faur 2004: 5–7).

Relations between public and private authority are complex: Sometimes public authority is wheeled in to control otherwise self-interested actors, and sometimes public intervention is encouraged or demanded by business. Consequently, self-regulation is largely politicised and appears in the form of regulated self-regulation. The actual mix of private and public legalisation, however, needs further scrutiny.

A third key element of self-regulation is the contribution by non-business actors. Whenever self-regulation is driven exclusively by business, demands and expectations in the immediate environment must be integrated into corporate strategy. Indeed, some industries and corporations adopt codes of conduct and other devices to improve relations with customers, sometimes with the express goal of preempting government action.

In cases of regulated self-regulation, an important public goal is to avoid bias in arrangements and represent the interests of weaker segments in society, which may find it difficult to organise in a collective format (Olson 1965). However, instances of standard setting are reported, wherein single corporations or a cluster of firms negotiate with their customers and, occasionally, with various civic groups (Cashore *et al.* 2004). These rules rarely span a whole industry; consequently, encompassing implementation often proves insufficient. Research has also emphasised the possibility of outside participation through the formalised integration of relevant stakeholders. These forces do not simply influence and change corporate perceptions and behaviour through their role in the economy (Gunningham and Rees 1997). They represent alternative and countervailing interests and are formal participants to self-regulatory arrangements, in which they take an active part in the formulation and implementation of rules (Boddewyn 1988).

This brief presentation of some of the key problems in self-regulation and how they have been dealt with in existing research shows that analyses have given considerable attention to the status of both domestic and international self-regulation, but not so much to how these are intertwined; that research heralds new forms of regulation beyond public authority but the involvement of public institutions is imperative in many arrangements; and that countervailing forces are not always represented just by proxy but may be formally involved as recognised players. These aspects of self-regulatory arrangements will be further analysed in the next chapters; indeed, at a time when private governance is unfolding and offered as an alternative to traditional public regulation, it is critical that we understand these challenges.

The history, infrastructure and mechanisms of the network

With the economic internationalisation of the financial industry, which forms part of a broader neoliberal practice, many service providers are today operating transnationally: Under these circumstances, legal action is particularly expensive, and consumers should expect lengthy dispute-resolution procedures. This is increasingly becoming a problem at a time when e-commerce is expanding rapidly and when consumer confidence is, consequently, at stake. This development has been triggered on the one hand by political decisions regarding the completion of the European internal market, and on the other hand by the unfolding of the internal market, which has led to new regulation to balance its economic and social consequences.

Indeed, most disputes can be resolved in national contexts, and national conflict-resolution schemes are the essential building blocks, but there is a growing demand for Europe-wide solutions. Various measures to upgrade consumer rights in relation to complaints procedures have been taken by the European Union (EU), but recent developments do not span much more than a decade and were sparked by the Commission's 1993 Green Paper on the Access of Consumers to Justice and the Settlement of Consumer Disputes in the Single Market (European Commission 1993).

A major step forward was made in 2000 when it was recognised that bodies not already covered by the Commission's 1998 Recommendation on the Principles Applicable to the Bodies Responsible for Out-of-Court Settlement of Consumer Disputes and its Communication on the Out-of-Court Settlement of Consumer Disputes could play an important role as well (European Commission 1998b, 1998c). Indeed, member states and the Commission set out to define common criteria for these bodies and give them formal recognition. To further solidify this arrangement, the Commission created in 2000 a European Extra-Judicial Network (EEJ-Net) that provides information and support to consumers who use these new complaints procedures, through 'Clearing Houses' set up in the individual member states (European Commission 2000a).

In 2001, the Commission launched a new and specific out-of-court complaints network for financial services and provided an institutional framework for resolving disputes. This was followed by the publication of a consumer's guide and a seminar to extend the network to the future member states.

In cases of dispute between a service provider and a consumer, where the conflicting parties are based in the same country of the EU, the consumer must address the national and designated out-of-court body. In cases, however, where there is a conflict between the local consumer and a financial service provider based in a foreign country, the consumer is obliged to contact the national scheme that is to assist the consumer and is obliged to transfer the complaint to the relevant foreign body in the network. The foreign body then solves the problem on the basis of the above Commission Recommendation and Communication entailing seven principles relating to independence, transparency, adversary, effectiveness, legality, liberty and representation that all bodies joining the Fin-Net must comply with (European Commission 2001a, 2001b). Therefore, a successful resolution of conflicts in the financial sector requires considerable issue-specific and legal resources that are not easily available to individual consumers.

Current principles of European self-regulatory schemes

The upgrading of the consumer in the financial industries is closely related to more general institution building in the EU. European institutions have increasingly become aware of the demand for more legitimate institutions. In recognition of the missing social dimension of the internal market, developments in some of the member countries and the debate on constitutional issues have propelled reforms and emphasised the role of the citizens and their organisations. This compelling philosophy found its way into the abortive constitutional treaty[1] and was at great length discussed in the Commission's White Paper (European Commission, 2001c).

In this context, self-regulation is viewed as an appropriate alternative to traditional public forum (European Commission 2001d) and a form of regulation that would include the affected interests in society and provide arrangements with a higher degree of legitimacy. In line with these efforts, major attempts have been made to create new and alternative dispute resolution mechanisms, the Fin-Net being the first example, but the introduction of which is envisaged in other sectors of the economy. Initiatives to create new forms of litigation are both linked to and fostered by general discussions on the legal instruments available in the EU and by attempts to facilitate the completion of the internal market.

These endeavours are concerned with the role of the consumer. Therefore, they must be seen not only in relation to general strategies of governance and reforms of participatory rights, but also as being closely related to the development of a European consumer policy. When the Fin-Net was launched, the then-

Internal Market Commissioner, Bolkenstein, stressed that 'markets thrive on confidence. Retail consumers want reassurance that cross-border shopping will be problem free. Fast, efficient and cheap methods of resolving disputes are essential to encouraging the development of a genuine pan-European market in retail financial services' (www.europa.eu.int/rapid/pressReleasesAction).

Consumers can still resolve disputes through the traditional court system, although the process takes longer and is more costly and, from the perspective of the consumers, less efficient. However, decisions made by self-regulatory bodies are not as a rule binding on business and not enforceable in the same way as they are in the ordinary court system, but financial institutions usually acquiesce with decisions of these private schemes.

The out-of-court complaints bodies are not only beneficial to the consumers but also advantageous from the perspective of the service providers in the financial industry. Simultaneously, initiatives have also been made to upgrade standards in business through rules of corporate governance, but again, the strategy has not been to enact a common and encompassing European Code of Corporate Governance. As emphasised by Charlie McCreevy, European Commissioner for Internal Market and Services, 'the basis of codes of corporate governance should come from the markets and/or national legislation. However, the EU has a role to play in encouraging convergence, where possible, in the efforts of member states to improve corporate governance practices'.[2] This strategy resembles the one subject to dispute resolution.

Essentially, disputes between the individual consumer and the individual service provider must be resolved, but confidence is a collective good that consumers and corporations at large will enjoy. To that end, an institutional framework that involves relevant stakeholders is needed. In this context, the individual consumer or corporation has no place. Instead, an important role is attributed to organisations representing business, consumers or various independent and expert bodies.

These regulatory innovations are of fairly recent origin. In the case of the Fin-Net, however, where existing domestic structures are the building blocks, a concerted effort – hammered out in a strategy and followed by a range of practical steps – has been required. There are some precursors to private-driven policy arrangements in Europe: for example, the pharmaceutical industry, which has even a global superstructure (Greenwood and Ronit 1991), is a precedent; but this example of regulated self-regulation was isolated and not a part of a new approach. The more a coherent strategy is adopted and put into practice, the more we are challenged to analyse this new strategy and assess its role both in European integration and in the context of self-regulatory theory.

Public and private complaints bodies

Disputes between parties in the market place can be settled in different ways. Both at national and at international levels, various private institutions are available for dispute resolution. A major motivation for the creation of the Fin-Net is that ordinary courts are usually very expensive and time consuming, especially for the consumer with limited time and resources and with little knowledge of the court system. Under these circumstances, an alternative to court rulings, and to traditional public regulation more generally, has been installed through the various complaints institutions.

Public authority has played a decisive role in the development of these new bodies. The Commission has been instrumental in bringing life to the network institution in general, and to the sectoral arrangement of retail financial services in particular. In a similar vein, political and economic support from governments in many member states was – and still is – decisive to the effective functioning of bodies.

At first glance, it may seem ironical that public authority directed a process that in some instances included alternatives to public regulation. However, research into the problems of self-regulation has shown that private regulation is not an entirely private process and that public goals can also be achieved through private means. In the case of the Fin-Net, however, it should be remembered that although the various European institutions launched the network, there was a domestic tradition of regulation before the Fin-Net emerged and began to coordinate regulation at the European level. This provides a case of international institutional embeddedness and can best be illustrated by examining the various arrangements that existed prior to the initiative, as well as the national arrangements that have since emerged.

The network principle, and its application in the financial services, is a kind of market regulation and a regulatory experiment that provides a superstructure for existing national out-of-court bodies. National bodies must comply with the rules formulated in the recommendation from the Commission, as must governments in the member states who are more familiar with and are entitled to report on the work of domestic schemes; but this framework was also formulated with a view to include those already in place. In other words, the criteria were not formulated to opportunistically allow any scheme into the network, but inspiration was found.

Many national schemes were private, and self-regulation was, from the outset, an inherent part of the network concept. The reason for recognising these private bodies alongside public-driven schemes was both principal – because regulation could be more flexible and include an element of subsidiarity and citizen participation – and pragmatic – because such arrangements were already available. Mindful of these arrangements when formulating the recommendation, and accepting them into the Commission's database, the Commission has given national bodies a license to operate both at the domestic level and as part of the transnational network.

Furthermore, because the network rests on the principle of mutual recognition, domestic public schemes have also mandated private schemes in other countries as partners. Likewise, self-regulatory bodies have recognised the work accomplished through public bodies in the financial services and do not see them as an imminent threat to private forms of regulation. Irrespective of their private or public status, they are embedded in a system of trust, and the same principles of exchange apply when complaints are transferred from one country to another since they all must comply with a set of minimum guarantees. Indeed, there are no plans to drive the domestic schemes in one particular direction or to give them a different status. Future members of the network are not encouraged to form a particular public or a private scheme, but they must adhere to the seven principles laid out in the Recommendation and to the criteria in the voluntary memorandum (Fin-Net 2001).

Domestic complaints bodies are unevenly distributed across the EU. In addition, great variation is found in the case of the Fin-Net. Some bodies are public, funded by the state and closely linked to relevant ministries, whereas others are part of an ombudsman scheme or created as conciliation bodies, with an independent status *vis-à-vis* the state and the affected interests. And yet another group of institutions emerge from business, are funded by the regulated industry itself and have become licensed by public authority from the beginning or have been recognised later and added to the European net.

Although great variation exists and although each national scheme has its own history and tradition, a general pattern can be found across the many out-of-court bodies. Thus, it is interesting to note that the majority of schemes are held in some kind of private format. In the German, French and Italian cases, for instance, we find a number of bodies run by private players in the different fields of the financial industry, but smaller cases of public schemes also exist in some areas. In Spain and Sweden, public-driven and centralised arrangements can be found and particular to the United Kingdom is that the complaints system is held in a public framework. Turning to smaller countries such as Belgium, Denmark, Ireland and The Netherlands, complaints bodies are – with minor exceptions – private, whereas Finland, Greece, Portugal and Luxembourg all display both examples of self-regulation and public regulation in the organisation of complaints bodies.

Although bodies can generally be ranked as either public or private, it would be wrong to establish a very simple dichotomy. On closer inspection, we find that public bodies are funded by the regulated industries and that private bodies are established according to a statutory scheme that embodies an element of public regulation and supervision.

All these far-from-exhaustive examples display a high degree of variation in terms of 'publicness' and 'privateness', but this diversity is found not only across countries but also across different services – banking, insurance and securities. In sum, however, they document a strong private character of the complaints bodies in the financial sector. Although the general economic and political conditions under which financial industries operate in each country are dissimilar, they have established a range of self-regulatory bodies and display a number of institutional and regulatory commonalities. These commonalities have in many ways facilitated the creation of a joint network.

National bodies and transnational coordination

The Fin-Net rests on a complex spatial and multilayered system of regulations. The various national bodies are not only horizontally related to each other but also vertically linked to a joint European scheme under which they enjoy a rather high degree of sovereignty. This rests on mutual acceptance and adaptation. Today, there are more than 40 very different bodies across the member states. National bodies must provide basic information about their schemes and report on changes. On the basis of the information provided by member states and the relevant out-of-court bodies, the Commission has established a database of the various schemes. In addition, some coordination is provided through the Commission's work with the EEJ-Net. Conferences and workshops have been organised in cooperation with the Commission, Clearing Houses and representatives from the member states and consumer organisations and business interest associations.

The very formation of national bodies along with their principles is not simply a top-down process with the Commission in the lead role. In banking and in the insurance sectors, mature institutions were already available in most member countries. Instead of building something quite new, regulators recognised from the start that national organisations had the experience and capacity to function as out-of-court complaints bodies. Coordination, however, was needed to bring these bodies into a Europe-wide scheme.

The many national bodies are now linked through the principle of mutual recognition, according to which bodies must provide consumers with information and assist in facilitating their access to the relevant dispute-resolution institution in the network. Annual conferences organised by the Commission have aimed at improving coordination between the national bodies in the network. These conferences serve a number of purposes: they are used as a control mechanism in an effort to guarantee compliance of national schemes with the core principles formulated in the recommendation.

The principles of their cooperation are not only dealt with in the commission initiatives but also outlined in a voluntary Memorandum of Understanding on a Cross-Border Out-of-Court Complaints Network for Financial Services in the European Economic Areas. This document, although backed by the Commission, is a declaration of intent and is not legally binding. New entities can become members of the network, but according to the recommendation schemes must first be submitted to the Commission, and the Commission therefore holds an important role in the implementation of rules.

Furthermore, to secure that the Commission is continually updated on the functioning of the network, the parties to the memorandum are requested to provide statistics on their handling of cross-border cases; in addition, they must issue annual reports. In this way, both authorities and customers are kept informed of the activities of these specialised and alternative out-of-court bodies.

Business and consumer participation

Pure industry self-regulation is not covered by the scheme, and none of the bodies in the Fin-Net are run independently by business and located within business interest associations or any other outfit representing business. In the process leading to the Commission Recommendation, it has been noted that many industries have developed their own mechanisms of self-regulation and that single corporations also have their schemes and codes that outline the general rules by which they must abide. However, these forms of self-regulation are not considered sufficiently legitimate.

They cannot replace public regulation, and they mainly rest on the moral obligation of businesses. These arrangements often tend to be seen in the light of a conspiracy – either against some other segments of business or against the consumers. Thus, 'the (here it is small case)recommendation is not intended to cover customer complaint mechanisms operated by business and conducted directly with the consumer or to such mechanisms carrying out such services operated by or on behalf of business' (European Commission 2001a: 6).

The exclusion of pure industry regulation was one of the crucial principles in the process of designing the Fin-Net. Industry regulation was simply seen as too problematic to gaining consumer confidence and, therefore, it heavily interfered with the criterion of impartiality in the recommendation: 'Impartiality should be guaranteed by ensuring those responsible have no perceived or actual conflict with either party' (European Commission 2001a: 6). Bodies relevant to this topic must have competence in regulatory issues and be impartial through all steps of the procedure and provide the necessary information to both parties. In other words, legitimacy is through participatory and procedural criteria that attribute a key role to countervailing forces.

The impartiality of these 'third-party bodies' does not suggest that their initiation is necessarily through forces outside of business. On the contrary, the formation of these national bodies is closely related to the financial industries, but the lead role in the early stages and in the financing of activities should not be confused with a decisive influence on the procedures and decisions adopted by these same bodies. They are independent of business, as well as consumers, and institutions that either operate as ombudsman schemes or have another legal and organisational status included. Also, the Commission Recommendation acknowledges this institutional plurality by referring to third-party bodies 'no matter what they are called' (European Commission 2001b: L 109/59).

In the eyes of governments and consumers, the strong input by industry has not been a serious threat to independence. Indeed, governments, EU institutions and consumer organisations have each in their own way corrected these asymmetries in the design of the out-of-court bodies and the network that links them, and the running of these bodies rests on a certain degree of value homogeneity.

The power of consumers as countervailing powers, however, varies across member states. Thus, some bodies consist of representatives of both the financial services and the consumers. In the Danish case, for instance, they include experts with a background in the industries and the consumers, with participation based on the principle of parity (Ronit 2005). The costs of running these bodies – including those of the participating consumer organisations – are inferred on the affiliated business interest associations exclusively. Business pays the piper but does not call the tune when some authority is surrendered to independent institutions or to consumers.

In French insurance, for instance, the National Consumer Association, as well as industry associations, is a member of the board appointing the Ombudsman. In the Netherlands, the national consumer organisation partakes in the Foundation for Dispute Settlement alongside with the Netherlands Bankers Association on a parity basis. In Dutch insurance, an almost similar pattern exists. Insurance in Luxembourg has applied the same model, with associations of insurance companies and consumers jointly running the scheme.

In Portugal, arbitration centres in banking and insurance settle consumer disputes; they owe their existence to the cooperation between municipalities, business interest associations and consumer associations. The Finnish case brings evidence of consumer participation as well: In insurance, the Ombudsman Bureau is created jointly by the Finish insurance companies and the national consumer agency, and consumer organisations are members of the executive committee on a parity basis.

These examples demonstrate that there is no single model of consumer participation across the many national schemes. As with any other issue in self-regulation, diversity is significant. However, there is a substantial consumer input where public and statutory arrangement are in place, and a more explicit influence is enjoyed by countries where consumer organisations have formally become the third leg in self-regulation together with business and public authority. They have invigorated national schemes and enhanced consumer confidence in the out-of-court bodies.

Conclusions

The Fin-Net is the first network of complaints bodies established in the EU. It pioneers the introduction of a new mode of regulation that ties together European and national bodies vertically and links the various national bodies horizontally through a subtle combination of public and private regulation. Similar projects are either underway in other industries or have already appeared in embryonic formats.

It is premature, however, to estimate the full potential of this particular regulatory strategy. On the one hand, many industries have developed their own patterns of private regulation with little or no interference from European authority, while regulated self-regulation is far from exhausted; on the other hand, there are also limits to self-regulation because it is essential to acquire the business capacity to initiate and run arrangements. Only some industries can provide the resources needed to lift such tasks, and with a high degree of concentration and international experience the financial services have a corporate structure that facilitates self-regulation.

National schemes have an established record of self-regulation, but the emergence of the Fin-Net has also accelerated the formation of new institutions. And with the creation of the Fin-Net, national bodies are included in a transnational and standardised scheme. This course of events shows that some national forms of institutional innovation predate European initiatives, but transnational governance systems are not merely aggregates thereof. In some cases, European coordination also became an incentive to reorganise existing bodies. Although the efforts to define regulatory principles and raise performance criteria must not be underestimated, the European initiative had to build on national schemes – rather than the other way round.

This suggests that a hierarchical instalment of transnational private governance is imaginable and a directive force is often demanded, but experience from national arrangements is essential as it helps to link different territorial levels. In our case, the successful development of a transnational governance system will include more territorial levels. The likelihood is that they will be confronted with different tasks of launching and coordinating regulation; however, these patterns must be further explored before they can be included in a theory of transnational governance.

The Fin-Net case also shows that regulation is neither completely public nor completely private but that rule-making is combined in different and interesting ways. The out-of-court complaints network displays a high degree of flexibility and offers a pragmatic approach to regulation. In other words, an authority system is not necessarily public nor private at all territorial levels or, indeed, at all national levels involved.

The coordinating unit at the European level is public, and, with national supervisory bodies involved in the process of notification, a public element is also added in the national context. In some countries, even the complaints institutions are public; in most cases, however, voluntary and statutory self-regulatory bodies are in place. The principle of mutual recognition facilitates cooperation between diverse national schemes. This pattern suggests that private-driven policy arrangements in other policy fields can also build upon a combination of public and private institutions.

Although the launching of the Fin-Net provides order, and benefits the financial services, the key ambition is to enhance consumer confidence and give consumers free and easy cross-border access to complaints bodies. However, in the process of designing and running the network, consumers are not seen as merely individualised actors in the market place. Both at the European and at the national levels, consumer associations have been invited to participate in the drafting of the recommendation and the Memorandum of Understanding. On top of that, they have in some national schemes been granted participatory rights and jointly run complaints bodies with the banking, insurance and securities industries. Scholarly work on the problems of self-regulation has primarily treated self-regulation on a continuum between public and private rule-making, but these examples demonstrate that self-regulation is neither an internal industry matter single-handedly managed by corporations or business interest associations nor a question involving business and government in a series of bilateral exchanges. Institutionalised outside participation by consumers, therefore, adds new dimensions to the practice and theory of self-regulation and must be integrated into the study of private governance and its multiple forms.

Notes

1 Treaty Establishing a Constitution for Europe, Conference of the Representatives of the Governments of the Member States, Brussels, October 2004.
2 Speech by Charlie McCreevy, 'Corporate Governance in Europe', European Corporate Governance Forum, Brussels, 20 January 2005.

15 Dispute resolution in international trade and investment law

Privatisation of the public?[1]

Noemi Gal-Or

Introduction

Global trade and foreign direct investment (FDI) have figured as critical facilitators in the communication and knowledge revolution beginning in the mid-1970s. Changes in these economic sectors effected transformations in known and accepted international and domestic rules of the game. They are challenging basic assumptions regarding three pillars of governance: law making, law adjudication, and law enforcement. As a result, they have brought international law into a swirl. It is now time to bring some theoretical and principled order into what has been born out of economic, political, and legal empirical experimentation.

Within this volume on transnational private governance (TPG), this chapter concentrates on the international legal ramifications of the privatisation of areas formerly under public governance. I argue that – important as they are to the clarifications of the legal and governance practises at the international and national levels – the discourses on the legalisation, judicialisation, and constitutionalisation of international relations rarely reach beyond the classic paradigm of public vs. private international law. And where exploring the overlap between these two spheres, they remain confined to symptomatic issues. For example, the debates address public's demand for transparency and private sector's need for confidentiality, or identify new private actors in international relations, yet without tackling the varying challenges these actors pose for public international law.[2]

Who are the new actors in international relations? Who is, and who can and should, be recognised as subject of international law? Why, and for what purpose? In other words, in the face of devolution and convergence of governance formats, can the state continue to be the primary (in most cases, the sole) subject of international law? Can it survive the empirical evolutions? If not, what are the rights and obligations that new international non-state actors enjoy and must be bound by as new de facto subjects of international law? Who among these actors can and should be recognised as subject of international law?

In the following pages, I trace the impact of the private sector on the public sphere by reviewing the major legal and political debates arising from the developments in global trade and investment. I will exemplify this by referring to the Third Draft of the Free Trade Area of the Americas (FTAA) Agreement as a case study representative of a revolutionary trend of recent developments in international trade and investment law.[3] I intend to show that in order to contribute to a coherent, relevant, and legitimate international legal system, each polemic must as a primary condition of clarification tackle the identity of subjects of international law. The first section of the chapter discusses the private–public nexus in regard to trade and investment and its reflection in international law. The second section analyses the intersection between the private and public in international trade and investment law by asking the question whether the public is co-opting the private sector, or vice versa. From this perspective, it examines whether trade and investment agreements are treaties or contracts and analyses the most pressing problems related to the mechanisms they provide for dispute settlements, namely privity of contract, juridicialisation of arbitration, the meaning of appeal, the enforcement of international arbitral awards, and the question about the need for specialised legal institutions. The chapter concludes with a call for a transdisciplinary discourse on the identity and definition of subjects of international law. Such debate is invaluable as a prerequisite for a 'principled' common ground upon which to establish a world rule-based governance.

Trade and investment

Trade and investment are the twin siblings of the globalised New Economy. Trade refers to commercial transaction between states, while commerce refers to commercial transactions, largely between private actors, and in specific cases (e.g. government procurement) also to state–private actor relations. In comparison, FDI constitutes the investment by private actors as well as by governments, and represents investment in both the private and public sectors. Consequently, it brings together private and public actors in a special relationship, and even where the private actor invests in the private sector, the latter is governed by the public jurisdiction. Indeed, FDI's impacts exceed the investment transaction itself and affect policies concerning investor protection under the foreign public jurisdiction. One way of addressing the investor's concerns has seen the practise of encouraging the development of FDI as a special sector. Treaty drafters have artificially and legally isolated investment from trade, although in real economic practice, such distinction remained impossible. Thus, governments have concluded special bilateral investment treaties regulating the investment regime between them, or as the case has increasingly been included investment provisions as special legal 'enclaves' within free trade agreements (FTAs).

These two approaches to investment have had a particular effect regarding international dispute resolution (DR). Due to the specialisation of international regimes (within trade, e.g. trade in goods, or involving intellectual property; and outside of trade, e.g. environmental law), it has further compounded the web of international treaty provisions, which are either contradictory or conflicting

(McRae 2004: 14). This, of course, has given rise to misunderstanding and uncertainty affecting the practical course of the economy and politics.[4] A noticeable by-product is the schism between civil society, governments, and IOs, the disillusionment of both business and the legal profession with treaty provisions and compliance.

Here is how the confusion manifests itself. The notion of trade evolves from the practise of exchanges of categories of goods (now also services) between large trading actors notably states or groups of states. It is premised on the needs of states, the pursuance of their individual interests, and their duty to regulate and manage their domestic economy. In this interstate exchange, governments act as representatives of their domestic economies seeking to secure the most favourable conditions for the most important sectors of their economy. *Public* international law is the instrument facilitating such arrangements by recognising the state, and its government, as the only representative of its citizenry, endowed with rights and bound by obligations arising out of this representative and delegated function. This still continues to figure as the theoretical and legal underpinning of the concept of 'subject of international law'.

Trade represents, of course, the aggregate activities carried out by many individual actors (natural and corporate) who engage in commerce and is reflected in two modes of relationship. First is commerce between individuals, legally characterised as a private party-to-private party transaction and governed by the designated domestic jurisdiction. Because of the variation among states' laws, when private-to-private commerce crossed state boundaries, it is governed by the state jurisdiction assigned to govern the transaction. This regime is known as *private* international law or the legal field of conflict of law.

The other variant of commerce relates to the exchange between the state (public actor) and a private actor. Traditionally, this has been governed by the domestic laws of the state entering the commercial relationship. Increasingly however, and propelled by various economic developments, state-to-private party commercial transactions have grown more complex, especially in matters of FDI. To meet the challenge, states have entered into interstate agreements in which they 'pulled' the private into the public fold. Nowhere has this practise been more confusing – and divorcing itself from the 'original' notions of legal relations between states – as in the specific area of investment.

Unlike trade and commerce, which involve already existing products, FDI is future oriented, hence carries a higher element of risk. As in trade, investment involves three main types of relationship. In the interstate relationship, one government invests in another state, e.g. in a public infrastructure enterprise. In the private party-to-state relationship, the private party invests directly in the public economic domain of another state, e.g. a concession type of activity to build and operate a waste site. In the inter-private party relationship, an individual person (natural or corporate) invests in a private economic activity, e.g. building and operating a hotel, and indirectly affecting the host state's economy. In other words, only the interstate investment relationship is purely public. The two others represent different type of public–private relations.

As noted before, in public international law, while the state is recognised as subject of international law – the private party is not. Consequently, in law the public–private relationship is one between non-equals. Traditionally in international law, the private party's rights and obligations have arisen and been recognised only in the context of a state's domestic law (private international law), or through the agency of the government acting as the individual's representative (public international law). However, particularly since the 1980s, and especially pronounced and proliferating since the 1990s, a new practise of managing these relations has been evolving. It is reflected in the various bilateral investment treaties or incorporated as part of bilateral, regional, or multilateral trade agreements. It has been argued that this new generation of treaties has caused the re-surfacing of an old Law Merchant (*Lex Mercatoria*) also called 'transnational law' (Berger 1996; Berger *et al.* 2004). Side-stepping the challenge of addressing the legal status of the economic actors (private and public), this development has congealed into a 'new' orthodoxy (Gal-Or 2006b) giving rise to a fragmented, incoherent, and inconsistent legal international trade and investment regime.

In contemporary Law Merchant, principles and rules of both conventional (treaty) and customary public and private international law have become intermingled. At times applied equally to the state and private party, the differences between these two legal systems (predicated on the particular political and legal status of either actor) have been overlooked. This 'blindness' is the cause of a major problem in current public international law. Inadvertently, it resulted in introducing a new type of conflict of law – not between states' domestic laws – but *within* international law (both public and private) and *between* international and domestic law. It has also unsettled the common notion of equality in law and is particularly apparent in the DR mechanisms developing under Law Merchant, where dispute settlement templates based on traditional legal conceptual foundations of equality (e.g. requirement for consent in contract) have been transplanted into relationships of legal inequality (state vs. private authority). Moreover, because this shift has been introduced in the area of investment, it contributed to the privileging of one type of individual – the investor – to the detriment and discrimination of other non-investor individuals. These might be affected by the investment but themselves are not part to the transaction (usually, non-state actors representing labour, environmental, human rights, subnational governments, and other interests). The prime example was provided in the North America Free Trade Agreement (Nafta) Investor Chapter (Chapter Eleven), which empowered the private party investor to directly (not through the agency of its national government) file a complaint against another government.[5] This provision was then followed suit in other bilateral investment treaties and larger agreements, and most notably in the Third Draft FTAA.

In summary, reconciling those differences by harmonising all investment treaty provisions will, alone, not satisfy the need of harmonising the system at large (Mann *et al.* 2004); nor will the goal be achieved by technical harmonisation of treaty provisions of investment and trade. The core of the fragmentation in public international law is not in a tension among industry sectors but rather in the tension between economic and economy-related sectors, e.g. labour, environment, immigration, security, culture, etc. In other words, the conflict is between the private and public interests. This tension calls for a shift in the conceptualisation of trade and investment, which has yet to be recognised by addressing the question of status in international law 'heads on'. To be sure, the debate on the subject of international law has figured as a constant undercurrent of public international law,[6] yet the deliberations have stalled at the threshold of a conscious and focused discussion on its re-definition.

Is the public sector co-opting the private sector or vice versa?

The intersection of international with domestic law, and of both with public and private law, has been challenging major legal and political assumptions. Is the old distinction in international law between the legal statuses of the state vs. the non-state actor still viable? In the negative, what implication does the 'status' of an actor[7] (state and non-state) have in regard to the actor's rights and responsibilities?

The main legal distinction between the public's and private party's status resides in the notion of representation for in large societies, it satisfies the requirement for equality. Only the public actor can represent a collectivity by delegation; the private actor represents only itself. While the public actor is constitutionally accountable to the represented collectivity (citizenry), the private actor is accountable to itself and only contractually bound to others (private and public parties). For instance, in its capacity as legal corporate personality, the private party is legally accountable by delegation to shareholders.[8] In addition to its constitutional duties, the state is also contractually bound to others (states and citizens of other states, and non-citizens). Thus, representation implies different rights and obligations and corresponds to the competences and capabilities of the representor – public or private. The state is self-governing, makes laws, enforces, and adjudicates them, hence possesses primary authority and power within the domestic realm. The private party's law making, enforcement, and adjudication competences are demarcated by the state's jurisdiction. Therefore, state and private actors are legally unequal. Indeed, the legal 'fiction' of equality in the interstate relationship originates in a conceptualisation which excludes the private party from the equation. Furthermore, the nature of state accountability to the *foreign* private party differs from its duty to its *national* private party. In addition, the state also maintains a relationship with domestic sub-level governing *public* actors (in both federal and unitary systems), which it represents in its foreign relations and which give rise to another differential as between the foreign private, and the sub-level public, actor. Brief, in international law, equality is rooted in a distinction between the interstate (equality among states) vs. intra-state (equality among private parties) planes. Recent developments in international trade and investment law, which have enfranchised the private party in its relations with the state, have been unsettling this epistemological differentiation.

I turn now to discuss specific issues which demonstrate this 'disturbance'. They arise out of the inclusion in international (interstate) agreements of new provisions affecting the status of the private party. In fact, so far only the investor private actor has been lifted out of the intra-state jurisdiction and transposed into, and endowed it with, legal capacity at the interstate level. This transformation in international investment DR provisions best manifests the blurring of the traditional distinctions between the public and private in international law.

FTAs and international investment agreements (IIAs): contracts or treaties?

'Treaty' is a concept embedded in international relations and law, which is meaningless outside this sphere for it pertains to interstate and state–international organisations relations only.[9] An FTA is an interstate agreement to eliminate tariff and non-tariff barriers blocking their mutual trade. An IIA is an interstate agreement to invest in their respective public or private markets, whether directly or indirectly. A certain type of IIA is the bilateral investment treaty which represents a contract between state and private party.

Conversely, a 'contract' is an agreement based on a promise between individuals which is governed by domestic law and regulated in international law through treaties respecting domestic governance in private matters. A special case involving state–private relationship arises, for instance, where a government concludes a commercial agreement (procurement) with a private party. The parties' inequality is reconciled by considering the state as a private party for the purpose of the transaction. The commercial relationship is then governed by the respective domestic law of the state or by private international law. Note, that in this relationship it is the state, which for the sake of the transaction, assumes a private party character, and not vice versa. Furthermore, private international law instructs that the relationship between the parties is governed by a *domestic* state jurisdiction.

Over time, the distinction between a state's commercial contract vs. trade treaty has become increasingly complex. The growing intricacy of economic relations in a globalising environment (Waelde 2004) and their ramification on tangential areas (labour, environment, security, and human rights) have introduced a new and different asymmetry in public–private relations. A significant corollary has been the proliferation of treaties, and consequently, of courts and tribunals with overlapping and cross-cutting jurisdictions (Shany 2003). This situation calls for the harmonisation, at least clarification, of the new rules if the legitimacy and relevance of international law are to be safeguarded. This is in the interest of both public and private actors.

The draft FTAA provides a good example for it reflects the latest 'legislative' mind set on a grand scale (of 34 American governments). Although modifying some of the Nafta Investor Chapter provisions, its Investment Chapter (Chapter Seventeen) preserves the core ingredients of the abovementioned asymmetry. On the one hand, it is a draft interstate treaty; on the other, it contains elements of a state–private party contract. The latter empower an investor of a signatory party to initiate legal proceedings against another party before an *international* panel, not only in addition but instead of a *domestic* court, and in spite of the fact that the investor is not party to the agreement (treaty).[10] So, in matters public–private, do these Chapter Seventeen provisions represent a treaty or a contract? And if both, how can this be reconciled in international law?

Regardless of the answer, the law developed in the FTAA suggests that the 'balance of power' has been tilting in favour of the private party. The treaty is elevating the private investor's legal status in international law to a par with the public and foreign party – state government (Gal-Or 2005). Therefore, in the treaty vs. contract debate, the public seems to be co-opting the private sector.

Dispute resolution

DR, which has now replaced the term of alternative dispute resolution (ADR), continues to embody the basic idea that DR encompasses all mechanisms except court litigation. DR mechanisms include the variety of negotiation, facilitation, conciliation, mediation, and arbitration (as stand-alone methods or combined). In the international trade and investment contexts, it originates in a mix of dispute settlement tools developed to address international public–private commercial disputes. In the past two decades, it has increasingly been acquiring characteristics of private party DR designed specifically to keep the disputed matter out of government reach. This body of rules came to be known as 'soft law' (Mistelis 2001).

The rationale for this development is usually found in business' distrust of courts of foreign governments, notably developing countries, which were failing to guarantee fair legal recourse to foreign investors. Moreover, as compared with court litigation, DR is considered as a cost-effective process saving resources, e.g. time and money. These rationales have now become redundant. First, most of the trade and FDI occur amongst developed countries with reputable judiciary systems. Second, the chief DR instrument – arbitration – has grown to resemble court litigation, losing its cost benefit edge. Concurrently however, DR has transformed into a large service sector, an industry with vested self-interest (Dezalay and Garth 1996, 2002; Gal-Or 2005). Encouraged by their success, the 'private legislators' of soft law have sought to refine and augment the scope of DR. The WTO and the Nafta, which spearheaded this trend, were replicated and refined in the Third Draft FTAA.

Is the private style adjudication permeating public DR? Or, is the public international dispute settlement transforming the private? Again, regardless of the answer, the developments are reverberating through international law, demanding to address the status of actors under and before the evolving law. In the following section, I will elaborate on the most intriguing aspects raised by the questions of treaty or contract, and DR.

Privity of contract

'Privity of contract' is the core premise of the ADR system, which segregates the private from the public adjudication processes in order to protect the former against the intrusion of the latter. The principles underlying privity of contract stipulate that the dispute settlement process and its outcome are deemed private and are governed exclusively by the consenting parties, which are legally equal. Because it is a private contract, the parties may keep it confidential.

Is the direct adjudicative relationship between state and investor (private actor) complying with the original logic of ADR? Is the presumed legal equality between the parties preserved also in the case of state–private party ADR?

In the FTAA Chapter Seventeen, the private party's status as claimant arises from the *treaty* concluded by mutual consent between equal public parties,[11] not from a *contract* for the ADR mechanism subsumed and fixed within the treaty. So, the private party is not a Party to the treaty hence also not to the agreement on its DR provisions (a privity of contract requirement).[12] A review of the definitions of 'investor of a Party' demonstrates that the investor (private actor) remains always subject to the jurisdiction of the contracting Party (state/public), i.e. the state and the investor are each governed by a different and separate legal order. This only reinforces the above-mentioned legal asymmetry between state and investor and emphasises the inconsistency with the underlying principle of privity of contract for the investor *cannot* be legally equal to the state. Consequently, the investor–state provisions in the draft FTAA Chapter Seventeen imputes to the private actor rights which are not recognised neither in public international law nor in ADR law.

According to the following statement by the NAFTA Free Trade Commission, which consists of cabinet-level representatives from the three member countries, 'The FTAA will build on the existing *FTAs* and on expanding the *links* that the *NAFTA* countries have *elsewhere in the hemisphere*, allowing them to take full advantage of emerging hemispheric markets'.[13] Indeed, FTAA drafters heeded concerns about the investor–state provisions raised already during the first decade of Nafta. Such issues regard both interstate and state–private party DR and include innovative provisions designed to secure business interests while simultaneously reassuring civil society and development concerns.[14] However, important as they are, they represent only symptoms of the core problem underlying this development in international law. The definition of the subject of international law remains undecided and arbitration continues to be administered without privity of contract.

Juridicialisation of arbitration[15]

Having examined the *inception* of the DR, I now turn to the DR *procedure*. As seen, in the case of investment DR, the process is tainted *ab initio* by problems flowing from the blurring of the legal statuses of private and public. In trade, the DR mechanisms (notably arbitration) also suffer deficiencies arising when transplanting elements of a process designed to settle *private* disputes into the *public* realm. The following non-exhaustive list illustrates typical issues in international trade and investment arbitration, which compromise to public policy and securing of the public good.

- Independence of the arbitrator: in the court system, the role and status of the judge is distinguished from the role and status of counsel and prosecutor, whereas in the arbitral procedure, duplication is tolerated (Mann 2005).
- Conflict of interest: the arbitrator selection procedure may be biased (even if in good faith) on political grounds, to satisfy the interests of the parties, or for personal interest in a specific legal outcome, etc. (ibid.).
- Qualifications: absence of transparent criteria guiding professional appointments.[16]
- Confidentiality and transparency: normally, proceedings are closed to the public before, during, and in state–private matters – also after the arbitral hearing. Confidentiality is also an impediment to preventing conflict of interest.
- Rules of evidence: arbitration is designed to avoid the intricate technicalities of court litigation by adopting a simplified process where a negotiated or mediated settlement is unattainable. This is increasingly changing due to the complex nature of the international trade and investment disputes.
- Legal precedent: due to its private and confidential nature, ADR rejects the notion of precedent based law. However, practice contradicts the theory (Bhala 1998/99; McRae 2004; Gal-Or 2005).

Government as well as the legal profession have acknowledged some of the problems and while still unresolved, progress is underway, e.g. governments' proposals regarding changes to the appointment of WTO panel members in order to rid the process of both politicisation and secure qualification.[17] Indeed, both the FTAA Chapter Seventeen Investment and Chapter Twenty Three on Dispute Settlement incorporate provisions designed to fill this void. The blurring of private and public dispute settlement procedures has placed panelists and arbitrators (as distinguished from judges) as sources of international law. The upshot is that arbitrators (private sector) and drafters of international treaties (lobbied by private counsel) effectively contribute to the creation of this special mix of public and private international law. In brief, the private is impressing on the public.

The concept of appeal

The concept of appeal suggests finality and finality infers the completion of a process. For long, the DR system has provided for gradation in the available procedures, e.g. moving from negotiation to mediation to arbitration to judicial review of arbitral awards by domestic courts. Generally, arbitration used to represent finality within the ADR system, yet DR rules de facto amounting to various forms of judicial review are gradually evolving (Shany 2003; Bishop 2004; McRae 2004; Gal-Or 2006a). The establishment of the WTO Appellate Body codified these cumulative steps by adding an 'in house' instance of arbitral appeal. The FTAA builds on this precedent by devising an adjudicative hierarchy with a final appeal procedure: 'The decisions of the Appellate Body are unappealable … [having] the force of *res judicata*'.[18]

Arguably, this progression suggests that the art of arbitration is transforming itself, indeed, emulating that of court litigation. Yet, while the trend is progressing, discussion regarding the purpose of appeal remains sparse. What implications will such development have on public international law? On lower level arbitration panels? Will this affect the status of the domestic courts of the disputing parties?[19]

Enforcement of international arbitral

Even if the mismatch of privity of contract, the juridicialisation of arbitration, and the notion of appeal were resolved, there still remains the challenge of compliance (or non-compliance) with, and enforcement of, the awards. Although the number of disputes and dispute settlements has been dramatically increasing, and despite a popular impression of poor state compliance, most awards are being adhered to by the disputing parties. The few digressions, however, have drawn the attention to the post-award issues (Sosnow 2005). And here as well, the international private party's impact on public practices at the international level is evident.

At the domestic level, courts and tribunals are called upon to render enforcement judgments which require knowledge of international law, and thus unintentionally, become partners to the institutionalisation of recent developments in international trade and investment law. In addition, the increase of cases representing the convergence of domestic with international and private with public illustrates the limits of domestic tools required in satisfying the interests of justice, on the one hand, and encourages adjustment to accommodate the new reality, on the other hand.

In Canada, two approaches have been developed to address this predicament. One strategy consists of changing the approach to national enforcement of international law. For instance, in *Baker*,[20] the court adopted a new interpretation method to determine whether to incorporate international legal norms within domestic law. Moving away from legal interpretation based on legislative intent and historical origins, it opted for a more engulfing contextual ('non-originalist') and persuasive approach. Consequently, a judge declining to incorporate international norms in the domestic law would now have to indicate so clearly; it would be more difficult for a judge to consider legislative silence as evidencing an intention to not conform to international law. A simple ascertainment of national and international law compatibility would suffice; in the absence of a compatibility conflict, the judge would remain free to give effect to international over domestic laws (Houle 2003: 2–3).

Deference to arbitral tribunal represents the other approach. In *Metalclad*,[21] a Nafta investment case, Mexico, supported by the Intervener Attorney General of Canada, urged the Supreme Court of British Columbia hearing the case to review the Canadian court's typical deferential approach to private commercial arbitral tribunals. It argued so on the grounds of privity of contract as well as public policy and public good concerns (Tollefson 2002). Similar to *Baker*, in *Metalclad*, the Court avoided addressing arguments which challenged the transposition of international within national law. Practically, it rejected the arguments while simultaneously affirming the applicability of the international law.

The Canadian deferential approach to international commercial arbitration forms part of a larger trend. In brief, a private adjudicatory system, bolstered by globalisation and promoted by influential non-state actors who participate in the process of international rule making, made inroads regarding the enforcement at the domestic level.

Is there a need – and justification – for specialised legal institutions?

In domestic jurisdictions, the growth in specialised courts and tribunals simplifies the adjudication process for 'justice users' in an ever-growing complex environment. For the sake of cohesion within the legal system, these bodies are subjected to the supremacy of the State. Moreover, at the domestic level, access to justice represents access to both input to legislation (e.g. elections and consultations) and the right to legal standing. Available to natural and legal persons alike, this is the backbone of the concept of democratic citizenship and civil rights.

Because the notion of citizenship is non-extant at the international level, other strategies have been pursued to secure a fair international playing field. Similar to the domestic justice system, they require substantive and procedural consistency.[22] Precisely, this is the challenge facing the international community at the backdrop of unprecedented proliferation in specialised courts and tribunals. That international legal cohesion depends on the harmonisation of specialised regimes (e.g. for trade and investment) is becoming increasingly evident to the legal profession. At the same time, it must be recognised by governments and private actors alike that harmonisation cannot be served by the private justice system's selective emulation of the public system's rules (and vice versa).

Conclusion

This article focuses on the most formal institutionalisation of transnational private governance, namely in the legal system. I argued that the common boundaries separating public from private international law have been gradually eroding in international trade and investment law. Ostensibly, the process – as seen also in the preceding chapters – is driven by the privatisation of international affairs. That this privatisation has permeated international law is evidenced in the many (2000 and more) bilateral investment treaties, regional, and global interstates treaties generating a build-up of legal inconsistencies. I argued that the recent developments in trade and investment law have strained the definition of the subject of law. I reviewed the most obvious manifestation of the pressure and called for an unambiguous debate of the issue.

Notes

1 I wish to acknowledge all those who contributed to this article by commenting on earlier drafts. These include especially the comments by Dirk Lehmkuhl and the colleagues at the ECPR workshop Transnational Private Governance in the Global Political Economy, Granada, Spain, 14–19 April 2005, as well as the editors of the volume.

2 Here are two examples from most recent international conferences. One is the discussion of the Draft Resolution No. 1/2006 of the International Commercial Arbitration Committee of the International Law Association, reading: '7. Lis pendens does not pertain to *public policy* and need not be raised on its own motion by an arbitral tribunal', 'The World Is Here', *72nd Biennial Conference of the International Law Association*, June 4–8, 2006, Toronto (emphasis added; on file with author). The other refers to panel deliberating on non-state actors (NSAs), which identified a range of international NSAs and assessed their impact on international relations, but was silent concerning the implications of such influence on international law. 'International Law: Who Needs It?' *European Society of International Law: Second Biennial Conference*, 18–20 May, 2006, Paris.

3 *Third Draft Agreement – November 21, 2003. Free Trade Area of the Americas Draft Agreement.* FTAA.TNC/w/133/Rev.3. Available online at: www.ftaa-alca.org/FTAADraft03/Index_e. asp [hereafter: FTAA]. Even before the collapse of the Doha Development Round in July 2006, there has been renewed pressure to revive the FTAA negotiations. See for instance: Letter from Canada to the FTAA Trade Negotiations Committee (TNC) Co-Chairs, 1 September 2005. Available online at: www.-dfait-maeci.gc.ca/tna-nac/FTAA/letter-en.asp.

4 Cutler juxtaposes the 'political' nature of the private with what she argues is a common misguided perception of the private as 'apolitical', and recognises the centrality of the definition of the subject of international law (Cutler 2003: 245–49).

5 North American Free Trade Agreement. Available online at: www.nafta-sec-alena.org/DefaultSite/index_e.aspx?DetailID=78.

6 Traditionally in legal parlance, part of this issue is often referred to under 'state immunity' and 'diplomatic protection', which correspond to the political debate on 'sovereignty' and 'public vs. private'.

7 I am using the terms 'actor' (international relations) and 'party' (law) interchangeably.

8 Depending on the type of NSA – some are legally accountable to their members or citizens (trade unions and sub-level government), while others are accountable only to 'themselves' (activists and loosely knit social movements); and civil society at large – is not accountable to anyone.

9 They are governed by public international law and are subject to the Vienna Convention on Treaties. United Nation, *Vienna Convention on the Law of Treaties 1969*, United Nations Treaty Series, vol. 1155, p. 331. Available online at: www.untreaty.un.org/ilc/texts/instruments/ english/conventions/1_1_1969.pdf.

10 The situation is different under international criminal and humanitarian law and is not relevant to the current discussion.

11 The Vienna Convention, *op. cit.*

12 It may be argued that by invoking the provision, the private claimant implicitly

consents to the contract. I dispute this argument but I am unable to elaborate on this point for lack of space.

13 'NAFTA Partners Celebrate Tenth Anniversary of Trade Agreement', 8 October 2003, p. 6. Available online at: http://ottawa.usembassy.gov/content/textonly.asp?section=can_usa&subsection1=trade&document=nafta_article_100803 (emphasis added).

14 Section C Procedures and Institutions, FTAA, *op. cit.* This may, among other things, match recent US innovative steps to reconcile social justice issues with trade and investment. For instance, the US–Jordan FTA is the first of its kind (for the US as a Party, followed by the USCFTA and CAFTA) to incorporate labour and environmental provisions within the main text of the trade agreement, and in addition, provide a single dispute resolution mechanism for both commercial and social issues. See J.F. Hornbeck (2003).

15 I use 'juridicialisation' to distinguish public court procedure from administrative and private procedures such as ADR.

16 The problems of the independence of the arbitrator, conflict of interest, and qualifications have been identified as rooted in symbolic (social) capital. The operation of sociopolitical networks may encourage a perception of bias consequently undermining the arbitrator's legitimacy; see Dezalay and Garth 1996, 2002; Gal-Or 2005; Sklair 2001.

17 See, for instance: European Commission, *Contribution From the EC and Its Member States to the Improvement and Clarification of the WTO Dispute Settlement Understanding*, 20 January 2003, European Commission, Directorate-General for Trade, Ref. 009/03-Rev2; Canada Department of Foreign Affairs and International Trade, *Contribution of Canada to the Improvement of the WTO Dispute Settlement Understanding*, undated. Available online at: www.dfait-maeci.gc.ca/tna-nac/wto_dispute-en.asp.

18 Chapter XXIII, article 302.

19 For reflections on the relations between European and domestic courts, see Schmitter 2000; see also new proposal for direct effect in Nafta: de Mestral and Winter 2005; Gal-Or 2005.

20 *Baker* marking a watershed in Canadian law.

21 A Nafta Chapter Eleven appeal heard by the Supreme Court of British Columbia, Canada. *United Mexican States* v. *Metalclad Corporation*, May 2, 2001 BCSC 664, Docket: L002904, Registry: Vancouver, 1–30. Available online at: www.courts.gov.bc.ca/jdb-txt/SC/01/06/2001BCSC0664.htm.

22 For a compelling analysis of fairness and justice, see Franck 1995.

Part V

Conclusions

16 Conclusion

The limits of transnational private governance[1]

Andreas Nölke and Jean-Christophe Graz

The central tenet of this volume is that transnational private governance in the contemporary world faces limits across three issues. There are limits on definition of each term of the concept. There are limits on framework conditions, as transnational private governance does not work in all situations. There are normative limitations, on the ability to solve economic, social, and ecological problems of global capitalism as well as deep reservations regarding the lack of democratic legitimacy. In highlighting these limitations, we want to take the debate on transnational private governance a step ahead; this debate so far has often been characterised by an optimistic undertone. By drawing conceptual, analytical and normative lessons from a pool of researchers in the fields of both comparative and global political economy, this volume should be of some help in stimulating a dialogue which until now was highly fragmented. The conclusion builds upon the categories developed in Chapter 1. It sums up the findings of the cases examined in each chapter in order to probe the theoretical claims presented in the introduction, nuance the argument, and differentiate between various strands of explanation. Far from aiming to ultimately prove the arguments developed in the introduction as a positivist would attempt, this conclusion will illustrate their internal theoretical coherence and empirical relevance (see Table 16.1).

The conceptual limitations of transnational private governance

Our contributions demonstrate that an empirically informed conceptualisation of transnational private governance has to acknowledge some limitations on all three elements of the concept, i.e. transnational, private, and governance.

Transnational: Limitations on the functional and spatial scope of private governance

Not all forms of transnational private governance have the same degree of 'transnationality', i.e. in how far they symbolise a shift away from territorial towards functional governance, and from spatially circumscribed units to global

Table 16.1 Transnational private governance: conceptual, empirical and normative limits.

Conceptual clarification	Transnational	Functional scope	More territorial than assumed
		Spatial scope	Less global than commonly assumed, many regional schemes, South largely excluded
	Private	Range of private actors	Only parts of the private sphere involved, focus on big firms, NGOs, professional associations
		State recognition	State and/or intergovernmental recognition always necessary
	Governance	Logic of power	Mostly consensual, but still unintentional domination
		Logic of action	Informal governance reinforced by more formal and hierarchical mechanisms
Framework conditions	Structural	Social system of production	Reliance on neoliberalism
		Forms of competition	Oligopolies, big MNCs, coordinated and branded global value chains
		International institutional embeddedness	Support by international institutions, in particular the EU
		Policy type	Regulatory policies, yet with significant distributional consequences
	Actor-based	Resources	Reliance on technical and professional knowledge of private actors
		Value homogeneity	Common values of private actors and their public counterparts
Normative implications	Socioeconomic concerns	Problem-solving capacity	Limited ability to solve large societal problems
		Neoliberalism	Stabilisation of neoliberalism, limited mitigation potential
	Procedural issues	Sovereignty	Restrictions on the public control over private actors
		Legitimacy	Limited transparency and accountability

reach. More specifically, we claim that there are inherent limitations on both the functional and spatial scope of transnational private governance.

The *functional* limitations of transnational private governance are obvious in many cases. Notwithstanding the drift from territorial to functional governance (van Waarden), cases which would first appear as primarily functional include a strong territorial component, as national networks of the Global Compact or the role of national chemical associations in case of Responsible Care clearly indicate (Conzelmann and Wolf). Whilst territoriality is here explored to enhance effectiveness, in other cases it proves to be less complementary. For example, accounting standards are hampered by legal variations across borders and more broadly between common law countries and Continental Europe (Botzem). Similarly, the European out-of-court network for financial services (Fin-Net) is institutionalised on the transnational level of the European Union (EU), but it is still heavily dependent on domestic arrangements (Ronit). The European social dialogue has also strong underpinnings in national industrial relations; as a result, it varies enormously across Europe (Smismans). Even the private governance of the Internet, which one would expect to be the most purely functional form of governance, is partially based on national and regional institutions. This is most obvious in the ties between ICANN and the US Department of Commerce (Bislev and Flyverbom). The creation of the European top-level domain (TLD) name (dot eu) for its part closely reflects the institutional peculiarities of the EU policy-making system (Christou and Simpson). Territoriality remains within the transnational private governance of global banking. Although the Institute of International Finance is an emanation of the global concerns of the big financial conglomerates, its most influential members still have strong ties with their respective national regulators (Tsingou).

The *spatial* limitations of transnational private governance first reflect the prominence of regional integration schemes as supports of such cooperative arrangements. Whilst the EU is obviously in the driver's seat here, private dispute resolution mechanisms in Nafta and developments in current Free Trade Agreement of the Americas (FTAA) negotiations (Gal-Or 2005) suggest that any other regional integration process is ready to embark on similar routes. Then there is the case of non-spatially limited forms of transnational private governance, such as norms of corporate social responsibility. As might be expected, areas with the most severe problems are more easily excluded, as tropical deforestation and the Forest Stewardship Council (FSC) clearly indicate (Conzelmann and Wolf). Many cases of transnational private governance, though in principle global, in fact depend on the implicit support of business from the core of the world economy. Whenever American firms control developments in an industry, governance arrangements will be based on the support provided by those firms (Muegge). The emergent e-commerce regime is thought of as global, yet strongly anchored in the United States and heavily influenced by large American corporations (Ibáñez). The same applies for global banking regulation, with the difference that European banks also play a major role (Tsingou). For their part, international accounting standards were first codified with some developing countries onboard; yet it is widely recognised that their role in decision making is minimal and even further reduced during the recent reform leading to a reinforced role for City standards. In general, actors from the South hardly play a significant role in transnational private governance, except for those cases that explicitly deal with development issues in the South (Conzelmann and Wolf; Merk).

Private: limitations on the involvement of private actors in transnational governance

The term private for considering such governance mechanisms is somewhat misleading, just as transnational is. From a political economy perspective striving to overcome the divide between its comparative or global understanding, private and public spheres remain closely related, and it is meaningless to analyse one without the other. Moreover, the 'private' should not be identified with the so-called private sector as a whole or a putative global civil society; ultimately, very small parts of it are involved in transnational private governance.

Therefore, private governance does not mean that the *state* is completely out of the picture. In contrast, our contributors emphasise in various ways the role of the state or intergovernmental institutions. Even where the state is not directly involved in self-regulation of business, it can always be called upon by parties who consider themselves disadvantaged (Muegge). The emergent regime of e-commerce, driven primarily by major US and European corporations, provides us with examples of how private self-regulation is backed by public authorities. These include public monitoring of implementation, support by public regulation where necessary (i.e. intellectual property rights), harmonisation of markets by intergovernmental regulation, and denial of public incentives to private initiatives of minor players such as the open source movement (Ibáñez). The extent of state involvement in Internet governance is particularly impressive given the widespread preference for private, self-managed governance within the libertarian-inclined Internet community (Bislev and Flyverbom; Christou and Simpson).

The EU has become particularly prominent as a public institution closely supervising transnational private governance. Although the European Registry of Internet Domains (Eurid) is a private, not-for-profit company, it still works under close supervision of its 'double principals', the European Commission and the EU Member States. Even during the policy process that has led to the dot eu governance framework, Commission representatives acted as participants in the process of 'self-regulation'. Still formally a case of private self-regulation, the 'domestication' of Eurid leads to a set up with close public supervision which echoes common EU-regulatory state practice (Christou and Simpson). The European social dialogue also takes places in the shadow of hierarchy. This is most obvious in case of the 'regulatory route' towards the implementation of its initiatives that relies on enforcement by public authorities. One may well question the 'private' character of this form of transnational governance. But even the main 'autonomous' European collective agreements have only emerged in response to initial regulation attempts by the Commission (Smismans). This close combination of public and private elements is also present in the Competitiveness Advisory Group (CAG) as participation from the public sector in its deliberations is a precondition to get the Commission to take over its recommendation (Holman). Smaller and more technical forms such as Fin-Net are based on a dense collaboration with the public sector alike (Ronit). Finally, International Accounting Standards Committee/International Accounting Standards Board (IASC/IASB) accounting standards only became a meaningful form of transnational private governance once adopted as a mandatory rule by the EU after each standard was assessed individually with the possibility of 'carve-outs' on certain rules, although the latter is more a defensive instrument (Botzem).

While this reinforces the assumption that transnational private governance has become a powerful tool of regional integration at the European level – thanks to an increasingly close relationship with the institutions of the EU – the involvement of intergovernmental organisations appears to be important at the global level too. Institutions such as the UN and its specialised agencies are directly involved in the field of corporate social responsibility and often offer additional guarantees for implementing particular codes (Conzelmann and Wolf, Fuchs, Merk). Similarly, out-of-court dispute resolution mechanisms are predicated in intergovernmental trade and investment agreements (Gal-Or), and the governance functions of the G30 and the IIF in the domain of global finance have been specifically delegated by governments organised in the Basel Committee (Tsingou).

Moreover, although the term private might lead us to believe that such transnational governance potentially concerns the *private sphere as a whole*, our cases show that only a limited range of actors is involved. The European social dialogue provides us with a clear-cut demonstration, as by definition it only includes peak associations of labour unions and employers' bodies. Yet, even within the broader category of labour, not all workers or their associations take part in the dialogue – especially in the Enlargement countries and in some sectors, major groups are notably absent. The same is true for capital, as the UEAPME case suggests that small- and medium-sized enterprises are underrepresented in the decision making of the European peak associations (Smismans). Many environmental corporate social responsibility (CSR) codes have been designed by large corporations of the North, without involving small- and medium-sized enterprises, not to speak of companies from developing countries bearing the cost of adopting the new standards. Conferences promoting CSR success stories frequently entail such high fees that critical NGOs cannot participate (Fuchs). Most importantly, the participation of labour remains a problem even for the most progressive and comprehensive CSR schemes (Merk). Furthermore, producers have much stronger incentives to invest in transnational private governance for the purpose of ordering markets than consumers do (Mügge). Whenever consumer associations are present, their participation remains uneven as the dispute resolution mechanisms of Fin-Net clearly suggest (Ronit).

Thus, unsurprisingly, big multinational companies frequently play a central role in transnational private governance. This observation not only applies to the usual suspects, such as large ICT firms in the Internet (Ibáñez), the G30 in global banking (Tsingou), or the ERT in the CAG set up by the European Commission (Holman), but also to big brand and retail firms from the industrialised countries as privileged targets of CSR concerns (Conzelmann and Wolf, Fuchs, Merk). More specifically, a distinct type of company seems to systematically gain advantages in transnational private governance – and sometimes only exists thanks to it: coordination service firms. In addition to the wide array of financial services provided by firms such as rating agencies or the Big Four auditing companies (Botzem), as well as legal services in dispute resolution mechanisms (Gal-Or, Ronit), a whole new industry has also emerged in response to the joint development of global commodity chains and CSR codes. Intertek, SGS, or Bureau Veritas have become the best-known firms specialised in inspection, tests, and certificates (Merk). The growing importance of social audits and other services provided by such firms reflects a trend towards the commoditisation of transnational private governance bought and sold on markets.

Governance: limitations to the consensual, non-hierarchical, and informal character of transnational private governance

The concept of governance is commonly understood as a form of political reorganisation that relies upon a mostly unintentional and consensual logic of power, and that implements in the same vein an informal and non-hierarchical logic of action. The accounts put together in this volume support, to a great extent, the cautionary tone we emphasised in the introductory chapter when we strongly qualified those four attributes of transnational private governance.

Accounting standards provide a prime example of how transnational private governance is inclined to be more *formalised* than is often acknowledged. Formalisation is a process which creates and strengthens authority. Private actors require such authority since international law does not acknowledge these actors as subjects. As private actors cannot create hard law, soft law becomes their first choice. Thus, in order to become effective private regulators, professions codify their knowledge in certain formal rules or programs (Botzem). This seems to be also true for financial markets in which professions have less say than oligopolistic groups of firms such as in Eurobond underwriting or auditing (Mügge). Similarly, codes of corporate social responsibility are increasingly formalised in order to reinforce their claim to trustworthily respond to political contestation targeting inconsistencies in implementation, monitoring, and verification (Merk). The formalisation of transnational private governance also affects dispute resolution mechanisms. Whilst it was originally conceived as a more informal and cost-effective tool than litigation in public courts, it now tends to take as much time and money, as well as detailed procedures (Gal-Or). Finally, within the European context, our cases on the European social dialogue (Smismans) and banking regulation (Tsingou) reinforce our assumption that the implementation of transnational private governance heavily hedges on the regulatory route.

To become truly effective, transnational private governance is neither informal, nor necessarily *consensual*. When incorporated in EU legislation, it is actualised *erga omnes*, including on those parties that did not delegate their sovereign rights or were not setting the rules. In cases of more stringent self-regulatory policies such as the dot eu governance framework, public policy imperatives prescribed by the Commission also circumscribe the consensual character by introducing various structural constraints (Christou and Simpson). Similarly, some of the standards developed by the International Accounting Standard Board have hardly succeeded in becoming consensual regulation, as they are still heavily contested, even after their final adoption (Botzem). In the financial sector, those companies largely excluded from the market by transnational private governance such as in Eurobond underwriting or auditing will probably not subscribe to the view that this form of governance is based on consensus (Mügge); nor will suppliers finding their GMO products banned from the shelves by big supermarket chains (van Waarden). Furthermore, many cases of transnational private governance reflect the unintentional form that may be taken by the structural and discursive power of business. Although not necessarily contested, it hardly remains consensual (Fuchs). In the domain of corporate social responsibility, our contributors emphasise, however, that more consensual forms of transnational private governance may well occur as a result of substantial learning processes (Conzelmann and Wolf) or negotiated social compromises (Merk).

Finally, the *non-hierarchical* character of transnational private governance also faces strong limits. For instance, UEAPME (which represents small- and medium-sized enterprises) had no other choice than to collaborate with UNICE – the organisation of larger industrial concerns – in order to be heard at the European negotiation table (Smismans 2000). Similarly, in setting up a European TLD name for the Internet, the European Commission has created a unique form of 'regulated self-regulation' (Christou and Simpson), of which Fin-Net can be seen as a variant for resolving some disputes in financial services (Ronit). For its part, the International Accounting Standard Board went through a tremendous transformation towards a hierarchical complex of boards and committees (Botzem). Even in the field of corporate social responsibility, the current 'anarchy' (Merk) of a myriad of schemes increasingly looks ineffective. Various initiatives are currently introducing more formal and hierarchical mechanisms. According to Conzelmann and Wolf, it is precisely this process of hierachisation that could lead to a more inclusive and democratic form of transnational private governance, as the case of the Forestry Stewardship Council would suggest.

Limitations on the empirical scope conditions for transnational private governance

In our attempt to explore in more detail the circumstances that appear to be essential for initiating, implementing, and sustaining transnational private governance, the introductory chapter identified six major framework conditions which presume a deep interrelationship between ideal and material conditions, as well as structural and more actor-centred forms of explanations. Each case studied in the volume, on its own way, provides significant accounts of how these conditions should be met for such new forms of governance to be effective. Whilst some reinforce shared assumptions on the topic (e.g. the importance of oligopolistic market structures, of neoliberal globalisation or the specialised knowledge of the private regulators), others – such as the role of the EU – are more counterintuitive or shed light on neglected issues in the existing literature.

A social system of production that is characterised by neoliberalism

Given the small role of long-term studies within the volume, we should be careful in claiming that transnational private governance would only exist in the current context of neoliberalism. As discussed by van Waarden, the private regulation of economic affairs was very prominent in the early evolution of capitalism, at least at the domestic level. However, many cases of transnational private governance examined in the book reflect a real shift in the organisation of the world economy in recent decades. When implemented within the EU arena, it is inextricably related to the neoliberal turn taken by the European integration since the 1980s (Holman). In governing the Internet revolution, it follows the dramatic deregulation of telecoms markets (Ibáñez). Another sector where the strong economic liberalisation has contributed to the evolution of transnational private governance is the financial sector (Botzem, Mügge, Tsingou). Similarly, the prime concern of codes of corporate social responsibility was from the outset the development of global value chains outsourcing business activities in the South (Merk). The focus of CSR on certificates and brands in no way undermines neoliberal core values such as consumerism. Transnational private governance can also mitigate a hindrance to the free operations of international markets, such as Fin-Net in financial services (Ronit) or distinct dispute resolution mechanisms in NAFTA and FTAA (Gal-Or). Finally, with some typical constraints brought forward by neoliberalism (such as the mobility of capital undermining the classical instrument of class struggle), labour is inclined to support transnational private governance as a 'second best' solution, as more forceful public redistributive options are politically difficult to enforce (Smismans).

Of course the effects of unfettered markets alone are not enough to explain such developments. The declining ability of states to regulate markets and the political unwillingness to do so play a crucial role too. In facing threats and uncertainties from abroad, states quickly run into the limits of their own legal jurisdictions. Resorting to (or tolerating) transnational private governance can therefore easily become a providential tool less bound to territorial jurisdiction (van Waarden), clearly related to the intellectual climate, the material reality, and the political project behind neoliberalism. The Internet appears to be a model case in this regard, as preferences of the US government were – before security concerns gained the upper hand – put forward to keep the net free from the public regulation that has been encountered in telecommunications or broadcasting (Christou and Simpson). More generally, self-regulation by business actors is easily promoted as the privileged route to overcome cumbersome or inefficient public regulations (Bislev and Flyverbom, Fuchs, Tsingou). The reliance of transnational private governance on neoliberalism, however, could also reduce its importance in the future, in accordance with the potential demise of such an intellectual climate (Fuchs).

A market structure that shows a limited degree of competition (an oligopoly)

One of the most specific mechanisms that support the evolution of transnational private governance is the pattern of interfirm cooperation in the markets that are being regulated. As Mügge shows in much detail with regard to the financial sector, it is much easier for private actors to promote such policies when only a few big players are involved and have settled early competitive struggles which any new market faces. By emphasising that mature markets are more prone to self-regulation, this finding adds a significant time dimension to the analysis of transnational private governance. The importance of market structures with a limited degree of competition cut across the three other cases focused on finance (Ronit, Tsingou, Botzem). Oligopolistic market structures are also important for those parts of Internet governance that deal with its technical infrastructure, since the latter is predominantly provided by a few big companies such as Cisco or HP (Bislev and Flyverbom). In the broader picture of e-commerce, strong concentration processes, if not oligopolies, are also evident. Thus, telecommunication operators, PC producers, software firms, or big content producers support transnational private governance initiatives (Ibáñez). The allocation of domain names – with a very competitive registration marketplace of 1500 or so companies for the dot eu name – could appear to be at great variance from such an assumption; yet incidentally, the initiative here did not come from the market, but from the European Commission, though the two developed a mutually supportive axis in the early stages (Christou and Simpson). Although oligopolies may differ from a genuine prominence of large firms (in well-defined market segments, small enterprises can form an oligopoly), in most cases these phenomena are closely interrelated. Company size also matters in corporate social responsibility. Here the mechanism works via easily identifiable branded names and retail companies that are more vulnerable to boycotts and political consumerism than others (Conzelmann and Wolf, Fuchs, Merk). Finally, transnational private governance in the EU is also largely supported by its exclusive focus on 'big business', as amply illustrated in the cases of the strategic importance of the CAG (Holman) or the underrepresentation of small- and medium-sized enterprises in the European social dialogue (Smismans).

The support by international institutions, in particular the EU

The EU in general, and the European Commission in particular, has come out as a major driving force behind the spread of transnational private governance. Promotion of this type of governance is part of a systematic and broad-based strategy towards regulatory innovation (Holman). A typical case in this respect is the dot eu TLD: the whole system around Eurid has been set up upon initiative of – and is responsible to – the European Commission (Christou and Simpson). The Commission is also the major player behind the launch of FinNet as a Europe-wide out-of-court complaints network (Ronit). The IASB accounting standards have become almost global, thanks to its adoption by the EU (Botzem). In auditing, the completion of the Single Market secured the recent drive towards a more comprehensive form of transnational private governance (Mügge). Without the active encouragement of the European Commission, there would not have been a social dialogue at the European level – and even here, its actual implementation via European-wide collective agreements only occurred when the Maastricht Treaty provided a higher degree of institutionalisation (Smismans).

To a more limited extent, we can identify the support of regional integration processes in a context of lower levels of institutionalisation, such as NAFTA (Gal-Or) or with other international institutions such as the Basel Committee (Tsingou). During the early stages of the IASB, for example, the involvement of the Basle Committee, the International Organisation of Securities Commissions (IOSCO), the International Monetary Fund (IMF), and the World Bank was decisive (Botzem). The private regulation of food security does not only rely on the oversight of the European Commission, but also of the Codex Alimentarius – a joint body of the World Health Organisation and the Food and Agriculture Organisation (van Waarden). Moreover, ILO conventions are a major backdrop for corporate social responsibility initiatives. Without them, a mobilisation for adequate labour conditions would be far more difficult (Merk). International organisations and agreements also stand behind the transnational private governance of the environmental sphere, as Agenda 21, CITES, and the International Tropical Timber Agreement indicate with regard to the Forest Stewardship Council (Conzelmann and Wolf). Beyond such an institutional embeddedness, the threat of public (national or intergovernmental) regulation can be a major factor leading to the evolution of transnational private governance. For example, the private governance of the Internet was conceived as a clear-cut alternative to public regulation, be it at the domestic and global level alike (Ibáñez). Similarly, the Responsible Care Program in the chemical industry was created after major crises and under the expectation that public regulation would be forthcoming, if not prevented by private initiatives (Fuchs). Still, not all cases of corporate social responsibility are as closely linked to the threat of public regulation. No public regulation, for instance, could be comprehensive enough to affect the 2000-odd companies from a variety of sectors that have joined the Global Compact (Conzelmann and Wolf).

A focus on regulatory policy (but with significant distributional consequences)

Except on private dispute resolution, the focus of transnational private governance on regulatory policies is more than obvious, be it the regulation of the Internet, financial markets, accounting rules, food safety, or social and environmental standards. Yet, these regulatory policies may have major redistributive effects. In derivatives trading or auditing, firms may be excluded from the market (Mügge); in the arena of Internet domain names trade-offs take place between actors claiming ownership of the same name (Bislev and Flyverbom forthcoming, Christou and Simpson); codes of corporate environmental responsibility can have serious distributive consequences, particularly for those companies that have not been involved in their development (Fuchs).

Policy issues other than regulatory policies, however, are usually not covered by transnational private governance, thereby limiting its empirical scope. While many of these 'missing' issues are quite obvious, given that they fall into the core competence of the nation state (e.g. the provision of military security or constitutional policies), the absence of explicitly (re-)distributive policies from transnational private governance is more striking. Even in the field of industrial relations – the most directly redistributive field potentially targeted – the focus is not on the main redistributive issues such as wage relations or social expenditures, but on mild regulatory concerns such as certain labour conditions (Smismans, Merk). According to Holman, however, this discrepancy can be fully explained, as it epitomises a form of 'asymmetrical regulation' where the distinct issues within the ambit of regulation at the transnational level limit the national capacity to act, notably in the field of social policies.

A strong reliance on highly specialised technical or professional knowledge

The existence of highly specialised technical or professional knowledge within the private sector appears to be another precondition of transnational private governance. This is all the more the case when public regulatory institutions lack the knowledge required to follow the pace of technical innovation. Under such circumstances, public authorities will be eager to subscribe to self-regulation, in order to prevent the costs for developing, implementing, monitoring, and enforcing regulation (Mügge, Tsingou, van Waarden).

Particularly in the case of Internet regulation, knowledge is a key resource, given that the core importance of the historic transformation that goes hand-in-hand with the rise of the Internet is based on fundamental changes of the traditional way of producing and transmitting knowledge. The sheer complexity of technical developments forces government officials to leave important governance functions to an expert-driven self-regulation. In the same time, this delegation of authority favours those private actors that have already accumulated a substantial amount of knowledge resources, be they big multinational companies in case of e-commerce, or experienced registry operators in case of the dot eu TLD (Bislev and Flyverbom forthcoming, Christou and Simpson, Ibáñez).

Private expert knowledge is also widely recognised as a core resource for governing global finance (Tsingou). This may even lead to a power shift between the actors concerned, as it is occurring in the domain of auditing from professional associations to globally operating service firms (Botzem). In the field of social regulation, the European Commission relies on the professional knowledge of top representatives of peak capital and labour organisations to draft its policy proposals (Smismans). In corporate social responsibility too, a growing professionalisation pervades the movement. As outlined above, the collection of data on company behaviour has become a major business (Merk). All participants in the governance structure of the FSC need to contribute specific problem-solving resources (Conzelmann and Wolf). Yet, we should remain wary in assuming that expert knowledge resources are essential in transnational private governance. As Fuchs reminds us, the discursive power of business has purposefully constructed the image that without its knowledge-intensive resources, effective regulation would not be possible.

The need for basic common values of private regulators (and their public counterparts)

Transnational private governance is frequently based on a common educational or professional background of those actors involved in it, supported by learning processes through regular meetings, or by a tradition of self-regulation as observed in the financial sector. Professions can play a major role here, as in accounting (Botzem). In a broader perspective, transnational private governance of e-commerce has been made much easier by the dominance of US-free market values among the participants (Ibáñez), as well as the general libertarian, state-sceptic attitude within the Internet community (Christou and Simpson). In the field of corporate social responsibility, the cooperation between stakeholders with varying backgrounds is made easier by common commitments for values such as sustainable growth, being reinforced by common learning processes (Conzelmann and Wolf). In contrast, the difficult and cumbersome development of transnational private governance in the European social dialogue may also be attributed to the basic value differences between capital and labour; together with their uneven power relationship, this precondition contributes at least to the limited scope of the social dialogue, confined to a few consensual issues such as occupational health and safety.

Value homogeneity, however, is not only an issue among the protagonists of transnational private governance, but also between them and the public regulators backing them up. Again, the case of the European social dialogue is very instructive here. Instead of propagating a comprehensive European welfare and industrial relations system, social partners, Member State governments, and the Commission all agree on narrowly circumscribing their agenda, so as to ensure its compatibility with a European project confined to the common market (Smismans). This value homogeneity between private regulators and public supervisors is furthermore epitomised in the case of the CAG, whose members are carefully selected on the basis of their shared commitment to the European market-making project (Holman). Shared values between private regulators and public authorities are a common feature beyond the EU, in other regional integration processes, and international institutions. In global banking, the tradition of 'revolving doors' between the public and private sectors provide a strong support for homogenising values shared by the transnational policy community (Tsingou). Finally, it should be noted that, at least partially, it was the considerable discursive power of business that purposely created such values in the first place (Fuchs).

Normative limitations of transnational private governance

Contributors to the volume may obviously diverge in assessing normative implications of transnational private governance. Here too, however, we can draw common lessons. Transnational private governance can undoubtedly lead to concrete results in specific issue areas. Yet, considering the significance of socioeconomic concerns at stake, most chapters emphasise the limited ability of transnational private governance to solve large societal problems. This contention reflects a lack of progressive prospect, according to which transnational private governance is likely to raise a number of concerns regarding state sovereignty, democracy, and the future of a neoliberal economic order.

A substantial, but ultimately limited ability to solve problems

Within the empirical limitations of the framework conditions outlined above, transnational private governance can contribute to solving concrete issues, in particular when a stable regulation of a single sector is at stake (Conzelmann and Wolf, Mügge, Tsingou, van Waarden). This is how, for example, the e-commerce regime has established and maintained a new form of Internet order, and made a significant contribution to the development of the sector (Ibáñez). Similarly, the dot eu TLD regime – newly established at the time of writing – appears to work well in the accreditation of Internet names and the dispute resolution on name ownership (Christou and Simpson). The IASB has been successful in establishing accounting standards used on a wide basis around the world – a task not achieved by public authorities such as the EU or the United Nations (Botzem). The same conclusion may be drawn regarding the ability of Fin-Net to solve cross-national disputes in specific consumer-oriented financial services, thereby sheltering consumers from lengthy and expensive procedures in public courts (Ronit). While the overall influence of the corporate social responsibility movement should not be overstated, it has led to some real improvements, particularly regarding the general acceptance of an obligation by business, and some procedural issues for a more effective implementation (Merk). The European social dialogue has also led to concrete outcomes on issues previously blocked for many years, such as parental leave (Smismans 2000). Yet, all cases studied in the volume emphasise strong limits in the ability of transnational private governance to solve problems, as it often leaves aside major socioeconomic concerns, such as rebalancing the relationship between capital and labour. Whilst most of them focus on specific sectors, they also underline how transnational private governance is at pains to provide an overarching, inter-sectoral framework. This type of meta-governance clearly remains a task of the public sector (Conzelmann and Wolf).

In contrast to what can be expected in the domestic arena, transnational private governance still requires the support of public administrations and courts to be implemented. In his chapter, Smismans provides an illustration of this feature in comparing the 'regulatory route' of European collective agreements (backed up by a Council Directive) to the 'autonomous route' of direct agreements between unions and employers' association. Whereas the former excludes the realm of private governance, the latter, while including the private, is difficult to implement effectively, particularly in the new Enlargement countries. The European social dialogue is not the only case where implementation of transnational private governance is delegated to public actors. The same can be observed as far as privately developed accounting standards are concerned; in the European Union, EU legislation made them binding (Botzem). In contrast, ongoing struggles to reinforce corporate social responsibility in global value chain and labour relations suggest that only independent private verification provides the required credibility of such forms of transnational private governance (Merk). The same problem arises in case of business self-regulation on environmental matters. Many of the most prominent standards such as Responsible Care do not necessarily lead to substantial environmental improvements in practice, or these improvements remain very controversial (Conzelmann and Wolf, Fuchs). Standards that have stringent requirements and verification schemes such as the FSC remain limited in their market share. Finally, if big firms have so widely joined the Global Compact, it may well be due to the fact that in pledging support to its ten principles, participants keep a free hand in deciding how and to which extent to implement them (Conzelmann and Wolf).

Whilst our contributors concur on the substantial, but ultimately limited ability of transnational private governance to address concerns other than specific issue areas, they vary in their normative assessment of the phenomenon (for a critical perspective see in particular Holman, Ibáñez, Gal-Or). The main criticisms point to its lack of democratic character and its propensity to contribute to further stabilisation of the current neoliberal economic order.

Stabilisation of the current neoliberal economic order

We have already noted that transnational private governance is supported by a neoliberal economic order, i.e. an order that is characterised by economic deregulation, the free play of markets, the preponderance of business over other societal constituencies, and a deep distrust towards public regulation. Actually, transnational private governance is not only supported by neoliberalism, but can also be viewed as its *supporter*, by contributing to its stabilisation. In other words, they are mutually reinforcing. For example, the CAG is part and parcel of the political project to reinforce the European neoliberal agenda (Holman). Dispute resolution mechanisms such as Fin-Net are meant to safeguard the smooth functioning of the Common Market in the field of financial services (Ronit). Voluntary regulations such as codes of conduct are perceived by business as non-threatening to the current (neoliberal) order, since they do not challenge – at least in a short-term perspective – basic pillars of this order (Merk). Other cases of transnational private governance have evolved in order to prevent governments from regulating markets, such as in Eurobond underwriting or Auditing (Mügge). Since public regulation is usually stricter, this also limits the problem-solving contribution by transnational private governance, as in the case of environmental protection (Fuchs).

Neoliberalism as an economic program is not equally benevolent to all parts of the business community. It generally favours big, transnationally mobile companies, in particular capital investors. The same can be stated for transnational private governance. One overriding concern of many of our contributions is that such governance particularly favours large and well-established multinational companies, in particular those from North America and the EU (Holman, Gal-Or, Ibáñez). More specifically, some cases of financial market regulation are meant to support a market order that primarily benefits the existing oligopoly (Mügge). Policies promoted by IASB benefits capital market actors such as institutional investors and financial analysts (Botzem). The flip side of these findings is that transnational private governance may lead to social closure, therefore disadvantaging small- and medium-sized enterprises (SMEs), newcomers, or business from outside of the Organisation for Economic Co-operation and Development (OECD), not to mention weakly organised labour or even more diffuse social movements.

Some of our contributions, however, notice that this prominent role of (big) business is also fragile, in particular if transnational private governance proves to be unable to fulfil those governance tasks assigned to it, thereby possibly leading to a backlash or, more generally, creating a site of contention between different social and economic forces (Fuchs, Merk). One of the potential counterweights to the neoliberal economic order, the European social dialogue – and particularly labour as its driving force – is too weak to force management to the negotiation table on important issues. Most European collective agreements have produced procedural than substantial norms, and are based on rather soft legal instruments. The further weakening of labour during the process of enlargement may also explain why capital now suddenly accepts autonomous implementation by the social partners as risks are limited. Yet, the European social dialogue can also be assessed as a small step in the right direction insofar as it has led to horizontal collaboration and mutual awareness of labour unions within different EU Member States (Smismans).

Restrictions on the (democratically legitimated) public control over private actors

Although none of our contributors would argue that a concerted effort by the most powerful states would be unable to reverse the allocation of governance tasks to private actors, we still can conclude that transnational private governance is in many cases effectively undermining the free and unrestricted choice of policy options and instruments of individual governments, in spite of the fact that most of these private institutions are somehow supported by intergovernmental institutions. In some cases of Internet regulation, for example, the regulatory competence of a few private companies has clearly exceeded those of most public actors. At the same time, these private actors follow a conscious strategy to keep public regulators out (Ibáñez). The same strategy can be observed in the financial sector, although it is not always successful (Mügge).

One of the most fascinating cases of a clash between private governance and public regulation is the dot eu TLD. Whilst the Internet community expects a laissez faire attitude, the EU extends its well-proven 'agencification approach' to this issue area (Christou and Simpson). It is still too early to assess, whether the complex dual agency model will be able to satisfy the expectations of the Internet community. A similar clash between private regulators and public regulators has occurred in the field of accounting standards (Botzem). Again, the EU has formally reserved the right to assess each standard before adopting it. But the carve-outs it has made have caused much controversy, thereby substantially raising the costs for the use of this type of authority. Another challenging case of transnational private governance with regard to the suspension of public authority is the European social dialogue, in which the Commission renounces its competence altogether if peak associations of capital and labour agree on an issue and, thus, bypasses any intervention from the European Parliament or even the Council (Smismans).

The EU is not the only institution where we can observe the tension between transnational private governance and public control. While the democratic character of many governments of the global South may be felt wanting, it is striking that hardly any of the CSR schemes discussed in the volume are concerned with whether the governments of producing states agree with improved labour standards that go hand in hand with effective CSR – or rather prefer to compete for investments on the basis of cheap labour or low environmental protection.

Limitations on the democratic character of transnational private governance

While transnational private governance receives a mostly favourable account in terms of problem solving or 'output legitimacy', most assessments of its 'input legitimacy' are more distrustful. As noted above, not all societal groups are equally represented within the decision-making institutions of transnational private governance, with a particularly powerful role being kept for major corporations or even oligopolies. If such governance is assessed against standard (domestic) models of democracy, it clearly remains inadequate, especially in terms of limited transparency and accountability (Holman, Ibáñez, Tsingou). This is particularly problematic in cases where private governance replaces public decision making, as in the European social dialogue (Smismans), or where private governance is further separated from democratic control by the dual agency role of the European Commission (Christou and Simpson). It does not only affect the making of laws, but also their adjudications, such as the rising importance of private dispute resolution mechanisms, suggests with regard to the limited independence of arbitrators, conflicts of interests, or transparency and confidentiality problems (Gal-Or).

As transnational private governance will always remain unsatisfactory *vis-à-vis* traditional theories of (domestic) democracy – an assumption that could be shared for most forms of intergovernmental cooperation (Conzelmann and Wolf) –, it is only against alternative models of functional democracy that more positive assessments can be made. Hence, tentative analyses of a 'constitutionalisation of international networks of technocrats' can be made (van Waarden). Some of our cases explore how to overcome the democratic deficit of transnational private governance. In spite of all of its shortcomings, the European social dialogue is one of them, by guaranteeing a structured participation of weak interest groups such as labour (Smismans). Similarly, Fin-Net as an inclusive scheme that involves consumer associations and is supervised by the EU is certainly to be preferred to pure industry self-regulation – although the reason for the inclusive model was less a concern of democratic legitimacy than of consumer confidence (Ronit). Probably the most democratically legitimate of all the cases is the Forestry Stewardship Council, based on an elaborate system for the effective participation of a broad range of stakeholders with decision-making power (Conzelmann and Wolf). Here, however, we may need to note a trade-off between the problem-solving contribution and the democratic legitimacy of transnational private governance, given the very limited market share of FSC-certified products. Since timber industries in many countries regard the FSC standard as being too strict, they have created competing labels with less severe criteria, thereby marginalising the FSC (Fuchs).

Conclusions and perspectives

At the heart of this volume is an examination of transnational private governance and its limits in conceptual, empirical, and normative terms. Devoting greater attention to such limitations appear to be particularly significant against the backdrop of a literature that tends to portrait transnational private governance as a major breakthrough towards more effective global governance. Hopefully, the more nuanced tone of this volume should contribute to a research agenda that draws attention to transnational private governance from a more critical perspective. Far from closing the books on the topic, it may thus broaden the field of future research and reinforce its analytical coherence, particularly on conceptual issues, theoretical implications, empirical coverage, and institutional design.

As far as future conceptual understanding is concerned, we hope that we were clear enough in showing that transnational private governance is not so transnational, not so private, and not so close to the ideal of 'governance' as described by many observers. Whilst this may leave us in need of a better-suited term for identifying on conceptual grounds future empirical research, further desegregation may also be required to generate new hypotheses and typologies on various forms of transnational private governance.

Regarding theoretical implications, this volume brings together theoretically pluralistic contributions; but this does not rule out building upon the inroads it made in explaining the emergence and potential developments of transnational private governance, including the identification of framework conditions for the advent of such forms of governance. Future research will hopefully probe and engage the analytical framework we put together in order to distinguish between conceptual, theoretical, and normative issues. The 16 or so core categories we set out in our introduction were from the outset not conceived as a rigid analytical grid. Whilst such tools may have been useful in enhancing coherence and dialogue among our contributors, they may not be useful in other cases or from distinct theoretical approaches.

Similarly, the empirical coverage of this volume is large enough to generate findings that allow drawing lessons at a high level of generalisation. It is not comprehensive though. Our understanding of transnational private governance should in particular pay more importance to the fast growing developments currently underway in the service sector. As services have assumed a crucial importance in our society and are increasingly internationalised, they also rely more on a mix of public–private standards and coordination practices as a result of regulatory reforms. Future research may thus focus on transnational private governance in domains such as consultancy, standardisation of consumer, and social services (quality support, transportation, tourism, healthcare, and higher education), or even on private military companies increasingly entwined in the security agenda.

Finally, this volume was not thought out as a direct contribution to institutional design. Nevertheless, important lessons could be drawn for engaging the concrete world in which transnational private governance is institutionally embedded. By providing an explicit discussion of its normative implications, it sets out the debate on how some forms of transnational private governance are likely to raise more concerns than others according to distinct criteria for organising and changing contemporary societies. For instance, whilst Conzelmann and Wolf see the Forestry Stewardship Council as a significant step in dealing with the usual democratic challenges of transnational private governance, Smismans and, more radically, Merk acknowledge that the European social dialogue and more generally worldwide codes of conduct can under certain circumstance be fruitfully invested by labour to undermine neoliberalism. These findings should help us thinking out institutional mechanisms in other areas of transnational private governance.

Note

1 We are very grateful to the contributors to this volume for their comments on an earlier version of this chapter.

Bibliography

Abbott, A. (1988) *The System of Professions. An Essay on the Division of Expert Labor*, Chicago: University of Chicago Press.

Abbott, K.W., Keohane, R.O., Moravcesik, A., Slaughter, A.-M., and Snidal, D. (2000) 'The Concept of Legalization', *International Organization*, 54, 3: 401–19.

The Accountant (1997) 'Top Firms Agree European Audit Blueprint', *The Accountant*, January.

Altvater, E. and Mahnkopf, B. (1996) *Grenzen der Globalisierung*, Münster: Westfälisches Dampfboot.

Anderson, B. (1991) *Imagined Communities*, London: Verso.

Ansell, C.K. and Weber, S. (1999) 'Organizing International Politics: Sovereignty and Open Systems', *International Political Science Review*, 20, 1: 73–93.

Ansoff, I. (1981) 'Die Bewältigung von Überraschungen und Diskontinuitäten durch die Unternehmensführung. Strategische Informationen auf schwache Signale', in H. Steinmann (ed.) *Unternehmensführung I: Planung und Kontrolle*, München: Vahlen.

Apeldoorn, B. van (2000) 'Transnational Class Agency and European Governance: The Case of the European Round Table of Industrialists', *New Political Economy*, 5, 2: 157–81.

Apeldoorn, B. van (2002) *Transnational Capitalism and the Struggle over European Integration*, London: Routledge.

Arrowsmith, J. and Marginson, P. 'The European Cross-Border Dimension to Collective Bargaining in Multinational Companies', *European Journal of Industrial Relations*, 12. Forthcoming.

Arts, B. (2003) 'Non-State Actors in Global Governance. Three Faces of Power', Preprint Max-Planck-Projektgruppe Recht der Gemeinschaftsgüter 003/4, Bonn: Max Planck Society.

Ashby, W.R. (1958) 'Requisite Variety and its Implications for the Control of Complex Systems', *Cybernetica*, 3: 83–99.

Bachrach, P. and Baratz, M. (1962) 'Two Faces of Power', *American Political Science Review*, 56: 947–52.

Baird, Z. *et al.* (2004) 'A New Model for Global Internet Governance', in D. MacLean (ed.) *Internet Governance: A Grand Collaboration*, New York: UN ICT Task Force.

Bakker, W. and Waarden, F. van (1999) 'Discretionaire ruimte bij de formulering en handhaving van regelgeving', in B. Wieger and F. van Waarden (eds) *Ruimte rond regels. Reguleringsstijlen vergeleken*, Amsterdam and Meppel: Boom.

Balanya, B., Doherty, A., Hoedeman, O., Ma'anit, A. and Wessel, E. (2000) *Europe Inc., Regional & Global Restructuring and the Rise of Corporate Power*, London: Pluto Press.

Bamber, G. and Cordova, E. (1993), 'Collective Bargaining', in R. Blanpain and C. Engels (eds) *Comparative Labour Law and Industrial Relations in Industrialized Market Economies,* Deventer: Kluwer.

Bardach, E. and Kagan, R.A. (1982) *Going by the Book: The Problem of Regulatory Unreasonableness,* Philadelphia: Temple University Press.

Barry, A., Osborne, T. and Rose, N. (eds) (1996) *Foucault and Political Reason: Liberalism, Neo-Liberalism and Rationalities of Government,* Chicago: University of Chicago Press.

Bartley, T. (2003) 'Certifying Forests and Factories: States, Social Movements, and the Rise of Private Regulation in the Apparel and Forest Products Fields', *Politics and Society,* 31, 3: 433–64.

Basel Committee on Banking Supervision (1998) *Enhancing Bank Transparency,* Basel: Bank for International Settlements.

Basel Committee on Banking Supervision (2002) *Public Disclosures by Banks: Results of the 2002 Disclosure Survey,* Basel: Bank for International Settlements.

Basel Committee on Banking Supervision (2004) *International Convergence of Capital Measurement and Capital Standards – A Revised Framework,* Basel: Bank for International Settlements.

Bayart, J.F. (2004) *Le gouvernement du monde. Une critique politique de la globalisation,* Paris: Fayard.

Becker, G. (1983) 'A Theory of Competition among Pressure Groups for Political Influence', *Quarterly Journal of Economics,* 98: 371–400.

Bendell, J. (2004) 'Barricades and boardrooms: a contemporary history of the corporate accountability movement', Technology, Business and Society Programme Paper no. 13, Geneva: UNRISD.

Benkler, Y. (2000) 'Internet Regulation: a Case Study in the Problem of Unilateralism', *European Journal of International Law,* 11: 171–85.

Benz, A. and Papadopoulos, Y. (eds) (2006) *Governance and Democracy,* London: Routledge.

Bercusson, B. (1994) 'The Dynamic of European Labour Law after Maastricht', *Industrial Law Journal,* 23: 1–31.

Bercusson, B. (1996) *European Labour Law,* London: Butterworths.

Bercusson, B. (1997), 'The Treaty of Amsterdam: Strengthening Social Dialogue and EC labour law', in E. Gabaglio and R. Hoffmann (eds) *European Trade Union Yearbook 1997,* Brussels: European Trade Union Institute.

Bercusson, B. (1999), 'Democratic Legitimacy and European Labour Law', *Industrial Law Journal,* 28: 153–70.

Berger, K.P. (1996) *Formalisierte oder 'schleichende' Kodifizierung des nationalen Wirtschaftsrecht. Zu den methodischen und praktischen Grundlagen der lex mercatoria,* Berlin: Walter de Gruyter.

Berger, K.P., Dubberstein, H., Lehmann, S. and Petzold, V. (2004) 'The CENTRAL Enquiry on the Use of Transnational Law in International Contract Law and Arbitration', Cologne: Center for Transnational Law, University of Cologne.

Bernard, N. (2000) 'Legitimising EU Law: Is the Social Dialogue the Way Forward? Some Reflections Around the UEAPME Case', in J. Shaw (ed.) *Social Law and Policy in an Evolving European Union,* Oxford: Hart.

Betten, L. (1998) 'The Democratic Deficit of Participatory Democracy in Community Social Policy', *European Law Review,* 23: 20–36.

Bhala, R. (1998/99) 'The Myth about Stare Decisis and International Trade Law (Part One of a Trilogy)', *American University International Law Review,* 14, 4: 845–956.

Bishop, D.P. (2004) 'The Case for an Appellate Panel and its Scope of Review', paper presented at the British Institute of International and Comparative Law, May 2004.

Bislev, S. and Flyverbom, M. 'Internet Regulation – on Modes of Governance and Entangled Authorities', in H. Krause Hansen and D. Salskov-Iversen (eds) *Critical Perspectives on Private Authority in Global Politics,* New York: Palgrave MacMillan. Forthcoming.

Bislev, S., Salskov-Iversen, D. and Krause Hansen, H. (2002) 'The Global Diffusion of Managerialism: Transnational Discourse Communities at Work', *Global Society,* 16, 2: 199–212.

Blundell, J. and Robinson, C. (1999) 'Regulation Without the State', Occasional Paper 109, The Institute of Economic Affairs: London.

Boddewyn, J.J. (1988) *Advertising Self-Regulation and Outside Participation: A Multinational Comparison,* New York: Quorum Books.

Boland, V. (2003) 'Chicago Exchanges to Fight Eurex' *Financial Times,* June 20.

Borrus, M. and Zyzman, J. (1997) 'Wintelism and the Changing Terms of Global Competition: Prototype of the Future?' Berkeley Roundtable on International Economy (BRIE) Working Paper 96B, Berkeley, CA: University of California.

Botzem, S. and Quack, S. (2006) 'Contested Rules and Shifting Boundaries: International Standard Setting in Accounting', in M.L. Djelic and K. Sahlin-Andersson (eds) *Transnational Governance: Institutional Dynamics of Regulation,* Cambridge: Cambridge University Press.

Braithwaite, J. and Drahos, P. (2000) *Global Business Regulation,* Cambridge: Cambridge University Press.

Branch, A. (2005) 'The Evolution of the European Social Dialogue Towards Greater Autonomy: Challenger and Potential Benefits', *International Journal of Comparative Labour Law and Industrial Relations,* 21, 1: 321–47.

Brand, U. (2005) 'Order and Regulation: Global Governance as a Hegemeonic Discourse of International Politics', *Review of International Political Economy,* 12, 1: 155–76.

Brand, U., Brunnengräber, A., Schrader, L., Stock, C. and Wahl, P. (eds) (2000) *Global Governance. Alternative zur neoliberalen Globalisierung?* Münster: Westfälisches Dampfboot.

Braun, R. (2001) 'Konzerne als Beschützer der Menschenrechte? Zur Bedeutung von Verhaltenskodizes', in: Brühl *et al.* (eds) *Die Privatisierung der Weltpolitik: Entstaatlichung und Kommerzialisierung im Globalisierungsprozess,* Bonn: Dietz.

Brkulic, D. (2001) *Herschrijven GMP+ Standaard,* Den Haag: Productschap Diervoeder.

Brühl, T., Debiel, T., Hamm, B., Hummel, H. and Martens, J. (eds) (2001) *Die Privatisierung der Weltpolitik: Entstaatlichung und Kommerzialisierung im Globalisierungsprozess,* Bonn: Dietz.

Brühl, T., Feldt, H., Hamm, B. and Hummel, H. (eds) (2004) *Unternehmen in der Weltpolitik. Politiknetzwerke, Unternehmensregeln und die Zukunft des Multilateralismus,* Bonn: Dietz.

Brunsson, N. (2000) 'Organization, Market, and Standardization', in N. Brunsson and B. Jacobsson (eds) *A World of Standards,* Oxford: Oxford University Press.

Brunsson, N. and Jacobsson, B. (eds) (2000) *A World of Standards,* Oxford: Oxford University Press.

Burchell, G., Gordon, S. and Miller, P. (eds) (1991) *The Foucault Effect: Studies in Governmental Rationality,* Harvester-Wheatsheaf: Hemel Hempstead.

Cameron, A. and Palan, R. (2003) *The Imagined Economies of Globalisation,* London: SAGE.

Carroll, A.B. (1996) *Business and Society – Ethics and Stakeholder Management*, 3rd ed., Cincinnati: South Western College Publishing.

Cashore, B. Auld, G. and Newson, D. (2004) *Governing through Markets: Forest Certification and the Emergence of Non-State Authority*, New Haven: Yale University Press.

Cawson, A. (1986) *Corporatism and Political Theory*, Oxford: Blackwell.

CEFIC and ICCA (2005) *Responsible Care 1985–2005*. Available online at: www.cefic.org/Files/Publications/RCStatusReport2005.pdf (accessed 27 September 2006).

Cerny, P.G. (1990) *The Changing Architecture of Politics*, London: SAGE.

Cerny, P.G. (ed.) (1993) *Finance and World Politics*, Aldershot: Edward Elgar.

Cerny, P.G. (2002) 'Webs of Governance and the Privatisation of Transnational Regulation' in D.M. Andrews, R. Henning and L. Pauly (eds) *Governing the World's Money*, Ithaca: Cornell University Press.

Chavagneux, C. (2001) 'Réglementation prudentielle: le forfait de la BRI?', *Revue d'économie financière*, 60: 47–58.

Checkel, J.T. (2002) 'Persuasion in International Institutions', ARENA Working Paper WP 02/14, Oslo: ARENA, University of Oslo.

Christensen, T. and Lægreid, P. (eds) (2001) *New Public Management*, Aldershot: Ashgate.

Christou, G. and Simpson, S. (2006) 'The Internet and Public–Private Governance in the European Union', *Journal of Public Policy*, 26, 1: 43–61.

Christou, G. and Simpson, S. (2007) *The New Electronic Marketplace: European Governance Strategies in a Globalising Economy*, London: Edward Elgar.

Church, C.H. and Phinnemore, D. (1994), *European Union and European Community. A Handbook and Commentary on the Post-Maastricht Treaties*, New York, London: Harvester Wheatsheaf.

Clapp, J. (1998) 'The Privatization of Global Environmental Governance: ISO 14000 and the Developing World', *Global Governance* 8: 295–316.

Clapp, J. (2001) *Toxic Exports. The Transfer of Hazardous Wastes from Rich to Poor Countries*, Ithaca: Cornell University Press.

Clean Clothes Campaign (2005) 'Looking of a Quick Fix: How Weak Social Auditing is Keeping Workers in Sweatshops', Clean Clothes Campaign Report. Available online at: www.cleanclothes.org/ftp/05-quick_fix.pdf (accessed 27 September 2006).

Clean Clothes Newsletter (2000) 'Using Codes of Conduct: Some Background for the CCC Strategy Debate' Clean Clothes Newsletter 13. Available online at: www.cleanclothes.org/news/newsletter13-codes.htm (accessed 27 September 2006).

Cohen, B.J. (1999) 'The New Geography of Money' in E. Gilbert and E. Helleiner (eds) *Nation-States and Money, The Past, Present and Future of National Currencies*, London: Routledge.

Colàs, A. (2002) *International Civil Society*, Cambridge: Polity Press.

Coleman, W. (1996) *Financial Services, Globalisation and Domestic Policy Change*, London: Macmillan.

Committee of European Securities Regulators (2004) 'U.S. Commodity Futures Trading Commission and the Committee of European Securities Regulators Announce Trans-Atlantic Cooperation Initiative and Statement of Intent to Develop an Action Plan on Cross Border Issues', Paris: Committee of European Securities Regulators.

Comor, E.A. (1999) 'Governance and the Nation-State in a Knowledge-Based Political Economy', in M. Hewson and T.J. Sinclair (eds) *Approaches to Global Governance Theory*, New York: SUNY Press.

Competitiveness Advisory Group (1997) *Competitiveness for Employment. Report to the President of the Commission and the Heads of State and Government,* Brussels: Competitiveness Advisory Group.

Competitiveness Advisory Group (1999) *Sustainable Competitiveness. Report to the President of the Commission and the Heads of State and Government,* Brussels: Competitiveness Advisory Group.

Connor, T. (1998) 'Independent Monitoring', Campaign for Labor Rights, 13 (April–May).

Connor, T. (2004) 'Time to Scale Up Cooperation? Trade Unions, NGOs, and the International Anti-Sweatshop Movement', *Development in Practice,* 14, 1–2: 61–70.

Conzelmann, T. and Wolf, K.D. 'Potenzial und Grenzen grenzüberschreitender politischer Steuerung durch privatwirtschaftliche Selbstregulierung', in A. Hasenclever (ed.) *Macht und Ohnmacht internationaler Institutionen. Festschrift für Volker Rittberger,* Baden-Baden: Nomos. Forthcoming.

Coriat, B., Petit, P. and Schméder, G. (eds) (2006) *The Hardship of Nations, New Horizons in Institutional and Evolutionary Economics*, Cheltenham, UK: Edward Elgar.

Covaleski, M.A., Dirsmith, M.W. and Rittenberg, L. (2003) 'Jurisdictional disputes over professional work: the institutionalization of the global knowledge expert', *Accounting, Organizations and Society,* 28: 323–55.

Cox, J. (2006) *The Suborning of American Democracy: The Triumph of Corporate Power,* Frederick: PublishAmerica.

Cox, R.W. (1983) 'Gramsci, Hegemony, and International Relations: An Essay in Method', reprinted in R.W. Cox (with T.J. Sinclair) (1996) *Approaches to World Order,* Cambridge: Cambridge University Press.

Cox, R.W. (1986) 'Social Forces, States and World Orders: Beyond International Relations Theory', in R.O. Keohane (ed.) *Neorealism and its Critics,* New York: Columbia University Press.

Cox, R.W. (1987) *Production, Power, and World Order,* New York: Columbia University Press.

Cox, R.W., with M.G. Schechter (2002) *The Political Economy of a Plural World. Critical Reflections on Power, Morals and Civilization,* London and New York: Routledge.

Cutler, A.C. (1997) 'Artifice, Ideology and Paradox: The Public/Private Distinction in International Law', *Review of International Political Economy,* 4, 2: 261–85.

Cutler, A.C. (1999) 'Private Authority in International Trade Relations: The Case of Maritime Transport', in A.C. Cutler, V. Haufler and T. Porter (eds) *Private Authority and International Affairs*, New York: SUNY Press.

Cutler, A.C. (2003) *Private Power and Global Authority: Transnational Merchant Law in the Global Political Economy,* Cambridge: Cambridge University Press.

Cutler, A.C., Haufler, V. and Porter, T. (eds) (1999a) *Private Authority and International Affairs,* New York: SUNY Press.

Cutler, A.C., Haufler V. and Porter, T. (1999b) 'Introduction', in A.C. Cutler, V. Haufler and T. Porter (eds) *Private Authority and International Affairs,* New York: SUNY Press.

Cutler, A.C., Haufler, V. and Porter, T. (1999c) 'The contours and significance of private authority in international affairs', in A.C. Cutler, V. Haufler and T. Porter (eds) *Private Authority and International Affairs,* New York: SUNY Press.

Dahl, R. (1957) 'The Concept of Power', *Behavioral Science,* 2: 201–15.

Dannreuther, C. and Petit, P. (2006) 'Post-Fordism, Beyond National Models: The Main Challenges for Regulation Theory', *Competition and Change,* 10, 2: 100–12.

David, P.A. and Greenstein, S. (1990) 'The Economics of Compatibility Standards: An Introduction to Recent Research', *Economics of Innovation and New Technologies,* 1: 3–41.

Dezalay Y. and Garth, B.G. (1996) *Dealing in Virtue. International Commercial Arbitration and the Construction of Transnational Legal Order,* Chicago: University of Chicago Press.

Dezalay Y. and Garth, B.G. (2002) *The Internationalization of Palace Wars. Lawyers, Economists, and the Contest to Transform Latin American States,* Chicago: University of Chicago Press.

De Schutter, O. and Deakin, S. (eds) (2005) *Social Rights and Market Forces: Is the Open Coordination of Employment and Social Policies the Future of Social Europe?* Brussels: Bruylant.

Dean, M. (1999) *Governmentality: Power and Rule in Modern Society,* London: SAGE.

Deinert, O. (2003) 'Modes of Implementing European Collective Agreements and Their Impact on Collective Autonomy', *Industrial Law Journal,* 32: 317–25.

Delarue, R. (1998) 'De Europese kaderakkoorden over ouderschapsverlof en deeltijdse arbeid: voorbereiding, totstandkoming, omzetting en perspectieven', paper presented at the Conference 'Sociaal Actieprogramma – Europese Sociale Dialoog' organized by ACW in the European Parliament, Brussels, November 1998.

Dicken, P. (1998) *Global Shift, Transforming the World Economy*, 3rd ed., London: Paul Chapman Publishing.

Djelic, M.L. and Sahlin-Andersson, K. (eds) (2006) *Transnational Governance: Institutional Dynamics of Regulation,* Cambridge: Cambridge University Press.

Douglas, M. and Wildavsky A. (1982) *Risk and Culture,* Berkeley: University of California Press.

Dryzek, J. (1999) 'Transnational Democracy', *The Journal of Political Philosophy,* 7, 1: 30–51.

Duffield, M. (2001) *Global Governance and the New Wars,* London: Zed Books.

Dunning, J. (1997) *Alliance Capitalism and Global Business,* London: Routledge.

Eberlein, B. and Kerwer, D. (2004) 'New Governance in the European Union: A Theoretical Perspective', *Journal of Common Market Studies,* 42, 1: 121–42.

EC-POP (2000a) *Interim Steering Group on the Proposed Dot eu Registry.* Available online at: www.ec-pop.org/0511/ (accessed February 2005).

EC-POP (2000b) 'The dot eu Registry Proposal'. Available online at: www.ec-pop.org/1009prop (accessed February 2005).

Egan, M. (2001) *Constructing a European Market: Standards, Regulation, and Governance*, Oxford: Oxford University Press.

Elam, M.J. (1990) 'Puzzling Out the Post-Fordist Debate: Technology, Markets and Institutions', *Economic and Industrial Democracy,* 11, 1: 9–37.

Engerling, F. (1996) 'The Multilateral Investment Agreement', *Transnational Corporations,* 5, 3: 147–61.

Ernst, D. (2003) 'The new mobility of knowledge: Digital Information Systems and Global Flagship Networks', East-West Center Working Papers no. 56, Honolulu: East-West Center.

Esbenshade, J. (2004) *Monitoring Sweatshops: Workers, Consumers and the Global Apparel Industry,* Philadelphia: Temple University Press.

Esping-Andersen, G. (1985) *Politics Against Markets,* Princeton: Princeton University Press.

Eurid (2006) 'Eurid's Quarterly Progress Report to the European Commission – First

Quarter 2006'. Available online at: www.eurid.eu/en/shared/documents/q-reports/q1-progress-report-final.pdf (accessed 27 September 2006).
European Accounting Bulletin (1998) 'Commission backs self-regulation for auditors', May 27.
European Commission (1985) 'Directorate General for Social Affairs', *Social Europe*, 2, 85.
European Commission (1993) 'Green Paper on Access to Justice and Dispute Settlement', COM 576 final, Brussels: Commission of the European Communities.
European Commission (1995a) 'Accounting Harmonisation: A New Strategy vis-a-vis International Harmonisation', COM 95 (508), Brussels: Commission of the European Communities.
European Commission (1995b) 'Social Dialogue – the Situation in the Community in 1995', *Social Europe*, 2, 95.
European Commission (1996) 'Action Plan on Consumer Access to Justice and the Settlement of Consumer Disputes in the Internal Market', COM (96) 13 final, Brussels: Commission of the European Communities.
European Commission (1998a) 'Adapting and Promoting the Social Dialogue at Community level', COM 32 final, Brussels: Commission of the European Communities.
European Commission (1998b) 'Commission Recommendation on the Principles Applicable to the Bodies Responsible for Out-of-Court Settlement of Consumer Disputes', (98/257/EC), Brussels: Commission of the European Communities.
European Commission (1998c) 'Commission Communication on the Out-of-Court Settlement of Consumer Disputes', COM 198 final, Brussels: Commission of the European Communities.
European Commission (2000a) 'Commission Working Document on the Creation of a European Extra-Judicial Network (EEJ-Net)'. Available online at: http://ec.europa.eu/ consumers/redress/out_of_court/eej_net/acce_just06_en.pdf (accessed 27 September 2006).
European Commission (2000b) 'The Creation of the .eu Internet TLD', Commission Working Paper no. 2, Brussels: Commission of the European Communities.
European Commission (2000c) 'Internet Domain Name System: Creating the .EU Top Level Domain, Communication from the Commission to the European Parliament and the Council', COM 421, Brussels: Commission of the European Communities.
European Commission (2001a) 'Communication from the Commission on "Widening Consumer Access to Alternative Dispute Resolution" ', COM 161 final, Brussels: Commission of the European Communities.
European Commission (2001b) 'Commission Recommendation of 4 April 2001 on the Principles for Out-of-Court Bodies Involved in the Consensual Resolution of Consumer Disputes, notified under document no. C (2001) 1016 (20001/310/EC)', Brussels: Commission of the European Communities.
European Commission (2001c) 'European Governance. A White Paper', COM 428 final, Brussels: Commission of the European Communities.
European Commission (2001d) 'White Paper on European Governance. Work Area No. 2. Handling the Process of Producing and Implementing Community Rules, Report of the Working Group "Better Regulation", Group 2c', Brussels: Commission of the European Communities.
European Commission (2003a) 'Commission Decision of 21 May 2003 on the Designation of the .eu Top Level Domain Registry', notified under document no. C(2003)1624, 2003/275/EC, OJL 128/29, Brussels: Commission of the European Communities.

European Commission (2003b) 'Contribution From the EC and Its Member States to the Improvement and Clarification of the WTO Dispute Settlement Understanding', Ref. 009/03-Rev2, Brussels: Commission of the European Communities.

European Commission (2004a) 'Communication on Partnership for Change in an Enlarged Europe – Enhancing the Contribution of European Social Dialogue', COM 557 final, Brussels: Commission of the European Communities.

European Commission (2004b) 'Green Paper on Public–Private Partnerships and Community Law on Public Contracts and Concessions', COM 327 final, Brussels: Commission of the European Communities.

European Commission (2004c) 'Commission Staff Working Paper "Annex to the European Electronic Communication Regulation and Markets 2004 (10th Report)", vol. 2', Brussels: Commission of the European Communities.

European Commission (2004d) 'Commission Regulation of 28 April 2004 Laying down Public Policy Rules Concerning the Implementation and Functions of the .eu Top Level Domain and the Principles Governing Registration', EC No 874/2004, OJL162/40, Brussels: Commission of the European Communities.

European Parliament and Council (2002) 'Regulation on the Implementation of the .eu Top Level Domain, (EC) No 733/2002. OJL133/1, 30.4.02', Brussels: European Parliament and Council.

European Round Table of Industrialists (1994) *European Competitiveness. The Way to Growth and Jobs,* Brussels: ERT.

European Round Table of Industrialists (1996) *Benchmarking for Policy-Makers. The Way to Competitiveness, Growth and Job Creation,* Brussels: ERT.

European Table of Industrialist (1993) *European Labour Markets. An Update on Perspectives and Requirements for Job Generation in the Second Half of the 1990s,* Brussels: ERT.

EWCB (2005) 'GM, Ford and GE Cases Highlight EWCs' Bargaining Role', *European Works Council Bulletin,* 56: 7–13.

Falkner, G. (1998) *EU Social Policy in the 1990s: Towards a Corporatist Policy Community,* London: Routledge.

Faure, S. (2001) 'The Role of Joint Voluntary Initiatives in the Promotion and Momentum of Social Dialogue in the Textile, Clothing and Footwear Industries', Sector Working Paper 170-2001, Geneva: International Labour Organization.

Fin-Net (2001) *Memorandum of Understanding on a Cross-Border Out-of-Court Complaints Network for Financial Services in the European Economic Areas,* Brussels: Fin-Net.

Fligstein, N. (1996) 'Markets as Politics: A Political-Cultural Approach to Market Institutions', *American Sociological Review,* 61, 656–73.

Fligstein, N. (2001) *The Architecture of Markets: An Economic Sociology of Twenty-First-Century Capitalist Societies,* Princeton: Princeton University Press.

Florio, M. (2002) 'Economists, Privatization in Russia and the Waning of the "Washington Consensus" ', *Review of International Political Economy,* 9, 2: 374–415.

Fluck, J. and Schmitt, T. (1998) 'Selbstverpflichtungen und Umweltvereinbarungen – rechtlich gangbarer Königsweg deutscher und europäischer Umweltpolitik?', *Verwaltungsarchiv,* 89: 220–63.

Flyverbom, M. (2005) 'Making the Global Information Society Governable: On the Governmentality of Multi-stakeholder Networks', PhD dissertation, Copenhagen Business School.

Franck, T.M. (1995) *Fairness in International Law and Institutions,* Oxford: Clarendon Press.

Franda, M. (2001) *Governing the Internet: The Emergence of an International Regime,* Boulder, CO: Lynne Rienner.

Frankel, C., (2004) 'Europæisk Netværksstyring af IKT', in J. Hoff (ed.) *Danmark som Informationssamfund,* Århus: Århus Universitetsforlag.

Freeriks, Mark (2004) 'Dutch Animal Feed Regulation: Its Theoretical Underpinnings and Evolution Through the Past Century', unpublished honors thesis, Utrecht University.

Friedman, M., 1970 'The Social Responsibility of Business is to Increase its Profits', *New York Times Magazine,* September 13: 32–3.

Friedman, R.B (1990) 'On the Concept of Authority in Political Philosophy', in J. Raz (ed.) *Authority,* New York: New York University Press.

Fuchs, D. (2005) *Understanding Business Power in Global Governance,* Baden-Baden: Nomos.

Fuchs, D. (2006a) 'Global Governance – an International Relations Perspective on Tropical Forests', in S. Spray and M. Moran (eds) *Understanding Environmental Challenges – A Multi-Disciplinary Approach on Tropical Deforestation,* New York: Rowman & Littlefield.

Fuchs, D. (2006b) '*Transnational Corporations and Global Governance: The Effectiveness of Private Governance*', in S. Schirm (ed.) *Globalisation State of the Art of Research and Perspectives,* London: Routledge.

Fuchs, D. and Lorek, S. (2005) 'Sustainable Consumption Governance: A History of Promises and Failures', *Journal on Consumer Policy,* 28, 3: 261–88.

Gallup International (1999) *Gallup International Millenium Survey,* London: Gallup International Association.

Gal-Or, N. (2003) 'Private vs. Public International Justice: The Role of ADR in Global and Regional Economic Treaties', in R.C. Thomsen and N.L. Hale (eds) *Canadian Environments: Essays in Culture, Politics and History,* Brussels: P.I.E.-Peter Lang.

Gal-Or, N. (2005) 'NAFTA Chapter Eleven and the Implications for the FTAA: The Institutionalisation of Investor Status in Public International Law', *Transnational Organisations,* 14, 2: 121–59.

Gal-Or, N. (2006a) 'Outsourcing of Justice: A New International Orthodoxy?' in K. van der Pijl and K.G. Giesen (eds) *Global Norms in the Twenty-First Century,* Cambridge: Cambridge Scholars Press.

Gal-Or, N. (2006b) 'The Concept of Appeal in International Dispute Resolution', paper presented at European Society of International Law Second Biennial Conference, Paris, May 2006.

Ganghof, S. (2005) 'Konditionale Konvergenz. Ideen, Institutionen und Standortwettbewerb in der Steuerpolitik von EU- und OECD-Ländern', *Zeitschrift für Internationale Beziehungen,* 12, 1: 7–40.

Garriga, E. and Melée, D. (2004), 'Corporate Social Responsibility Theories: Mapping the Territory', *Journal of Business Ethics,* 53: 51–71.

Gereffi, G. (1994) 'The Organization of Buyer-Driven Global Commodity Chains: How US Retailers Shape Overseas Production', in G. Gereffi and M. Korzeniewicz (eds) *Commodity Chains and Global Capitalism,* Westport, CT: Praeger Publishers.

Germain, R. (2004), 'Globalising Accountability within the International Organisation of Credit: Financial Governance and the Public Sphere', *Global Society,* 18, 3: 217–42.

Germain, R.D. (ed.) (1999) *Globalization and its Critics: Perspectives from Political Economy,* London: Macmillan.

Gill, S. (1990) *American Hegemony and the Trilateral Commission,* Cambridge: Cambridge University Press.

Gill, S. (1993a) 'Epistemology, Ontology and the 'Italian School'', in S. Gill (ed.) *Gramsci, Historical Materialism and International Relations,* Cambridge: Cambridge University Press.

Gill, S, (ed.) (1993b) *Gramsci, Historical Materialism and International Relations,* Cambridge: Cambridge University Press.

Gill, S. (1994) 'Structural Change and Global Political Economy: Globalizing Élites and the Emerging World Order', in Y. Sakamoto (ed.) *Global Transformation,* Tokyo: United Nations University Press.

Gill, S. (ed.) (1997) *Globalisation Democratization and Multilateralism. Multilateralism and the UN System,* London: Macmillan.

Gill, S. (1998) 'New constitutionalism, democratisation and global political economy', *Pacific Review,* 10, 1: 23–38.

Gill, S. and Law, D. (1993) *The Global Political Economy. Perspectives, Problems and Policies,* 4th ed., Baltimore: The Johns Hopkins University Press.

Gillingham, J. (2006) *Design for a New Europe,* Cambridge: Cambridge University Press.

Golub, P. (2004) 'Imperial Politics, Imperial Will and the Crisis of US Hegemony', *Review of International Economy,* 14, 4: 763–86.

Goodhart, C., Hartmann, P., Llewellyn, D., Rojas-Suarez, L. and Weisbrod, S. (1998) *Financial Regulation: Why, How and Where Now?* London: Routledge.

Gordon, K.M. (2000) 'Rules for the Global Economy: Synergies Between Voluntary and Binding Approaches', Working Papers on International Investment 1999/3, Paris: OECD.

Gordon, K.M. and Miyake, M. (2000) 'Deciphering Codes of Corporate Conduct: A Review of their Contents', Working Papers on International Investment 1999/2, Paris: OECD.

Graz, J.C. (2003) 'How Powerful are Transnational Elite Clubs? The Social Myth of the World Economic Forum', *New Political Economy,* 8, 3: 321–40.

Graz, J.C. (2005) 'International Standardisation and Corporate Democracy', in K.G. Giesen and K. van der Pijl (eds) *Global Norms for the 21st Century,* London: Palgrave.

Graz, J.C. (2006a) 'Theorizing Hybrids in the Global Political Economy', *Competition and Change,* 10, 2: 230–45.

Graz, J.C. (2006b) 'International Standardisation and Corporate Democracy', in K.G. Giesen and K. van der Pijl (eds) *Global Norms for the 21st Century,* Cambridge: Cambridge Scholars Press.

Graz, J.C. and Palan, R. (2004) 'La régulation globale du capitalisme – n° spécial', *A Contrario* 2:2.

Greenwood, J. and Ronit, K. (1991) 'Pharmaceutical Regulation in Denmark and the UK: Reformulating Interest Representation to the Transnational Level', *European Journal of Political Research,* 19, 2–3: 327–59.

Greenwood, R., Suddaby, R. and Hinings, C.R. (2002) 'Theorizing change: the role of professional associations in the transformation of institutionalized fields', *Academy of Management Journal,* 45, 1: 58–80.

Group of Thirty (1997) *Global Institutions, National Supervision and Systemic Risk,* Washington, DC: Group of Thirty.

Gunningham, N. (1995) 'Environment, Self-regulation, and the Chemical Industry: Assessing Responsible Care', *Law & Policy,* 17, 1: 67–108.

Gunningham, N. and Rees, J. (1997) 'Industry Self-Regulation: An Institutional Perspective', *Law & Policy*, 19, 4: 363–412.

Haas, P.M. (1992) 'Introduction: Epistemic Communities and International Policy Coordination', *International Organization*, 46, 1: 1–37.

Hajer, M. (1997) *The Politics of Environmental Discourse. Ecological Modernization and the Policy Process*, Oxford: Clarendon Press.

Hall, P.A. and Soskice, D.W. (2001) *Varieties of Capitalism*, Oxford: Oxford University Press.

Hall, R.B. and Biersteker, T.J. (eds) (2002) *The Emergence of Private Authority in Global Governance*, Cambridge: Cambridge University Press.

Haller, A. (1993) 'Die Rolle des International Accounting Standards Committee bei der weltweiten Harmonisierung der externen Rechnungslegung', *Der Betrieb*, 46, 26/27: 1297–305.

Halliday, F. (2001) 'The Romance of Non-state Actors', in D. Josselin and W. Wallace (eds) *Non-State Actors in World Politics*, London: Palgrave.

Hansen, H.K., Salskov-Iversen, D. and Bislev, S. (2000) 'Governmentality, Globalization and Local Practice: Transformations of a Hegemonic Discourse', *Alternatives*, 25: 183–220.

Hart, J.A. and Sangbae, K. (2002) 'Explaining the Resurgence of U.S. Competitiveness: The Rise of Wintelism', *The Information Society* 18, 1: 1–12.

Hartog, J. den (2003) 'Feed for Food: HACCP in the Animal Feed Industry', in *Food Control*, 14: 95–9.

Haufler, V. (1993) 'Crossing the Boundary Between Public and Private: International Regimes and Non-State Actors', in V. Rittberger (ed.) *Regime Theory and International Relations*, Oxford: Clarendon Press.

Haufler, V. (1997) *Dangerous Commerce: Insurance and the Management of International Risk*, Cornell University Press: Ithaca.

Haufler, V. (1999) 'Self-Regulation and Business Norms: Political Risk, Political Activism', in A.C. Cutler, V. Haufler, T. Porter (eds) *Private Authority and International Affairs*, New York: SUNY Press.

Haufler, V. (2001) *A Public Role for the Private Sector: Industry Self-Regulation in a Global Economy*, Washington, DC: Carnegie Endowment for International Peace.

Haufler, V. (2002) 'Public and Private Authority in International Governance: Historical Continuity and Change', paper prepared for the Conference on New Technologies and International Governance, Washington, DC.

Havinga, Tetty (2003) 'Private regulering voedselveiligheid. De supermarkt als regelgever en handhaver', *Recht der werkelijkheid*.

Hawkins, R. (1995) 'Introduction: Addressing the Problematique of Standards and Standardisation', In Hawkins, R., Mansell, R., and Skepi, J. (eds) *Standards, Innovation and Competitiveness?: The Politics and Economics of Standards in Natural and Technical Environments*, Aldershot: Edward Elgar.

Held, D., McGrew, A.G., Goldblatt, D. and Perraton, D. (1999) *Global Transformation: Politics, Economics and Culture*, Cambridge: Polity Press.

Helleiner, E. (1994) *States and the Reemergence of Global Finance: From Bretton Woods to the 1990s*, Ithaca: Cornell University Press.

Héritier, A (2002a) 'New Modes of Governance in Europe: Policy-Making without Legislation?', in A. Héritier (ed.) *Common Goods*, Lanham, MD: Rowman & Littlefield.

Héritier, A. (ed.) (2002b) *Common Goods*, Lanham, MD: Rowman & Littlefield.

Hermet, G. (2005) 'La gouvernance serait-elle le nom de l'après démocratie?

L'inlassable quête du pluralisme limité', in G. Hermet, A. Kazancigil and J.F. Prud'homme (eds) *La gouvernance. Un concept et ses applications,* Paris: Karthala.
Hibou, B. (ed.) (1999) *La privatisation des Etats,* Paris: Karthala.
Higgott, R., Underhill, G. and Bieler, A. (eds) (1999) *Non-State Actors and Authority in the Global System,* London and New York: Routledge.
High-Level Group (2004) 'Facing the Challenge. The Lisbon Strategy for Growth and Employment', Report from the High-Level Group chaired by Wim Kok. Available online at: ec.europa.eu/growthandjobs/pdf/kok_report_en.pdf (accessed 27 September 2006).
Hirst, P. and Thompson, G. (1996) *Globalization in Question,* London: Polity Press.
Hix, S. (1998) 'The Study of the European Union II: The "New Governance" Agenda and its Rival', *Journal of European Public Policy,* 5,1: 38–65.
HM Treasury (2005) 'EU and US Agree Priorities for Future Cooperation on Financial Markets Regulation', HM Treasury Press Release, December 2.
Hollingsworth, J.R. and Boyer, R., (eds) (1997) *Contemporary Capitalism: The Embeddedness of Institutions,* Cambridge: Cambridge University Press.
Holman, O. (2004) 'Asymmetrical Regulation and Multidimensional Governance in the European Union', *Review of International Political Economy,* 11, 4: 714–35.
Holman, O. (2006), 'Socialising Structural Policy', paper presented at the 4th Convention of the Central and East European International Studies Association, Tartu, June 2006.
Hopwood, A.G. (1994) 'Some Reflections on the Harmonization of Accounting in the EU', *European Accounting Review,* 3, 2: 241–53.
Hornbeck, J.F. (2003) 'A Free Trade Area of the Americas: Status of Negotiations and Major Policy Issues', CRS-4 Report for Congress, Washington, DC: Congressional Research Service.
Houle, F. (2003) 'Le rôle des juges de l'administration publique dans la réception du droit international conventionnel en droit interne Canadien', paper presented at the conference 'International Norms for the 21st Century: Political Science, Philosophy, Law. An International Symposium', Aix-en-Provence, September 2003.
Hummel, H. (2001) 'Die Privatisierung der Weltpolitik. Tendenzen, Spielräume und Alternativen' in T. Brühl, T. Debiel, B. Hamm and H. Hummel (eds) *Die Privatisierung der Weltpolitik: Entstaatlichung und Kommerzialisierung im Globalisierungsprozess,* Bonn: Dietz.
Humphrey, J. and Schmitz, H. (2001) 'Governance in Global Value Chains', *IDS Bulletin,* 32, 3: 19–29.
Humphreys, P. and Simpson, S. (2005) *Globalisation, Convergence and European Telecommunications,* Cheltenham: Edward Elgar.
Hurd, I. (1999) 'Legitimacy and Authority in International Politics', *International Organization,* 53, 2: 379–408.
Hymer, S. (1975) 'The Multinational Corporation and the Law of Uneven Development', in H. Radice (ed.) *International Firms and Modern Imperialism,* Harmondsworth: Penguin.
IASC (1998) 'Shaping IASC for the Future', discussion paper issued for comment by the Strategy Working Party of the International Accounting Standards Committee, London: International Accounting Standards Committee.
IASCF (2002a) *Annual Report 2001,* London: International Accounting Standards Committee Foundation.
IASCF (2002b) *IASC Constitution* (revised), London: International Accounting Standards Committee.
IASCF (2006) *Annual Report 2005,* London: International Accounting Standards Committee Foundation.

Ibáñez, J. (2004) 'Sociedad postinternacional', in C. García and E. Vilariño (eds) *Comunidad internacional y sociedad internacional,* Bilbao: UPV/UCM/UPF.

Ibáñez, J. (2005) *El control de Internet. Poder y autoridad en los mercados electrónicos,* Madrid: Los Libros de la Catarata.

Inglehart, R. (1977) *The Silent Revolution,* Princeton: Princeton University Press.

Institute of International Finance (1997) *Report of the Task Force on Conglomerate Supervision,* Washington, DC: Institute of International Finance.

International Labour Organisation (2000) *Labour Practices in the Footwear, Leather, Textile and Clothing Industries,* Geneva: International Labour Organisation.

IOSCO (2000) 'A Resolution on IASC Standards, passed by the Presidents' Committee', *May 2000,* International Organisation of Securities Commission. Available online at: www.iosco.org/library/resolutions/pdf/ IOSCORES19.pdf (accessed 8.8.2006).

Jenkins, R. (2002) 'The Political Economy of Codes of Conduct', in R. Jenkins, R. Pearson and G. Seyfang (eds) *Corporate Responsibility & Labour Rights; Codes of Conduct in the Global Economy,* London: Earthscan Publications.

Jessop, B. (2003) 'Governance and Metagovernance: On Reflexivity, Requisite Variety and Requisite Irony', online paper published by the Department of Sociology, Lancaster University.

Joerges, C., Inger-Johanne S. and Teubner, G. (eds) (2004) *Transnational Governance and Constitutionalism,* Oxford: Hart Publishing.

Johnson, A. (2005) *European Welfare States and Supranatinoal Governance of Social Policy,* Houndmills: Palgrave.

Jordana, J. and Levi-Faur, D. (eds) (2004) 'Introduction', in J. Jordana and D. Levi-Faur (eds) *The Politics of Regulation. Institutions and Regulatory Reforms for the Age of Governance,* Cheltenham: Edward Elgar Publishing.

Jordana, J. and Levi-Faur, D. (eds) (2005) *The Politics of Regulation,* Cheltenham: E. Elgar.

Kagan, R.A. (2001) *Adversarial Legalism. The American Way of Law,* Cambridge, MA: Harvard University Press.

Kahn-Freund, O. (1972) 'Labour Relations and International Standards. Some Reflections on the European Social Charter', in W.J. Miscellanea (ed.) *Ganshof Van der Meersch,* vol. 1, Brussels: Bruylant.

Kaplinsky, R. (2000) 'Spreading the Gains from Globalisation: What can be Learned from Value Chain Analysis?' *IDS Working Paper 110,* Brighton: Institute of Development Studies.

Kapstein, E. (1991) 'Supervising International Banks: Origins and Implications of the Basle Accord', Princeton Studies in International Economics 185, Princeton: Princeton University.

Kapstein, E. (1999) 'Distributive Justice as an International Public Good', in I. Kaul, I. Grunberg and M.A. Stern (eds) *Global Public Goods,* Oxford: Oxford University Press.

Kassim, H. and Menon, A. (2005) 'The Principal Agent Approach and the Study of the European Union – Promise Unfulfilled?' in E. Jones and A. Verdun (eds) *The Political Economy of European Integration – Theory and Analysis,* London: Routledge.

Kearney, N. (1999) 'Corporate Codes of Conduct: the Privatized Application of Labour Standards' in S. Picciotto and R. Mayne (eds) *Regulating International Business. Beyond Liberalization,* London: Macmillan.

Kelly, J. (1996) 'An Independent Line', *Financial Times,* November 28.

Keohane, R.O., Moravcsik, A., Slaughter, A.M. and Snidal D. (2000) 'The Concept of Legalization', *International Organisation,* 54, 3: 401–19.

Keohane, R.O. and Nye, J. (1974) 'Transgovernmental Relations and International Organizations', *World Politics*, 27, 1: 39–62.

Kerkow, U., Martens, J. and Schmitt, T. (2003) *Die Grenzen der Freiwilligkeit. Handlungsmöglichkeiten und Erfahrungen von NGOs und Gewerkschaften bei der Anwendung freiwilliger Selbstverpflichtungen der Wirtschaft*, Berlin: Weed.

Kern, K. (2004) 'Globale Governance durch transnationale Netzwerkorganisationen. Möglichkeiten und Grenzen zivilgesellschaftlicher Selbstorganisation', in D. Gosewinkel *et al.* (eds) *Zivilgesellschaft – National und Transnational*, Berlin: Edition Sigma.

Kersbergen, K. van and Waarden, F. van (2001) 'Shifts in Governance: Problems of Legitimacy and Accountability. Background Study on the Theme "Shifts in Governance" as Part of the Strategic Plan 2002–2005 of the Netherlands Organization for Scientific Research (NWO)', The Hague: NWO-MAGW Social Science Research Council.

Kersbergen, K. van and Waarden, F. van (2004) ' "Governance" as a Bridge between Disciplines. Cross-Disciplinary Inspiration regarding Shifts in Governance and Problems of Governability, Accountability, and Legitimacy', *European Journal of Political Research*, 43: 143–71.

King, A.A. and Lenox, M.J. (2000) 'Industry Self-Regulation without Sanctions: The Chemical Industry's Responsible Care Program', *Academy of Management Journal*, 43, 4: 698–716.

King, M.R. and Sinclair, T.J. (2003) 'Private Actors and Public Policy: A Requiem for the New Basel Capital Accord', *International Political Science Review* 24, 3: 345–62.

Kleekämper, H. (1995) 'Aktuelle Entwicklungen beim IASC', *Betriebswirtschaftliche Forschung und Praxis (BFuP)*, 4: 414–31.

Klein, H. (2003) 'Understanding WSIS: An Institutional Analysis of the UN World Summit on the Information Society', *Information Technologies and International Development*, 1, 3–4: 3–13.

Klein, N. (2000) *No Logo: Taking Aim at the Brand Bullies*, Toronto: Knopf.

Kleinman, Mark (2002) *A European Welfare State?* Houndmills: Palgrave.

Kollman, K. (2003) 'Marketing Good Behavior: The Role of Transnational Business Networks in Promoting Standards of Corporate Responsibility', paper presented at the ISA/IEESA conference, Budapest, June 2003.

Kooiman, J. (2002): 'Governance. A Social-Political Perspective', in J.R. Grote and B. Gbikpi (eds) *Participatory Governance: Political and Social Implications*, Opladen: Leske + Budrich.

Kooiman, J. (2003) *Governing as Governance*, London: SAGE.

Korten, D. (1995) *When Corporations Rule the World*, West Hartford: Kumarian Press.

KPMG (2005) *KPMG International Survey of Corporate Responsibility Reporting 2005*, Amsterdam: KPMG.

Krasner, S.D. (ed.) (1983) *International Regimes*, Ithaca/London: Cornell University Press.

Kratochwil, F. (1993) 'Contract and Regimes. Do Issue Specificity and Variations of Formality Matter?', in V. Rittberger (ed.) *Regime Theory and International Relations*, Oxford: Clarendon Press.

Ledgerwood, G. and Broadhurst, A.I. (2000) *Environment, Ethics, and the Corporation*, New York: St. Martin's Press.

Lessig, L. (1999) *Code and Other Laws of Cyberspace*, New York: Basic Books.

Lessig, L. (2001) *The Future of Ideas. The Fate of the Commons in a Connected World*, New York: Random House.

Levy, D., Egan, D. (2000) 'Corporate Political Action in the Global Polity', in R. Higgott, G. Underhill and A. Bieler (eds) *Non-State Actors and Authority in the Global System*, London: Routledge.
Levy, D., Newell, P. (2002) 'Business Strategy and International Environmental Governance: A Neo-Gramscian Synthesis', *Global Environmental Politics*, 2, 4: 84–101.
Lipschutz, R. and Rowe, J.K. (2005) *Globalization, Governmentality and Global Politics: Regulation for the Rest of Us?* London: Routledge.
Lisbon European Council (2000), Presidency Conclusions, 23 and 24 March 2000.
Lo Faro, A. (1999) *Funzioni e finzioni della contrattazione collettiva comunitaria*, Milano: Giuffrè Editore.
Low, N., Gleeson, B. (2000) 'Ecosocialisation and Environmental Justice', paper presented at Conference of the International Critical Geography Group, University of Taegu, August 2000.
Lowi, T.J. (1972) '4 Systems of Policy, Politics, and Choice', *Public Administration Review*, 32, 4: 298–310.
Lukes, S. (1974) *Power, A Radical View*, London: Macmillan.
Macdonald, K.M. (1995) *The Sociology of the Professions*, London: SAGE.
Macdonald, K.M. (2000) 'Social Closure and Occupational Registration', in J.R. Edwards (ed.) *The History of Accounting. Critical Perspectives on Business and Management. Professionalisation of Accounting*, vol. IV, London: Routledge.
MacLean, D. (ed.) (2004) *Internet Governance: A Grand Collaboration*, New York: UN ICT Task Force.
Majone, G. (ed.) (1996) *Regulating Europe*, London: Routledge.
Majone, G. (2000) 'The Credibility Crisis of Community Regulation', *Journal of Common Market Studies*, 38, 2: 273–302.
Majone, G. (2001) 'Two Logics of Delegation: Agency and Fiduciary Relations in EU Governance', *European Union Politics*, 2, 1: 103–21.
Majone, G. (2002) 'International Economic Integration, National Autonomy, Transnational Democracy: An Impossible Trinity?', EUI Working Papers RSC no. 2002/48.
Mann, H. (2005) 'The Emperor's Clothes Come Off: A Comment on Republic of Ghana v. Telekom Malaysia Berhard, and the Problem of Arbitrator Conflict of Interest', *Transnational Dispute Management*, 2, 1.
Mann, H., Cosbey A., Peterson, L. and Moltke, K. von (2004) 'Comments on ICSID Discussion Paper "Possible Improvements of the Framework for ICSID Arbitration" ', Winnipeg: International Institute for Sustainable Development. Available online at: www.iisd.org/pdf/2004/investment_icsid_response.pdf (accessed 27 September 2006).
Mansbridge, J.J. (1992) 'A Deliberative Theory of Interest Representation', in M.P. Petracca (ed.) *The Politics of Interest. Interest Groups Transformed*, Boulder: Westview Press.
Mansbridge, J.J. (1995) 'A Deliberative Perspective on Neocorporatism', in J. Cohen and J. Rogers (eds) *Associations and Democracy. The Real Utopias Project*, London: Verso.
Marginson, P. (2000) 'The Eurocompany and Euro Industrial Relations', *European Journal of Industrial Relations*, 6, 1: 9–34.
Martinez-Diaz, L. (2005) 'Strategic experts and improvising regulators: explaining the IASC's rise to global influence, 1973–2001', *Business and Politics*, 7, 3: Art. 3.
Marx, K. (1939) *Grundrisse der Kritik der Politischen Ökonomie (Rohentwurf)*; trans. M. Nicolaus (1973) *Foundations of the Critique of the Political Economy (Rough Draft)*, Harmondsworth: Penguin.

Mathiason, J., Mueller, M., Klein, H., Holitscher, M. and McKnight, L. (2004) 'Internet Governance: the State of Play', online paper, New York: Internet Governance Project.
Mattli, W. (2003) 'Public and Private Governance in Setting International Standards', in M. Kahler and D. Lake (eds) *Governance in a Global Economy: Political Authority in Transition,* Princeton: Princeton University Press, pp. 199–225.
McDonough, W. (2002) 'The Review of the Capital Accord', *BIS Review,* 75.
McKinsey&Company (2004) *Assessing the Global Compact's Impact*, New York: Global Compact Office. Available online at: www.unglobalcompact.org/NewsAndEvents/news_archives/2004_06_09.html (accessed 2 August 2006).
McRae, D. (2004) 'What is the Future of WTO Dispute Settlement?' *Journal of International Economic Law,* 7, 1: 27–41.
Mello, B.D. (2003) 'Reebok and the Global Footwear Sweatshop', *Monthly Review,* 54, 9: 26–40.
Mengin, F. (2004) *Cyber-China: Reshaping National Identities in the Age of Information*, London: Palgrave.
Merritt, G. (1986), 'Knights of the Roundtable: Can They Move Europe Forward Fast Enough?', *International Management,* 26, July: 22–6.
Mestral, A. de and Winter, J. (2005) 'Giving Direct Effect to NAFTA', in T.J. Courchene, D. Savoie and D. Schwanen (eds) *The Art of the State Volume II: Thinking North America,* Montréal: Institute for Research on Public Policy.
Meyer, Laurence (2000) 'The Challenges of Global Financial Institutions Supervision', *BIS Review,* 68.
Milgrom, P.R., North, D.C. and Weingast, B.R. (1990) 'The Role of Institutions in the Revival of Trade: The Law Merchant, Private Judges and the Champagne Fairs', *Economics and Politics,* 2, 1: 1–23.
Miller, D. (2003) 'Preparing for the Long Haul: Negotiating International Framework Agreements in the Global Textile, Garment and Footwear Sector', *Global Social Policy,* 4, 2: 215–39.
Miller, P., Rose, N. (1992) 'Political Power Beyond the State: Problematics of Government', *The British Journal of Sociology,* 43, 2: 173–205.
Mistelis, L. (2001) 'Is Harmonisation a Necessary Evil? The Future of Harmonisation and New Sources of International Trade Law', in I. Fletcher, L. Mistelis and M. Cremona (eds) *Foundations and Perspectives of International Trade Law,* London: Sweet and Maxwell.
Mittelman, J. (ed.) (1996) *Globalization. Critical Reflections,* Boulder: Lynne Rienner.
Moffet, J., Bregha, F. and Middelkoop, M.J. (2004) 'Responsible Care: A Case Study of a Voluntary Environmental Initiative', in K. Webb (ed.) *Voluntary Codes: Private Governance, the Public Interest and Innovation,* Ottawa: Carleton University.
Moran, M. (1991) *The Politics of the Financial Revolution: The USA, UK and Japan,* London: Macmillan.
Moran, M. (2002) 'Understanding the Regulatory State', *British Journal of Political Science,* 32, 391–413.
Morgenthau, H. (1948) *Politics Among Nations: The Struggle for Power and Peace,* New York: Knopf.
Mueller, G.G. (1979) 'St. Louis to Munich: The Odyssey of the International Congresses of Accountants', *The International Journal of Accounting,* 1–12.
Mueller, M.L. (2002) *Ruling the Root. Internet Governance and the Taming of Cyberspace,* Cambridge, MA: MIT Press.

Multidisciplinary Working Group on Enhanced Disclosure (2001) *Final Report*, Basel: Bank for International Settlements.

Murphy, C. (1994) *International Organization and Industrial Change*, Oxford/New York: Oxford University Press.

Murphy, C. (2000) 'Global Governance: Poorly Done and Poorly Understood', *International Affairs*, 76, 4: 789–803.

Murphy, C. (2002) 'Why Pay Attention to Global Governance?' in Wilkinson, R. and Hugues, S. (eds) *Global Governance. Critical Perspectives*, London: Routledge.

Nadvi, K. and Wältring, F. (2002) 'Making Sense of Global Standards', INEF Report no. 58, Duisburg: Institute for Development and Peace.

Newman, A. and Bach, D. (2001) 'In the Shadow of the State: Self-Regulatory Trajectories in a Digital Age', paper prepared for the 2001 Annual Convention of the American Political Science Association, San Francisco, August/September 2001.

Nobes, C. (1985) 'Harmonisation of Financial Reporting', in C. Nobes and R. Parker (eds) *Comparative International Accounting*, New York: St. Martin's Press.

Nobes, C. and Parker, R. (eds) (2004) *Comparative International Accounting*, Essex: Pearson Education.

Nölke, A. (1995) *Geberkoordination für die Länder Afrikas südlich der Sahara*, Baden Baden: Nomos.

Nölke, A. (2000) 'Regieren in transnationalen Politiknetzwerken? Kritik postnationaler Governance-Konzepte aus der Perspektive einer transnationalen (Inter)Organisationssoziologie', *Zeitschrift für Internationale Beziehungen*, 7, 2: 331–58.

Nölke, A., Overbeek, H. and Apeldoorn, B. van (2003) 'The Transnational Political Economy of Corporate Governance Regulation: A Research Outline', Working Papers Political Science no. 05/2003, Amsterdam: Free University of Amsterdam.

Nölke, Andreas (2003a) 'Transnationale Politiknetzwerke. Eine Analyse grenzüberschreitender politischer Entscheidungsprozesse jenseits des regierungszentrischen Modells', unpublished manuscript (Habilitationsschrift).

Nölke, Andreas (2003b) 'Private International Norms in Global Economic Governance: Coordination Service Firms and Corporate Governance', Working Papers Political Science No. 06/2003, Amsterdam: Free University of Amsterdam.

Nowrot, K. (2005) 'The New Governance Structure of the Global Compact. Transforming a "Learning Network" into a Federalized and Parliamentarized Transnational Regulatory Regime', Essays in Transnational Economic Law 47/2005, Halle: Institute for Economic Law.

Nugent, N. (2006) *The Government and Politics of the European Union*, Houndmills: Palgrave.

Nye, J.S. and Owens, W. (1996) 'America's Information Edge', *Foreign Affairs*, 75, 2: 20–36.

Ohmae, K. (1990) *The Borderless World*, London: Collins.

Olson, M. (1965) *The Logic of Collective Action. Public Goods and the Theory of Groups*, Cambridge: Harvard University Press.

Olson, M. (1995) 'The Varieties of Eurosclerosis: The Rise and Decline of Nations since 1982', EUI Working Papers Jean Monnet Chair Papers 32.

Ong, E. and Glantz, S. (2000) 'Tobacco Industry Efforts Subverting International Agency for Research on Cancer's Second-hand Smoke Study', *The Lancet*, 355: 1253–59.

O'Rourke, D. (2002) 'Monitoring the Monitors: A Critique of Corporate Third-Party Labor Monitoring', in R. Jenkins, R. Pearson and G. Seyfang (eds) *Corporate Responsibility & Labour Rights: Codes of Conduct in the Global Economy*, London: Earthscan Publications.

O'Rourke, D. (2003) 'Outsourcing Regulation: Analysing Non-Governmental Systems of Labor Standards and Monitoring', *Policy Studies Journal,* 31, 1, 417–37.

O'Rourke, D. (2004) 'Community Monitoring and Corporate Accountability' in. J. Ruggie, C. Kolb, D. O'Rourke and A. Kuper (eds) *The Impact of Corporations on Global Governance,* New York: Carnegie Council on Ethics and International Affairs.

Ottaway, M. (2001) 'Corporatism Goes Global: International Organizations, Nongovernmental Organization Networks, and Transnational Business', *Global Governance,* 7, 3: 265–92.

Overbeek, Henk (2004) 'Global Governance, Class, Hegemony: A Historical Materialist Perspective', Working Papers Political Science No. 01/2004, Amsterdam: Free University of Amsterdam.

Panzieri, R. (1976) 'Surplus Value and Planning: Notes on the Reading of Capital', in Conference of Socialist Economists (ed.) *The Labour Process and Class Struggle,* London: Stage 1.

Parker, A. (2003) 'EU Urged to Set Up an Audit Watchdog', *Financial Times,* September 13.

Pattberg, P.H. (2004) 'Private Environmental Governance and the Changing Nature of Authority', paper prepared for the International Studies Association Annual Meeting, Montréal.

Pauly, L. (1997) *Who Elected the Bankers?* Ithaca: Cornell University Press.

Pauly, L. (2002) 'Global Finance, Political Authority, and the Problem of Legitimation', in R.B. Hall and T. Biersteker (eds) *The Emergence of Private Authority in Global Governance,* Cambridge: Cambridge University Press.

Peltzman, S. (1989) 'The Economic Theory of Regulation after a Decade of Deregulation', *Brooking Papers on Microeconomics,* 1–59.

Perry, J. and Noelke, A. (2005) 'International Accounting Standard Setting: A Network Approach', *Business and Politics,* 7, 3: 1–32.

Petit, P. (1999) 'Structural Forms and Growth Regimes of the Post-Fordist Era', *Review of Social Economy,* 57, 2: 220–43.

Picciotto, S. (2000) 'Liberalization and Democratization: The Forum and the Hearth in the Era of Cosmopolitan Post-Industrial Capitalism', *Law and Contemporary Problems,* 63, 4: 157–78.

Picciotto, S. and Haines, J. (1999) 'Regulating Global Financial Markets', *Journal of Law and Society,* 26, 3: 351–68.

Pierre, J. and Peters, B.G. (eds) (2000) *Governance, Politics and the State,* Basingstoke: Macmillan.

Pijl, K. van der (1993) 'The Sovereignty of Capital Impaired: Social Forces and Codes of Conduct for Multinational Corporations', in H. Overbeek (ed.) *Restructuring Hegemony in the Global Political Economy: The Rise of Transnational Neo-Liberalism in the 1980s,* Routledge: London and New York.

Pijl, K. van der (1998) *Transnational Classes and International Relations,* London: Routledge.

Pijl, K. van der (2004) 'Two faces of the transnational cadre under neo-liberalism?', *Journal of International Relations and Development,* 7, 2: 177–207.

Pochet, P. (2005) 'The Emergence and Evolution of the Sectoral and Interprofessional Social Dialogue? A Quantitative Analysis', NEWGOV Project. Available online at: www.eu-newgov.org/database/DELIV/D01D29_Policy_Memo_Emergence_European_social_dialogue.pdf (accessed 29 September 2006).

Polanyi, K. (1944) *The Great Transformation,* Boston: Beacon Press.

Pollack, M.A. (1997) 'Delegation, Agency and Agenda Setting in the European Community', *International Organization,* 51, 1: 99–134.

Pollack, M.A. and G.C. Shaffer (2001) 'Transatlantic Governance in Historical and Theoretical Perspective', in M.A. Pollack and G.C. Shaffer (eds) *Transatlantic Governance in the Global Economy,* Lanham: Rowman & Littlefield.

Pollitt, C. and Bouckaert, G. (2000) *Public Management Reform,* Oxford: Oxford University Press.

Porter, T. (1999) 'Hegemony and the Private Governance of International Industries', in A.C. Cutler, V. Haufler and T. Porter (eds) *Private Authority and International Affairs,* New York: SUNY Press.

Porter, T. (2001) 'The Democratic Deficit in the Institutional Arrangements for Regulating Global Finance', *Global Governance,* 7, 4: 427–39.

Porter, T. (2005) 'Private Authority, Technical Authority, and the Globalization of Accounting Standards', *Business and Politics,* 7, 3: Art. 2.

Portnoy, B. (1999) 'Alliance Capitalism as Industrial Order: Exploring New Forms of Interfirm Competition in the Globalising Economy', in R.A. Higgott, G.R.D. Underhill and A. Bieler (eds) *Non-State Actors and Authority in the Global System,* London and New York: Routledge.

Prakash, A. (2000) 'Responsible Care: An Assessment', *Business and Society,* 39, 2: 183–209.

Prakash, A. (2002) 'Beyond Seattle: Globalization, the Nonmarket Environment and Corporate Strategy', *Review of International Political Economy,* 9, 3: 513–37.

Prakash, A. and Hart, J.A. (1999) 'Globalisation and Governance: An Introduction', in A. Prakash and J.A. Hart (eds) *Globalisation and Governance,* London: Routledge.

Price, M.E. and Verhulst, S.G. (2000) 'In Search of the Self. Charting the Course of Self-Regulation on the Internet in a Global Environment', in C.T. Marsden (ed.) *Regulating the Global Information Society,* London: Routledge.

Princen, S. (2002) *The California Effect in the External Trade Relations of the European Union,* Deventer: Kluwer.

Quintin, O. (1998) 'Bilan et perspectives du dialogue social en Europe', *Petites Affiches,* 79, 3.

Radice, H. (1975) *International Firms and Modern Imperialism,* Harmondsworth: Penguin.

Raikes. P., Jensen, M.F. and Ponte, S. (2000) 'Global Commodity Chain Analysis and the French filière Approach: Comparison and Critique', CDR Working Paper 00.3, Brighton: Centre for Development Research.

Ramirez, C. (2001) 'Understanding Social Closure in its Cultural Context: Accounting Practitioners in France (1920–1939)', *Accounting, Organizations and Society,* 26, 4/5: 391–418.

Reed, M.I. (1996) 'Expert Power and Control in Late Modernity: An Empirical Review and Theoretical Synthesis', *Organization Science,* 17, 4: 573–98.

Reich, R.B. (1991) *The Work of Nations,* New York: Knopf.

Reinicke, W. (1997) 'Global Public Policy', *Foreign Affairs,* 76, 6: 127–38.

Reinicke, W. (1998) *Global Public Policy. Governing without Governments?* Washington: Brookings Institution.

Rhodes, M. and Apeldoorn, B. van (1998) 'Capital Unbound? The Transformation of European Corporate Governance', *Journal of European Public Policy,* 5, 3: 406–27.

Rhodes, R.A.W. (1996) 'The New Governance: Governing without Government', *Political Studies,* 44, 4: 652–67.

Rhodes, R.A.W. (1997) *Understanding Governance,* Buckingham: Open University Press.

Richardson, K. (1997) 'Het Primaat van Concurrentievermogen: het Europese Bedrijfsleven en de Intergouvernementele Conferentie van 1996', in O. Holman (ed.) *Europese Dilemma's aan het Einde van de Twintigste Eeuw. Democratie, Werkgelegenheid, Veiligheid, Immigratie,* Amsterdam: Het Spinhuis.

Rieth, L. (2004) 'Corporate Social Responsibility in Global Economic Governance: A Comparison of the OECD Guidelines and the UN Global Compact', in: S.A. Schirm (ed.) *New Rules for Global Markets: Public and Private Governance in the World Economy,* Houndmills: Palgrave Macmillan.

Risse, T. (2006) 'Transnational Governance and Legitimacy', in A. Benz and Y. Papadopoulos (eds) *Governance and Democracy. Comparing National European and International Experiences,* London: Routledge.

Risse-Kappen, T. (ed.) (1995) *Bringing Transnational Relations Back In,* Cambridge: Cambridge University Press.

Ronit, K. (2001) 'Institutions of Private Authority in Global Governance: Linking Territorial Forms of Self-Regulation', *Administration & Society,* 33, 5: 555–78.

Ronit, K. (2005) *Selvregulering og de private ankenævn i dansk forbrugerpolitik,* Copenhagen: Multivers.

Ronit, K. and Schneider, V. (eds) (2000) *Private Organizations in Global Politics,* London, New York: Routledge.

Rosenau, J.N. and Czempiel, E.O. (eds) (1992) *Governance Without Government: Order and Change in World Politics,* Cambridge: Cambridge University Press.

Rosenzweig, R. (1998) 'Wizards, Bureaucrats, Warriors, and Hackers: Writing the History of the Internet', *American History Review,* 103: 1530–52.

Ross, G. (1995) 'Assessing the Delors Era and Social Policy', in S. Leibfried and P. Pierson (eds) *European Social Policy: Between Fragmentation and Integration,* Washington, DC: Brookings Institution.

Ryan, Bernard (2003) 'The Charter and Collective Labour Law', in T. Hervey and J. Kenner (eds) *Economic and Social Rights under the EU Charter of Fundamental Rights,* Oxford: Hart.

Sala, V. della (2004), 'Maastricht to Modernization: EMU and the Italian Social State', in A. Martin and G. Ross (eds) *Euros and Europeans. Monetary integration and the European Model of Society,* Cambridge: Cambridge University Press.

Salter, L. (1999) *The Standards Regime for Communication and Information Technologies' Private Authority and International Affairs,* Albany: SUNY Press.

Samuels, J.M. and Piper, A.G. (1985) *International Accounting: A Survey,* London: Croom Helm.

Sassen, S. (1999) 'Digital Networks and Power', in M. Featherstone and S. Lash (eds) *Spaces of Culture. City, Nation, World,* London: SAGE.

Sassen, S. (2003) 'Globalization or Denationalization?' *Review of International Political Economy,* 10,1: 1–22.

Sassen, S. (2006) *Territory, Authority, Rights,* Princeton: Princeton University Press.

Savoie, D. (1994) *Thatcher, Reagan, Mulroney: In Search of a New Bureaucracy,* Pittsburgh: University of Pittsburgh Press.

Schaper, M. (2005) 'Applying Financial Leverage to Green Infrastructure Development: Environmental Policies of World Bank, Export Credit Agencies, and Private Banks', paper presented at the Conference on Business Power in Global Governance, Wittenberg, December 2005.

Scharpf, F. (1998) 'Demokratie in der transnationalen Politik', in U. Beck (ed.) *Politik der Globalisierung,* Frankfurt a.M.: Suhrkamp.

Schiek, D. (2005) 'Autonomous Collective Agreements as a Regulatory Device in European Labour Law: How to Read Article 139 EC', *Industrial Law Journal,* 34, 1: 23–56.

Schimmelfennig, F. (2003) 'Internationale Sozialisation: Von einem "erschöpften" zu einem produktiven Forschungsprogramm?', in G. Hellmann, K.D. Wolf and M. Zürn (eds) *Die neuen Internationalen Beziehungen. Forschungsstand und Perspektiven in Deutschland,* Baden-Baden: Nomos.

Schmidt, S.K. and Werle, R. (1998) *Coordinating Technology: Studies in the International Standardization of Telecommunications,* Cambridge, MA: MIT Press.

Schmitter, P.C. (1979) 'Still the Century of Corporatism?', in P.C. Schmitter and G. Lehmbruch (eds) *Trends Toward Corporatist Intermediation,* London: SAGE.

Schmitter, P.C. (1983) 'Democratic Theory and Neo-Corporatist Practice', EUI Working Paper No. 74.

Schmitter, P.C. (1993) 'Corporatism as Organizational Practice and Political Theory', in W.M. Lafferty and E. Rosenstein (eds), *International Handbook of Participation in Organizations,* vol. 3, Oxford: Oxford University Press.

Schmitter, P.C. (2000) 'Designing a democracy for the Euro-Polity and revising democratic theory in the process', in I. Shapiro and S. Macedo (eds) *Designing Democratic Institutions,* New York: New York University Press.

Scott, J. (ed.) (1990) *The Sociology of Elites,* three vols, Aldershot: E.Elgar.

Seidman, H. and Gilmour, R. (1986) *Politics, Position, and Power: From the Positive to the Regulatory State,* 4th edn, New York: Oxford University Press.

Sell, S. (2003) *Private Power, Public Law,* Cambridge: Cambridge University Press.

Sennett, R.B. (1978) *The Fall of Public Man,* New York: Vintage.

Shany, Y. (2003) *The Competing Jurisdictions of International Courts and Tribunals,* Oxford: Oxford University Press.

Sinclair, T. (1999) 'Bond-Rating Agencies and Coordination in the Global Political Economy', in A.C. Cutler, V. Haufler and T. Porter (eds), *Private Authority and International Affairs,* New York: SUNY Press.

Sinclair, T.J (1994) 'Passing Judgement: Credit Rating Processes as Regulatory Mechanisms of Governance in the Emerging World Order', *Review of International Political Economy,* 1, 1: 133–59.

Sinclair, T.J. (2005) *The New Masters of Capital,* Ithaca: Cornell University Press.

Sinclair. T.J. (1999) 'Bond-Rating Agencies and Coordination in the Global Political Economy', in A.C. Cutler, V. Haufler and T. Porter (eds) *Private Authority and International Affairs,* New York: SUNY Press.

Siochrú, S.Ó and Girard, B. (2002) *Global Media Governance: A Beginner's Guide,* New York: Rowman and Littlefield.

Sklair, L. (2001) *The Transnational Capitalist Class,* Malden, MA: Blackwell Publishers.

Slaughter, A.M. (2004) *A New World Order,* Princeton: Princeton University Press.

Smismans, S. (2000) 'The European Economic and Social Committee: towards deliberative democracy via a functional assembly', European Integration Online Papers vol. 4 no. 12. Available online at: http://eiop.or.at/eiop/texte/2000-012a.htm (accessed 28 September 2006).

Smismans, S. (2004) *Law, Legitimacy and European Governance: Functional Participation in Social Regulation*, Oxford: Oxford University Press.

Smith, C.W. (2002) *Digital Corporate Citizenship: the Business Response to the Digital Divide,* Bloomington: Center on Philanthropy.

Smith, M. (2000) *American Business and Political Power: Public Opinion, Elections, and Democracy,* Chicago: University of Chicago Press.

Soederberg, S. (2003) 'The Promotion of "Anglo-American" Corporate Governance in the South: Who Benefits from the New International Standard', *Third World Quarterly,* 24, 1: 7–27.

SOMO (2003) 'Monitoring and Verification Terminology Guide for the Garments and Sportswear Industries'. Available online at: www.somo.nl/monitoring/reports/terminology.htm (accessed 11 March 2006).

Sosnow C. (2005) 'Softwood Lumber as Case Study: Canada–U.S. Dispute Resolution under NAFTA and the WTO', *Canadian International Lawyer,* 6, 3: 131–43.

Spar, D.L. (1999) 'Lost in (Cyber)space: The Private Rules of Online Commerce', in A.C. Cutler, V. Haufler and T. Porter (eds) *Private Authority and International Affairs,* New York: SUNY Press.

Stigler, G. (1971) 'The Theory of Economic Regulation', *Bell Journal of Economics,* 2: 113–21.

Stone, D. (2001) 'Learning Lessons, Policy Transfer and the International Diffusion of Ideas', ESRC Centre for the Study of Globalisation and Regionalisation Working Paper no. 69/01, Warwick: CSGR.

Strange, S. (1988) *States and Markets,* London: Pinter.

Strange, S. (1996) *The Retreat of the State: The Diffusion of Power in the World Economy,* Cambridge: Cambridge University Press.

Strange, S. (1998) *Mad Money: When Markets Outgrow Governments,* Ann Arbor: University of Michigan Press.

Streeck, W. (1996) 'Neo-Voluntarism: A New European Social Policy Regime', in G. Marks, F.W. Scharpf, P.C. Schmitter and W. Streeck (eds) *Governance in the European Union,* London: SAGE.

Streeck, W. (1997), 'Citizenship Under Regime Competition: The Case of the European Works Councils', European Integration Online Papers Vol. 1, no. 5. Available online at: http://papers.ssrn.com/sol3/papers.cfm?abstract_id=302665 (accessed 27 September 2006).

Streeck, W. and Schmitter, P.C. (1985) 'Community, Market, State – and Associations? The Prospective Contribution of Interest Governance to Social Order', in W. Streeck and P.C. Schmitter (eds) *Private Interest Government. Beyond Market and State,* London: SAGE.

Streeck, W. and Schmitter, P.C. (1985) 'Community, Market, State – and Associations?', *European Sociological Review,* 1: 119–38.

Streeck, W. and Schmitter, P.C. (1991) 'From National Corporatism to Transnational Pluralism: Organized Interests in the Single European Market', *Politics and Society,* 1: 133–64.

Sum, N.L. (2005) 'From "New Constitutionalism" to "New Ethicalism": Global Business Governance and the Discourses and Practices of Corporate Social Responsibility', paper prepared for the ECPR Joint Sessions Workshop Transnational Private Governance in the Global Political Economy, Granada, April 2005.

Sundgren, J. (1997) 'Self-Regulatory Initiatives in the Global Economy: Exploring the Concept of Private Regimes', paper prepared for the International Studies Association Annual Meeting, Toronto.

SustainAbility (2004) *Final Report for the Global Strategic Review of Responsible Care. External Stakeholder Survey*, Washington: SustainAbility.

Synnott, T. (2005) 'Some Notes on the Early Years of the FSC', unpublished manuscript. Available online at: www.fsc.org/keepout/en/content_areas/45/2/files/FSC_Founding-Notes.doc (accessed 2 August 2006).

Tamm Hallström, K. (2004) *Organizing International Standardization. ISO and the IASC in Quest of Authority*, Cheltenham: Edward Elgar.

Thatcher, M. (1999), *The Politics of Telecommunications: National Institutions, Convergence, and Change*, Oxford: Oxford University Press.

Thatcher, M. (2001), 'The Commission and National Governments as Partners: EC Regulatory Expansion in Telecommunications 1979–2000', *Journal of European Public Policy*, 8, 4: 558–84.

Thomas, R.D. (1970) 'The Accountants International Study Group – The First Three Years', *International Journal of Accounting*, Fall: 59–65.

Thomson Financial (2003) 'All About Equities', *European Capital Markets League Table*, Third Quarter 2004.

Tilly, C. (ed.) (1975) *The Formation of National States in Western Europe*, Princeton: Princeton University Press.

Tollefson, C. (2002) 'Metalclad v. United Mexican States revisited: Judicial oversight of NAFTA's Chapter Eleven investor-state claim process', *Minnesota Journal of Global Trade*, 11, 2: 183–231.

Treu, T. (1996) 'European Collective Bargaining Levels and the Competences of the Social Partners', in P. Davies, A. Lyon-Caen, S. Sciarra and S. Simitis (eds) *European Community Labour Law: Principles and Perspectives*, Oxford: Clarendon Press.

True, J., Jones, B. and Baumgartner, F. (1999) 'Punctuated Equilibrium Theory: Explaining Stability and Change in American Policy Making', in P. Sabatier (ed.) *Theories of the Policy Process*, Boulder: Westview Press.

Turner, L. (1998) 'The Europeanization of Labour: Structure Before Action', in E. Gabaglio and R. Hoffmann (eds) *The ETUC in the Mirror of Industrial Relations Research*, Brussels: European Trade Union Institute.

Unmüßig, B. (2005) 'Freiwilligkeit und ihre Grenzen. Zur gesellschaftspolitischen Verantwortung globaler Unternehmen', *Süddeutsche Zeitung*, July 28.

Urminsky, M. (2001) 'Self-regulation in the Workplace: Codes of Conduct, Social Labeling and Socially Responsible Investment', MCC Working Paper No. 1 Series on Management Systems and Corporate Citizenship, Geneva: International Labour Office.

Urry, M. (1985) 'New Advisory Body for Issuers Seeks to Add Order to the Market', *Financial Times*, February 19.

Utting, P. (2000) 'Promoting Socially Responsible Business in Developing Countries: The Potential and Limits of Voluntary Initiatives', Report of the UNRISD Workshop, Geneva, October 2000.

Versluis, E. (2003) 'Enforcement Matters. Exploring Enforcement and Compliance Practices in Four EU Member States', PhD thesis, Utrecht University.

Vogel, D. (1986) *National Styles of Regulation: Environmental Policy in Great Britain and the United States*, Ithaca: Cornell University Press.

Vogel, D. (1995) *Trading Up. Consumer and Environmental Regulation in a Global Economy*, Cambridge, MA: Harvard University Press.

Vogel, D. (2003) 'Risk Regulation in Europe and the United States', *Yearbook of European Environmental Law*, 3: 1–30.

Waarden, F. van (1999a) 'European Harmonization of National Regulatory Styles?', in

J.A.E. Vervaele (ed.) *Compliance and Enforcement of European Community Law*, Deventer: Kluwer Law.

Waarden, F. van (1999b) 'Elk land zijn eigen trant', in W. Bakker and F. van Waarden (eds) *Ruimte rond regels. Reguleringsstijlen vergeleken*, Amsterdam and Meppel: Boom.

Waarden, F. van (2002) 'Market Institutions as Communicating Vessels: Changes between Economic Coordination Principles as a Consequence of Deregulation Policies', in J.R. Hollingsworth, K.H. Mueller and E.J. Hollingsworth (eds) *Advancing Socio-Economics. An Institutionalist Perspective*, Lanham: Rowman and Littlefield.

Waarden, F. van (2006) 'Taste, Traditions and Transactions: The Public and Private Regulation of Food', in C. Ansell and D. Vogel (eds) *What's the Beef? The Contested Governance of European Food Safety*, Cambridge MA: MIT Press.

Waarden, F. van and Drahos, M. (2002) 'Courts and (Epistemic) Communities in the Convergence of Competition Policies', *Journal of European Public Policy*, 9, 6: 913–34.

Waelde, T.W. (2004) 'The "Umbrella" (or Sanctity of Contract/pacta sunt servanda) Clause in Investment Arbitration: A Comment on Original Intentions and Recent', BIICL Paper.

Wagner, J. (2003) 'Chicago Exchanges Shake Off Electronic Reluctance', *The Banker*, February 1.

Walter, I. (1988) *Global Competition in Financial Services*, Cambridge, MA: American Enterprise Institute/Ballinger.

Webb, K. (ed.) (2004) *Voluntary Codes: Private Governance, the Public Interest and Innovation*, Ottawa: Carleton University.

Weintraub, J. (1997) 'The Theory and Politics of the Public/Private Distinction', in J. Weintraub and K. Kumar (eds) *Public and Private in Thought and Practice*, Chicago: University of Chicago Press.

Weiss, Linda (2003) 'Introduction: Bringing Domestic Institutions Back In', in L. Weiss (ed.) *States in the Global Economy*, Cambridge: Cambridge University Press.

Weiss, M. (2004) 'Enlargement and Industrial Relations: Building a New Social Partnership', *The International Journal of Comparative Labour Law and Industrial Relations*, 20, 1: 5–26.

Werhane, P. and Freeman R. (eds) (2005), *The Blackwell Encyclopedia of Management, vol. II: Business Ethics*, Oxford: Blackwell.

West, D. and Loomis, B. (1999) *The Sound of Money: How Political Interests Get What They Want*, New York: Norton.

Wick, I. (2003) *Workers' Tool or PR ploy? A Guide to Codes of International Labour Practice*, Bonn: Südwind.

Willmott, H., Cooper, D.J. and Puxty, T. (2000) 'Maintaining Self-Regulation: Making "Interests" Coincide in Discourses on the Governance of the ICAEW', in J.R. Edwards (ed.) *The History of Accounting: Critical Perspectives on Business and Management. Professionalisation of Accounting*, Vol. IV, London: Routledge.

Wolf, K.D. (1999) 'The New Raison d'État as a Problem for Democracy in World Society', *European Journal of International Relations*, 5, 3: 333–63.

Wolf, K.D. (2002) 'Civil Society and the Legitimacy of Governance Beyond the State: Conceptional Outlines and Empirical Explorations', paper prepared for the International Studies Association Annual Meeting, New Orleans.

Wood, D. (2005) *Governing Global Banking*, Aldershot: Ashgate.

World Bank (2003) 'Strengthening implementation of corporate social responsibility in global supply chains'. Available online at: www.bsr.org/CSRResources/Environment/Strengthening.pdf (accessed 25 January, 2006).

Yanz, L. and Jeffcott, B. (1997) 'El Salvador Conference Debates Independent Monitoring', *Asian Labour Update,* 26, 1.

Zago, A.M. (1999) 'Quality and Self-Regulation in Agricultural Markets: How do Producer Organisations Make the Rules?', *European Review of Agricultural Economics,* 26, 2: 199–218.

Zahn, E. and Foschiani, S. (2000) 'Strategien und Strukturen für den Hyperwettbewerb', in F. Wojda (ed.) *Innovative Organisationsformen: Neue Entwicklungen in der Unternehmensorganisation.* Stuttgart: Schäffer-Poeschel.

Zeitlin, J. and Pochet, P. (eds) (2005) *The Open Method of Co-ordination in Action*, Brussels: Peter Lang.

Zürn, M. (1998) *Regieren jenseits des Nationalstaates. Globalisierung und Denationalisierung als Chance,* Frankfurt/Main: Suhrkamp.

Index